German Unification

Process and Outcomes

EDITED BY

M. Donald Hancock

AND

Helga A. Welsh

Westview Press

BOULDER • SAN FRANCISCO • OXFORD

Copyright © 1994 by Westview Press, Inc.

Published in 1994 in the United States of America by Westview Press, Inc., 5500 Central Avenue, Boulder, Colorado 80301-2877, and in the United Kingdom by Westview Press, 36 Lonsdale Road, Summertown, Oxford OX2 7EW

Library of Congress Cataloging-in-Publication Data
German unification : process and outcomes / edited by M. Donald
  Hancock and Helga A. Welsh.
    p. cm.
  Includes bibliographical references and index.
  ISBN 0-8133-8125-8. — ISBN 0-8133-1965-X (pbk.)
    1. Germany—History—Unification, 1990.   I. Hancock, M. Donald.
  II. Welsh, Helga A.
  DD290.25.G47   1994
  943.087'9—dc20   92-6822
                                                                                CIP

Printed and bound in the United States of America

The paper used in this publication meets the requirements
of the American National Standard for Permanence of Paper
for Printed Library Materials Z39.48-1984.

10   9   8   7   6   5   4   3   2   1

To the memories of

Donald Schoonmaker
Rudolf Wildenmann

Valued friends and colleagues

Contents

Preface   *ix*

Introduction: Models of Unification, *M. Donald Hancock
    and Helga A. Welsh*   1

**PART ONE
Background and Impetus**

1   The Collapse of Communism in Eastern Europe and
     the GDR: Evolution, Revolution, and Diffusion,
     Helga A. Welsh   17

2   West German Policy Toward East Germany: A Motor
     of Unification? *Johannes L. Kuppe*   35

**PART TWO
Process and Outcomes**

3   Delegitimation of the Old Regime: Reforming and
     Transforming Ideas in the Last Years of the GDR,
     Henry Krisch   55

4   Steps Toward Union: The Collapse of the GDR and
     the Unification of Germany, *Michael G. Huelshoff
     and Arthur M. Hanhardt, Jr.*   73

5   Exiting the GDR: Political Movements and Parties
     Between Democratization and Westernization,
     Michaela W. Richter   93

6   Parties and Problems of Governance During
     Unification, *Gert-Joachim Glaeßner*   139

7   An Unwelcome Enlargement? The European
     Community and German Unification, *Andreas Falke*   163

PART THREE
Consequences and Problematics

8   An Impossible Dream? Privatizing Collective Property
     in Eastern Germany, *Peter H. Merkl*   199

9   Social Policy at a Crossroads, *Gunnar Winkler*   223

10   Economic and Political Performance: Patterns and
     Prospects, *M. Donald Hancock*   245

11   German Security Policy in Post-Yalta Europe,
     James Sperling   261

12   Germany in Transition: The Challenge of Coping
     with Unification, *Petra Bauer-Kaase*   285

Conclusion: Beyond Unification, *Helga A. Welsh and*
     M. Donald Hancock   313

Appendix 1: Chronology of German Unification   325
Appendix 2: A Ten-Point Program for Overcoming the
     Division of Germany and Europe   329
Appendix 3: Treaty on Establishing a Monetary, Economic, and
     Social Union   339
Appendix 4: Unification Treaty   353
Appendix 5: German Elections, 1949-1993   371

Select Bibliography   375
About the Editors and Contributors   381
About the Book   384
Index   385

Preface

This volume is an international collaborative effort based on personal and professional witness by American and German social scientists to German unification as both process and outcome. Their contributions are addressed to students of comparative politics, public and private officials, and all citizens who seek to understand the causes, course, and enormous political, economic, and social consequences of one of the decisive international events of the late twentieth century.

Throughout the volume, we have followed two linguistic conventions which are not necessarily shared by others. Accordingly, a few explanatory remarks seem in order. The first concerns the use of the plural form of "Germany." William A. Safire, in an op-ed article in the *New York Times Magazine* published on 1 April 1990, persuasively advocates the use of the grammatical rule governing the plural of proper names in the case of German unification. "We're talking about uniting the two *Germanys*," Safire observes. "Although the plural of nouns ending in *y* after a consonant is *ies*, the plural of proper names overrides the rule to preserve the name itself: Mr. and Mrs. Murphy and their two daughters are the *Murphys*; if both girls are confusingly named Mary, they're the *Marys*." Accordingly, we consistently used the plural *Germanys*, rather than *Germanies*, a clarification which we welcomed and adopted for this book.

In addition, we have preferred the term "unification" to "reunification." Although we realize that "reunification" is commonly used by scholars and others, reunification would literally mean the reestablishment of a united Germany within the boundaries of 1937—and therefore should be avoided. Former Chancellor Willy Brandt deserves the credit for sensitizing the German and international public to the historical meaning of "reunification" and its misapplication to contemporary events in Germany. Indeed, unified Germany in its present borders is a new territorial entity that has not previously existed; therefore, strictly speaking, any reference to German *re*unification is historically imprecise.

The German Information Center in New York generously provided English-language translations of Chancellor Helmut Kohl's "Ten-Point

Program for Overcoming the Division of Germany and Europe," the Treaty on Monetary, Economic, and Social Union," and the "Unification Treaty" which are included in this volume as Appendixes 2-4. The appendixes are slightly abridged versions of the original documents.

We gratefully acknowledge the institutional support and technical assistance of colleagues at the Center for European Studies at Vanderbilt University and the Department of Political Science at the University of Arizona, in particular Jan Thompson, Robert Francis, Stacy McMillen, Robert Wilson, and Suzan McIntire. We are also grateful to Ian Wallace for translating the chapter by Gert-Joachim Glaeßner and Anita M. Mallinckrodt and Britta Luehr for providing English-language drafts of the chapters by Johannes L. Kuppe and Gunnar Winkler, respectively. The final responsibility for the translations rests with the editors.

A special note of appreciation is due Susan McEachern at Westview Press. Her patient encouragement has made this volume possible.

M. Donald Hancock (Vanderbilt University)
Helga A. Welsh (Wake Forest University)

Introduction

Models of Unification:
Integration Theory and Democratization

M. Donald Hancock and
Helga A. Welsh

Germany's unification in 1990 encompassed multiple processes of fundamental system change. On the international level, unification entailed the creation of a new political community through the merger of two previously separate political, economic, and social systems. In terms of regime transition, unification involved the extension of established democratic principles, institutions, and decisionmaking procedures in the Federal Republic of Germany to the former German Democratic Republic. In comparative perspective, the democratization of eastern Germany coincided with what Samuel Huntington has termed the "third wave" in a successive series of global democratic transformations dating from the early part of the eighteenth century.[1]

These simultaneous outcomes test two hitherto disparate bodies of theoretical literature in social science: integration theory and general concepts of democratization. Integration theory addresses underlying socio-economic and political factors encouraging the formation of new political communities. In the specific German case, it also explicates the range of alternative regime choices implicit in the events of 1989-90 which spelled the demise of the German Democratic Republic as well as the actual outcome that ensued. Democratization theory, meanwhile, emphasizes the necessary conditions for successful transitions to viable post-authoritarian regimes.

The historical record provides contradictory evidence concerning Germany's democratic prospect. The nation's first attempt at constitutional democracy—the proclamation of the Weimar Republic in November 1918—ended ignominiously with the rise of the Third Reich fifteen years later. In contrast, the formation of the Federal Republic in 1949 yielded a stable and effective democratic regime that served as a veritable international model of successful political and economic performance. The "new

Germany" of the expanded Federal Republic poses unprecedented political
and economic challenges not only to the Germans themselves but also to
social scientists who seek to explain the process of unification and assess
its consequences.

Integration Theory Revisited

"Classical" integration theory, as it evolved from the 1930s through
the late 1960s, primarily addresses the transformation of autonomous nation-states into new forms of trans- or supranational political authority
characterized by a shared sense of community among relevant political
actors (including governments, organized interest groups, and citizens). A
minimum common denominator of various conceptions of integration,
Charles Pentland succinctly summarizes, is *"a process whereby a group of
people, organized initially in two or more independent nation-states, come
to constitute a political whole which can in some sense be described as a
community."*[2] While Pentland correctly observes that there is no consensual definition of "community" among international relations scholars, the
concept minimally consists of a shared sense of national or regional identity and fundamental political values among elites and a majority of citizens. Subsumed under Pentland's broad definition of integration are four
distinctive theoretical approaches to the integrative process: pluralism,
federalism, functionalism, and neo-functionalism.

Theorists preoccupied with the first two of these approaches—pluralism and federalism—emphasize in common the dual primacy of political
power and what Pentland describes as "high politics" (that is, international
diplomacy and security issues).[3] For both pluralists and federalists, the
primary unit in international relations is thus the nation-state—either in the
traditional sense of autonomous national actors or in the form of emergent
federal systems whose powers transcend those of previously independent
national units, respectively. This difference in focus is crucial, in that pluralist theorists concentrate on the political and social factors conducive to
the peaceful adjustment of conflicts *among* independent states, while federalist theorists emphasize the transfer of national sovereignty to *new* regional centers of recognized political authority.

A notable example of the pluralist approach is Karl Deutsch, who
sought to define political conditions conducive to the peaceful resolution
of social conflict in a conceptual analysis of political community in the
North Atlantic area.[4] To explicate such conditions, Deutsch developed a
four-fold typology of international and national communities which dis-
tinguishes between two types of "integrated security communities" and

two types of "not integrated not security" communities. Integrated systems consist of (1) "not amalgamated" security systems such as the North Atlantic region and (2) "amalgamated" security systems such as stable nation-states.[5] Characterizing both international and national security communities are a shared belief among national leaders "that common social problems must and can be resolved by 'peaceful change. . . .'" and "institutions and practices strong enough and widespread enough to assure, for a 'long' time, dependable expectations of 'peaceful change' among [their] population."[6] In contrast, non-integrated communities consist of either (3) "not amalgamated not security" systems—for example, antagonistic national rivals such as the United States and the Soviet Union during the Cold War—and (4) "amalgamated not security communities" such as unstable empires or nation-states confronting the prospect of disintegration and/or civil war.[7]

Other federalist theorists such as Amitai Etzioni and K.C. Wheare view integration less as a condition and more as a political and social *process* culminating in the emergence of new supranational states in which political power is constitutionally divided between a national (federal) government and its previously independent sub-units.[8] Successfully-established federal systems possess central features associated with political modernity among traditionally autonomous nation-states which have resisted or escaped pressures of supranational integration: territoriality, an effective governing political-administrative apparatus, and citizen allegiance to the national level of government.

Functionalists and neo-functionalists affirm with pluralists and federalists the importance of political "community" and the peaceful resolution of social and political conflict within the boundaries of such a community, but they are primarily concerned with the "low politics" of underlying socioeconomic factors—rather than deliberate political and constitutional acts—that facilitate integration over time. Common to both approaches, as Pentland notes, is an emphasis on "the economic, social and technological factors which, by much less direct processes, are said to bring about political change."[9] Thus, both groups view political change as "an incremental process . . . based on the need to resolve social and economic problems."[10]

Beyond these similarities, however, functionalism and neo-functionalism differ sharply with respect to their scope of inquiry and theoretical orientation. The functionalist approach—closely identified with the proliferate work of a single scholar, David Mitrany[11]—emphasizes *global* processes of increased international cooperation based on "material interdependence" among nations and their citizens rooted in industrialization and the expansion of international trade.[12] In Mitrany's view, material interdependence has not only undermined the "formal separation" of individual nations but also facilitates "innumerable private and public international arrangements" which in turn have welded the world "into one organic whole."[13] While Mitrany's formulation of functionalist theory is unabashedly idealistic with strong prescriptive overtones, the expanding trans-national economic and social linkages which he describes help explain and justify the formation of twentieth century international organizations—including the League of Nations and the United Nations—and "functional" or task-specific agencies such as the World Health Organization (WHO) and the Food and Agricultural Organization (FAO).

A postwar generation of scholars drew on Mitrany's sweeping global perspectives to develop more rigorous theoretical explanations of the emergence of West European economic integration and its institutionalization in the form of the European Coal and Steel Community (ECSC) and the European Economic Community (EEC) as particular regional expressions of functional cooperation. The most influential formulation of the neo-functionalist definition of integration remains Ernst B. Haas, who focused on the ECSC as a prime example of an emergent supranational political community characterized by a shift in *"loyalties, expectations and political activities"* among political elites *"toward a new centre, whose institutions possess or demand jurisdiction over the pre-existing national states."*[14] The relevant actors among such elites are "officials of trade associations, the spokesmen of organised labour, higher civil servants and active politicians."[15]

Distinctive to Haas' definition of an integrated political community is his insistence on the need for institutionalized political power at the center. In his view, such power embodies a national agreement or consensus on deliberative means to resolve group conflict and process binding decisions on the community-at-large.[16] "While the co-existence of conflict and harmony within the same social system can no doubt be achieved without the attributes of a single statehood," Haas observes, "the deliberate creation and perpetuation of a new national consciousness can hardly be expected to come about without the presence of formal governmental institutions and practices."[17] At the same time—and herein lies another distinctive feature of neo-functionalist theory—the integrative process is driven by "the perception of interests and . . . the articulation of specific values on the part of existing political actors," notably economic and political elites.[18] That is, integration does not merely "happen." Nor does it occur, as Mitrany would have it, because of a diffuse "anti-state" normative preference throughout the world. Instead, the "ideologies" of private and public groups provide the central political impulse for both promoting and opposing the integration process.[19]

Other neo-functionalists contributed additional conceptual components of integration theory in light of the subsequent development of the EEC through the early 1960s. Leon Lindberg, for example, stipulated four key variables that facilitate the integration process: (1) the development of central institutions and policies, (2) a sufficient level of importance of tasks assigned central institutions "to activate socio-economic process to which conventional international organizations have no access," (3) the inherent expansiveness of such tasks, and (4) the perception among member-states that their interests are "consistent with the enterprise."[20] Although Lindberg draws heavily on Haas' reformation of functionalist theory, he eschews Haas' insistence on the formation of a national political community as the logical "end state" of the integrative process. Instead, he endorses the view of Jan J. Schokking and Nels Anderson that the emergent European Community "'might very well permit to a great extent the participating nations to retain their identity while yet joined in the organization that transcend nationality.'"[21] Lindberg also elaborated a notion of integrative "spill-over" which is implicit in Haas' earlier work: "In its most general formulation, 'spill-over' refers to a situation in which a given action, related to a specific goal, creates a situation in which the original goal can be assured only by taking further actions, which in turn create a further condition and a need for more action. . . ."[22]

A noteworthy feature of these contrasting approaches to integration theory—pluralism, federalism, functionalism, and neo-functionalism—is that they are complementary rather than contradictory explanations of international political and economic change. As shown schematically in Figure 1, each approach depicts different community and organizational realities. Moreover, the fundamental notion that integration is inherently a dynamic process implies the possibility of systemic transformation from one cell to another. Therein lies the significance of integration theory for the particular case of German unification.

Models of Unification

Integration theory suggests different possibilities for the conceivable course of German unification once regional reform tendencies ensued in Eastern Europe in the mid-1980s. Of these possibilities—each of which comprises a distinct "model of unification"—only one actually materialized. All of them were implicit, however, as potential alternative outcomes of political change during the formative months of 1989-90.

Figure 1
Overview of Theoretical Approaches to Political and Economic
Integration with Empirical Examples

	End Product	
	Intergovernmental Cooperation	Supranational Authority
Integrative Process Direct: political variables primary	Pluralism NATO	Federalism United States
Indirect: socio-economic variables primary	Functionalism United Nations, WHO	Neo-Functionalism ECSC, EEC

Adapted from Charles Pentland, *International Theory and European Integration* (New York: The Free Press, 1973), 23.

Prior to the incipient collapse of communism in Eastern Europe and the former Soviet Union, West and East Germany comprised what Deutsch classifies as a pluralist "not amalgamated not security" community. The Federal Republic and the German Democratic Republic consisted of mutually antagonistic socioeconomic and political systems: one capitalist-democratic, the other socialist-authoritarian. Moreover, each belonged to rival military-political alliances (NATO and the Warsaw Pact) whose basic purpose was selective security—including preparedness for the eventuality of all-out war—directed against each other. The absence of an elite-level consensus on procedures for the peaceful resolution of social conflict was clearly evident in the postwar historical record of mutual suspicion, incessant political recriminations, and repeated resort to violence along the German-German border.

Partially mitigating the division of West and East Germany into separate political systems were cultural attributes of a common national identity. These included the same language; common religious traditions; shared historical memories; and a rich legacy of classical and modern art, literature, and music. Reinforcing a trans-German sense of community were West German media penetration throughout most of the GDR and innumerable personal contacts which had been sustained since 1945 despite the physical division of the country. On a cultural and citizen level, then, East and West Germans remained loosely integrated in a social community that transcended political boundaries. A residual national German identity was buttressed by the GDR's efforts to sustain and expand intra-German trade, parallel pride in postwar Germany's two "economic miracles," and the policy of "small steps" on the part of West German Social Democratic leaders intended to bring East and West Germans closer together.[23]

Hence, the onset of incipient reforms in the East German Party and state in 1989 initially pointed toward the prospect that Germany's existing "not amalgamated *not security* community" could evolve into a "not amalgamated *security* community." Such a transformation would have presupposed the continued existence of the Federal Republic and the German Democratic Republic as separate states, but the repudiation of orthodox Marxist-Leninist norms and political authoritarianism by a new governing East German counter elite could have facilitated the emergence of an trans-German consensus affirming a joint commitment to the peaceful resolution of mutual social and other problems. A not amalgamated German security community could have facilitated in turn an expanding network of public and private contacts that would correspond to Mitrany's vision of increased interdependence on the basis of functional cooperation between the two systems.

The rapid escalation of popular demands for political unification on the streets of Leipzig, Berlin, and other East German cities—as recounted in the chapters in this volume by Henry Krisch, Michael G. Huelshoff and Arthur M. Hanhardt, Jr., and Michaela W. Richter—quickly negated such a prospect. Instead, Chancellor Helmut Kohl's proclamation of a "Ten-Point Program"[24] for German unification on 28 November 1989 raised the imminent prospect of a second model of unification: that of a political confederation.

Kohl's call for the creation of "confederative structures" between the two German states which would include joint government and parliamentary committees to facilitate "standing consultations" and joint political decisions was at sharp variance with established West German policy not to accord full legal equality to the East German regime.[25] The Chancellor's tentative blueprint, which was hastily formulated to dispel widespread criticism of West German passivity in the face of the growing liberalization movement in the GDR,[26] included proposals to provide immediate assistance to East Germany for humanitarian purposes, extensive economic assistance "as soon as the GDR has embarked on a fundamental transformation of its political and economic system, . . ." and an "opening" of the European Community to the GDR and other East European states.[27]

Although Chancellor Kohl's proposal remained politically still-born in light of subsequent international and domestic events, the concept of a German confederation is closely akin to Haas' neo-functionalist notion of a supranational political community characterized by a shift in "loyalties, expectations, and political activities" by political elites to new centers of power.[28] Such a system would have approximated Etzioni's vision of an emergent federal system, although it would have been achieved on the basis of statutory law rather than a new constitution. In all probability, a German confederation would have proved only a transitional arrangement, with Lindberg's concepts of "inherent expansiveness" of important tasks and policy "spill-over" pointing in time toward full political and economic integration.

As events proved, policymakers in the two Germanys and the former wartime Allies chose a third model of unification: that of direct transition from a pluralist "not amalgamated not security system" to full-fledged federalism. This bold move evoked memories of early postwar aspirations among idealistic West European integrationists to create a United States of Europe as a new regional political community comprising previously independent nation-states, although it was achieved on a far more limited territorial scale. The flurry of international diplomatic activity and direct negotiations between German public officials during the spring of 1990 which culminated in Allied endorsement of German unification and state treaties between the two Germanys providing for monetary, economic, and political union resulted in an extension of established constitutional norms and political institutions in the Federal Republic to Germany as a whole. The result was the establishment, by diplomatic and legislative fiat, of a new all-German political community on a federal model. The process thus vindicated federalist rather than functional or neo-functionalist theories of integration as the empirical basis of German unification.

Beyond Unification: Democratization as Habituation

Integration theory usefully clarifies the alternative choices that Allied and German elites confronted in 1989-90, but it singularly fails to address a crucial consequence of integration on both a regional and national level: that of accompanying democratization. None of the postwar theorists of integration—from Deutsch to Haas, Etzioni, and Lindberg—even consider how political integration might affect elite accountability and citizen participation in any new transnational political enterprise.[29] This omission is significant in light of contemporary criticism of the "democratic deficit" within the European Community and ongoing efforts by the Germans themselves to transform formal unity into an integrated economic and social system and political stability.

As a distinct body of conceptual and empirical literature, democratization theory addresses this omission—albeit without respect to simultaneous processes of regional or national political integration. The German case underscores the imperative to bring both theoretical perspectives together.

An early but still highly relevant formulation of general principles involved in regime transformation from autocracy to democracy—applicable to Germany as well post-authoritarian countries in Eastern Europe and other regions—is Dankwart A. Rustow's general model of democratic transitions.[30] Rustow depicts a three-stage process of democratization: (1) a preparatory stage, (2) a decision stage, and (3) a habituation stage. The first of these involves "a prolonged and inconclusive political struggle" among protagonists representing "well-entrenched forces (typically social classes)" which "is likely to begin as a result of the emergence of a new elite that arouses a depressed and previously leaderless social group into concerted action. . . ." The second stage entails "a deliberate decision on the part of the political leaders to accept the existence of diversity in unity and, to that end, to institutionalize some crucial aspect of democratic procedure. . . ." The third stage unfolds as leaders of political parties and organized interests accept—either out of convenience or conviction—newly-established democratic practices and institutions.[31]

For democratization to succeed, Rustow contends, a prior sense of national unity must exist in the sense that "the vast majority of citizens in a democracy-to-be must have no doubt or mental reservation as to what political community they belong to."[32] The ultimate viability of democracy rests, in Rustow's judgment, on the acceptance by contending elites of the legitimacy of opposing views. "[Politics] is, above all, a process for resolving conflicts within human groups—whether these arise from the clash of interests or from uncertainty about the future."[33] Whether such a process will yield a more—or less—stable democracy in particular instances is uncertain. As Samuel Huntington observes: "Democratic and non-democratic systems may be created but they may or may not endure. The stability of a system differs from the nature of the system."[34]

The essential ingredients in any struggle to implement and maintain democracy, then, include a prior struggle among opposing elites representing diverse social groups over basic rights of representation, a conscious decision to establish democratic norms and procedures, and a willingness on the part of political and other group leaders and their constituents to accept interim policy outcomes in a joint quest for approximate solutions to important socioeconomic and other issues. Alongside these domestic factors of democratization, international influences may also influence the onset of democratic transitions in particular nations as a result of what Lucian Pye has identified as recurrent global crises of authoritarianism[35] and what Huntington describes as a "snowballing effect" of successful transitions elsewhere.[36]

The particular course of German unification—as a compelling instance of the political integration of two previously separated systems—reveals the salience of Rustow's general theory of democratization, both with respect to the process itself and its subsequent consequences. The onset of a preparatory struggle on behalf of regime liberalization ensued in the form of citizen protests during the fall of 1989 and promptly led to efforts by reform groups and even dissident members of the governing Socialist Unity Party (SED) itself to initiate fundamental social and political change.[37] Because of the authoritarian nature of the regime, none of the dissident groups and nascent political parties which began to emerge by November 1989 represented what Rustow terms "well-entrenched [social] forces," much less distinct social classes. Nonetheless, the various opposition groups and parties provided an organizational voice for previously leaderless and silent regime opponents throughout all strata of East German society.

The struggle for liberalization gained official legitimacy when SED leaders agreed in December 1990 to consult with opposition leaders on a continuing basis in a series of informal "Roundtable" political discussions.[38] By early 1990 government and opposition representatives reached a fateful decision to schedule East Germany's first competitive national election to the Volkskammer in March. With this step, East German elites and counter-elites embarked on the second stage of Rustow's analytical assessment of the democratization process: the dual acceptance of "diversity in unity" and "some crucial aspect of democratic procedure."

Contributors to this volume describe in detail the subsequent international and domestic events that culminated in the attainment of constitutional-institutional unity on the basis of Rustow's first democratization criterion of a "prior sense of national unity." National election results on 2 December overwhelmingly vindicated the prior preparatory struggle and elite decisions in favor of both democracy and political integration of the two postwar German republics. These historic outcomes thus set into motion the third phase of democratization as process: habituation.

On the elite level of unified Germany, democratic habituation is well underway in the requisite acceptance by most government, party, and interest group leaders of the legitimacy of opposing political views and their shared commitment to the peaceful resolution of social conflicts. Yet, as repeated instances of violence against persons and electoral volatility during the early 1990s soberly demonstrated, not all groups and individuals share elite norms affirming sociopolitical diversity and "uncertainty about the future."[39]

Germany's first attempt at democratic habituation failed during the late 1920s and early 1930s as a result of elite disunity and economic crisis. Its second effort, within the territory of the Federal Republic, succeeded after 1949 because of the political irrelevance of anti-system elites and unprecedented economic development. The central political challenge confronting the unified nation's leaders and citizens into the twenty-first century is whether Germany's third democratic transition can likewise succeed. The reestablishment of a national German political community demonstrates the relevance of integration theory, but democratization theory emphasizes the fundamental importance of democratic habituation in the day-to-day behavior of political elites and citizens for ensuring unified Germany's political effectiveness and stability.

Notes

1.   Samuel Huntington, *The Third Wave. Democratization in the Late Twentieth Century* (Norman and London: University of Oklahoma Press, 1991). Huntington dates the "first wave" from 1828 to 1926, the "second wave" from 1943 to 1962, and the "third wave" from the mid-1970s onward.

2.   Charles Pentland, *International Theory and European Integration* (New York: The Free Press, 1973), 21. Author's italics.

3.   Ibid., 109.

4.   Karl W. Deutsch, *Political Community and the North Atlantic Area. International Organization in the Light of Historical Experience* (Princeton, New Jersey: Princeton University Press, 1957).

5.   Ibid., 5-7.

6.   By peaceful change Deutsch understands "the resolution of social problems, normally by institutionalized procedures, without resort to large-scale physical force." Ibid., 5.

7.   Ibid., 6-7.

8. See Amitai Etzioni, *Political Unification. A Comparative Study of Leaders and Forces* (New York: Robert E. Krieger Publishing Company, 1974), and K.C. Wheare, *Federal Government*, 4th ed. (New York: Oxford University Press, 1964). An important contribution to theoretical aspects of federalism is W.H. Riker, *Federalism. Origin, Operation, Significance* (Boston: Little, Brown and Company, 1964).

9. Pentland, 22.

10. Ibid.

11. Mitrany's principal publications include *The Progress of International Government* (London: Allen & Unwin, 1933); *A Working Peace System. An Argument for the Functional Development of International Organisation* (London: RIIA, 1943); "The Functional Approach to World Organisation," *International Affairs*, 24 (London, 1943): xxx; *A World Peace System* (Chicago: Quadrangle Books, 1966); and *The Functional Theory of Politics* (New York: St. Martin's Press, 1975).

12. Mitrany, *The Progress of International Government*, 100-101.

13. Ibid., 43 and 101.

14. Ernst B. Haas, *The Uniting of Europe. Political, Social and Economic Forces 1950-1957* (Stanford, Calif.: Stanford University Press, 1958), 16. Author's italics.

15. Ibid., 17.

16. Ibid., 6. Haas adds: "Stated in constitutional terms, the agreement on the means of political action is equivalent to the acceptance of the doctrine of respect for the rule of law. Official decisions, once made according to procedural rules accepted as binding by all, are carried out."

17. Ibid., 7.

18. Ibid., 13.

19. Ibid.

20. Leon N. Lindberg, *The Political Dynamics of European Economic Integration* (Stanford, Calif.: Stanford University Press, 1963), 7-8. Also see Leon Lindberg and Stuart A. Scheingold, *Europe's Would-Be Polity* (Englewood Cliffs, N.J.: Prentice-Hall, 1970).

21. Ibid., 6. See Jan J. Schokking and Nels Anderson, "Observations on the European Integration Process," *Journal of Conflict Resolution*, IV (1960): 385-410.

22. Lindberg, *The Political Dynamics of European Economic Integration*, 10.

23. On the latter, see in particular the chapter in this volume by Joannes L. Kuppe on "West German Policy Toward East Germany: A Motor of Unification?"

24. See Appendix 2.

25. Former East German First Secretary Walter Ulbricht had first proposed the creation of a German confederation in 1956. At the time West German officials vehemently rejected the plan.

26. *The New York Times*, 28 November 1989.

27. "Kohl vor dem Bundestag: Konföderation der deutschen Staaten," *Deutschland-Nachrichten*, 30 November 1989.

28. Haas, 16.

29. The entry "democracy" or "democratization" does not even appear in any of the indexes of the works cited.

30. Dankwart A. Rustow, "Transitions to Democracy: Toward a Dynamic Model," *Comparative Politics*, 2 (April 1970): 337-63.

31. Ibid., 350-58.

32. Ibid., 350.

33. Ibid., 358.

34. Huntington, 11.

35. Lucian W. Pye, "Political Science and the Crisis of Authoritarianism," *The American Political Science Review*, 84 (1990): 3-19.

36. Huntington, 32 and 46.

37. See in particular the chapters in this volume by Henry Krisch and Michaela Richter.

38. Various contributors to this volume discuss the Roundtable sessions in Part Two.

39. See Chapter 10.

PART ONE
Background and Impetus

1

The Collapse of Communism in Eastern Europe and the GDR: Evolution, Revolution, and Diffusion

Helga A. Welsh

In the fall of 1989 the magnitude of political change and the speed with which it occurred in Central and Eastern European countries caught the world by surprise. Despite national variations in the demise of communist rule, the causes and manifestations of the politico-economic crisis of the regimes in Eastern Europe displayed remarkable similarities. Likewise, the goals of establishing pluralist political systems and market-oriented economies are cornerstones in the transition processes currently underway in the region of Central and Eastern Europe.

One after another, ruling communist parties were forced to renounce their leading roles in politics and society and had to negotiate the transition to substantially altered political and economic structures. Although the interdependence of these developments was striking, from a more global perspective Central and Eastern European countries and, in 1991, the Soviet Union were among the last hold-outs in the "third wave" of democratization that had started in the middle of the 1970s.[1]

The spread of polyarchy in the 1970s and 1980s reflected global developments[2] but the events themselves were nevertheless relatively independent,[3] at least among those countries where a shift from right wing, often military-based regimes occurred. This was different in the setting of Eastern European communist systems, partly because their goals were not limited to the maintenance of power and the implementation of selective policies but instead were aimed at implementing an alternative form of political, social, and economic development. The failures of this effort were evident throughout the region. In addition, existing institutionalized networks of communication and interaction were finely meshed, and the "model" or "demonstration" effect of the pluralist countries of Western Europe, and the "West" more generally, was particularly strong; the transition processes were and remain substantially influenced by external forces from within and without the region. Therefore, the domino-effect fall of communist regimes points to particularly strong *inter*dependence effects in Central and Eastern Europe; within-system and across-system diffusion effects coincided.[4] Graffiti found in Prague captured this notion nicely: *Poland, Ten Years. Hungary, Ten Months. East Germany, Ten Weeks. Czechoslovakia, Ten Days.*[5]

Communism's demise showed variations across national settings in Central and Eastern Europe but it was the outcome of long-term processes of regional change which came to fruition in the late 1980s. By the 1980s, the evolutionary changes in Hungary and Poland and the almost complete lack of these changes in the rigid, conservative regimes in Bulgaria, Czechoslovakia, and East Germany had become emblematic of divergent political developments within the Soviet sphere of influence. In those countries where elite intransigence had been prevalent, changes occurred with rapid speed. In Poland and Hungary, by contrast, factions within the Communist parties opened up channels of communication with the opposition, thereby allowing for a more gradual change.

During the 1980s the survival skills of the Solidarity movement were an indicator of the growing weakness of the Polish United Workers' Party. Finally, in the spring of 1989, the startling outcome of the Roundtable negotiations and the stunning electoral success of Solidarity removed any doubts about the erosion of trust and public rejection of the ruling Communist party. But it was the decision by the Hungarian government to dismantle the border fortifications to the West, known as the iron curtain, that set in motion unprecedented and unexpected developments. East German citizens on vacation in Hungary took the opportunity to voice their frustration with the lack of political and economic reform in their country and decided to emigrate to West Germany. The following events are well-known and well-documented: The mass exodus acted as catalyst for popular upsurge in the GDR, then in Czechoslovakia, in Bulgaria and finally in Romania.[6]

Although there was genuine surprise at "how seemingly stable, enduring social systems fail and collapse"[7] in such short order, ex post facto explanations abound.[8] James N. Rosenau, for example, suggests five global dynamics that contributed to the legitimacy crisis of authoritarian regimes.[9] In addition to the Gorbachev factor, he cites "the impact of technology, the consequences of new interdependence issues, the advent of authority crises, and the greater competence of subgroups and citizens" as major contributing factors for the changes in Central and Eastern Europe and elsewhere. J.F. Brown points to six interrelated causes that reflect some of these themes in the specific setting of Eastern Europe: forty years of failure, in particular economic failure; the illegitimacy of communism; societal opposition; the loss of confidence in the ability to rule and the accompanying lack of willingness to apply means of force to maintain rule; the improvement in East-West relations; and, finally, the Soviet factor.[10]

These issues will be taken up by analyzing the situation in the former GDR but with a view to developments in the other Central and East European countries as well. Although the interdependence of national and international factors in the demise of communism was striking, the emphasis in this chapter is on within-system developments which were nevertheless influenced by external factors. In addition, the focus is on the underlying causes and not on singular political events that preceded the implosion of the political regimes in the GDR and in the rest of Central and Eastern Europe.

The Dilemmas of Reform and Modernization

Social scientists have long been interested in the link between socioeconomic and political development. According to the reasoning underlying much modernization literature, the higher levels of socioeconomic achievement, the greater the pressures towards a more human, open, competitive, and ultimately more pluralist society.[11] Socioeconomic modernization in turn creates pressures for changes in the political environment, including greater participation, social differentiation, and secularization. Although attention was first given to the study of developing countries, by the end of the 1960s students of communist affairs increasingly addressed the links between modernization and political change in Eastern Europe and the Soviet Union. Partly the result of the growing dissatisfaction with the totalitarian political model, it was also encouraged by economic reforms in European socialist systems.[12]

Indeed, measured in terms of socioeconomic modernization, Central and Eastern European countries had reached a level that was considered conducive to the emergence of pluralistic policies. The absence of far-reaching system transformation in them was attributed almost exclusively to the veto power of the Soviet Union.[13] Therefore, seen from the perspective of the modernization approach, these nations were viewed as "anomalies in socioeconomically highly-developed countries where particularly intellectual power resources have become widespread."[14]

Apart from the pressures of modernization it has been argued that the imperatives of economic reform ultimately would lead to political democratization (but not necessarily system transformation), albeit "gradually through incremental changes."[15] The severity of economic problems required drastic economic changes leading to painful consequences for large segments of the population, e.g., high rates of inflation, rising levels of unemployment, declining levels of real income, and greater pressure toward qualitative performance. In order to offset disturbing effects of economic reform, broad-based support and thus rewards like enhanced civil and political rights would be required.

However, even if the negative side effects of economic reform could be contained, economic restructuring entailed, among other things, diffusion of decisionmaking power and the necessity of providing accurate economic data to planners and politicians. In the long run, participation and openness could not be limited to the economic sphere alone and had to be extended to the political realm as a whole.

Signs of Systemic Crises

The Limits of Political Participation

By the end of the 1960s the political situation in Eastern Europe seemed consolidated, both domestically and internationally. Party domination through the exercise of command and violence had been largely replaced by manipulation and persuasion. Jowitt termed this the "inclusion phase." In contrast to the revolutionary and the consolidation phases, the inclusion period seemed to be characterized by "attempts by the party elite to expand the internal boundaries of the regime's political, productive, and decisionmaking systems, to integrate itself with the non-official (non-apparatchik) sectors of society rather than insulate itself from them."[16] In short, elements of political participation were addressed.

In communist-governed political systems such as those in Eastern Europe where educational achievements and political mobilization were highly valued, demands for independent political participation and political articulation could not be oppressed or ignored forever. As these demands became more forceful, the weaker the perceptions of the political system became.

Adopted in 1976, the latest version of the SED's program incorporated the main characteristics of a "developed socialist society." The interpretation of developed socialism and its adaptations to national conditions have varied widely in Central and Eastern Europe and have served mainly to undergird existing policies that were often quite different from one another in different political settings. However, some common denominators were obvious. It was asserted that the communist party would remain the centerpiece of political life and that its importance would actually increase. The doctrine of developed socialism stressed the growing significance of the scientific-technological revolution for a productive national economy. Continuing development and perfection of socialist democracy were particularly stressed, and it was asserted that citizen participation in state and economic affairs was on the way to becoming the most distinctive feature of life under socialism.[17] However, to political leaders in the communist bloc the paradox of how a political system can become more democratic "while still guaranteeing that the party will continue to guide, if not control, the governing of society"[18] proved intractable.

Efforts to enhance political participation witnessed the additions of new political actors, adaptations of political structures, and changes in political functions as seen in the changing roles of the mass organizations and non-communist parties, the emphasis on local politics, and the emerging role of the Protestant churches in the GDR.[19] In many cases, however, changes were limited to form rather than substance,[20] i.e., they were largely quantitative. At the same time, the potential for merely quantitative increases in the existing arenas of participation was virtually exhausted by the middle of the 1980s. For example, on the average every citizen over fourteen years of age in the GDR was a member in at least three mass organizations and/or political parties.[21]

In an effort to mobilize and integrate ever greater sectors of society to the communist community, most communist parties in Central and Eastern Europe had distanced themselves from the Leninist idea of the vanguard party of the best and brightest and had switched to mass membership parties. This is evidenced, among other things, by the continuous increase in membership numbers. In the GDR, the membership of the SED had grown consistently from 1.6 million in 1961 to 2.3 million in 1988—which was the equivalent of roughly 20 percent of the adult population.

Although the reasons for entry into the Communist Party should not be explained solely or even predominantly with careerism, party membership nevertheless had lost much of its ideological fervor and was often an act of pragmatism. With the advent of Gorbachev's policies of *glasnost* and *perestroika*, it became increasingly difficult to defend the orthodox conservatism of the GDR leadership at the level of the party cells. The growing dissatisfaction among ordinary party members is partly evidenced by the fact that the number of proceedings against SED members (23,000) and resignations from the SED (11,000) reached new heights in 1988.[22] However, neither mass resignations nor organized factionalism within the SED occurred at any noticeable scale. Reluctance to undertake personal risks, diffuse support for different reform concepts, and a belief in the possibility to exert pressure on the party leadership that would result in reform processes were important factors in the failure of organized opposition to emerge within the ranks of the SED.[23]

At the same time, in the words of Bradley Scharf, "a kind of 'hidden' evolution of authority patterns emerged. Continuing personnel changes in institutional leadership produced a moderation of authoritarian relationships," which affected paternalistic patterns of behavior at work places where educational standards were high.[24] This applied not only to the intelligentsia in research institutes, in universities, and among the cultural elite in general but reached the level of the SED as well[25] and contributed to growing diversification of political thinking. Although it became possible to articulate reformist ideas, such ideas were nonetheless ignored by the political leadership.[26]

The Honecker era by no means was totally inflexible to external influences. Periods of domestic relaxation and tightening of control alternated, depending on the leadership's perception of the extant level of political stability—as seen in shifts from limited liberalization to stricter control of cultural and political activities in 1976 and 1987-88. Generally speaking, repression had been replaced by a more flexible mode of conflict resolution that was characterized by selective and/or preventive repression and co-optation efforts. As a result, individuals had become aware of the limits of permissible behavior and did become more outspoken. Once the limits of permissible behavior were expanded, it was still possible to implement more restrictive policies but at the expense of even greater disillusionment among the population since expectations had been raised. The cycle of repression and liberalization became another indicator of how limited reform efforts were and how encrusted political decisionmaking had become.

The Erosion of the Social Contract

The transition in Central and Eastern Europe is at least dual in nature.[27] It encompasses the political as well as the economic sphere. This cannot be otherwise, since politics and economics were closely intertwined and interconnected in communist political systems. "Under state socialism, economic problems are, by definition, political problems as well. When the distribution of goods—and the income needed to purchase them—are centrally controlled, the government is thereby held responsible for the total quality of social life."[28]

This has direct relevance to the question of legitimacy in modern societies which have seen at least a partial shift from charisma, tradition, law, or fear of sanction to performance-related criteria as the basis for acceptance and support of a particular regime.[29] This holds particularly true for socialist regimes in which the erosion of ideology increasingly forced them to base their right to rule on socioeconomic criteria. It has become commonplace to explain past compliance of the populations in the region with the delivery of certain social and economic benefits, a sort of "social contract." The inherent danger was obvious: once the communist regimes had linked their legitimacy to the provision of material resources, economic and political reforms became indispensable. If these reforms did not result in visible economic betterment, dominant party rule was automatically in danger.

As a result of worsening global economic conditions and the inability to reform the command economies adequately, the economic difficulties of the communist regimes in Central and Eastern Europe entered a new stage in the 1980s. In particular, the indebtedness to the West—the need to repay the foreign debt—and the reliance on imports from the West for a widening selection of goods had eroded the past economic isolationism of Comecon countries. In relation to other countries in Eastern Europe, the economic crisis in the former East Germany was more modest but continued to accelerate. Economic indicators started to decline; for example, international competitiveness suffered and environmental damage became more visible.[30] But it was still true that the GDR was generally considered the best performing and most effective of the planned economies in Central and Eastern Europe and the economic setbacks were considered less serious than in some of the neighboring countries.[31]

The need to meet rising social and economic expectations in the 1980s contributed to the political and economic liberalization of most of the systems in Central and Eastern Europe, albeit to different degrees. Efforts of legitimation started to shift at least partially from the economic to the political sphere.[32] This holds true even for countries such as the GDR whose leadership was considered conservative and risk-adverse. At the beginning of the 1980s, when domestic spending as a proportion of total national expenditures was cut in order to reduce the substantial foreign debt, consumer sectors suffered. Outspoken public criticism may have contributed to the partial reversal of this policy decision. The GDR's leadership made an effort to protect the consumer sector, whereas significant cuts were made, for example, in industrial investment.[33] In addition, growing discontent with the inadequate supply and the quality of goods (the "1000 little things") and shortages in the provision of housing encouraged the distribution of power to local organs by 1985. But in the long run such efforts proved futile. The concentration of investments in selected areas of production led to the neglect of others—for example, the health care sector. By 1988, the head of the State Planning Commission of the GDR, Gerhard Schürer, felt compelled to inform Erich Honecker that even under conditions of good economic performance the current economic policy could no longer be maintained without severe repercussions.[34]

The Decline in Leadership Authority

There is general agreement that "the failure of most of these regimes to establish or retain political authority, that is, to win the acknowledgment of the populations that the regimes had a right to rule" was one of the primary causes of the collapse of communism in Central and Eastern Europe.[35] When the crisis of authority takes places under disequilibrated conditions, the conditions for revolutionary action are in place. Mancur Olson asserted that the upheavals in Eastern Europe in the fall of 1989 should not be interpreted primarily as the "mass action of unhappy people."[36] Rather, the "successful insurrection against an autocratic regime" is "normally due to the problems, divisions, irresolutions, or other weaknesses of the regime, not because of an increase in the animosity of the population."[37] According to this argument, authoritarian regimes base their power on the servitude and discipline of their officials, civilian and military—or, in the words of Chalmers Johnson, the non-deviant actors of society.[38] The motives for public obedience are manifold and range from incentives (in the form of access to scarce material goods and upward social mobility) to the acclaimed *Untertanengeist* (individual submissiveness), i.e., a psychological predisposition that obeys authority without questioning the right or wrong of certain actions. Authoritarian regimes are secure as long as they can count on individuals to enforce the prevailing rules of the system. As Mancur Olson states: "(I)f the cadre observe a moment of vacillation, an incident of impotence, a division in the leadership, or even the collapse of analogous regimes, all the power of an imposing regime can vanish in night air."[39]

In the case of GDR, the factors encouraging such an erosion of authority were manifold. Among them were the perception that the leadership was old, sick (Erich Honecker), and incapable of reform, as seen in the response to Soviet reform efforts; electoral manipulations in the communal elections in the spring of 1989; attempts to ignore and then to defend the harsh actions by the Chinese leadership at the Tiananmen Square demonstrations; the inauguration of a government that was led by non-communists in Poland; and negotiations between opposition forces and representatives of the Hungarian Socialist Workers' Party in the summer of 1989.

In many ways, then, the crisis of authority was closely tied to the incapability of an aging leadership to respond to new and challenging demands. One factor was the succession dilemma, that is the perception that leadership succession was accompanied by some sort of crisis—a perception that was nurtured by the fact that no institutionalized channel for leadership replacement existed. As a result, successions within the communist party elites were relatively infrequent and a gerontocratic leadership became a marked feature of socialist societies in Central and Eastern Europe. In 1988, Todor Zhivkov had been at the helm of the Bulgarian Communist Party since 1954, János Kádár had been in leadership positions in Hungary since 1956, Nicolae Ceausescu had led the Romanian Workers' Party since 1965, Gustáv Husák had became First Secretary in Czechoslovakia in 1969, and

Erich Honecker had succeeded Walter Ulbricht in 1971. Ailing, stubborn, and often out of touch with reality, they no longer represented the ideals of communism but the weaknesses of power and privilege.

For Erich Honecker, the achievement of socialism was largely synony-mous with the elimination of unemployment and homelessness, and he failed to understand the forces of political and economic change. There was visible disappointment in the GDR when he—at the advanced age of sev-enty-four—still refused to relinquish power on the occasion of the XI Party Congress in 1986. However, the aging of the leadership was not limited to the national level. In 1988, seventy-eight of 215 members of the Central Committee of the SED were over 62 years of age, and 104 were 49 years or older. [40] Nor was there any significant leadership change at the regional level. The average age for heads of the district Councils was 59 years, as compared to 62.5 years for the district first secretaries. In the spring of 1989, no district first secretary was younger than 59 years of age. Indeed, three of the fifteen district first secretaries had passed the retirement age of 65, and eight were in the age group between 60 to 65 years of age. With one exception, all first district secretaries were appointed to elite positions (at either the national or local level) during the formative years of the GDR, which had been characterized by international isolation and internal turmoil. On the average, the district first secretaries who left office in the 1980s had been in this position for 11.4 years while the average length of tenure for the heads of district Councils who were replaced in the 1980s was 18 years.[41]

Other factors that had contributed to acquiescence and loyalty toward the regime had also begun to falter. For example, professional and social mo-bility—once a characteristic of communist regimes—had been severely af-fected. Upward channels of mobility became limited to selective elites; in general self-recruitment—and not competition—became a distinctive feature of society. The continued reductions in those permitted to enter universities, the lack of upward mobility, and the selective use of material privileges—in particular for the political elites—furthered feelings of deprivation and disil-lusionment.

The living standard of the general population was, on the one hand, characterized by relatively small income differentials. In addition, the lack of quality in the assortment of goods, the lack of services and infrastructure, and the limited nature of travel possibilities further evened out potential dis-parities. But the reduction of inequalities that helped maintain power also undermined it, since efficiency, innovation, and development had been paralyzed. In addition, the relative high levels of equality in many areas of life contrasted sharply with the extreme inequality in the access to and the use of power.[42] In the words of two Hungarian observers: "Socialism achieved an 'equality of injustice.'"[43]

Privileges associated with leadership positions—including modern housing, foreign cars, access to otherwise almost inaccessible western goods, and travel to the West—increasingly attracted attention and furthered frustration. The long duration in positions of power had removed leaders from everyday life and from the concerns of the people for whom they were allegedly pursuing the communist goal. In addition, since the socialization of the aged leadership of the GDR had taken place under conditions of war, poverty, and political persecution, their perceptions of global relations were still heavily influenced by the dichotomy between communism and capitalism. Gorbachev's "new thinking," which aimed at abandoning class struggle as the determining feature of present-day East-West relations and to put in its place relations based on trust and cooperation, led to early signs of disagreement between the Soviet leader and Erich Honecker.[44]

The Erosion of Trust

The monopoly of information—i.e., access to, the distribution of, and the shaping of the content of information—was securely in the hands of the communist parties. Whereas the monopoly of information was severely undermined in Poland and was gradually liberalized in Hungary, the control of media continued to be extremely tight in the case of the GDR with one major exception. East Germans were in the privileged position of having almost unrestricted—and since 1973—officially sanctioned access to West German television and radio broadcasting.

The dilemma between the necessary restriction of access to information and the inability to control the influx of Western media could not be resolved in the long run; it had to backfire. Thanks to the use of new electronic media such as facsimile machines, videos, and computer disks, the transmittal of ideas became ever more sophisticated and efforts to censor and restrict information increasingly obsolete.

The domestic situation was presented with selective information and inappropriate praise for achievements. As one citizen observed in a letter to the official newspaper of the trade union, the daily life of the people in the GDR was not accurately reflected in the media coverage with the result that one might conclude that the media "report about a totally different country. The supposedly enthusiastic endorsement of the masses to the decrees of the government is not felt."[45]

Policies of *perestroika* and *glasnost* that had been inaugurated by Mikhail Gorbachev shortly after his ascent to power in 1985 were not met with universal approval by party officials in Central and Eastern Europe.

But the East European public earnestly hoped that a new era of relations between the Soviet Union and Eastern Europe would lead to greater national self-determination. Selective consent to particular Soviet-initiated reform policies confronted several East European leaders—with the notable exception of those in Hungary and Poland—with dilemmas since they felt an obligation to praise Soviet policy initiatives as usual but could not agree with some of the basic propositions. The Politburo under Erich Honecker was no exception. It favored relaxation of tensions in East-West relations but disapproved of a fundamental reconceptualization of foreign policy toward the West. *Perestroika* and *glasnost*—that is, efforts at reforming domestic policies—were ignored, condemned, and simply considered irrelevant for the GDR. Media functionaries felt compelled to censor Gorbachev's speeches and to restrict distribution of specific issues of Soviet magazines.

Daily broadcasts from West Germany enabled East Germans to make independent judgments on Soviet reform efforts and provided them with "a window through which they could witness the revolutionary changes taking place around them."[46] Whether it was the attempt by the SED leadership to keep the Tiananmen Square uprising from their news, the claim that the exodus of East Germans leaving Hungary in the summer of 1989 was the result of organized smuggling of human beings by West Germans, or the manipulation of electoral outcomes in the spring of 1989—all of these occurrences contributed to the further erosion of trust. Finally, the lack of credibility overcame any remaining loyalty and obedience.

The Failure of Political Socialization

The longevity of a political system is dependent upon the political elite's skills in adjusting to changing influences from the environment. These influences can be internal and external, supportive, constraining, negative or positive in character, but they cannot be ignored over long periods of time without major repercussions. In view of this all-too-common view, Western scholars tended to count on the adaptability and responsiveness of communist elites, which might explain at least partly why systemic crises were analyzed but no appropriate conclusions regarding the maintenance of communist regimes were drawn.

Generally speaking, the greater the exposure to the West, the more difficult it became to ignore the wishes of the population. In East Germany, building positive support for the communist regime was particularly difficult because of the existence of the Federal Republic of Germany. In the public eye, social and economic achievements were compared primarily to those of the West, not to those of other socialist political systems. The continued exodus to the West throughout the 1950s was just one sign of the lack of widespread positive support for the system. Building the Berlin Wall in August 1961 was a major watershed since it enabled the East German leadership to pursue the issue of a separate identity of the German Democratic Republic with greater vigor. In retrospect, system support seemed greatest in the 1970s and started to decline at the beginning of the 1980s.

The leadership succession from Walter Ulbricht to Erich Honecker in 1971, the signing of the Basic Treaty between the two Germanys in 1972, and the process of détente in East-West relations nourished hopes for a better future among the general population. However, the anxiously-sought-after international recognition had its impact both on the government and the governed.[47]

Some of the new issues with which the leadership of the GDR was confronted were tied to the relaxation of tensions between East and West Germany and to the Helsinki Final Act to which both German states were signatories. Growing numbers of tourists from the West in the GDR, the expanded possibilities for GDR citizens to travel within Eastern Europe and the Soviet Union, and the increase in the number of people from the GDR who were allowed to travel to the West contributed to a widening of the political spectrum and increased political and economic expectations. For example, at the beginning of the 1980s, on the average only about 40,000 people below retirement age were allowed to travel to West Germany in so-called urgent family matters. After 1983 the number had increased steadily to approximately 1.2 million in 1987 and in 1988.[48] If the government had hoped that these measures would alleviate feelings of isolation and therefore foster regime stability, its calculations proved wrong. On the contrary, the fact that the criteria for selection were not always transparent and that the privilege of travel to the West could be revoked at any time without recourse reinforced the absolute power of the state organs.

In particular, young people took the fulfillment of consumer needs, a secured place of work and a finely-meshed social protection net for granted. For some small but outspoken segments of the population quality of life became slowly associated with non-materialistic values, fostering the emergence of an alternative political culture at least among some segments of the youth. Peace and ecological movements were not just opposition to the narrow boundaries of the official political culture; they were also an expression of growing self-confidence. In contrast to Poland and Hungary, the emergence of political opposition groups—in 1989 there were approximately 160 civic groups with a membership of roughly 2,500 people—occurred only relatively late in the middle of the 1980s. The fragmentation into small groups facilitated their survival but limited their public outreach. By and large, they were committed to socialist ideals but differed in their concrete policy goals.[49] These limitations notwithstanding, the peace, ecological, and church-related civic groups proved to be the backbone of the "revolution" in the former GDR.

However, even at the height of identification with the GDR in the middle of the 1970s, the reasons for this identification were to be found primarily in professional security, feelings of attachment to one's native land and in personal relationships rather than in ideological and political justifications.[50] According to a study of the Youth Institute in Leipzig in 1975, 66 percent of students and 57 percent of apprentices identified themselves "strongly" with the GDR. At the beginning of the 1980s this number started to decline and by the late 1980s the approval rating had dropped to 19 percent among apprentices and to 34 percent among students.[51]

Although the available survey data are limited to attitudes among youth, the decline is striking and it can be assumed that similar attitudes were prevalent in other societal groups as well. However, the decline of system support—in particular among the younger population—must have been particularly disturbing to the regime because it conclusively demonstrated the failure of socialist socialization. Even considering that younger people had not lived through the periods of more overt state terror, "had not seen their parents shamed into submission,"[52] and that their attachment to material and professional achievements might have been less pronounced, it is still noteworthy that of almost 344,000 refugees emigrating from East to West Germany in 1989, roughly 51 percent fell into the age group of 18 to 29 years.[53] Shortly before unification, in September 1990, the preference for unification was most pronounced among those 45 years of age or older. At the same time, unification still was approved by 86.5 percent in the age groups between 18 and 44, i.e., among those who had spent their whole lives in the communist-governed part of Germany.[54] The lack of identification with a socialist future among younger age groups is also indicated by the fact that, as of December 1990, 47.8 percent of all members of the Party of Democratic Socialism (the successor party to the Socialist Unity Party) were retired people and only 8.9 percent were under 30 years of age.[55] In short, not only did the socialist regimes in the GDR—and more generally throughout Central and Eastern Europe—fail to create the socialist person but, even more importantly, they could not even instill regime loyalty.

Conclusion

Since the unification of Germany, research on the GDR has been excluded almost completely from studies that focus on the collapse of communism and the ensuing transition processes in Central and Eastern Europe.

To be sure, the question of nationality and national identity—and the accession of the GDR to the Federal Republic of Germany—made the GDR a special case in the transition processes in Central and Eastern Europe. However, the case of the (former) GDR's singularity should not be taken to extremes. Nationalism defined as the desire to unify initially was not a driving force in the revolutionary upheaval in the former GDR, and most underlying causes in the demise of communist rule and the uncertainties and difficulties of the transition are shared by the former GDR and its Central and East European neighbors.

Some of the developments that led to the events of 1989 have been highlighted in the chapter. I have argued that forces of modernization and the need to reform the economies have presented the communist regimes in Central and Eastern Europe with intractable dilemmas. The ensuing legitimacy crisis was made even more prevalent by external forces, but it was based on the inability of the political elites to respond to political, economic, and social changes around them. The lack of system support had reached such dimensions that even any notion of a "third way" between capitalism and communism became unacceptable to the general public. Whether major reforms that might have been implemented in the 1960s and 1970s before the crisis of legitimacy had become multi-dimensional and insurmountable would have allowed for a new form of political, economic, and political system will remain an open question. However, it seems assured that in the absence of the veto of the major powers unification was inevitable once the systemic differences between the GDR and the Federal Republic became superfluous.

Notes

1. Samuel P. Huntington, *The Third Wave. Democratization in the Late Twentieth Century* (Norman and London: University of Oklahoma Press, 1991). According to this classification, the first wave started in the United States in 1820 and ended after 1926. A second wave began in the early 1940s and ended at the beginning of the 1960s.

2. Cf. Harvey Starr, "Democratic Dominoes. Diffusion Approaches to the Spread of Democracy in the International System," *Journal of Conflict Resolution*, 35 (1991): 356-81; and James N. Rosenau, "The Relocation of Authority in a Shrinking World," *Comparative Politics*, 24 (1992): 253-72.

3. Terry Lynn Karl and Philippe C. Schmitter, "Modes of Transition in Latin America, Southern and Eastern Europe," *International Social Science Journal*, XLIII (1991): 269-84, 274.

4. The power of diffusion has always been one key element underlying the fear of the spread of reform efforts in Central and Eastern Europe; the Brezhnev doctrine of limited sovereignty was the ultimate expression of this concern. By stating that any internal or external threat to socialism was the responsibility of all socialist countries and not just the domestic affair of any particular state in the socialist camp, the internationalist character of socialism was emphasized.

5. Cited in William Echikson, *Lighting the Night. Revolution in Eastern Europe* (New York: William Morrow and Company, 1990), 11.

6. See the chapter by Michael G. Huelshoff and Arthur M. Hanhardt, Jr., in this book.

7. Daniel Chirot, "What Happened in Eastern Europe in 1989?" in Daniel Chirot, ed., *The Crisis of Leninism and the Decline of the Left. The Revolutions of 1989* (Seattle and London: University of Washington Press, 1991), 3-32, 3. See also Nancy Bermeo, ed., *Liberalization and Democratization. Change in the Soviet Union and Eastern Europe* (Baltimore and London: The Johns Hopkins University Press, 1992).

8. For an interesting account see Lucian W. Pye, "Political Science and the Crisis of Authoritarianism," *The American Political Science Review*, 84 (March 1990): 3-19.

9. Rosenau, "Relocation of Authority," 253-72.

10. J.F. Brown, *Surge to Freedom. The End of Communist Rule in Eastern Europe* (Durham and London: Duke University Press, 1991), 2-4.

11. For a recent attempt to apply modernization theories to Eastern Europe, see Klaus Müller, "Modernizing Eastern Europe. Theoretical Problems and Political Dilemmas," *Archives Européenes de Sociologie*, 33 (1992): 109-50.

12. Excellent examples of this trend are Charles Gati, ed., *The Politics of Modernization in Eastern Europe. Testing the Soviet Model* (New York, N.Y.: Praeger, 1974); Jan F. Triska and Paul M. Cocks, eds., *Political Development in Eastern Europe* (New York, N.Y.: Praeger, 1977).

13. See, for example, Samuel P. Huntington, "Will More Countries Become Democratic?" *Political Science Quarterly*, 99 (Summer 1984): 193-218, 214. "In terms of cultural tradition, economic development, and social structure Czechoslovakia would certainly be a democracy today (and probably Hungary and Poland also) if it were not for the overriding veto of the Soviet presence."

14. Tatu Vanhanen, *The Process of Democratization. A Comparative Study of 147 States, 1980-88* (New York: Crane Russak, 1990), 170.

15. Ibid., 172.

16. Kenneth Jowitt, "Inclusion and Mobilization in European Leninist Regimes," in Triska and Cocks, eds., *Political Development*, 93-118, 93.

17. *Programm und Statut der Sozialistischen Einheitspartei Deutschlands vom 22. Mai 1976* (Berlin: Dietz, 1976), 41.

18. David W. Paul, "Hungary and Czechoslovakia: Rationalizing the Prevailing Policies," in Jim Seroka and Maurice D. Simon, eds., *Developed Socialism in the Soviet Bloc: Political Theory and Political Reality* (Boulder, Colorado: Westview Press, 1982), 37-59, 52.

19. Helga A. Welsh, "Participation in a Developed Socialist Society: The Case of the GDR." Paper delivered at the Tenth Annual Conference of the German Studies Association, Albuquerque, New Mexico, 26-28 September 1986.

20. Donald E. Schulz, "On the Nature and Function of Participation in Communist Systems: A Developmental Analysis," in Donald E. Schulz and Jan S. Adams, eds., *Political Participation in Communist Systems* (New York, N.Y.: Pergamon, 1981), 22-78, 52-59.

21. Cf. Dietrich Staritz, "Neue Akzente in der DDR-Bündnispolitik," *DDR-Report*, 16 (1983): 70-3.

22. Heinrich Bortfeldt, *Von der SED zur PDS. Wandlung zur Demokratie?* (Bonn and Berlin: Bouvier, 1992), 38-39.

23. Jan Wielgohs and Marianne Schulz, "Reformbewegung und Volksbewegung. Politische und soziale Aspekte im Umbruch der DDR-Gesellschaft," *Aus Politik und Zeitgeschichte*, B 16-17 (1990): 15-24, 16-17.

24. C. Bradley Scharf, "Social Services in the GDR: Administrative Co-Ordination and Citizen Participation." Paper delivered at the Third Biennial Conference of the GDR Studies Association, Washington, D.C., 13-15 October 1989, 10.

25. Cf. Gregor Gysi and Thomas Falkner, *Sturm aufs Große Haus. Der Untergang der SED* (Berlin: Edition Fischerinsel, 1990), 25-26.

26. See the chapter by Henry Krisch in this book.

27. In some cases—East Germany, Czechoslovakia, and Yugoslavia as well as in the former Soviet Union—it also encompassed a redefinition of national identity within different geographical and institutional settings. Cf. Claus Offe, "Capitalism by Democratic Design? Facing the Triple Transition in East Central Europe," *Social Research*, 58 (1991): 865-92.

28. Barbara Heyns and Ireneusz Bialecki, "Solidarnosc: Reluctant Vanguard or Makeshift Coalition?" *American Political Science Review*, 85 (1991): 351-70, 352.

29. James N. Rosenau, *Turbulence in World Politics. A Theory of Change and Continuity* (Princeton: Princeton University Press, 1990), 381.

30. Jürgen Becher, "Das Ringen um die Wirtschaftsreform in der DDR," *Deutschland Archiv*, 22 (1990): 687-96, 687.

31. Phillip J. Bryson and Manfred Melzer, *The End of the East German Economy. From Honecker to Reunification* (New York: St. Martin's Press, 1991), 22.

32. Stephen White, "Economic Performance and Communist Legitimacy," *World Politics*, 38 (1986): 462-82.

33. *Informationen des Bundesministeriums für innerdeutsche Beziehungen*, No. 24, 20 December 1985, 13. The rate of investment in the productive sector declined from 16.1 percent in 1970 to 9.9 percent in 1988. See "Schürers Krisen-Analyse," in *Deutschland Archiv*, 25 (1992): 1112-20, 1114.

34. Hans-Hermann Hertle, "Der Weg in den Bankrott der DDR-Wirtschaft. Das Scheitern der 'Einheit von Wirtschafts- und Sozialpolitik' am Beispiel der Schürer/Mittag-Kontroverse im Politbüro 1988," *Deutschland Archiv*, 25 (1992): 127-31.

35. Cf. Zvi Gitelman, "The Roots of Eastern Europe's Revolution," *Problems of Communism*, XXXIX (1990): 89-94, 89.

36. Mancur Olson, "The Logic of Collective Action in Soviet-type Societies,"*Journal of Soviet Nationalities*, 1 (1990): 8-27, 8.

37. Ibid., 15-16

38. Chalmers Johnson, *Revolutionary Change*. 2nd ed. (Stanford, Cal.: Stanford University Press), 94-104.

39. Olson, "The Logic of Collective Action," 16.

40. Gerd Meyer, *Die DDR-Machtelite in der Ära Honecker* (Tübingen: Francke Verlag, 1991), 158.

41. Helga A. Welsh, "Continuity and Change in the Local Political Elite in the GDR, 1952-1989." Paper delivered at the GDR Studies Association Conference, Washington, D.C., 13-15 October 1989, 13, 22.

42. Frank Adler, "'Das Bermuda-Dreieck' des Realsozialismus: Machtmonopolisierung — Entsubjektivierung — Nivellierung. Rückblicke auf die Gesellschafts- und Sozialstruktur der DDR und ihre Erosion," *BISS public*, no. 2 (1991): 5-46, 14.

43. György Csepeli and Antal Örkeny, "From Unjust Equality to Just Inequality," *The New Hungarian Quarterly*, 33 (1992): 71-76, 72.

44. See Daniel Küchenmeister, "Wann begann das Zerwürfnis zwischen Honecker and Gorbatschow? Erste Bemerkungen zu den Protokollen ihrer Vier-Augen-Gespräche," *Deutschland Archiv*, 26 (1993): 30-40.

45. Cited in Bortfeldt, *Von der SED zur PDS*, 48.

46. Tara Sonenshine, "The Revolution Has Been Televised," *The Washington Post* (National Weekly Edition), 8-14 October 1990.

47. Cf. Kazimierz Wasiak, "Gesellschaftliche Auswirkungen wachsender Teilnahme der DDR am internationalen Leben," *Deutschland Archiv*, 18 (1985): 727-40.

48. Walter Süß, "Perestrojka oder Ausreise. Abwehrpolitik der SED und gesellschaftliche Frustration," *Deutschland Archiv*, 22 (1989): 286-301, 296.

49. Rolf Reißig, "Der Umbruch in der DDR und der Niedergang realsozialistischer Systeme," *BISS public*, no. 1 (1991): 35-64, 45; Vladimir Tismaneanu, "Nascent Civil Society in the German Democratic Republic," *Problems of Communism*, XXXVIII (1989): 90-111.

50. Harry Müller, "Lebenswerte und nationale Identität," in Walter Friedrich and Hartmut Griese, eds., *Jugend and Jugendforschung in der DDR. Gesellschaftliche Situationen, Sozialisation und Mentalitätsentwicklung in den achtziger Jahren* (Opladen: Leske and Budrich, 1991), 124-35, 131-32.

51. Ibid., 138-39.

52. Rita R. Rogers, "Glasnost and the Emotional Climate in Eastern Europe," *Political Communication and Persuasion*, 7 (1990): 247-55, 252. See also Dietrich Staritz, "Ursachen und Konsequenzen einer deutschen Revolution," *Der Fischer Weltalmanach. Sonderband DDR* (Frankfurt am Main: Fischer Taschenbuch Verlag, 1990), 13-44, 24.

53. Cf. Dieter Voigt et al., "Die innerdeutsche Wanderung und der Vereinigungsprozeß," *Deutschland Archiv*, 23 (1990): 732-46, 732-34.

54. Walter Friedrich and Peter Förster, "Ostdeutsche Jugend 1990," *Deutschland Archiv*, 24 (1991): 349-60, 353.

55. Heinrich Bortfeldt, "The German Communists in Disarray," *The Journal of Communist Studies*, 7 (1991): 522-32, 524.

2

West German Policy
Toward East Germany:
A Motor of Unification?

Johannes L. Kuppe

Since 3 October 1990 the two German states—the Federal Republic of Germany (FRG) and the German Democratic Republic (GDR)—are again unified, scarcely a year after the collapse of the communist system of government in the GDR. After more than forty years of sociopolitical and, more recently, also mental separation of sixty million Germans in the West and sixteen million in the East, a unique and extraordinary event occurred in German history: by peaceful means, the Germans became a nation-state again. Other separated peoples, for example, the Vietnamese, had to fight wars for that goal; others, such as the Koreans, have not yet achieved it.

When the path toward unification seemed inevitable, the possible causes and motives for the collapse of the communist-governed system in the German Democratic Republic and the expressed desire for national unity on the part of the East German people were extensively discussed. Multiple causes and motives for the collapse of the SED government have been identified,[1] but the relative significance of each of them is disputed. There is also widespread agreement that some of the causes and motives for the collapse of the GDR were responsible for the unexpectedly swift pace of unification. In particular, the Soviet Union's rapid loss of hegemony under Gorbachev's leadership played an important role both in the demise of communist rule in East Germany and in clearing the way to unification.[2]

In contrast, the role of Bonn's inter-German policy (*Deutschlandpolitik*) vis-à-vis unification so far has not been analyzed in a systematic fashion; instead it has been largely left to heated political debates. It is this aspect of unification that I will address in this chapter. In particular, I will consider the question of whether successive West German governments were successful in the pursuit of unification which, according to the Preamble of the constitution (the Basic Law) was supposed to be the primary goal of German policy. This chapter is intended to contribute to the discussion of whether German unification more or less fell into the laps of the German people as a "historical present"—or whether West German policy toward the GDR actively pursued the goal of unification and was finally rewarded in 1990. According to the first scenario, the main reasons for unification can be found in an advantageous international situation, accompanied by the collapse of the regime in the GDR. In the latter case, the advantageous international environment was a major facilitator but not the main reason for unification. Instead, unification occurred largely as the result of a goal-oriented West German policy.

German-German Policy During the East-West Conflict

Unification and Western Integration: Incompatible or Mutually Reinforcing Goals?

Following World War II and the division of Germany into four zones of occupation, politicians of nearly all political persuasions—from Jakob Kaiser (CDU) to Kurt Schumacher (SPD)—sought to secure a role for a united Germany between East and West based on neutrality and national sovereignty. These concepts, however, were made obsolete by the outbreak of the Cold War, which manifested itself in the announcement of the Truman Doctrine and the adoption of the Marshall Plan in the spring and summer of 1947[3] and in a speech at the founding conference of the Cominform by Andrei Zhdanov, Stalin's confident and Leningrad party secretary, in September of the same year. Zhdanov confirmed the bipolar nature of postwar politics and characterized the cold war as an intense struggle between the two major camps. As a consequence, the first chancellor of the Federal Republic, Konrad Adenauer, had to abandon the achievement of (re)unification as a short-range policy goal.[4] Instead, his foremost goals became the attainment of West German sovereignty and the Federal Republic's firm economic, political, and military incorporation in the North Atlantic Community. Indisputably, Adenauer considered the Western integration of the Federal Republic as the cornerstone of his foreign policy. However, his motives for this policy decision are still a matter of scholarly debate. According to one view, Western integration was his primary concern and the acknowledgment of German unity was only a political declamation dictated by domestic imperatives. Another view holds that Western integration can be interpreted as an instrument that would strengthen the West generally and would ultimately force the surrender of the GDR by the Soviet Union. In any case, Adenauer's policy of Western integration made (re)unification a long-range goal; therefore, it was not a concern of day-to-day political operations.

Bonn's formula for its inter-German policy for the 1950s read as follows: (Re)unification is a task of the future and it will ensue on the basis of Western strength (*"Politik der Stärke"*) according to Western prerequisites.[5] Western integration was the order of the day, and the ratification of the Paris Treaties, the entry of West Germany into the North Atlantic Treaty Organization (NATO) in 1955, and Germany's membership in the European Coal and Steel Community (1951) and the European Economic Community (1957) firmly embedded the Federal Republic into the Western alliance. At the same time, the West German government—as well as the Western powers—rejected any political contacts with the East German government, which they considered illegitimate since it was not based on democratic elections.[6]

In addition, West Germany and its Western allies rejected any consideration of Stalin's proposal of 1952 in which the Soviet leader offered the conclusion of a peace treaty with Germany as a whole, provided that Germany would become a neutral state. Indeed, the Federal Government and its Western allies rejected all advances made by the Soviet Union and the GDR that aimed at maintaining German division and international recognition of the GDR—including First Secretary Nikita Khrushchev's advancement of his two-state theory in the mid-1950s.

This policy applied in particular to the offer by the East German Minister-President Otto Grotewohl in 1950, in which he proposed the creation of a politically-balanced "All-German Council"—a proposal repeatedly advanced by the Socialist Unity Party of Germany (SED) until well into the 1960s. It applied also to the proposal of the First Secretary of the Central Committee of the SED, Walter Ulbricht, at the end of 1956 in which he offered a confederation of the two German states.[7] Above all, it applied to the Soviet policy toward West Berlin. Among other demands, the Soviet leadership called for the transformation of West Berlin into a "Free City of Berlin," accompanied by a military withdrawal of Allied forces from West Berlin.

The GDR was not only not taken seriously as a negotiation partner but was ignored altogether, since the West German leadership viewed the GDR as a Soviet satellite whose international diplomatic recognition—and enhanced political status through political contacts—must be prevented under all circumstances. Therefore, an active and operational inter-German policy was not considered imperative. The functional instrument of this policy was the so-called Hallstein Doctrine, named after one of Adenauer's chief foreign policy aides. It stated that the Federal Republic would break off diplomatic relations with states that diplomatically recognized East Germany.

Announced in 1955, this doctrine contributed significantly to the international isolation of the GDR until the 1960s. Independent of whether one agreed with this particular policy approach, it is at the least uncertain whether a policy of close cooperation between the two German states would have even been feasible in view of the continuing deterioration in relations between East and West.

In retrospect, Adenauer's policy of Western integration can be interpreted as creating the prerequisites for the unification of Germany, even if the then-largest opposition party—the Social Democratic Party of Germany (SPD)—condemned Adenauer's policy (at least until the passage of its Bad Godesberg program in 1959)[8] as the greatest barrier to overcoming Germany's division.

Deutschlandpolitik in the 1960s: A Time of Change

During the 1960s, the domestic and foreign policy coordinates of Bonn's policy toward East Germany changed. After the Soviet Union's political and military retreat in the 1962 Cuban missile crisis, relations between the United States of America and the Soviet Union began to improve. This policy continued even after Khrushchev's dismissal and the political takeover of a new Moscow troika under the leadership of Leonid Brezhnev in 1964. However, the evolving climate of détente suffered a serious—if temporary—blow when Warsaw Pact troops invaded Czechoslovakia in August 1968 to halt the reforms known as the "Prague Spring."

The domestic situation in the Federal Republic had also changed significantly. By the time the Adenauer era ended in 1963, the Federal Republic had been elevated to a recognized and equal partner of the West. (Re)unification, however, was farther off than ever, for Bonn's policy toward the other German state consisted for the main part in emphasizing that the four former wartime allies bore responsibility for "all of Germany and Berlin" according to the Potsdam Agreement of 1945 and article 7 of the Paris Treaties of 1954.

This ritualized declamation provoked neither the Western allies to independent actions nor did it stimulate activities in inter-German relations. The construction of the Berlin Wall in August 1961 demonstrated beyond doubt that the political rhetoric which the two German states had exchanged during the 1950s would not contribute to mitigating but, instead, to deepening the division of Germany. It became paramount to brake the stalemate situation.

Already under Federal Chancellor Adenauer, the changing political situation in East-West relations began to affect German policy. Increased foreign policy activities toward Eastern Europe manifested themselves in particular through the establishment of West German trade missions in Poland,

Romania, and Hungary in 1963; Bulgaria in 1964; and Czechoslovakia in 1967. These foreign policy initiatives were motivated in part by hopes that the GDR could be isolated from its allies—thereby reducing its value to the Soviet Union, which might then be willing to give up one of its most important East European partners. Federal Chancellor Ludwig Erhard (in office between 1963 and 1966) advanced this new political thinking in the so-called Peace Note of 25 March 1966, which was communicated to all states which the Federal Republic had recognized diplomatically and in which renunciation of force treaties were offered to the East European states and the Soviet Union. As usual, the GDR was excluded from this offer.[9]

In response to Chancellor Erhard's diplomatic offer, the SED leadership was compelled to take a stand since it feared encirclement and the isolation of the GDR. This fear was enhanced by other West German policy moves that signaled the beginnings of a more active foreign policy toward the East.[10] Given the unchanged position of West Germany toward the East German state—"reunification only through free elections"—these moves continued to question the legal existence of the GDR. The "Ulbricht doctrine" was a direct outcome of this fear. It stated that the GDR considered diplomatic relations between countries of the Warsaw Pact and West Germany a violation of a declaration signed by the members of the Warsaw Treaty Organization in 1966 in Bucharest.

The West German government initiated a policy toward the socialist-governed countries in the East that combined pragmatic flexibility with firmness in basic principles. This policy was later elaborated and became known as the "policy of small steps" (*Politik der kleinen Schritte*). Egon Bahr, SPD politician and a close adviser of Berlin's governing mayor, Willy Brandt, had called for "change through rapprochement" (*Wandel durch Annäherung*) which was based on the assumption that increased communication and cooperation with the East would result in the liberalization of domestic relations within the Eastern bloc. It was seen as a significant first step toward improved relations with East Germany when the German federal government, in conjunction with the Senate of [West] Berlin as the leading negotiator, concluded four agreements with the GDR government between 1963 and 1966. For the first time since the building of the Berlin Wall, these agreements allowed citizens of West Berlin the opportunity to conduct short-term family visits to East Berlin.[11]

At the end of 1966 the conservative CDU/CSU-FDP coalition government collapsed and was replaced by a Grand Coalition (*Große Koalition*) made up of the CDU/CSU and the SPD. For the first time since the end of World War II, a member of the Social Democratic Party, Willy Brandt, was represented at the level of the federal cabinet headed by Chancellor Kurt Georg Kiesinger (CDU). Already prior to the formation of the Grand Coalition and Brandt's elevation to foreign minister, the SPD had become a driving force in inter-German relations and relations with Eastern Europe in general.[12] With the SPD's takeover of the foreign office during the Grand Coalition government, the voices of those in the CDU/CSU who had been supportive of a more active East European and inter-German policy (*Ost- und Deutschlandpolitik*) gained in influence. Under pressure from the SPD, Chancellor Kiesinger joined the forces calling for change.

Thus, in 1967 an exchange of letters between Kiesinger and the Chairman of the GDR's Council of Ministers, Willi Stoph, opened a new era in inter-German relations. Previously official letters from GDR political elites would be routinely returned unopened by Western officials. The GDR was simply seen and treated as if it did not exist; it was a "phenomenon," as Kiesinger once said. At this point, however, the Federal Chancellor offered negotiations at all levels without previous international recognition of the GDR. For the first time the federal government dealt directly with East German politicians in matters concerning the German question, thereby compelling the SED to react. The West German government expected that these new semi-official contacts below the level of international recognition would ease the situation for the people in the divided country. However, the government in East Berlin foreclosed major accomplishments and indeed ended this inter-German initiative when it realized that its main goal of international diplomatic recognition by the West was not attainable.

The invasion of Czechoslovakia by Soviet-led Warsaw Pact troops in August 1968 adversely affected inter-German relations and impeded further steps toward the normalization of relations between the two German states. The SED, which had actively supported this action of socialist internationalism against a fraternal state, did not grow weary of relentlessly seeking to blame the West (in particular the Federal Republic) for the Czechoslovak reform development. In reality, however, the East German political elite was already retreating. When the Soviet Union attempted to break out of its foreign policy isolation after the Czechoslovak debacle and sought to introduce new measures of détente toward the West,[13] Walter Ulbricht—who, as First Secretary of the SED and chairman of both the State Council and the National Defense Council, had become the indisputable leader of East Germany—demonstrated considerable reluctance toward an opening to the West and thus toward the policy of détente.

The desire of the Soviet leadership to base its foreign policy on a relaxation of tensions with the West changed its attitude toward the major point of controversy in German-Soviet relations: the issue of West German ties to West Berlin. According to the Western interpretation, West Berlin was an integral part of the Federal Republic of Germany. In contrast, the Soviet Union, the GDR, and other East European countries adamantly denied West

Berlin's ties to the Federal Republic. In 1969, however, Moscow hesitantly agreed that the election of Gustav Heinemann as Federal President could be held in West Berlin and thereby acknowledged the special ties between West Berlin and the Federal Republic. Ulbricht, however, was not prepared to make concessions even if this policy collided with Soviet aspirations to improve relations with the West. The SED's defensive posture toward the Federal Republic expressed itself in stereotypical repetitions of unattainable demands. The SED's attitude toward the solution of the German question became hollow since it was based on verbal acrobatics full of internal contradictions. Into the 1960s, SED functionaries had been satisfied to justify Germany's national division as a supposedly natural development on the way to socialism[14] while still maintaining the facade of a unified nation. Toward the end of the decade, however, they began proclaiming that the divided country had developed into two nations: one that was socialist and one that was capitalist. But even from a Marxist-Leninist point of view this reasoning could not be justified, and the communist allies in the East, including the Soviet Union, refused to follow the SED's interpretation.

Treaty Policy of the Social-Liberal Coalition

For the first time in the history of the Federal Republic of Germany, a coalition government between the Social Democrats and the Free Democrats took office in the fall of 1969. From the very outset, the new administration took decisive steps to change West German policy toward the East. In doing so, it adjusted its policy to the new political environment in Europe more generally and responded to Soviet policy initiatives in particular. Starting in 1969 the Soviet leadership signaled to the Western powers its willingness to tackle the pending Berlin question in a way that should neither burden the Allies nor bring new threats to the people residing in West Berlin.

In his inauguration speech, newly-elected Chancellor Willy Brandt declared that West German policy toward its Eastern counterpart would be based on the formula of one nation but two separate states. This formula—which in essence remained valid until unification—permitted continued affirmation of the goal of national unity while opening up possibilities of cooperation that would benefit the population in both parts of Germany.

Although the GDR was thereby recognized as an equal partner in negotiations, it still had not come a step closer to its major foreign policy goal of diplomatic recognition by the West German state. The West German government refused to view East Germany as a foreign state; instead it reaffirmed the special character of relations between the two Germanys. West Germany's continued affirmation of the concept of an indivisibly unified

German nation was considered a permanent denial of the GDR's right to an independent, nationally-defined existence.

The political elites in the East felt compelled to respond with an ideology of complete separation from the West to counter the emerging climate of détente and the new West German initiatives toward the East. However, this policy, which was carried to its extreme, lacked credibility and persuasiveness. The policy of relaxation between East and West pressured the SED into expanding instruments of delimitation (*Abgrenzung*)[15] and defense, which in turn increasingly separated the regime from the population. Ultimately, this policy would contribute significantly to the downfall of the SED regime in the fall of 1989.

The developments in the spring of 1970 demonstrated the increased pressure under which the East German leadership was forced to operate. In March and May two governmental delegations, led by West German Chancellor Willy Brandt and Willy Stoph, Chairman of the Council of Ministers of the GDR, met in Erfurt (East Germany) and Kassel (West Germany). These meetings did not result in any immediate results[16] since the SED leadership continued to demand that the international diplomatic recognition of the GDR was a sine qua non if inter-German normalization were to commence and succeed. On instructions of SED First Secretary Walter Ulbricht, the "exchange of thoughts" with the West German leaders was stopped. Ulbricht's stubborn attitude toward détente and his misperception of the changed international environment in all likelihood was not the decisive reason for his removal as First Secretary of the SED, but it contributed to his replacement by Erich Honecker in 1971.

Decreasing East-West confrontation made possible a flurry of East-West diplomatic activity during the remainder of the decade. West Germany concluded treaties recognizing existing state boundaries with some of its East European neighbors and the Soviet Union, which were duly ratified by the respective parliaments.[17] In 1971, the United States, the United Kingdom, France, and the Soviet Union endorsed the Berlin Accord governing regulated access to West Berlin. Thirty-three European states, the United States, and Canada signed the Final Act of the Conference for Security and Cooperation in Europe (CSCE) in 1975.

This evolving international network of détente provided the background for rapprochement in inter-German relations. The Berlin Accord made possible the conclusion of a Transit Agreement and a Transportation Agreement between the two German states, and the Senate of [West] Berlin and the GDR government reached an agreement concerning inter-city traffic and the regulation of territorial questions.

By the end of 1972, Bonn and East Berlin completed negotiations on a Treaty of Basic Relations (the Basic Treaty).[18] The treaty did not solve the question concerning Germany's future nor did it alter the four victorious powers' responsibility for the solution of the German question.[19] Nonetheless, some foreign observers interpreted the treaty as a kind of "substitute peace treaty" that sealed the existence of two German states.[20] In the Federal Republic, the treaty was met with almost unanimous rejection by the conservative opposition of CDU/CSU in the parliament. Having lost the vote, the opposition asked the Federal Constitutional Court to review the question whether the Basic Treaty violated provisions of the West German constitution (Basic Law). However, the Federal Constitutional Court affirmed that the negotiated Basic Treaty did not violate the obligation to unite the two countries as has been set forth in the Preamble to the Basic Law.

In many ways the Basic Treaty was the "mother treaty" for more than three dozen successor treaties and agreements, protocols, and other contractual agreements concluded with the GDR until the 1980s.[21] It was the contractual foundation on which the Federal Republic's desired special relations with the GDR could be developed, although the SED leadership interpreted it in a way that violated its letter and spirit numerous times. The SED soon made clear that the Basic Treaty was not a modus vivendi for the foreseeable future and that it desired to pursue its ultimate goal of international recognition through the Treaty. The special character of the relations and the refusal by West Germany to consider the GDR a foreign country were reconfirmed once again in 1974 when "Permanent Representations" with quasi-diplomatic status instead of embassies were opened in Bonn and East Berlin.[22]

The foundations on which the policy of rapprochement was based remained unchanged after Helmut Schmidt succeeded Willy Brandt as federal chancellor when it was discovered in 1974 that a close aide to Brandt had spied for the East German government. Nor did the policy change in 1982 when the SPD-FDP coalition government was replaced by a coalition government made up of the CDU/CSU and FDP under the leadership of Chancellor Helmut Kohl.

During the 1980s, however, the international environment changed considerably, allowing the two German states to gain independence and flexibility in their relations with one another.[23] The death of Leonid Brezhnev in November 1982 signaled the beginning of a continuing decline of Moscow's foreign policy dominance in its sphere of influence—and thereby also of its hegemony over Eastern Europe and the GDR. In particular following the ascent of Mikhail Gorbachev to the position of General Secretary of the CPSU in March 1985, the tense bipolar relationship between the United States and the Soviet Union began to waver—to the advantage of a multipolar division of power. Thus, the foreign policy coordinates changed for the most important Allies of both superpowers, the Federal Republic of

Germany, on the one hand, and the German Democratic Republic, on the other.

The Détente Process: Pros and Cons

It is not essential here to clarify the individual phases of Bonn's treaty policy nor to assess the numerous setbacks and obstacles to its implementation. Instead, the primary question is whether—and to what extent—the policy of rapprochement might have obstructed or facilitated the policy goal of achieving German unification.

To be sure, the policy of "small steps" initially contributed significantly to the international prestige of the GDR. Virtually all members of the United Nations shortly accorded diplomatic recognition to the East German regime, albeit sometimes with minor qualifications (as was the case with the United States). In 1973 the Federal Republic and the German Democratic Republic became the one hundred thirty-third and one hundred thirty-fourth members of the United Nations, respectively. The international reputation of the GDR was undoubtedly given a boost when Federal Chancellor Schmidt and the Chairman of the State Council and General Secretary of the SED, Erich Honecker, met in Schorfheide, north of Berlin, in December 1981, and in particular by Honecker's official visit during the fall of 1987 to the Federal Republic, which carried with it almost all the attributes of a state visit.

One could argue that the international recognition of the GDR also helped stabilize communist rule at home and therefore undermined the goal of unification.[24] Yet, as events proved, Bonn's treaty and dialogue policies during the seventeen years following the signing of the Basic Treaty had a decisive consequence which seems to be more important than all other considerations: it forced the GDR to relax its policy of closed borders. In a drastic departure from past policies, each year millions of Western visitors traveled to the GDR. Restrictions on travel to the West changed over the years as well. Increasing domestic pressure made possible the legal visit or emigration of tens of thousands of people per year. In relaxing its previous travel restrictions, the SED had to take into account that its propaganda depiction of the allegedly superior path of socialist development to Western conceptions of modernization would be challenged by the reality of competing and diametrically opposed socio-political concepts and experiences. Moreover, those competitive images were strengthened by the persuasive power of a highly attractive way of life and consumer world in the West which impressed visitors from the GDR.

One can therefore contend, with considerable plausibility, that the real success of Bonn's German-German policy during the 1970s and 1980s lay in the expansion of channels of communication between the two states.

Following Germany's political unification, Bonn's German-German policy of the past two decades has nevertheless become a hotly debated domestic political issue regardless of political affiliation. The implosive manner of the SED regime's collapse demonstrated that it was significantly more unstable than most professional and other observers could determine from the outside or had wanted to believe. The question is often posed whether the ruling elites in the GDR would have had to abandon their power hegemony earlier had they not profited from the "policy of small steps." In answering this question, one has to be aware of the dilemma in which policy makers found themselves: It seemed that the consequences of the division of Germany could only be modified and eased at the price of negotiations with communist rulers, i.e., their limited recognition.

Today, however, one can legitimately ask whether West German administrations did go beyond the level of courtesy needed for intergovernmental interaction. One can argue that the activities of citizen movements during the 1980s in the GDR were seen in the West as isolated developments and not as a sign of the growing internal weakness of the system. The Kohl/Genscher administration continued the policies of their predecessors without major policy changes, albeit with stronger nationalist overtones. But it is also true that they contributed even further to the international recognition of the GDR. For instance, in the last years before the collapse of the GDR, high-ranking officials at the level of the federal as well as the state administrations never seemed to miss an opportunity to pay their respect to Erich Honecker. Who, after all, wanted to be seen as an opponent of détente?

The SPD, after its march into opposition, even intensified its contacts with the SED and behaved almost as if it were still the party in charge of inter-German relations. Joint working groups composed of representatives of SPD and SED developed "initiatives," "ground rules," and "suggestions" for a corridor that was supposed to be free of atomic weapons and for further arms reductions in Europe.

In early September 1987, the Basic Values Commission of the SPD's Board of Directors and a group from the Academy of Social Sciences of the SED's Central Committee jointly published a paper entitled *Ideological Controversy and Mutual Security*.[25] The paper reflected many years of discussion on issues of mutual recognition, peace, and reform. Its publication had two contradictory effects. On the one hand, the joint paper proved a stimulus for internal party discussions within the SED which at times became quite tumultuous since it called for a willingness to engage in political dialogue with domestic opponents. On the other hand, the paper accorded the SED enhanced legitimacy since its existence was not only confirmed but also taken seriously by the largest Social Democratic party in the West.

The advocates of increased inter-German dialogue still stand by their position.[26] However, one can ask whether it was not a sign of "company blindness" and "loss of distance," or perspective, to certify the SED's reform capability precisely at a time when its defense against Soviet-initiated reforms accelerated into grotesque measures, such as the censoring of Soviet publications and in particular Gorbachev's speeches.[27]

Conclusion

In the 1980s both the government in power and the opposition acted on the assumption that German unification could only be achieved within the context of European unification processes. Consequently, unification was not an operative goal of day-to-day political measures. The only difference between the two major partisan positions was that the CDU/CSU was more outspoken in emphasizing the long-range goal of unification while the SPD opposition was more reserved in stating such policy goals. According to numerous opinion polls conducted in the 1980s, scarcely anyone in East or West Germany believed in unification in the foreseeable future. However, it seems nevertheless true that West German policy toward East Germany did contribute to unification.

In response to the question at the beginning of this chapter "Was German policy toward the East a motor of unification?" two answers seem plausible: (1) Although it cannot be tested on empirical grounds, it seems reasonable to speculate that the SED regime would have collapsed as a result of the decline of Soviet power even if the Federal Republic of Germany had continued Adenauer's policy of strength in inter-German relations which rejected negotiations and communication with the GDR leadership. In retrospect, one can argue that many policy initiatives which contributed to the legitimacy of the communist political system and which lend credibility to a system that suffered from irrefutable structural defects proved unnecessary. The "policy of small steps" was, after all, always tied to the hope that the communist power structure could be reformed from the top down—that is, liberalized and continued for the foreseeable future.[28] Today this hope is seen as illusory, but it seemed a valid policy option when détente was first initiated. (2) In the 1970s, the domestic and international situation called for changes in inter-German policy, and there was no reasonable alternative to the path that was pursued. The policies of small steps and rapprochement contributed significantly to tying the East German communists into a network of treaties which they could not renounce without confronting the possibility of renewed international isolation even within the Soviet-dominated bloc. At the same time, the treaties between West and East Germany made growing communication possible which ultimately helped to undermine the legitimacy of the regime. The political and economic systems in the GDR—and elsewhere in the Eastern bloc—collapsed because of their own structural deficiencies, a process that was accelerated when the Soviet Union removed its protective shield. The policy of détente in inter-German relations might well have contributed to the defeat of lingering Stalinist practices.

In the early 1970s, former GDR Foreign Minister Otto Winzer had called Bonn's inter-German policy "an aggression in felt house shoes." He was correct, although certainly in a way he did not anticipate. Bonn's policy was a defensible form of "aggression" because it sought to achieve unification in a peaceful manner. Inter-German policy was always interventionist—even though West German politicians denied such claims—because it affected the stability of the regime in the GDR. One can even call the policy ingenious because it was willing to grant some measure of stabilization for the East German regime while revealing the structural weaknesses of the system and its lack of legitimacy vis-à-vis the population in East Germany. It is for these reasons that German unity was not an accidental by-product at the end of the East-West conflict but was also the result of continued efforts aimed at achieving unity.

Notes

1. An extraordinarily extensive body of literature discussing these aspects is available. The following sources also contain further significant bibliographic information: Eckhard Jesse and Armin Mitter, eds., *Die Gestaltung der deutschen Einheit. Geschichte-Politik-Gesellschaft* (Bonn and Berlin: Bouvier Verlag, 1992), and Werner Weidenfeld and Karl-Rudolf Korte, eds., *Handwörterbuch zur deutschen Einheit* (Frankfurt/M.: Campus Verlag, 1991). For the history of both German states prior to unification see Werner Weidenfeld and Hartmut Zimmermann, eds., *Deutschland Handbuch. Eine doppelte Bilanz 1949-1989* (Munich: Carl Hanser Verlag, 1989); Rolf Reißig and Gert-Joachim Glaeßner, eds., *Das Ende eines Experiments. Umbruch in der DDR und deutsche Einheit* (Berlin: Dietz Verlag, 1991); and Gert-Joachim Glaeßner and Ian Wallace, eds., *The German Revolution of 1989: Causes and Consequences* (New York: Berg Publishers, 1992).

2. Hannes Adomeit, "Gorbachev and German Unification: Revision of Thinking, Realignment of Power," *Problems of Communism,* 39 (1990): 1-23.

3. See, for example, Joseph L. Nogee and Robert H. Donaldson, *Soviet Foreign Policy Since World War II,* 4th ed. (New York: Macmillan, 1992), 85-100.

4. On this point see Frank R. Pfetsch, *West Germany: Internal Structures and External Relations* (New York: Praeger, 1988).

5. Cf. Henry Ashby Turner Jr., *The Two Germanies since 1945* (New Haven and London: Yale University Press, 1987), 67-82.

6. For a discussion of the controversy surrounding the proposal by Stalin, see Gerd Meyer, *Die sowjetische Deutschland-Politik im Jahre 1952* (Cologne: Böhlau Verlag, 1970) and, more recently, Gerhard Wettig, "Die Stalin-Note vom 10. März 1952 als geschichtswissenschaftliches Problem," *Deutschland Archiv,* 25 (1992): 157-67.

7. For a summary presentation of the "Deutschlandpolitik der SED," see Bundesministerium für innerdeutsche Beziehungen, *DDR Handbuch,* vol. 1, 3d ed. (Cologne: Verlag Wissenschaft und Politik, 1985), 279-305.

8. In this program, the SPD relinquished a number of basic theoretical positions and then unqualifiedly acknowledged the Federal Republic's integration into the Western defense alliance. Cf. Turner, *The Two Germanies,* 80-82.

9. A proclamation of the Evangelical Church in Germany preceded this "Peace Note" by two weeks. The Church paper called for an independent policy toward Eastern Europe by Bonn. In the East, therefore, the impression was strengthened that the Federal Republic was prepared to move beyond repetitions of German-German legalisms and was interested in expanding its political activities in Eastern Europe.

10. The pressures for change are elaborated by Wolfram F. Hanrieder, *Germany, America, Europe. Forty Years of German Foreign Policy* (New Haven and London: Yale University Press, 1989), 170-94.

11. In order to conclude these agreements both sides had been willing to exclude certain principal policy positions—for example, the question of international recognition and the question of ties between West Berlin and the Federal Republic of Germany. This was exceedingly more difficult for the GDR side, which could expect no diplomatic gain from signing the treaty. In contrast, West Berlin had negotiated the agreement in close coordination with the Federal Republic and with the permission of the Western Allies and had thereby reaffirmed its ties with the Federal Republic of Germany.

12. At the behest of SED First Secretary Ulbricht and as a result of tedious preliminary talks, the SED and SPD had agreed that high-ranking party functionaries ("guest speakers") would meet in July 1966 in Karl Marx City (Chemnitz) and in Hannover. However, after much discussion the SED canceled the "speakers exchange program."

13. These measures included, inter alia, the beginning of uninterrupted conversations with the Federal Republic about a renunciation of force treaty.

14. An expression of this effort was passage in 1962 of the so-called "National Documents" in which "Adenauer's divisive clique" was no longer alone said to be guilty of dividing Germany. Instead, the formation of a second sovereign (later the only sovereign) German state was said to be the unavoidable result of natural historical developments. This concept results from the deterministic aspect of Historical Materialism, which, according to Soviet interpretation, sees historical developments influenced by "laws" resembling those valid for the natural sciences.

15. See the entries "Abgrenzung," "Nation und nationale Frage," and "Deutschlandpolitik der SED" in the *DDR Handbuch*. An overview of the SED's view of the national question is provided by Gottfried Zieger in *Die Haltung der SED und DDR zur Einheit Deutschlands 1947-1987* (Cologne: Verlag Wissenschaft und Politik, 1988), 322.

16. In the long run, however, the meeting was not inconsequential, for Chancellor Brandt put forth a twenty-point program in Kassel which, although totally rejected by Stoph, nevertheless later was seen to be completely realized in German-German agreements.

17. Renunciation of force treaties were concluded with the USSR and Poland in the summer and fall of 1970, and a "Treaty of Mutual Relations" was concluded with Czechoslovakia in 1973. The most comprehensive presentation of these treaties of the Federal Republic is found in Benno Zündorf, *Die Ostverträge. Die Verträge von Moskau, Warschau, Prag, das Berlin-Abkommen und die Verträge mit der DDR* (Munich: Verlag C.H. Beck, 1979).

18. The significance of the Basic Treaty for inter-German relations is addressed by Ernst D. Plock in *The Basic Treaty and the Evolution of East-West German Relations* (Boulder and London: Westview Press, 1986).

19. Dettmar Cramer provides a lucid political assessment of the Basic Treaty in *Deutschland nach dem Grundvertrag* (Stuttgart: Verlag Bonn Aktuell, 1973). See also Wilhelm Bruns, *Deutsch-deutsche Beziehungen. Prämissen - Probleme - Perspektiven*, 3d. ed. (Opladen: Verlag Leske und Budrich, 1982).

20. Eberhard Schulz and Peter Danylow have put together the international view of the German question in *Bewegung in der deutschen Frage? Die ausländischen Besorgnisse über die Entwicklung in beiden deutschen Staaten*, 2d ed. (Bonn: Europa Union Verlag, 1985).

21. Cf. "Zehn Jahre Deutschlandpolitik" and "Innerdeutsche Beziehungen" in the series, *Die Entwicklung der Beziehungen zwischen der Bundesrepublik Deutschland und der Deutschen Demokratischen Republik*, for

the periods 1969-1979 and 1980-1986 (Bonn: Bundesministerium für innerdeutsche Beziehungen, 1980 and 1986).

22. In addition, Bonn's Permanent Representation in the GDR (unlike other diplomats) was not part of the Foreign Ministry but was responsible instead directly to the Chancellor's Office.

23. For detailed accounts of the developments in inter-German relations in the 1980s, see A. James McAdams, "Explaining Inter-German Cooperation in the 1980s," *German Studies Review* (DAAD Special Issue 1990): 97-114; F. Stephen Larrabee, ed., *The Two German States and European Security* (London: Macmillan, 1989); and Ronald D. Asmus, "The Dialectics of Détente and Discord," *Orbis*, 28 (1985): 743-74.

24. On this question see Claus-Dieter Ehlermann, et al., *Innerdeutsche Wirtschaftsbeziehungen* (Baden-Baden: Nomos Verlag, 1975). For more recent discussions of the economic benefits which the GDR derived from improved inter-German relations, see Jeffrey Michel, "Economic Exchanges Specific to the Two German States," *Studies in Comparative Communism*, 20 (1987): 73-83, and Sandra Peterson, "Inter-German Relations: Has the Cost Risen for the West?," in Gale A. Mattox and J. Vaughan, eds., *Germany Through American Eyes* (Boulder: Westview Press, 1989), 47-65. The current discussion centers around two main issues: (1) To what extent did the government of the Federal Republic contribute in 1982 and 1983 to the international credit worthiness of the GDR and postponed the collapse of the East German economy by securing two bank credits for the GDR, each amounting to a billion DM? (2) Even the nature of the payments for the release of approximately 30,000 political prisoners from the GDR between 1963 and 1989 has come under attack. What was officially declared as the delivery of goods in the amount of three billion DM turned out to be payment of hard currency to the GDR.

25. The paper was reprinted in *Deutschland Archiv*, 21 (1988): 86-91. It also appeared in *Neues Deutschland*, the central organ of the SED, on 28 August 1987. For a detailed analysis see Ann L. Philipps, *Seeds of Change in the German Democratic Republic: The SED-SPD Dialogue*. Research Reports No. 1 (Washington, D.C.: American Institute for Contemporary German Studies, December 1989).

26. The SPD's leading negotiator, Erhard Eppler, has specifically justified the Ideology Paper by arguing that it strengthened GDR opposition inside and outside of the SED and therefore facilitated a peaceful change in the GDR government. See "Die Geschichte im Rückspiegel," in *Die Zeit*, 28 February 1992.

27. The question was put this way by, among others, Robert Leicht in "Trübungen auf der Netzhaut," in *Die Zeit*, 20 March 1992.

28. The question remains an open one whether Bonn's "policy of small steps" would also have achieved unification if—as all professional observers presumed—the Soviet Union had not disintegrated and had not agreed to unification. In hindsight was West German policy correct only because it was helped by an unexpected and incalculable change in foreign policy calculations within the Soviet leadership? Clearly, no one can persuasively answer this speculative question.

PART TWO

Process and Outcomes

3

Delegitimation of the Old Regime: Reforming and Transforming Ideas in the Last Years of the GDR

Henry Krisch

Looking back upon eighteen astonishing months of political upheaval, the East German philosopher, Hans-Peter Kröger, asked how the East German regime could have maintained itself after 1968 with relative ease, only to collapse like a house of cards in the fall of 1989.[1] This sense of surprise over the rapid and total collapse of what had been widely regarded as one of the more stable of the communist regimes was widely shared by Western observers.[2] Moreover, judging by memoir literature, this outcome certainly caught GDR leaders by surprise. Although many members of the SED leadership had become aware in the years after 1986 that serious reforms were needed, they continued almost to the end to think in terms of persuading party chief Erich Honecker to accept minimal reforms.[3]

Although the political leadership of the GDR was notably set in its policies and personnel, this hard crust of authority was rendered increasingly hollow and brittle by a steady erosion of the regime's legitimacy.[4] The legitimacy of the system that proclaimed itself as "real existing socialism" (*Realsozialismus*) ebbed through a number of channels. Its failures in economic policy produced a massive popular secession, one made more painful because it included so many young and highly trained people. Moreover, the regime's blatant aping of Western consumption values and its nearly total surrender to the international youth culture undermined its moral claim to an alternative way of life.[5] The regime's increasingly overt mobilization of the all-German national past left its legitimacy vulnerable to West Germany's embodiment of the same legacy.[6]

An important factor in this decline of legitimacy was the inability of the regime to respond positively to, or generate itself, new impulses in social and political thought. The growing divergence between the regime's assumptions and the outlook of a changing society deprived the GDR of political legitimacy, leaving it vulnerable to any sudden adverse blow.

In addition to the increasingly problematical domestic situation, the regime faced new and difficult external challenges. These included developments in Eastern Europe, particularly the rise of Solidarity in Poland, and the challenge of Gorbachev's reform programs in the USSR after 1985.[7] The regime itself increasingly fostered comparisons with West Germany, and it sponsored an improved image of Germany's national heritage. However, it faced an increasingly critical response from a population quite capable of making its own judgments of Western reality, based on information derived from increased travel abroad and from the almost ubiquitous West German television.

One of the groups challenging the regime were traditional critics of Leninist one-party systems—the literary intelligentsia. Both under Walter Ulbricht and throughout the Honecker era, writers were either driven to emigrate (as was the case with Reiner Kunze), expatriated (Wolf Biermann), jailed and then expelled (Erich Loest), or simply harassed by the authorities (Stefan Heym). The most prominent GDR novelist, Christa Wolf, was for a time shadowed by the secret police (the *Stasi*). These writers—as well as many others—provided an independent and often critical overview of such issues as the Nazi past of the GDR "everyman" (*Jedermann*), the ecological damage wrought by the GDR's overriding production imperative, the special concerns of women, and numerous other problems.

Such writers undeniably contributed to the delegitimation of the regime by addressing moral and social issues otherwise excluded from public discussion, and they provided otherwise unavailable information through their fiction, dramas, and films. As important as they were, however, the real challenge to the old order came from a variety of professional and social groups whose ideas emerged slowly and indirectly from within official institutions such as universities, research institutes, party and government offices, and a semi-tolerated penumbra of church-related peace, feminist, ecological, and civil rights circles. Some of this material was known before the *Wende* of October 1989; much more has become known since then. The contributions of such groups is the principal focus of this chapter.

"New Thinking" About Politics and Society

Two aspects of "new thinking" about the future course of East German development that surfaced during the 1980s are of special interest: the first deriving from social science research, and the second emerging from civic action movements. These two strands, emerging in different segments of GDR society, converged during the fall of 1989 to generate the "peaceful revolution" that envisioned a reformed GDR.

New thinking about politics and society presented an important challenge to the regime. Through the Honecker ascendancy, and with increasing force during the last half decade of the regime, a variety of individuals and social groups raised a series of claims against the justification of the regime's arbitrary exercise of authority. My objective is to analyze the new thinking that emerged during the final months of the old order and the first months of the new order, focusing on those ideas that most directly challenged the existing system and on the institutions and persons that generated and nurtured them. Such delegitimizing ideas derive their political significance from the nature of the society being challenged. In the GDR, as in the rest of communist Europe, the "revolutionary" ideas often seemed commonplace borrowing from the world of pluralist "bourgeois" democracy. This suggests that the political revolution was undergirded by a culture shift in which the GDR (and Eastern Europe generally) accepted Western norms as their own. The relative weakness of "third way" ideas (to be discussed below) probably reflects this cultural aspect of the revolution.

An important, if ultimately ineffective intellectual challenge to the regime, came from the GDR's intellectual and academic establishment. Centered in university and academic institutions, especially (but not exclusively) in disciplines ranging from state law (*Staats- und Rechtswissenschaft*) to philosophy and sociology, reform thinking in these fields resulted from several developments inherent in the relative stabilization achieved in the dozen years or so after Honecker's accession to power in 1971.

Throughout the 1970s and 1980s, the ruling party-state elite in the GDR faced the task of managing an increasingly complex society. The GDR's ability to compete internationally, and especially within Germany, depended on qualitative improvements in the economy and society and on adapting to a growing demand for effective citizenship. A consequence of these changing tasks of governance was the regime's growing acceptance of empirical social research as a tool of effective economic and social management.[8] As a result, reform thinking spread throughout the scholarly world and into lower and middle ranks of the party itself. It included such fields as the nature of international relations, the comparative study of communist regimes, the question of clashing social interests, the individual's relationship to society, the nature of citizenship, and the concept of the political system.

One aspect of reform thinking in the GDR was a redefinition of the nature of world affairs generally and international relations between the two ideological blocs in particular. In this, as in other efforts to modify the received official dogmas, East German thinking paralleled and was heavily

influenced by similar Soviet developments.[9] A central feature of this strand
of reform thought was a new evaluation of the essential nature and international role of "imperialism," i.e., the capitalist democracies and, in the GDR
context, especially West Germany.[10] The essence of this argument was that
contemporary political and economic conditions provided the "imperialists"
strategic, ecological, and financial incentives to modify their aggressive policies. Consequently, they would seek new ways of maximizing their social
and economic advantages; this would lead in turn to the emergence of an international constituency favoring peaceful relations.

This change in interpretation presented a useful rationale for accepting
policies that would allow the GDR and, more significantly, its people to
have contact with the imperialist West. Since such contacts would not necessarily strengthen a hostile rival, the prospect of mutual borrowing and
learning emerged. That is, one could accept a Western position while remaining loyal to the GDR.

Increased attention to the issue of human rights, particularly in international comparison, also influenced reform thought in the GDR.[11] Moving
away from the traditional communist view that Western emphasis on human
rights was but political aggression, GDR scholars now saw human rights—
measured by common criteria—as a peaceful and generally beneficial arena
of East-West competition. Even in the more careful phrasing of published
work, it was possible to declare that international human rights criteria
should also serve as yardsticks for measuring the human rights record of the
GDR and other socialist states.[12] Moreover, the source of these ideas was
almost as important as their content. The fact that so many of these scholars
held important positions (and hence were also party members) in some of
the most prestigious universities and academies of the GDR reflects the extent to which reform thinking had permeated deeply within the temples of
the official belief system. An entirely different question is whether such
scholars were able to influence the top Party and state leadership with their
new ideals. By their own admissions, as noted below, their achievements in
this regard were meager.

A good example of rather modest reform thinking, which was nonetheless too bold for publication prior to the *Wende*, appeared in the final
issue of *Staat und Recht*.[13] The East German scholar, Karl-Heinz Schöneberg, had observed in an address to the journal's editorial board in 1987 that
too many of the journal's articles amounted to little more than exercises in
expounding prior SED resolutions, providing a theoretical justification for
political-tactical decisions previously adopted, and pretending to develop original arguments and legal theory from them. He added that such failings
were characteristic of Marxist-Leninist theorizing as influenced by the
personality cult in the USSR (and, he added, not only there). His critical re-

flections sufficed to prompt the censure to ban publication of his presentation in the journal in January 1988.

The difficulties and problematical prospects of such "inside" efforts at reform have caused some of those who participated in these efforts to look back in self-critical scorn. In Steding's view, East German theorists, despite occasional efforts, had generally failed to develop either meaningful critical dialectical thinking or a "culture of clashing views."[14] Another self-critic, Heinz Niemann (a historian at East Berlin's Humboldt University), has described in bitter and cynical tones the work of young reform-minded scholars who were (like himself) "victims to the bitter end of their illusions regarding the system's capacity for reform."[15]

The assessment of changes in the Soviet Union and Eastern Europe led to conflict between the empirical and theoretical findings of GDR scholars and their patrons in the Party leadership.[16] In the GDR, as in the Soviet Union, the field of comparative communist studies had always been neglected for tactical political reasons. One consequence of the rise of Solidarity in Poland, for both Soviet and East German scholars, was to legitimize this field by convincing political leaders of its immediate utility. In the GDR, this took the form of an internal party resolution of November 1982.[17]

The resulting research illuminated three main features of communist development in Eastern Europe. One was the likelihood of systemic crises akin to the one that had shaken Poland in 1980-81; another was the increasing differentiation between communist states and systems; a third concerned problems in the GDR and other East European states that might result from indigenous factors and therefore not be exclusively due to external "imperialist" influence.

Scholars working in this field sought to foster a more realistic view of GDR politics by drawing parallels to the Soviet and East European experience. They were especially attracted by the Hungarian example, including the semi-reformed election procedures of 1985. Interest in Hungary may have been sharpened by the brief episode of parallel and mutually-supportive GDR and Hungarian foreign policies in the mid-1980s. These scholarly efforts paralleled the work on GDR affairs proper. By stressing the reality and "normality" of conflicts of interest in the GDR and similar societies, reform-minded scholars tried to justify political reforms in the GDR.[18] In their view, domestic reforms were eminently justified as a means of making political institutions more responsive to the people and allowing citizens ever more effective opportunity for participation in politics.[19]

GDR authorities had their own motives for sponsoring such research.[20] To a decreasing degree, they hoped to learn from the mistakes of other regimes. Thus, a more accurate description of politics in other developed socialist societies could serve to guide GDR policy toward those regimes. In addition, the acceptance of underlying differences among communist regimes could justify the growing reluctance among GDR leaders to follow Gorbachev's policy innovations.

Despite such benefits, political control over comparative and innovative research became steadily more onerous, and the impact of such scholarship on policymaking diminished. The hostile reaction of leaders to the results of this research led to a degree of self-censorship, as scholars did not wish to be seen as bearers of ill-tidings. Hence, research, as well as institutional and personnel policies in the field, became increasingly subject to supervision at Politburo levels. Not surprisingly, some 70 to 80 percent of all research on this subject was devoted to studies that were withheld from publication.

One set of ideas that reformers sought to introduce into GDR political thinking concerned the notion of a political system.[21] This was a controversial concept because it assumed a network of institutions and relationships characterized by mutual interaction and response rather than purpose or deliberative direction from the center (i.e., the Party). Moreover, the task of guiding society in a manner that would be both politically orthodox and technologically effective was becoming ever more difficult. Under these circumstances, it was not clear how much (and what kind of) political direction might be required for optimum technological development. The intellectual and political challenge confronting GDR reformist scholars was that the elements in such a political system—including parties, interest groups, and political institutions—would have to be understood as representing real and conflicting (if not necessarily contradictory) interests. Any viable political system must include and represent such interests. This, in turn, implied that individuals and social groups would (and should) seek new institutions and relations to express such interests. Social scientists would have to examine the social landscape empirically in order to comprehend the nature and direction of future political development.

A key element in this reform program was the search for structures that would facilitate more popular participation in decisionmaking. Among GDR scholars, this search usually led in the direction of greater autonomy for social groups and increased authority for formal government structures such as elected assemblies and local government bodies. A reflection of the GDR experience was the notion of increasing mass participation by allowing factory and local government personnel to address substantive political issues during formal deliberations concerning the formation of national economic plan targets.[22]

One outcome of such reforms would have been to increase greatly the complexity of political and social relations. Logically, therefore, GDR reformers stressed the role of formal legal regulations in directing the country's future development. This resurrection of the old notion of the *Rechts-staat* was common to GDR reformist thinking in the political field. It represented a clear break with a Leninist notion, widespread in the GDR in the 1950s and later, that posited the superiority of political decisions over legal restraints.[23]

Law and political structure were thought of, in turn, as resting on a social foundation of clashing interests.[24] The notion of clashing interests had a dual background. Theoretically, it involved a revival (without acknowledging its source) of Walter Ulbricht's earlier concept of socialism as a long-term historical process with its own stable political and social characteristics. According to this view, clashing interests and their representation in political structures and processes were neither a reluctant concession to subjective error nor a "remnant" of capitalism. Moreover, economic differences of interest among workers, managers, experts, and others could justify supporting differential reward or other policies of deliberate social advancement in the name of more efficient production.

The growing acceptance of the reality that various social groups, institutions, and indeed individuals might have interests that did not coincide automatically with each other or with any overarching political purpose—indeed that, say, an individual might need protected, formal access to seek redress against political authorities—provided the theoretical framework for advocating greater political autonomy. As I note below, much of the political program of 1989-90—including efforts to draft a new democratic constitution for the GDR—reflected this line of thought.

By 1988, the GDR's social scientists had thus developed a systematic critique of GDR doctrine in social and political questions. The elaboration of such a critique paralleled developments in the Soviet Union and other East European countries. In the GDR, as in the rest of the European communist world, the legitimacy of the Leninist political and social order had been dissipated largely among the very groups and individuals whose task it was to elaborate and propagate the system's values.

On the eve of the political crisis that overwhelmed the GDR, the ideas and projects expressed by reform-minded social scientists were synthesized in an extraordinary document: the "reconstruction program" (*das Umbau-papier*), which was drafted by younger scholars at the very heart of the GDR's political-academic establishment.[25] Their proposals clearly aimed at a restructured GDR in which social forces and their initiatives would have priority in setting goals, in which political pluralism and constitutionally-guaranteed rights would be the foundation for politics, and in which the intellectual hegemony of the Party would be challenged.[26]

Reform Thinking in the Social Opposition

The ultimate collapse of the GDR, however, was not the work of "insiders" such as these. Instead, the ideas that fueled the civic action revolt against "actual socialism" during the crisis of 1989 came from a variety of groups and individuals who were, by preference and often by necessity, outsiders. The latter consisted of groups and individuals who were gathered under the organizational shelter of the Evangelical church. They stressed concrete issues of daily life—including peace, the environment, and the position of women—rather than more general political questions.

In the heat of the crisis, some of the opposition groups focused more directly on political goals. During the summer of 1989, a number of political organizations were founded to challenge the regime on grounds broader than specific issues. Groups such as New Forum (*Neues Forum*) and the newly-reestablished Social Democratic Party acted on, and in turn, helped generate political critiques of the established political order. These critiques, along with the social science reform thinking described above, constituted the program of the peaceful revolution of 1989 before that movement was overtaken in early 1990 by the drive for German unification.

A common theme of these programmatic efforts was to bring about increased mass participation in political decisionmaking. Different dimensions of participation were involved. One was the demand for *broader* participation. This meant eliminating restrictions on political activity by such groups as practicing religious believers and citizens who were not members of the SED or one of the bloc parties. In addition, there was a widespread demand for the transformation of existing and future political arrangements to ensure effective political participation by GDR citizens. Reforms along these lines included competitive elections, a meaningful role in setting targets and procedures, and the transformation of social organizations such as trade unions into genuine interest groups.

In raising such demands, East German citizens acted in ways parallel to political developments in Eastern Europe and the Soviet Union. In all of these countries, as Hubertus Knabe has pointed out, demands had been raised for the "separation of party, state, and society and for the creation of democratic procedures to formulate [and] arrive at decisions."[27]

A central element in reform arguments for participation was the call for more structured communication concerning public issues. Such communication was to take place both between regime and citizens as well as among groups in society. A typical expression of such ideas may be found in the manifesto of the best-known of the opposition groups, New Forum, which contains a prominent call for a "democratic dialogue" required because "communication about the general situation" was too restricted.[28] Other ideas in this manifesto—which were characteristic of reform thinking from unofficial levels of society—included the subordination of economic development to ecological concerns and to dimensions of individual, personal growth.

An important element of reform thinking in society—especially in light of subsequent political events—was the widespread commitment to some form of socialism, albeit a socialism intended to be very different from the *Realsozialismus* of the old GDR. Opposition forces frequently accused the regime of discrediting the very notion of socialism and insisted on the validity of their own socialist credentials. For example, in its declaration at the fortieth anniversary of the GDR, New Forum denounced "attempts of the regime to portray us as enemies of socialism."[29] In this same declaration, New Forum appealed to rank-and-file members of the SED to put their knowledge and experience to work in reforming the GDR. After the opening of the Berlin Wall in early November 1989, a group that included many prominent writers, artists, and social scientists (some of them SED members) issued the widely-noted appeal: "For Our Country" (*Für unser Land*). The signatories called for a "socialist alternative" to West Germany, warning that economic pressures could resulted in a "fire sale" (*Ausverkauf*) of East Germany's "moral and material values."[30]

During the fall of 1989, many other social and political groups, each with its declarations and appeals, appeared on the public stage. As indicated previously, they typically called for social dialogue, political rights, greater concern for the environment, needs of women, the Third World, and peace—usually coupled with a sometimes vague commitment to socialism. Such groups came from one or another of two intertwined traditions, and many, of course, represented both.[31] One was that of informal and unofficial discussion in the "niches" of GDR life; the other was related to the proliferation of church-related groups.

Jens Reich, one of the founders of New Forum, has described a dissenting discussion club, the *Freitagskreis*, which after some twenty years of meetings became almost identical with the group that founded New Forum.[32] Originally, it was a "private philosophical seminar, a sort of 'flying university,'" which became broader in scope and more varied in participants over the years.[33] Some meetings drew a sufficiently large audience to warrant electronic surveillance by the security forces.

Another strand of new thinking came through the many groups sheltered under the organizational umbrella of the Evangelical church. The church provided material and moral backing for a variety of studies and reports that helped dissenters break through the official monopoly of political discourse. During the last years of the GDR, even visitors to the GDR could readily witness (and sometimes participate in) discussions—startling in their candor

and courage—which were held openly at church services, in post-perfor-
mance theater discussion groups, and in private homes.[34] Eventually, the
church itself began taking a political stand. In mid-September 1989, a
church synod meeting in Eisenach issued a statement directly linking the exodus of GDR citizens to the West with political and social deficiencies of the
regime.[35]

Finally, there was a widespread erosion of support for the official ideology, both among its "natural" constituents among workers and within the
ranks of the Party itself. Opinion research conducted during the final years
of the GDR revealed, for example, that the proportion of apprentices who
identified strongly with Marxism-Leninism dropped from 46 percent in
1975 to an astonishingly low 9 percent in May 1989. Not surprisingly, by
May 1990 only 14.3 percent of workers preferred the PDS over other parties.[36]

The reform ideas described thus far were widely shared by members of
the ruling party, particularly those in research and educational institutions.
The growing disaffection of ordinary party members with their own leadership was reflected in a rising number of internal disciplinary actions, resignations, dissenting statements sent to higher party bodies, and vigorous discussion in party meetings.[37] When in the course of the winter of 1989 the
SED permitted the very un-Leninist formation of internal party factions
(styled *Plattformen*), a number of such groups emerged. The issues raised
by these groups were strikingly similar to those enunciated by the non-SED
opposition—internal party democracy, pluralism, and a formal democratic
and constitutional framework for political action. They provided the basis
for the PDS's 1990 election campaigns.

In the elections of 1990, the PDS was clearly identified as the party up-
holding the idea of GDR identity and the possibility of a socialist "third
way" between the old GDR and the present Federal Republic.[38] The idea of
such an alternative path soon lost any political basis in Germany, but it continued to be an attractive notion to political forces seeking a rationale for opposing the (West) German sociopolitical consensus. A common element in
this thinking is that the institutional arrangements of the Federal Republic,
both before and since the *Wende*, need to be reformed.[39]

Many of the ideas discussed thus far were brought together in a document that in some ways is both monument and epitaph to the effort at re-
thinking the conditions for a worthy and humane existence in the GDR.
That document was the draft constitution which was commissioned in the
first meeting of the Roundtable on 7 December 1989.[40] A Roundtable
working group, *Neue Verfassung der DDR* (New Constitution of the
GDR), handled the work of constitutional creation. Its members included

leading figures of the opposition movement as well as notable members of the reform wing of the SED.[41]

The tone for this document was set in its preamble, which was authored by Christa Wolf. In striking contrast to the previous constitution, the preamble to the proposed new constitution contained no mention of Marxism, the working class, a vanguard party, or ties with the (former) Soviet Union. The text began with a reference to the German people's humanistic traditions, acknowledged the Germans' responsibility for their history, and called for revolutionary renewal as a basis for building a democratic and integral (*solidarische*) political community. This community would be characterized by peaceful international relations, respect for gender equality, and concern for the environment. It would be the work, not of "the people" in the abstract, but instead by the citizens of the GDR. In its detailed provisions, the draft constitution represented both liberal and participatory strains of current democratic thought. It called for widespread rights for political and social organizations, the use of referenda, and the enfranchisement of resident aliens in local elections. As one of its co-authors, the West German juridical scholar Ulrich Preuß, commented: the integrity of the political process was to rest on a foundation of constitutional rights for social activism by groups and individuals.[42]

According to the Roundtable's plans, the draft was to be approved by a newly-elected Volkskammer and submitted to the general population in a referendum. But when the completed draft was duly submitted in April to the Volkskammer elected on 18 March 1990, a majority of its members rejected the proposal in favor of rapid unification with West Germany. Instead, piecemeal changes designed to remove the most obvious excesses of the old constitution and to smooth the road to unification were approved in June. Nonetheless, some of the ideas of the draft constitution have been brought into the continuing discussion of the Commission on Constitutional Changes that was mandated by the Unification Treaty of 1990.[43]

Conclusion

The demands for substantive participation and for social and political self-determination by the people of the GDR were a direct challenge to the Leninist system of party-state control. They demonstrated that the "democratically mature" population of the GDR—as in many other communist countries—insisted on participation in public life of a degree and kind that, if realized, would have moved the locus of decisionmaking power from self-selecting elites to the mass of the population. This movement, which in the final years of the GDR encompassed ever-larger numbers of citizens from ever more varied elements of society, may be characterized as a movement from *subject* to *citizen*.

In addition to this fundamental shift in political culture among East Germans,[44] the regime was increasingly seen as irrelevant to important policy concerns such as militarism, the environment, gender equality, and intellectual freedom. By failing to engage its population in meaningful dialogue on these issues, the regime ensured that such issues would be discussed in those very circles (described above) that were, for participatory reasons, hostile to its power.

Finally, the styles of thought characteristic of both policy and participatory dissent were far removed from the official ideology of Marxism-Leninism "in the colors of the GDR." As Antonia Grunenberg has pointed out, the increasing emptiness of the official ideology—characterized by its decay into a politicized *Leerformel* —helped to engender the varied alternative "scene" in which thoughtful East Germans could find their concerns addressed in a meaningful way.[45] It was this shift in legitimacy in the realm of thought that prepared and accompanied a shift in political legitimacy that ultimately doomed the GDR regime.

Notes

1. Hans-Peter Kröger, "Eine Krake im Kampf mit sich selbst," *Frankfurter Allgemeine Zeitung*, 13 June 1991.

2. For one of many examples, see Fred Oldenburg, "Die Implosion des SED-Regimes. Ursachen und Entwicklungsprozesse," *Berichte des Bundesinstituts für ostwissenschaftliche und internationale Studien*, 10 (1991). Oldenburg notes that even after the *Wende* in 1989, most analysts expected a slow pace of political change, in part because of European and global strategic implications of change in Germany. Ibid., 3.

3. This was certainly true of Egon Krenz, who succeeded Honecker; Günter Schabowski, who initiated the old leader's overthrow; and Hans Modrow, who before 1989 had been widely regarded as an alternative party head. See Günter Schabowski in Frank Sieren and Ludwig Koehne, eds., *Das Politbüro* (Reinbek bei Hamburg: Rowohlt, 1990); Egon Krenz, *Wenn Mauern fallen* (Vienna: Paul Neff Verlag, 1990); Reinhold Andert and Wolfgang Herzberg, *Der Sturz. Erich Honecker im Kreuzverhör* (Berlin: Aufbau Verlag, 1990); and Walter Süß, "Bilanz einer Gratwanderung. Die kurze Amtszeit des Hans Modow," *Deutschland Archiv*, 24 (June 1991), 596-608. Krenz (pp.26-28) describes the eerie stillness at SED headquarters during the summer of 1989; his and others' efforts to induce Honecker to

act involved such minor steps as hardly to be commensurate with the true gravity of the regime's situation.

4. Comparing the two German states in retrospect, the East German sociologist Thomas Koch describes GDR society as resting on an "ebbing basic consensus." Koch, "Statusunsicherheit und Identitätssuche im Spannungsfeld zwischen 'schöpferischer Zerstörung' und nationaler Reintegration," *BISS public*, 2 (1991): 83.

5. Few GDR voices questioned the policy of aiming at Western (especially West German) levels of consumption. One isolated decrier of this line was Wolfgang Harich; see his *Babeuf and the Club of Rome*. In a number of novels, some writers questioned the unthinking acceptance of material-technical "progress" (e.g., Christa Wolf's *Störfall* and Hans Cibulka's *Swantow*). A good study of the relationship of planned consumption levels to general regime policy is Ralf Rytlewski, "Kommunismus ante Portas? Zur Entwicklung von Massenkultur und Massenkonsum," in Gert-Joachim Glaeßner, ed., *Die DDR in der Ära Honecker* (Opladen: Westdeutscher Verlag, 1988), 633-43.

6. There is a vast literature on the GDR's more positive attitude toward eras and persons from the German past. For a brief survey of the situation as of the mid-1980s, see Henry Krisch, *The GDR. The Search for Identity* (Boulder, Colo.: Westview Press, 1985), 83-87. A final GDR treatment of this theme can be found in Helmut Meier and Walter Schmidt, eds., *Erbe und Tradition. Geschichtsdebatte in der DDR* (Cologne: Pahl-Rugenstein, 1989).

7. Walter Süß provides a good survey of the importance of external events for domestic East German developments in "Größere Eigenständigkeiten im Dienste des Status Quo. Die DDR und ihre Blockführungsmacht," in Glaeßner, 186-213. See also his earlier study, "Kein Vorbild für die DDR? Die sowjetische Reformbemühungen aus der Sicht der SED," *Deutschland Archiv*, 19 (1986): 967-88.

8. A far-sighted early statement of this idea was Peter Christian Ludz's final work, *Mechanismen der Herrschaftssicherung* (Munich: Carl Hanser Verlag, 1980), especially 49-57, 183-223. Ludz anticipated the escalation of tensions between regime and people during the last years of the old regime when he observed (p. 286) that GDR citizens, by taking the regime at its promised word, felt they deserved continuous improvements in the conditions of their daily lives and were increasingly ready to speak out in this direction.

9. See Michael Sodaro, *Moscow, Germany, and the West from Krushchev to Gorbachev* (Ithaca, N.Y.: Cornell University Press, 1990), 370-76, and Fred Oldenburg, "Moskau und die Wiedervereinigung

Deutschlands," *Berichte des Bundesinstituts für ostwissenschaftliche und internationale Studien*, 38 (1991), especially 5-13.

10. I base this section on the excellent summary by Heinz Albert Hutmacher, *Friedensfähigkeiten des Imperialismus: Aspekte einer aktuellen Ideologie-Diskussion in the DDR* (Bonn: Friedrich-Ebert-Stiftung, 1989). A central East German statement of the new outlook is Dieter Klein, *Chancen für einen friedensfähigen Kapitalismus* (Berlin: Dietz Verlag, 1988), especially 53-88. The role of such new thinking in the international rivalries of the early 1980s is analyzed in Rudolf H. Brocke and Clemens Burrichter, "'Neues Denken' in der Systemkonkurrenz," in Glaeßner, 167-85.

11. A center for such study was the Institute of Scientific Socialism of the SED Central Committee's Social Science Academy, which served as a locus of reformist thinking within the Party's scholarly establishment. A new research focus on "human rights in East-West relations" was established there in 1987.

12. Frank Berg and Rolf Reißig, "Menschenrechte in der Politik des Sozialismus," *Deutsche Zeitschrift für Philosophie*, 36 (1988): 599-610.

13. Rolf Steding, "Editorial," *Staat und Recht*, 40 (1991): 161-64. Here, Steding paraphrases Schöneberg's 1987 remarks cited in the text.

14. Ibid.

15. Heinz Niemann, "Der sogenannte 'Bund Demokratischer Kommunisten Deutschlands' in der Opposition und Dissidenz der DDR," *Deutschland Archiv*, 24 (1991): 533-38. Nieman has little but (perhaps excessive) scorn for the plans of such reformist scholars to send an "open letter" to the once-forthcoming XII Congress of the SED.

16. See the survey by Erhard Crome and Jochen Franke, both former researchers at the Akademie für Staats- und Rechtwissenschaft at Potsdam-Babelsberg, "Die Osteuropaforschung der DDR in den achtziger Jahren. Strukturen und Schwerpunkte," *Berichte des Bundesinstituts für ostwissenschaftliche und internationale Studien*, 5 (1991): 303-10.

17. Ibid., 12. The resolution of the Central Committee Secretariat, dated 17 November 1982, set forth goals and assigned institutional roles for such research. Little of this work, however, ever reached public view prior to the *Wende*.

18. Interviews with scholars prior to the *Wende* indicated that research on Eastern Europe and the Soviet Union was, in part, a roundabout way of examining sensitive issues at home—including party-state relations, the quality of democratic participation in decision making, and the political role of social organizations such as trade unions.

19. How difficult it was to use East European experiences as a template for change in the GDR may be judged by an episode regarding Poland. When the Polish ruling Party decreed in late 1988 that certain opposition

forces might be legalized, providing that they did not question the foundations of socialism and were prepared to accept government responsibility, the reaction among SED ideology and propaganda officials was one of "unrest and sharp rejection." See Robert Weiss and Manfred Heinrich, "Der Runde Tisch. Konkursverwalter des 'realen' Sozialismus. Analyse und Vergleich des Wirkens Runder Tische in Europa," *Berichte des Bundesinstituts für ostwissenschaftliche und internationale Studien* 14 (1991): 13 and 42.

20. Crome and Franke, 20-25.

21. Interview with Rolf Reißig in May 1988.

22. Interviews with Rosemarie Will (Humboldt University) and Peter Zotel and Robert Weiss (GeWi Academy) in May 1988.

23. This was an important point for GDR legal scholar Uwe-Jens Heuer and many of the reform-minded scholars who had been his students. For Heuer, see *Überlegungen zur sozialistischen Demokratie* (Berlin: Akademie Verlag, 1987), especially 28-29. Also see Heuer, Gerd Quilitzsch, and Dieter Segert, "Sozialistische Politik als Gegenstand vergleichender Wissenschaft," *Deutsche Zeitschrift für Philosophie*, 36 (1988): 900-908.

24. From the mid-1980s onward, a voluminous scholarly literature appeared on this subject. A useful survey is Dietrich Staritz, "Tendenzen des Wandels im politischen System der DDR," in Glaeßner, 305-10. Also see Gerd Quilitzsch, Dieter Segert, and Rosemarie Will, "Interessenwidersprüche und politisches System. Uwe-Jens Heuer zum 60. Geburtstag," *Staat und Recht*, 56 (1987): 656-63. Interview with Uwe-Jens Heuer, April 1988.

25. Rainer Land, ed., *Das Umbaupapier (DDR). Argumente gegen die Wiedervereinigung* (Berlin: Rotbuch Verlag, 1990). The heart of this study is a long essay entitled "Studie zur Gesellschaftsstrategie," which is the work of Rainer Land, Michael Brie, Hannelore Petsch, Dieter Segert, and Rosemarie Will. It was the product of a research project on the theory of socialism (*Forschungsprojekt Sozialismustheorie*) at Humboldt University and appeared as the first brochure in the series "Sozialismus in der Diskussion" (Berlin: Dietz Verlag, 1989).

26. Ibid., especially 118-22. The authors had noted (ibid., 116) that "the more radical and serious any effort [to change the relationship of social forces and political institutions] is, the more closely it touches on the relationship of party and state." The existing processes of political leadership would have to be broken up (*durchbrochen*).

27. Hubertus Knabe, "Democratization and Political Reform. On the Critical Discussion of Legitimacy and Legitimization in the GDR," in Margy Gerber, ed., *Studies in GDR Culture and Society*, 10 (Lanham, Maryland: University Press of America, 1991), 33.

28. Neues Forum, *Gründungsaufruf*. Reprinted in Gerhard Rein, ed., *Die Opposition in der DDR* (Berlin: Wichern Verlag, 1989), 13-14.

29. Ibid., 15-16.

30. "Für unser Land" appeared in *Neues Deutschland* on 26 November 1989. A convenient source that lists the appeal's signers is Charles Schüddekopf, ed., *"Wir sind das Volk!" Flugschriften, Aufrufe und Texte einer deutschen Revolution* (Reinbeck bei Hamburg: Rowohlt, 1990), 240-41.

31. An enormous and growing literature, in both German and English, deals with these groups. One study that places the data concerning such activity in the conceptual framework of "civil society" is Vladimir Tismaneanu, "Against Socialist Materialism. The Independent Peace Movement in the German Democratic Republic" in Tismaneanu, ed., *In Search of Civil Society* (London: Routledge, 1990).

32. Jens Reich, *Rückkehr nach Europa. Bericht zur neuen Lage der deutschen Nation* (Munich: Carl Hanser, 1992).

33. Reich (ibid.) recounts that he thought of the group as a "Jakobinerklub."

34. The author attended a "peace service" at the Saint Nicholas Church in Leipzig on a Monday evening in June 1988. He was startled to hear a public appeal for funds to aid "political prisoners in the GDR."

35. "Was nötig ist, damit Menschen auch in unserem Lande gerne leben," in Rein, *Die Opposition*, 214-17. The declaration included a damming list of unfulfilled promises and unresponsive reactions by the regime in areas ranging from ecological to military, from social to political problems. In early September, church leaders sent Honecker an open letter in which they voiced many of the same sentiments. See Micha Wimmer, et al., *"Wir sind das Volk!" Die DDR im Aufbruch* (Munich: Heyne, 1990), 24-25.

36. On attitudes of workers, see Evelyne Fischer and Dietmar Wittich, "Zur Sozialstruktur des politischen Verhaltens im Gebiet der ehemaligen DDR," *Informationen zur soziologischen Forschung*, 26 (1990): 1. The attitudes of apprentices are reported in Peter Förster and Günter Roski, *DDR zwischen Wende und Wahl* (Berlin: Links/Druck Verlag, 1990), 39-44.

37. For a general discussion of this process, see Heinrich Bortfeldt, *Von der SED zur PDS* (Bonn: Bouvier Verlag, 1992), especially 40-41. A detailed account of the conflict of ideas within the SED can be found in Henry Krisch, "From SED to PDS. The Struggle to Revive a Left Party," in Russell J. Dalton, ed., *Germany Votes 1990. Reunification and the Creation of a New German Party System* (Oxford: Berg, 1993).

38. Speaking at the extraordinary party congress of the SED in December 1989 at which he became the party's leader and spokesman, Gregor Gysi declared that "the crisis of administrative-centralist socialism in our

country can only be solved by having the GDR pursue a third way beyond Stalinist socialism and rule by transnational monopolies." Gysi, "Wenn wir alle für unsere neue Partei streiten, wird sie stark bleiben!" *Außerordentlicher Parteitag der SED/PDS. Materialien* (Berlin: Dietz Verlag, 1990), 13-28.

39. An example was the "Three Stage Plan" for German unity publicized in December 1989 by the movement, *Demokratie Jetzt,* which called for reforms in West Germany to achieve greater social equality, decreased unemployment, and a more ecologically-sensitive productive apparatus. See Volker Gransow and Konrad Jarausch, eds., *Die deutsche Vereinigung. Dokumente zu Bürgerbewegung, Annäherung und Beitritt* (Cologne: Verlag Wissenschaft und Politik, 1991), 111. Similar views were expressed after unification by three former SED "in-house" political reformers who are currently active in the PDS: Uwe-Jens Heuer, Ekkehard Liberam, and Michael Schumann, "Die PDS und ihr Verhältnis zu Demokratie und Rechtsstaat," *Utopie kreativ,* 13 (September 1991): 26-34.

40. Helmut Herbst and Edward Rose, eds., *Vom Runden Tisch zum Parlament* (Bonn: Bouvier, 1990), 23-24.

41. For details on the membership of the working group and its "expert group," as well as pertinent letters of authorization and transmission, see the booklet published by Neue Verfassung, *Entwurf: Verfassung der Deutschen Demokratischen Republik* (Berlin: BasisDruck, 1990).

42. Ulrich K. Preuß, "Auf der Suche nach der Zivilgesellschaft," *Frankfurter Allgemeine Zeitung,* 28 April 1990. Cited in Gert-Joachim Glaeßner, *Der schwierige Weg zur Demokratie. Vom Ende der DDR zur deutschen Einheit* (Opladen: Westdeutscher Verlag, 1991), 142.

43. Ibid., 141-43. For example, a thirty-two member joint parliamentary commission, which was established in 1991, was instructed to deal, inter alia, with environmental protection as a goal of state action, means to make the idea of a "social state" more concrete, and steps to strengthen participatory opportunities by citizens.

44. For a discussion of the relationship of changing political culture to political change as such, see Henry Krisch, "Changes in Political Culture and the Transformation of the GDR, 1989-1990," in Gert-Joachim Glaeßner and Ian Wallace, eds., *The German Revolution of 1989* (Oxford: Berg, forthcoming).

45. Antonia Grunenberg, *Aufbruch der inneren Mauer. Politik und Kultur in der DDR 1971-1990* (Bremen: Edition Tremen, 1990), 229-31.

4

Steps Toward Union:
The Collapse of the GDR
and the Unification of Germany

Michael G. Huelshoff and
Arthur M. Hanhardt, Jr.

A great deal has been written about the collapse of the German Democratic Republic (GDR) in 1989-90 and the subsequent unification of the two Germanys. Fred Oldenburg has spoken of an "implosion" of the GDR in which chance and circumstance played large, unpredictable and, perhaps, inexplicable roles.[1] Heinrich Bortfeldt has written about the inability of the Socialist Unity Party (SED) to respond effectively to growing threats in the late 1980s.[2] He points to the centralization of power in the Party, its inability to tolerate intra-party dissent, and the growing disparity between Party rhetoric and reality in explaining why the SED was unable to maintain discipline within its own ranks in the autumn of 1989. The SED was also unable or unwilling to use force in quelling demonstrations. Other explanations note the importance of international factors, including pressures from Gorbachev's policies of *glasnost, perestroika*, and the "new thinking" in Soviet foreign policy; the reformist examples set by Poland and Hungary; and, depending upon one's point of view, either conspiratorial or benign pressures from the West.

In fact, all these explanations, with the possible exception of the conspiracy theories, offer parts of the explanation for the events of 1989-1990. The "revolution" was unique, but it is not our argument that each revolution is unique. A plethora of theories has been developed in the social sciences to explain the phenomenon of revolution. Yet these theories are of little help in understanding the collapse of the GDR and the unification of Germany. While there are many cases of foreign intervention in revolutions, we could find few cases of foreign powers effectively initiating change and then refusing direct intervention, as the Soviets did in 1989. Additionally, there are few cases of revolution in one part of a divided nation and no theories that can explicate the interactions of divided nations in revolutionary conditions.[3] Finally, the events of 1989 constitute a fundamental change in international and European politics—a change in intellectual paradigm so comprehensive that it can only be compared to the world wars in their significance for twentieth-century history. Thus, the conventional theories of revolution are insufficient guides to explaining the breakdown of the GDR and subsequent German unification.

A more satisfactory explanation for the events of 1989 can be developed from the observation that domestic and international politics are inseparably intertwined. Few major international and domestic events can be explained without reference to variables from both levels of analysis. Important variables in this case include, at the international level, the attitudes of the former wartime Allies toward reform and later unification. Domestically, the key variables explaining the events of 1989-90 included the quality of the SED leadership and the leaders and goals of the opposition. These variables and levels of analysis are displayed in Figure 4.1. From this perspective, the necessary condition for the GDR revolution is found in the relaxation of Soviet control over the Eastern bloc (cell 1,1). Without the clear rejection of the Brezhnev doctrine by Mikhail Gorbachev, it is unlikely that the SED would have collapsed. The application of *glasnost, perestroika,* and "new thinking" in Soviet foreign policy, however, is insufficient in explaining the revolution. Instead, domestic developments provide the sufficient elements of the explanation, including the collapse of the SED noted by Bortfeldt and the disorganized, if eventful, politics in the streets of the GDR during the fall of 1989 (cell 1,2). Thereafter, the events leading to unification on 3 October 1990 were more or less improvised responses to the internal collapse of the GDR. At this point, the necessary and sufficient variables reversed: domestic developments drove unification (cell 2,2) and international actors were only able to shape them at the margins (cell 2,1). This chapter will assess, by time periods, the major domestic and international actors and events that affected and effected the East German implosion and led to German unification.

7 May to 10 September 1989: The Politics of Rejection

Growing dissent and dissatisfaction with the domestic situation in the GDR were observable throughout the 1980s. Beginning with the unofficial peace movement protesting the arms policies of both East and West and continuing with an expanding environmentalist movement,[4] predominantly young people sought answers to questions the SED considered illegitimate in "socialism in the colors of the GDR." Although principally located in the Protestant churches of the GDR, dissent did not question socialism nor did

Figure 4.1
Explaining the Collapse of the SED
and German Unification

Levels of Analysis

	International	Domestic
	Necessary Variable	Sufficient Variable
Collapse of SED	Soviet foreign policy. Without "new thinking," Brezhnev doctrine prevented reform.	SED leadership's willingness to reform. SED responses to Soviet pressure ineffectual, unable to reform.
	Sufficient Variable	Necessary Variable
German Unification	Views of Four Powers could not slow or block unification driven by domestic pressures. All external actors constrained by previous positions.	Domestic demands for unification. Masses reject "third way," demand unification.

it posit German unification among its goals.[5] Moreover, the dissidents of the 1980s produced no comprehensive reform program of their own. Those who were dissatisfied and disaffected demanded responsiveness from the regime; they wanted answers to questions that the SED never recognized as justified.

On 7 May 1989, communal elections were held in the GDR. The ruling SED and its National Front expected and in fact obtained results—98.85 per cent—that were in excess of those observed by poll watchers representing unofficial grassroots groups in the GDR. Egon Krenz, in his role as national election supervisor, ignored questions about the outcome and certified the results. Irrefutable evidence of election fraud subsequently focused and fanned growing popular dissatisfaction, resulting in a demonstration involving 123 arrests in Berlin on 7 June. This demonstration was a forerunner of the famed "Monday night demonstrations" emanating from the Nikolaikirche in Leipzig and thereafter spreading throughout the GDR during the late summer and autumn of 1989.[6] Between June and September, a "political culture of demonstrations" quickly established itself in the GDR.

Increasing manifestations of popular dissatisfaction in the GDR were met with official praise for the "Chinese solution" to dissent demonstrated in Tiananmen Square on 4 June. Right up to the fortieth anniversary of the Chinese revolution in October, the SED regime—and particularly Egon Krenz—declared solidarity with the Chinese Communist party and its treatment of "counter-revolutionaries."[7] Yet, as the summer of 1989 progressed, it became stunningly clear that the SED and its governmental institutions were unable to react effectively, short of violence—thus setting the scene for a confrontation between an orthodox party and government leadership and "the people." During this process, East Germans lost their awe of a comprehensively repressive party-and-state apparatus that was simply unable to function without instilling fear among its subjects. In many ways the willingness of the citizens of the GDR to take to the streets to confront the SED was perhaps the most remarkable phenomenon of the summer and fall of 1989. After all, the last time East German citizens had taken to the streets to protest against the state, in June 1953, their demonstrations had been brutally suppressed by Soviet troops.

While it is unlikely that we will ever be able to fully understand why so many were so brave, some reasons can be discerned. The demonstrators undoubtedly hoped that this time the Soviets, bent on their own reforms and hoping for Western financial support, would not intervene, even though the GDR was considered the Soviet's most important economic partner within the Council for Mutual Economic Assistance and the Warsaw Treaty Organization. Also, the SED had successfully dealt with dissent both within and without the SED through jail sentences and subsequent expulsions to the West (in exchange for hard currency). Protest after the 1950s was never a matter of life or death. Finally, protesters in the 1980s initially demanded reform of the socialist system—not its replacement. This limitation on the reformists' demands must also have eased possible fears of arrest and mistreatment. Although violence did occur, it was arguably at a level lower than might have been otherwise expected, given the size of the state security apparatus, or as it was experienced elsewhere in Eastern Europe.[8]

A dialectic of internal dissatisfaction, met by inept or inapt regime responses, characterized the domestic side of the collapse of the GDR. So, too, did the regime's appeal for external support in quelling growing dissent. Obviously the Chinese were unable to help, except as an exemplary but decreasingly credible example of repression. Certainly other communist regimes could normally be counted upon to aid a fraternal party in need, as was the case in Czechoslovakia in 1968. This, too, proved impossible in the Gorbachev era of *glasnost, perestroika,* and the end of the "Brezhnev doctrine." With Hungary and Poland following their own paths, the (still) orthodox regimes of Czechoslovakia, Bulgaria, and Romania could not be expected to provide much useful support for the increasingly beleaguered Erich Honecker and his colleagues. Instead, they were being left to their own devices even—and especially—by the Soviet Union.

In June, General Secretary Mikhail Gorbachev visited the Federal Republic. During his stay, Gorbachev was treated to the wonders of West German high technology and quality production. The contrasts between the two Germanys were clear. Even though the GDR was the most important trading partner of the Soviet Union, the prospects of hard currency financial support and know-how transfer from West Germany were most tempting. At the same time "Gorbymania" swept the Federal Republic. The supposed attractions of doing business with the Soviet Union assumed rapturous heights in the minds of German business elites. East German policy makers, feeling the GDR's position vis-à-vis the Soviet Union threatened, prevailed upon a hospitalized Erich Honecker to publicly introduce the GDR's very own 32-bit microchip as a triumph of socialist technology. That the chip was obsolescent and that its development had cost prodigal amounts of precious investment funds only highlighted the relative backwardness of the GDR.

During the summer of 1989 emigration pressures grew among GDR citizens. Applications for legal emigration had risen into the tens of thousands in the late 1980s. Slow and bureaucratic responses to these applications inspired those wishing to leave to explore alternative means. The dismantling (and marketing) of the Hungarian "iron curtain" inspired East Germans to "vacation" in Hungary and take their chances in crossing the "green boundary" into Austria and hence to the Federal Republic. Soon GDR vacationers in Poland and Czechoslovakia were occupying West German embassies to acquire travel documents and a West German passport. The GDR expected the fraternal socialist governments at least to hold to the line that it was illegal for GDR citizens to travel to third countries for which they had no visas issued by East Berlin. Yet this was inconsistent with the reforms then being contemplated and implemented in Hungary and Poland. Poland and Czechoslovakia initially refused the mostly young East Germans the opportunity to leave legally. Hungary began softening in August, as the numbers of GDR citizens in Hungary grew. Hungary sent signals to the East Germans and the international community through its foreign minister, Gyula Horn, that the borders might be opened on humanitarian grounds. The borders were formally opened at midnight on 11 September.[9] The number of East Germans leaving was growing quickly, from 4,600 in January 1989 to 10,600 in May, 21,000 in August, 33,000 in September, and 57,000 in October, reaching a monthly high of 133,000 in November.[10]

Through the summer of 1989, few observers saw German unification as an implication of the quickening pace of developments in and around the two Germanys. The SED was under growing pressure to reform. Encouraged by the examples being set in Hungary, Poland, and even the Soviet Union, alternatives to the Stalinist central control were being articulated in the GDR, as in Rolf Henrich's *Der vormundschaftliche Staat* (*The Tutelary State*).[11] The SED ban on reformist literature and films from the Soviet Union and Eastern Europe only accentuated the realization in an increasingly broad range of the public that the current government was incapable of reform. During this period, variables at the international level pushed the SED to attempt some domestic reforms in the areas of travel and political pluralism. Its inability to reform effectively and credibly only accelerated the collapse of the SED. The necessary conditions for reform (that is, Soviet "new thinking") interacted with the inability of the SED to contemplate and initiate reform. The SED would ultimately collapse, then, not just because of Soviet pressure, but because it could not respond to Soviet pressure.

11 September to 9 November: The Politics of Collapse

Even as late as November 1989, only a few voices either favoring or predicting the possibility of German unification could be heard. One such voice was that of the U.S. Ambassador to West Germany, General Vernon Walters, who opined that the existence of two Germanys was abnormal and speculated that unification might come about soon.[12] Apparently this view was not shared by the Department of State, since nothing more was mentioned on this subject for some time.

Walters' musings were also not shared by the West German foreign policy establishment. Bonn was at pains to dampen any expectations regarding possible unification during this period. The official line was that the internal problems driving dissent within and emigration from the GDR must be solved by the East Germans themselves. West German policy was directed toward stabilizing the regimes to the east. By stimulating discussion of the tabu question of German unification, old insecurities and fears would be aroused among Germany's neighbors and in the Soviet Union, with possibly disastrous consequences. This position was articulated by Chancellor

Helmut Kohl's foreign policy adviser, Horst Teltschik, in early September.[13] The Kohl government was thus continuing the *Ost- und Deutschlandpolitik* of the early 1970s, seeking to improve East German living conditions and encouraging hoped-for liberalization without directly confronting the issue of unification.

Meanwhile, within the GDR, dissent and dissatisfaction grew. The political culture of demonstrations spread from Leipzig and East Berlin to other parts of the GDR, including major cities such as Dresden, Karl-Marx-Stadt (Chemnitz), Magdeburg, and Halle. Increasingly, demonstrations also took place in smaller cities such as Arnstadt, Ilmenau, Neubrandenburg, Greifswald, Halberstadt, Großräschen, Lauchhammer, Güstrow, Greiz, and Senftenberg. The famous Leipzig Monday demonstrations grew from a few hundred demanding the right to travel during the spring and summer of 1989 to 6,000-8,000 on 25 September, over 10,000 on 2 October, 70,000-100,000 on 9 October, about 120,000 on 16 October, 250,000-300,000 on 23 October, 200,000-300,000 on 30 October, and about a half a million on 6 November.[14]

While the demonstrations grew, efforts were undertaken to focus dissatisfaction and to give it a programmatic and organizational framework. Chief among these was New Forum. New Forum was the work of the artist Bärbel Bohley and the attorney Rolf Henrichs, who had been prominent voices in efforts to encourage reform in the GDR. New Forum's commitment to reform was evidenced in its formal application for recognition under the GDR constitution. This recognition was swiftly denied by the government, as was an appeal of the denial. Nonetheless, New Forum continued to push for reforms while refusing to declare itself to be a political alternative to the SED. Rather, New Forum saw itself as an organizational framework within which reformist policies could be formulated, debated, and brought to the attention of the East German government.

At the same time the Social Democratic Party (SDP) was founded in secret, as were other political formations and nascent parties. Common to all of these new organizations was the belief in the reformability of socialism in the GDR. None of their programs included a call for German unification. This was also the position of the "bloc parties," which included the Christian Democratic Union (CDU), the Liberal Democratic Party of Germany (LDPD), and others that had loyally served the SED for decades. As these parties responded to change and recognized the need for reform in the early autumn of 1989, they also did not envisage any prospect for German unification.

The most important GDR internal development was the continuing collapse of the SED and with it the government. Most governmental authority was focused on the person of Erich Honecker, who was old and ill in the late summer of 1989. During much of the growing disagreement with Hungary over emigration, Honecker was hospitalized. He turned his authority over to Günter Mittag, rather than to his heir-presumptive, the vacationing Egon Krenz.[15] Mittag's inability to cope paralyzed the GDR government at a critical time in early September. As shown by the reports of the *Stasi*, the SED leadership knew in precise detail what was happening in the GDR.[16] Yet these leaders were utterly incapable of formulating a coordinated response to a growing crisis that was unaffected by their incantation of the customary Marxist-Leninist slogans and police-state techniques.

The ineptness of the party-state apparatus was demonstrated with chilling clarity in its response to the GDR citizens in the West German embassies in Prague and Warsaw. When internal and external pressures demanded action, a recuperating Honecker himself decided that East Germans would be allowed to legally emigrate with the proviso that the East Germans would transit the GDR to pick up proper visas on their way to the Federal Republic. On 30 September, trains bearing the emigrants passed before the eyes of those in the GDR who either also wished to emigrate or who were still hoping to reform the GDR. In either case, the trains were a cruel affront to the dissidents still in the GDR and an occasion of violence at train stations. This mistake was repeated on 4 October, three days before the GDR's fortieth anniversary celebrations.[17]

The chaos churning through the streets of the GDR came to a head on 6 and 7 October when Gorbachev visited East Berlin to help celebrate four decades of communist rule.[18] From the beginning it was clear that Gorbachev was participating in a formality. In his meeting with the SED Politburo, Gorbachev asserted that he would not support SED efforts to block reform in the GDR. Unification, however, was not a voiced alternative. Thus, Gorbachev reaffirmed the implications for the GDR of "new thinking" in Soviet policy, first expressed during the spring and summer of 1989.

The conduct of the police toward demonstrators at the anniversary and the anticipation of violence at the first Monday night demonstrations after the celebration strained the GDR's faltering political system to the limit. There were significant violent incidents from 4 through 7 October in Berlin and Leipzig. Demonstrators were beaten up, arrested, and held in demeaning circumstances.[19] The prospect for reform was becoming ever bleaker.

Under conditions of escalating crisis, the reigning Politburo pressured Honecker to resign on 18 October in a symbolic move of renewal. He was replaced by Egon Krenz who, together with other newly-elevated members in the Politburo, were all formed in essentially the same old SED mold. This mold was bound to crack under street-generated pressures.[20] Although Krenz promised reform, it was clear that he could not jump over his own shadow—nor that of his peers, either. Günter Schabowski, Wolfgang Herger, Heinz Keßler, Hans Modrow, and the others who replaced the "old" SED elite were not people who were capable of instituting the far-reaching reforms that would be necessary in the GDR. Moreover, Gorbachev, who met with Krenz in Moscow on 1 November, did not provide Krenz with any meaningful support. In fact, contrary to the customary practice, Gorbachev did not participate in the usually joint press conference prior to Krenz's departure from Moscow. Left alone, Krenz was visibly "twisting in the wind." After forty-one days as general secretary of the SED and a total of forty-four days in office as chair of the Council of State and the National Defense Council, Krenz became a completely private citizen on 6 December.

Krenz's ineffectuality characterized the collapse that cleared the way for unification. The decision to open the Berlin Wall on 9 November, was a bundle of errors and misunderstandings that remains unclear.[21] The inability of the "new team" even to formulate a clear policy on border controls and foreign travel regulations demonstrated their incapacity to pull together in the face of rapid change.

The character of the time was revealed in the massive demonstration on the Alexanderplatz on 4 November. The distinguished list of speakers included Christoph Hein, Christa Wolf, Marcus Wolf, Stephan Heym and Schabowski. Marcus Wolf and Schabowski were hardly able to speak over the protests of the crowd. The thrust of the speeches, the banners, and the mood of the crowd was to throw the rascals out and to renew the GDR as a socialist state. Their vision was of a state that had never really experienced socialism. The "socialist reality" of the GDR was in fact Stalinism plus "state monopolistic capitalism." With the bad old GDR now purged, a new GDR would be able to proceed along a "third path" between capitalism and the socialism of the past.[22] The Alexanderplatz rally was the last major demonstration in the waning GDR to emphasize reform rather than unification with the Federal Republic.

The door to unification was opened with the masses that streamed through the Brandenburg Gate and other German-German border crossings on and following 9 November. Once the Berlin Wall had opened, there was a manifest mood-swing. Now the crowds were increasingly demanding unification. The overwhelming majority of those visiting the West picked up their 100 DM in *Begrüßungsgeld* (greeting money), looked around, and returned to the GDR. Their impressions were enough to confirm what they had seen on western television and learned from visiting friends and relatives. In spite of the communist rhetoric, they were neither living as well as their "brothers and sisters" nor were they, after four decades of sacrifice, anywhere near grasping a constantly deferred socialist utopia. Heinz

Kallabis, a reform socialist, has presented a devastating analysis of the disparity between pretense and reality in the GDR of the 1980s.[23] Kallabis' work demonstrates what drove the people of East Germany toward speedy unification: the reality of the West with all of its shortcomings was a more accessible utopia than that promised by the SED.

The importance of international and domestic variables in the collapse of the GDR and the unification of the Germanys reversed during this period. The long-standing reformist movement in the GDR blossomed into an effective opposition only in the context of international pressures. Now, with growing numbers of demonstrators demanding unification, the politics of the street began to push reform in the international system, particularly the elimination of Four Powers rights over the two Germanys. Street-level developments also pushed the leadership of both the Federal Republic and the rapidly crumbling GDR to confront unification. At precisely this point the unification process was forced to move from rhetorical pieties in the West and fearful hopes in the East to the difficult task of giving shape to a unification plan. Unification, then, did not come into discussion because of international pressures, but because of domestic developments. Unification was possible only because domestic groups in the GDR demanded it, rather than any conceivable "third way."

10 November to 18 March 1990:
The Politics of the Street

Neither the GDR nor the Federal Republic was really prepared for unification. The same was true of the United States and the Soviet Union. The Soviet Union opposed unification but supported a closer association between the two otherwise sovereign Germanys. Yet Soviet "new thinking" in foreign policy was quickly outpaced by domestic developments in the GDR. Street-level politics pushed them all to come to grips with unification.

The collapse of the SED after the opening of the Wall was swift. A series of mild reform programs was proposed throughout November, December, and January, each of which was shouted down in the streets. To maintain some form of order in the country, the remnants of the SED, led by the reborn reformist Hans Modrow, were forced to share power with a growing number of new and reformed political parties and groups in a common Roundtable based on the Polish model.[24] The interim GDR government of Hans Modrow became mired in inept attempts to reform the *Stasi* (foolishly renamed the Ministry for National Security, or *Nasi*) and to save what it could for the Party of Democratic Socialism (PDS, the renamed and supposedly reformed SED). Efforts of the interim government to make itself more palatable to the people of the GDR only further undermined public confidence in those who were identified with the old, corrupt system.[25] Under growing public pressure, free parliamentary elections scheduled for May were moved up to March.

The Volkskammer election of 18 March 1990 was dominated by a coalition of newly formed and reformed center-right parties that campaigned for quick unification and received strong support from popular West German politicians. The election firmly established that a majority of East Germans favored unification.[26] The voices of the reformers in the New Forum and the PDS were lost in the clamor of demands for immediate unification.

The politics of the street dominated developments in the international system, as they also dominated the domestic situation. Helmut Kohl's "Ten-Point Plan" of 28 November for some form of German confederation was less a careful and thoughtful blueprint than an effort to get "something/ anything" before the people to slow the rate of emigration from east to west.[27] The French expressed concern for their rights as one of the Four Powers, and sought to stabilize the East German regime with a state visit by President François Mitterrand to East Berlin in December. The British also claimed their rights as one of the Four Powers and expressed misgivings about possible German neutrality. The only Western Power to support unification quickly was the United States,[28] after a short policy review in December 1989. As did the French and British, the US demanded that a unified Germany remain a full member of NATO.[29] Initially, the Soviets seemed unprepared for the changes they helped to place in motion in the GDR. Soviet policy on unification was clarified at the Malta summit between General Secretary Gorbachev and American President George Bush in December 1989. While Western discussion of Germany's role in NATO heated up in the winter of 1989-1990,[30] the Soviet position hardened.[31] Two central security questions were raised by German unification: Germany's alliance status and Germany's borders.

Security considerations were the central problem for the Four Powers, which had retained elements of sovereignty in the two Germanys after World War II, and in the Four Power Agreement of 1971. Before unification could be achieved, a treaty formally ending World War II and transferring full sovereignty to a united Germany had to be approved by all parties. Both sides insisted that a united Germany had to remain loyal to its previous alliance partners. The Soviets were willing to consider a neutral Germany, as they had often proposed since 1950, but with specific guarantees of Germany's neutrality. Neutrality was unacceptable to France, which feared losing its close association with Germany; the United Kingdom, which feared a loss of its influence in Europe; and the United States, which also wanted to assure its future role in Europe. All three Western powers also feared that the Soviets would come to dominate a neutral Germany. During the Ottawa "open skies" conference to discuss conventional arms reductions in Europe in February 1990, all four agreed to convene the so-called "Two-Plus-Four" talks to address the eventual alliance status of the united Germany.

Related was the issue of Germany's borders. The redrawing of the eastern border by the Soviets in 1945 was not recognized by the West German Basic Law. Poland began to fear that a unified German government would not be bound by its commitments to respect European borders embodied in the Helsinki accords.[32] To compound matters, Chancellor Kohl, in an ill-advised effort to shore up political support on the right wing of his party, waffled on the issue of Germany's eastern borders. It was not until 7 and 8 March 1990 that Chancellor Kohl and the West German Bundestag dropped all preconditions and recognized the postwar Oder-Neiße line as the Polish boundary with Germany.[33] Nonetheless, the Poles insisted that they be included in those portions of the Two-Plus-Four talks dealing with borders.

Despite the Soviets' efforts, and in the face of concerns raised by Poland, German unification was not to be stopped. During this phase of unification, domestic events pushed along the politicians, both domestic and international. The attempts of the remnant PDS to reform within a socialist structure were rejected by the demonstrators. The continued emigration of tens of thousands of East Germans to the West each week threatened to lead, as some quipped, to German unification on West German soil. The triumph of the conservative pro-quick unification parties in the Volkskammer election of March signaled that German unification was virtually unstoppable. Domestic developments pushed the Four Powers to address their role in German unification, with varying reservations on the part of each of them.

19 March to 3 October:
The Politics of Unification

While it was clear after the Volkskammer election of 18 March that Germany would be unified, questions remained regarding how and under what domestic and international conditions. Domestically, the questions concerned the legal framework to be applied to unification. Internationally, the Two-Plus-Four talks quickly devolved into one (the Soviets) versus the rest. Since the Soviets expressed strong security concerns, and given that they had some 340,000 troops stationed in the GDR, the Soviets could not be ignored. The international conditions for uniting Germany revolved around ways to reassure the Soviets of their security and to buy them off.

The domestic battle over unification had two elements: the form of economic unification and the form of political unification. Economic unification entailed both the extension of the West German D-Mark to the GDR (the East German mark was nonconvertible and had no prospects of future convertibility) and the extension of Western social and economic benefits to the East. Economic unification was driven by the continuing waves of East Germans leaving for the West, even if in somewhat lessened numbers after the March election. Additionally, the fall of the Wall was revealing the bankruptcy of the East German economy, and demands for a leveling of standards of living in East and West were growing. Bonn, which had campaigned in the East on improving economic conditions, was forced to deliver.

The debate about the form of economic union was sharp. Oskar Lafontaine, the SPD's popular chancellor-candidate in the national election scheduled for December 1990, argued that unification had to be slowed, until it could become clear what the costs would be for West German taxpayers. Kohl was able to deflect this criticism by contending that unification would be relatively cost-free, since East German firms could continue to export to Eastern Europe. Kohl also appealed to the need to meet East German demands for better standards of living and the emotionally-charged historical drive to unify the divided nation. Kohl was unable to avoid the pressures posed by the Bundesbank. Bank president Karl-Otto Pöhl feared that Kohl's earlier pledge to exchange East and West marks at a rate of 1:1, coupled with higher federal borrowing to pay for reconstruction and social programs in the East, might touch off inflation in the German economy. Kohl adroitly reduced the Bundesbank's influence by naming Pöhl the head of the group to oversee economic unification, which meant that Pöhl would be the first to blame if the process proved too slow. Apparently to placate the powerful head of the independent Bundesbank, Kohl agreed to tighten Germany's stance on European monetary integration along lines proposed by Pöhl. The two Germanys concluded a Treaty on Monetary, Economic, and Social Union on 18 May, and on 1 July economic union was effected.

Politically, the two German states could be united either by formal treaty between the two sovereign states and the adoption of a new all-German constitution (via Article 146 of the West German Basic Law) or by the dissolution of the GDR and the application of its constituent parts to join the Federal Republic (via Article 23). The former was preferred by the West German Social Democrats and much of the left in the East. This strategy would have slowed unification and improved the SPD's chances in the December 1990 election. Legally, the two states would have had to be unified by August to hold a united election. Article 146 unification was opposed by many West German conservatives. Unification via Article 23 seemed to be quicker, provided a cleaner break with the GDR's past, and maintained the important democratic elements of the Basic Law. It also improved the likelihood that Kohl could win the first national election in the newly-unified Germany, since Kohl was more popular in the East than in the West. Buttressed by a strong showing in the May communal elections in the GDR, and despite criticism from the left, East-West negotiations were conducted on the basis of Article 23.[34] After long and occasionally acrimonious bargaining, with key points of contention such as abortion laws deferred, a treaty unifying the two Germanys was signed on 31 August 1990.

Technically, German economic and political union was not possible as long as the Four Powers maintained their rights in Germany. The large number of Soviet troops on East German soil was a reminder that unification was contingent upon external developments. Yet the internal domestic pressures for unification were so strong, and the Soviet military and political position so weak, that the Soviets could at best slow unification. The efforts of the Western Powers, led by the United States, were directed at inducing the Soviets graciously and quickly to bow out of the GDR, while saving face and assuring Soviet security. The Western Powers followed two tracks to convince the Soviets to support quick German unification.

Multilateral negotiations constituted the first track of the Western strategy. In the course of the Two-Plus-Four talks, and later at the London NATO summit on 5-6 July 1990, the Western Powers sent clear signals to Moscow that they viewed the Cold War as over, that future NATO strategy would not take advantage of collapsing Soviet influence in Eastern Europe, and that German unification was imminent. The second track focused upon bilateral assurances to the Soviets, especially during the U.S.-Soviet summit in May-June 1990. Kohl and Foreign Minister Genscher also sought to reassure the Soviets during a visit to Moscow in February as well as during meetings in Copenhagen, Brest, and Münster in June. The Soviets tried vainly to either neutralize Germany or keep both parts in their respective military blocs. With the Warsaw Pact rapidly disintegrating, these efforts lacked credibility.

Kohl's visit to Gorbachev on 17 July finally broke the logjam. The Soviets and Germans agreed that the Soviets would withdraw their troops gradually from the GDR, that no NATO Bundeswehr troops would be stationed in the East until after the Soviets were gone, and that after the Soviets left no non-German NATO troops would be deployed in the East. The Germans also agreed to extend economic support to the Soviet Union and to construct housing for the soldiers returning from the GDR to the Soviet Union. Soviet-German friendship was formalized in a treaty signed on 9 November 1990.

Much has been made of the Kohl-Gorbachev talks of July 1990. These discussions seemed to push along an understanding on the part of the Soviets that Germany was fully dedicated to peace and that war would not begin in Germany again. Yet the agreement itself only constituted Soviet recognition of long-standing Western positions in the Two-Plus-Four talks. The Soviets had few options, as economic unification had been achieved smoothly, and the pressures for quick political unification, from both the Germanys and the international system, were reaching a peak. The Soviets undoubtedly held out for the best deal they thought they could get, but it was a far cry from past Soviet demands.

With the Soviets on board and the economic and political treaties signed, all that was left was for the Four Powers to suspend their rights over Germany. This was unceremoniously accomplished on 1 October 1990. The Germanys were formally unified on 3 October 1990.

Conclusion

The events from the summer of 1989 through the unification of the two Germanys on 3 October 1990 have been characterized as a "revolution." Viewed against the literature on revolutions, the German-German case appears exceptional. The flow of events and the virtually unique interplay of domestic and international elements make it difficult to order the German case among those in the theoretical literature on revolutions. The necessary conditions leading to the collapse of the SED are found in the Soviets' "new thinking" in foreign policy and Soviet unwillingness to use force to support the SED. Yet the sufficient conditions explaining the collapse are found in domestic politics. The SED's unwillingness and inability to contemplate reform, coupled with inept and incompetent leadership, led to its fall. External pressures alone can not explain the collapse of the SED, which had ruled East Germany for forty years.

Once the SED was no longer in power, the way was open for unification. Yet unification was not the only possible outcome. Most of the organized opposition to the SED desired an ill-defined "third way" between capitalism and socialism. The Soviets, initiators of reform in the GDR, were also not pushing for unification. At this point, the necessary and sufficient variables shifted, and domestic developments drove unification. The politics of the street in the GDR pushed all international actors—notably the United States, the Soviet Union, France, and Great Britain—to come to grips with the demands of the people. Street-level developments and the March 1990 election also convinced the political leadership of both Germanys that unification must be achieved. From then on it was mainly a matter of negotiating terms.

The political significance of the 1989 revolution in the GDR, coupled with the curious role of international factors and the implications of the division of Germany, defies generalization. Nonetheless, abstracting from the particulars of the revolution to more general conceptual analysis underscores the importance of necessary and sufficient variables in the achievement of German unification and the ways in which these variables interacted and changed over time as the issues changed.

The unifying Germany offers social scientists and German specialists a unique opportunity to study and analyze the integration of two political and economic systems that had previously been seen as growing apart from one another. The rapidity of disintegration and unification make the united Germany a fascinating new case in the seemingly endlessly compelling political history of Germany.

Notes

1. Fred Oldenburg, "Die Implosion des SED-Regimes: Ursachen und Entwicklungsprozesse," *Berichte des Bundesinstituts für ostwissenschaftliche und internationale Studien*, 10 (1991).

2. Heinrich Bortfeldt, "Die SED ihr eigener Totengräber?" *Deutschland Archiv*, 24 (1991): 733-36.

3. Ray Edward Johnston, ed., *The Politics of Division, Partition and Unification* (New York, N.Y.: Praeger, 1976).

4. Anita M. Mallinckrodt, *The Environmental Dialogue in the GDR* (Lanham, Maryland: University Press of America, 1987).

5. Robert F. Goeckel, *The Lutheran Church and the East German State* (Ithaca, N.Y.: Cornell University Press, 1990).

6. See Günter Gaus, "Kopf aus der Nische," *Süddeutsche Zeitung*, 9/10 September 1989.

7. Egon Krenz, *Wenn Mauern fallen* (Vienna: Paul Neff Verlag, 1990), 130-34. Here, Krenz does his best to revise his involvement in, for example, the election fraud. Ibid., 125-29.

8. Neues Forum Leipzig, *Jetzt oder nie—Demokratie Leipziger Herbst '89* (Leipzig/Munich: Forum Verlag/C. Bertelsmann, 1989/1990).

9. Gyula Horn, "Wir mußten es wagen," *Der Spiegel*, 2 September 1991: 114-126.

10. Data are from Volker Ronge, "Loyalty, Voice or Exit? Die Fluchtbewegung als Anstoß und Problem der Erneuerung in der DDR," in Göttrik

Wewer, ed., *DDR—Von der friedlichen Revolution zur deutschen Vereinigung* (Opladen: Leske and Budrich, 1990), 40.

11. Rolf Henrich, *Der vormundschaftliche Staat* (Hamburg: Rowohlt, 1989). Although published in West Germany, the substance of Henrich's book was widely known in the GDR.

12. "Nur Deutsche wollten die Wiedervereinigung," *Die Welt*, 15 September 1989

13. Horst Teltschik, "Auf dem Weg zu einem neuen Europa?" *Frankfurter Allgemeine Zeitung*, 9 September 1989.

14. Data on numbers of participants vary significantly, not the least as the East German media, when they reported on the demonstrations, significantly underreported the figures. These data are from Neues Forum Leipzig, *Jetzt oder nie;* Hubertus Knabe, ed., *Aufbruch in eine andere DDR: Reformer und Oppositionelle zur Zukunft ihres Landes* (Reinbek bei Hamburg: Rowohlt Verlag, 1989); and *Geschichte der Deutschen 1949-1990* (Frankfurt am Main: Insel Verlag, 1990). (No author cited.).

15. While Krenz was the annointed successor to Honecker, he had fallen somewhat out of favor and was not encouraged to cut short his vacation to try to tackle the growing problems in the GDR.

16. Excerpts from Mittag's forthcoming book, *Um jeden Preis*, along with an interview, are to be found in *Der Spiegel*, 9 September 1991: 80-104.

17. See Armin Mitter and Stefan Wolle, eds., *"Ich liebe Euch doch alle!" Befehle und Lageberichte des MfS Januar-November 1989* (Berlin: BasisDruck, 1990).

18. See Oldenburg, "Die Implosion," 14; Arthur M. Hanhardt, Jr., "Demonstrations, Groups, Parties and the *Volkskammer* Election: Aspects of Political Change in East Germany." Paper presented at the annual meeting of the American Political Science Association in San Francisco, Calif., September 1990; and Krenz, *Wenn Mauern fallen*, 31-32.

19. Excerpts from a verbatim report of Gorbachev's meeting with the SED Politburo are printed in *Der Spiegel*, 9 September 1991: 107-110. See also Fred Oldenburg, "Sowjetische Europa-Politik und die Lösung der deutschen Frage," in *Osteuropa*, XLI (August 1991): 757-58.

20. Many texts document these events. For an impressive account of the situation in Leipzig during the entire autumn, see *Jetzt oder nie*. Also see Charles Schüddekopf, ed., *"Wir sind das Volk!" Flugschriften, Aufrufe und Texte einer deutschen Revolution* (Reinbek bei Hamburg: Rowohlt, 1990).

21. Günter Schabowski has described his version of Honecker's replacement in *Das Politbüro* (Reinbek bei Hamburg: Rowohlt, 1990), 83-110. For Egon Krenz's account, see *Wenn Mauern fallen*, 141-145. Erich

Honecker has given his account in Reinhold Anert and Wofgang Herzberg, *Der Sturz. Erich Honecker im Kreuzverhör* (Berlin and Weimar: Aufbau Verlag, 1990), 25-37.

22. Krenz, 161-95, and Schabowski, 112-151.

23. See, for example, Gregor Gysi, ed., *Wir brauchen einen dritten Weg* (Hamburg: Konkret Literatur Verlag, 1990). This volume contains essays by Michael and Andre Brie, Hans Modrow, and others as well as the program of the SED successor party, the Party of Democratic Socialism (PDS). Also see Knabe, *Aufbruch in eine andere DDR*.

24. Heinz Kallabis, *"Realer Sozialismus"—Anspruch und Wirklichkeit* (Berlin: Treptower Verlagshaus, 1990). The two studies in this volume were completed in 1987 and between April and July 1989.

25. Uwe Thaysen, *Der Runde Tisch. Oder: Wo blieb das Volk? Der Weg der DDR in die Demokratie* (Opladen: Westdeutscher Verlag, 1990).

26. On SED corruption, see Hannes Bahrmann and Peter-Michael Fritsch, *Sumpf: Privilegien. Amtsmißbrauch. Schiebergeschäfte* (Berlin: LinksDruck Verlag, 1990).

27. Dieter Roth, "Die Volkskammerwahl in der DDR am 18. März 1990. Rationales Wahlverhalten beim ersten demokratischen Urnengang," in Ulrike Liebert and Wolfgang Merkel, eds., *Die Politik zur deutschen Einheit. Probleme–Strategien–Kontroversen* (Opladen: Leske and Budrich, 1991), 115-138.

28. The text of the "Ten-Point Program" can be found in Gebhard Diemer, ed., *Kurze Chronik der Deutschen Frage* (Munich: Olzog Verlag, 1990), 210-16. See also Appendix 2.

29. This was also reflected in American public opinion. See Arthur M. Hanhardt, Jr., "Die deutsche Vereinigung im Spiegelbild der amerikanischen öffentlichen und veröffentlichten Meinung," in Wolfgang Friedrich, ed., *Die USA und die Deutsche Frage* (Frankfurt/New York: Campus Verlag, 1991).

30. See Secretary of State James Baker's statement, "A New Europe, A New Atlanticism: Architecture for a New Era." Address to the Berlin Press Club, Berlin, 12 December 1989.

31. The element of reaction to Western proposals can be seen in "On Germany," Statement by the Soviet Foreign Ministry Collegium, Moscow, 24 February 1990.

32. Prime Minister Tadeusz Mazowiecki, "Belonging to Europe." Speech to the Council of Europe, Strasbourg, 30 January 1990, and Minister of Foreign Affairs Krzysztof Skubiszewski, "Problems of Peace and Security in Europe." Speech to an Extraordinary Session of the Assembly of the Western European Union, Luxembourg, 22 March 1990.

33. Marc Fischer, "Kohl, in a Turnaround, Affirms Polish Border," *The International Herald Tribune*, 7 March 1990, and Wolfgang Benz, *Deutschland seit 1945* (Munich: Moos & Partner, 1990), 173.

34. See Wolfgang Schäuble, *Der Vertrag. Wie ich über die deutsche Einheit verhandelte* (Stuttgart: Deutsche Verlags-Anstalt, 1991).

5

Exiting the GDR:
Political Movements and Parties
Between Democratization
and Westernization

Michaela W. Richter

Hindsight is no substitute for the careful reconstruction and analysis of how party systems develop and function. It may now appear inevitable that, as unification became possible and then probable, the GDR's party system would fall under the control of the principal parties from the Federal Republic. Yet for those civic movements that had compelled the GDR regime to yield power, this outcome was unanticipated and disappointing.

Those who challenged the regime in the fall of 1989 did not adequately understand that two competing conceptions of change were at work in the GDR. The first was to reform the existing system from within. This was the goal of those who mobilized mass demonstrations to demand democratization of the GDR's political practices, while retaining its socialist ideals. The second alternative was to abandon the GDR altogether and to become part of the Federal Republic. Beginning in the summer of 1989, this was the implicit, if unarticulated premise of all those who participated in the mass exodus from East Germany to the Federal Republic. By the time of the 18 March 1990 Volkskammer election, a majority of East German voters had decided to exit the GDR as well by supporting parties that promised a speedy and painless union with West Germany.

Initially, these two tendencies reinforced each other and, in the process, created powerful pressures that the regime, even with its massive repressive apparatus, proved incapable to withstand. But once the Berlin Wall was opened, these two models of change increasingly competed with one another. In the end, the opposition's vision for a sovereign GDR with new democratic institutions and a more humane version of socialism lost out to the East German electorate's pragmatic desire of merging with the Federal Republic and thus becoming the immediate beneficiaries of its political and economic system.

The inherent tensions between advocates of reform from within and those who preferred the ready-made West German model shaped as well the transformation in the GDR's party system from the fall of 1989 onward. Initially, the forty-year-old party structure, dominated by the communist SED and its subservient bloc party allies, was challenged by newly emerging civic movements demanding democratic and economic reforms. But with the opening of the Wall and the setting of an early election date during the first Roundtable meeting in mid-December, the East German party system underwent another series of shocks.

In the second phase, developments increasingly centered less on internal reforms than the speed and form of unification with the Federal Republic. During the transition from the first to the second phase, the confrontation was no longer between regime and opposition parties. Instead, it was between partisans of rapid union and those desiring a more gradual path, with West German parties actively intervening to shape the outcome. The result was the marginalization of those who made the revolution and the virtual reproduction of the West German party system in the East.

This chapter seeks to chart and explain this dual restructuring of the East German party system. What were the major changes during the democratic revolution of the fall 1989?[1] What changed in the aftermath of the opening of the Berlin Wall? How and why did the West German parties succeed in displacing the opposition groups responsible for the rout of the old regime? In accounting for the unexpected outcome of "their" peaceful revolution, opposition groups have blamed the intervention of the West German parties (and media). But these complaints ignore the importance of both external exigencies, created by the opening of the Berlin Wall and Gorbachev's readiness to acquiesce in the new international conditions thereby created, and internal pressures resulting from the rapidity of the regime's collapse, the unwillingness of the East German population to submit to yet another economic and political experiment, and the lack of concrete alternatives offered by the East German opposition and reformed regime parties.

After a brief survey of the origins of the East German party system and its structure prior to the events in the fall of 1989, I will examine in the second part of this chapter the impact of Gorbachev's reforms on the SED regime. The third section then considers the effects on the structure of East German parties of the consequent peaceful revolution in the GDR. Part four charts and explains the critical changes between the first and second phases in the restructuring of East German parties.

Origins and Structure of the East German Party State

Party formation in the Soviet-occupied zone (SBZ) began with the Soviet Military Administration (SMAD) Decree No. 2 of 10 June 1945, which allowed the formation of "antifascist" democratic parties and trade unions. Within three weeks, four parties were licensed: the Communist Party (*Kommunistische Partei Deutschland*, KPD), the Social Democratic Party (*Sozialdemokratische Partei Deutschlands*, SPD), the Christian Democratic Union (*Christlich-Demokratische Union*, CDU), and the Liberal Democratic Party (*Liberal-Demokratische Partei Deutschlands*, LDPD).[2] SMAD's apparent acceptance of a pluralistic party system reflected Soviet interests at this stage. By avoiding the impression of imposing its own political designs on the SBZ, the Soviet Union hoped to strengthen relations with its Western Allies, whose cooperation was vital to satisfy Soviet reparation claims. Furthermore, as the first to license what were clearly viewed as national rather than zonal parties (hence their Berlin headquarters), SMAD expected to shape the subsequent development of an all-German party system in ways conducive to Soviet influence.[3]

Nonetheless, party pluralism in the SBZ was from the outset limited. Until 1948, no other parties were licensed either at the zonal or sub-zonal level. Licensing itself required programmatic conformities (e.g., to anti-fascism, democracy, and civil rights), prior approval of leaders and members, and adherence to SMAD instructions. Despite their formally equal status, SMAD consistently favored the KPD at the expense of its competitors in everything from registrations of local party organizations to allocations of vital resources (office space and furniture, paper and newsprint) and political and administrative appointments. Most importantly, all four parties could operate only as members of the "common front of anti-fascist parties."[4] Constituted on 14 July 1945, this "anti-fascist bloc" was altogether new in German party tradition. Its members subscribed to a minimal programmatic consensus; its decisions had to be unanimous, were binding on all parties, and were made by party leaders without prior intra-party consultations.[5]

Communist electoral defeats in the summer of 1945 in Hungary, Austria, Bavaria, and Hesse, combined with increasing Allied resistance to Soviet reparation claims, altered Soviet strategy. From late 1945 onward, SMAD took a number of steps that linked the East German occupation zone ever more tightly to the Soviet Union. SMAD first eliminated the KPD's main leftwing rival through the forcible KPD/SPD merger in April 1946.[6] Especially after their surprising electoral strength in the communal and Landtag elections of 1946, SMAD also moved to curb the bourgeois bloc parties (the CDU and LDPD). It not only removed leaders willing to resist Soviet economic policies but, using the principle of "anti-fascist unity," forced the bloc parties into all-party coalitions in which communists invariably received the key positions.[7]

The process of Sovietization was hastened by a series of major East-West confrontations (including the proclamation of the Truman Doctrine, the Czech coup, and the Berlin airlift) and Stalin's inability (after the failed Moscow and London Conferences of 1947) to reverse the transformation of the Western zones into a sovereign democratic state within the Western camp. Between 1948 and 1949, SMAD systematically converted the SBZ into a Soviet-style managed economy and communist state under SED control.[8] In 1948, the SED itself underwent a restructuring into a centrally led, hierarchical, and disciplined "Marxist-Leninist party of a new type." This was accompanied by a series of purges to ensure the dominance of those with proven loyalty to Stalin and the Soviet Communist Party.[9] Finally, SMAD destroyed the remaining independence and political leverage of the CDU and LDPD through purges of "reactionary" and "anti-progressive" elements and their replacement by more pliant leaders.[10] As a further check, SMAD helped to found (in April 1948) two new bourgeois parties ready to accept the SED's "leading role": the German Democratic Peasants' Party (*Demokratische Bauernpartei Deutschlands*, DBD) and the National Democratic Party of Germany (*National-Demokratische Partei Deutschlands*, NDPD). Their purpose was to support SED policies in the bloc (which they joined in September 1948), draw away members from the CDU and LDPD, and maintain the fiction of multi-party bloc decisions should the latter two parties veto SED policies or withdraw from the bloc.[11] Finally, for the May 1949 elections to the Third People's Congress, which finalized the SBZ's transition into a separate state that October, the bloc parties had to join the SED on a "unity list" (*Einheitsliste*) and agree to a fixed distribution of seats. The consolidation of the SED's political and economic power thus coincided with the establishment of the GDR as a separate political and economic system.[12]

The system that had emerged at the time of the GDR's founding remained fixed for the next forty years. After 1948, no additional parties were allowed, nor could any party leave the bloc and operate on its own.[13] The *Gleichschaltung* (forcible subordination) of the CDU and LDPD was completed in 1952, when the SED forced them to recognize formally the SED's leading role, to accept the achievement of socialism along the Soviet model, to adopt the SED's structure of "democratic centralism" and to abandon all activities in trade unions, factories, and the public administration.

Henceforth, the SED selected the bloc candidates for the People's Chamber (Volkskammer) and allocated official posts among them. Irrespective of their actual votes, the bloc parties always held 208 of the 500 seats in the Volkskammer. Though each had one seat in the thirty-one member State Council (*Staatsrat*) and the forty-five member Council of Ministers (through which "collective leadership" was exercised), these were positions without real policy influence or political leverage.

The bloc parties maintained separate (but neither equal nor autonomous) organizations and publications. From 1958 on, the costs of maintaining the party apparatus and media were covered increasingly by state contributions that provided the SED with an additional lever of control.[14] Following repeated purges (the last after the 1953 uprising), membership in the bloc parties was strictly regulated. They could not publicly recruit members, and every new member required prior approval by the SED. Since the SED defined itself as the party of the proletariat, the bloc parties were allowed only a small contingent of working class members.[15]

Despite effusive and constant professions of friendship and the proven loyalty of their leaders, the SED never accepted the bloc parties as real partners. Attempts at any independent policies were forbidden, and reform suggestions were ignored. Ever fearful of possible opposition, the SED prohibited direct contacts or negotiations between the bloc parties and sought to prevent common interests or collusion by playing each off against the other in allocating mandates, positions, and other rewards.[16] Yet the SED found it useful to retain the bloc system. Externally, it maintained the fiction of the GDR as a multi-party system. Internally, the bloc parties served as convenient transmission belts for the official party line as mechanisms for the socialization of, and control over, those parts of the population that the SED could not or did not want to recruit and as sources of information about grievances of certain social interests. For many East German citizens, in turn, the bloc parties provided a certain cover, enabling them to pursue careers without having to join the SED and accept its "Leninist" discipline. At the same time, much of the population cynically dismissed them as *Blockflöten*, i.e., as flutes playing to the SED's tune.

Until the 1980s, this system survived. Following the construction of the Wall, the GDR achieved a modicum of economic growth and prosperity and with it some domestic legitimacy. Externally, the Cold War and Soviet interests in the division of Europe ensured the system's continued survival. But as these internal and external pillars weakened, both the SED's power and the GDR's survival came under threat.

Exit and Voice: East Germany's Path to Democracy

The collapse of the SED regime was, of course, part of a larger breakdown of communism in Eastern and Central Europe. By the mid-1980s, the cumulative impact of the economic, political, and social problems in all communist systems, on the one hand, and the external challenges of the CSCE process and reformist pressures from Gorbachev, on the other, undermined whatever little legitimacy the Eastern and Central European communist regimes had enjoyed in the past.[17] These developments presented the GDR's leaders with even graver problems and choices than its communist bloc allies.

Internally, the GDR's economic decline in the 1980s was doubly resented by East Germans because, having achieved relative prosperity and security in the preceding decade, they suddenly saw not just an erosion of past gains but waning chances for future improvements. Popular resentments were exacerbated by easy accessibility to West German television, which made the Federal Republic the standard of comparison rather than other communist nations or the grim post-war years. The net effect was to weaken the implicit bargain after 1961—accommodation with the regime in return for a minimum of comfort.[18]

As for external challenges, although the CSCE agreements legitimated the GDR's statehood by formally acknowledging the inviolability of post-1945 borders, these accords also undermined the foundations on which the GDR rested. Since it owed its existence to irreconcilable tensions between East and West, it could only be weakened by the reduction of East-West tensions as well as greater trans-bloc military and economic cooperation so central to the CSCE process. The GDR's response of encouraging "external" dialogue within the CSCE framework while foreclosing it at home (by criminalizing and silencing reformists and dissidents) worked reasonably well until Gorbachev came to power.[19]

Gorbachev's commitment to fundamental democratic and economic change within the Soviet Union and his public backing for the reform process in Hungary and Poland (including the Roundtable talks and free elections) directly threatened the SED. No longer could domestic reform pressures be deflected by blaming external constraints set by Soviet interests and concerns. More seriously, after forty years of proclaiming the Soviet Union as the only acceptable political and economic model for the GDR, the SED had no alternative German model of socialism to fall back on. Its only response was to deny the existence of a crisis in the GDR and hence the need for the changes the Soviet leader espoused.[20]

In the end, the gap between the bunker mentality of the Politburo and popular impatience with the lack of change could not be maintained. Yet the GDR's distinctive geopolitical origins and status also made the East German revolution different from those of its communist neighbors.

In terms of Albert Hirschman's theory of alternative responses to disaffection with declining firm performance or organizational dysfunctioning, opposition to the GDR regime could be expressed either through "exit" or "voice."[21] Until the revolution of 1989, "exiting" for East Germans entailed emigrating to the Federal Republic, which gave them automatic citizenship and material assistance to ease their integration into West German society. In this case, individuals dubious about the GDR's reformability opted to change their own life. Exiting was thus a form of individual protest (and was treated as such by the regime).

By contrast, "voice" entailed efforts to force regime change and reforms through public protest actions: distribution of anti-regime materials, oppositional meetings, public challenges, demonstrations. Voice, though riskier than exit, was the preferred option for those East Germans who, while critical of the system's political and economic performance, retained faith in its reformability.

From 1988 on, the SED leadership's sought to neutralize Gorbachev's reform pressures through ever greater repression. This intensified protest through both exit (in the form of surging visa applications) and voice (such as the unofficial Rosa Luxemburg demonstrations of January 1988; the Leipzig demonstrations of January 1989 for freedom of opinion, press, and assembly; and protests against the communal election frauds in June 1989). The transformation from such individual acts of protest to revolutionary upheavals began in the summer of 1989. From July through early October 1989, the revolutionary process was essentially exit-driven. No longer content to wait for exit visas, tens of thousands of East Germans flooded into West German embassies in Hungary, Poland, and Czechoslovakia, refusing to leave until granted direct entry to the Federal Republic.

What ultimately produced systemic changes in the GDR, however, was the added impact of voice. The seemingly unstoppable outward flow of East Germans and the SED's unwillingness to recognize, much less redress, the causes for these mass exits finally galvanized not just the small opposition groups but also those East Germans who refused or could not take the exit option. From late September on, the revolutionary process was essentially "voice-driven." Once marginal dissident groups and an ever larger number of ordinary East Germans entered the public sphere demanding to be heard, to be talked to, and to be treated as responsible citizens. This time, efforts to contain popular protest with violence (notably the arrests of demonstrators in Dresden, Leipzig, and East Berlin throughout September, as well as attacks by security forces on pro-Gorbachev demonstrators during his visit on 6 October in Berlin) proved counterproductive. They enraged and mobilized rather than intimidated the population; they stimulated rather than retarded the formation of opposition groups; they raised demands from dialogue to fundamental change.

The combined impact of exit and voice finally brought the regime down. On 18 October 1989, Erich Honecker was ousted and replaced by his former protégé, Egon Krenz. Over the next three weeks, Krenz revamped the Politburo, opened a dialogue with the church and opposition, and announced an "action program" of reforms—all to no avail. Unable to stop further mass flight and popular demonstrations, an SED spokesman finally announced on 9 November the opening of all border crossings to Berlin and to the West. Rather than help shore up the crumbling SED regime, however, this move only hastened its demise. But it also changed the dynamics and direction of the democratic revolution.

First, unification which up to this point had not been on the political agenda, now moved to the center of attention both internationally and within the two Germanys. Externally, it was first raised by former Chancellor Willy Brandt in his speech of 10 November in which he demanded that "what belongs together, must grow together." Chancellor Kohl then seized the initiative with his Ten-Point Program of 28 November, which provided for the first time a coherent framework for eventual unification. By the time of the 18 March 1990 election in the GDR, Kohl and Foreign Minister Hans-Dietrich Genscher had won not only the West's but also the Warsaw Pact's consent to accept the decision of East German voters in favor of union with the Federal Republic.[22]

November 9 also altered the revolution's internal context. The sudden exposure to the prosperous reality of West Germany came as a shock to East Germans long accustomed only to experiencing life in the West vicariously through television. On the one hand, the contrast increased the fury of the population to the point that the SED regime was forced to share power with the democratic opposition. On the other hand, the opening of East German borders undermined these reformers' original agenda of an East German path to democracy and economic reform. First, the dramatic difference between "real existing socialism" and "real existing capitalism" convinced even more East Germans to head West rather than to wait for the GDR to catch up—an average of 2,000 per week did so between 9 November 1989 and 18 March 1990. Second, an ever larger part of the East German public now realized that their only chance of reaching an analogous standard of living was integration with the Federal Republic. Beginning with demonstrations on 4 December in Leipzig, Dresden, and Halle, the early voices for a new, reformed GDR were drowned out by pro-unification demands. This amounted in effect to a call for a collective exit from the GDR. The result was that by 18 March the issue was no longer internal reform but in what manner and how quickly the GDR would yield its sovereignty to the Federal Republic.

From December onward, therefore, one can see a *Wende in der Wende*, or a revolution within the revolution. Much the same pattern emerged in the transformation of the East German party system. Here, too, two distinctive phases were discernible. The first entailed essentially the "democratization" of East German party politics; the second, its "Westernization." Roughly speaking, the first phase began with the demonstrations in late September/early October and, though it "symbolically" ended with the opening of the Wall, it formally concluded with the establishment of the Roundtable and an all-party government in December. Informally, phase two also began on 9 November, since this changed the over-all context of East German party developments. Formally, however, it began on 12 December 1989 with the setting of the date (subsequently changed) for the Volkskammer elections during the Roundtable's first meeting and ended with the Volkskammer election of 18 March. Between phase one and two, significant changes occurred among the central political actors, the political agendas of the competing parties, and the structure of party competition and party alignments.

The Democratization of the East German Party System

The mass demonstrations transformed the once frozen landscape of East German party politics into a pluralistic, open, and competitive arena. The key developments during this revolutionary first phase included (1) the appearance of new political actors ready to challenge the ruling parties for control, (2) the "renewal" of the bloc parties, and (3) the disintegration and ostensibly democratic "rebirth" of the SED.

Enter the Opposition

The initiators of this new political pluralism and the central actors of the initial revolutionary phase were the citizen movements and new parties that came out of the long-suppressed and small opposition. In the 1980s, a number of dissident groups had formed around specific themes or issues, including human rights, peace, environment, and the role of women. These groups generally shared a vision of a socialist, ecological, peaceful, communal, and democratic society. Most saw in *glasnost* and *perestroika* a chance of revitalizing the GDR and reforming the regime rather than destroying it.[23]

The various opposition groups found protection in the Protestant churches, which provided them with space and protection as well as limited public exposure through such sponsored activities as environmental forums, peace vigils or prayers, special exhibits, and discussion evenings.[24] It was from such weekly peace vigils in the Nikolaikirche in Leipzig that the first Monday demonstrations emerged. Moreover, beginning in the 1980s, elements within the churches began to call for greater dialogue between the regime and dissident voices, encourage reforms, and offer a forum for alternative voices.

Around 1988, however, some of the dissidents began to leave the "ghetto of the church" and to build a second public sphere of their own through self-published newspapers, clandestinely produced brochures and flyleafs, samizdat circulation of Western publications, and critical materials produced by East German dissidents. They also began to challenge the regime more directly through open demands for reform and demonstrations.[25] Yet the GDR's opposition remained numerically and politically insignificant. As of June 1988, there existed some 160 movements with a total of 2,500 members. They worked in small, informal, and often conspiratorial groups to escape the detection of the state security apparatus, i.e. the *Stasi*.[26] The mass exodus and the regime's intransigence finally altered the political context in favor of the opposition groups. But even as they seized the political initiative in the fall of 1989, they did so through separate associations that often competed against each other rather than form a common opposition front such as KOR in Poland or Civic Forum and Public Against Violence in Czechoslovakia. This persisting fragmentation made it all the more difficult both to stabilize the mass support the East German opposition had achieved in the early phase of the revolution and to withstand the onslaught of the West German parties after December 1989.

Among the most important of the newly formed political groups in the first phase were Democratic Awakening (*Demokratischer Aufbruch*), the Social Democratic Party (*Sozialdemokratische Partei*, SDP), the New Forum (*Neues Forum*), Democracy Now (*Demokratie Jetzt*), the Initiative for Peace and Human Rights (*Initiative für Frieden und Menschenrechte*), the Greens (*Die Grünen*), the Independent Women's Association (*Unabhängiger Frauenverband*), and the United Left (*Vereinigte Linke*). All of these groups participated in the Roundtable discussions and, between 28 January and 18 March 1990 in the all-party "Government of National Responsibility."

From the outset, these new political groupings were divided over whether to function as a political party or as citizen movements. Those who favored the formation of parties, notably the founders of Democratic Awakening and the SDP, believed the opposition had to challenge the regime directly by openly competing against the existing parties and thus offering East Germans a clear political alternative. The citizen movements, on the other hand, saw their task not just as providing an alternative government but as helping ordinary people to assume for themselves responsibility and power for areas that affected their everyday lives.

In the initial months of the fall 1989, the pace of political change was essentially dictated by the citizen movements. The largest, most broadly based, and most prominent was the New Forum. During the critical period between Krenz's ascent to power and the formation of the Roundtable, it acted as the opposition's principal negotiator with the regime.

The New Forum presented itself to the public on 12 September 1989 with a manifesto that had been deliberately released the day before to the foreign press via two prominent dissidents and co-founders of the Forum, Bärbel Bohley and Katja Havemann. The manifesto constituted a triple challenge to the regime. Its prior publication in the West violated East German law, but the attendant publicity also offered its signatories protection. Most importantly, it gave the New Forum far greater access to the East German population than would have been possible through traditional opposition channels within the church. Proclaiming its readiness to register as a legal political association under Article 29 of the GDR's constitution, the New Forum made it psychologically easier for timid "law-abiding" East Germans to associate themselves with it. Finally, the manifesto provided the addresses and telephone numbers of the signatories so that interested citizens could contact them directly. All three elements contributed to the New Forum's early success. Not even the Ministry of Interior's rejection, on 21 September, of the New Forum's application and its infiltration by the *Stasi* impeded its rapid growth.[27] The number of people who signed petitions for its legalization or declarations of support grew from 4,000 at the end of September to 100,000 by the end of October and to 200,000 by the end of November. Popular demands for its legalization in demonstrations throughout East Germany finally convinced the Krenz government on 8 November to recognize it as a lawful political organization.

The New Forum's founders saw it as an open political platform in which citizens of every political persuasion could, through a "broad, all-encompassing and solidaristic dialogue," arrive at a consensus about the future shape of the GDR. It demanded concrete economic and political reforms (including freedom of the press, opinion, association, assembly, and travel; free elections; the abolition of political crimes; the separation of party and state; and an end to economic privileges, inefficiency, and environmentally damaging policies). Yet, New Forum steadfastly refused to offer ready-made solutions and preconceived programmatic ideas or to tell citizens what to think or do. Thus, its rapid growth between September and December resulted less from public approval of the New Forum's program than from its courageous public challenge to the regime, and, no less importantly, to its prominent exposure in West German media as one of the first visible opposition groups.

With the opening of the Berlin Wall, however, New Forum's popularity declined. One reason was its continued refusal to offer a clear program for the future at a time of rapid change. Another was the obvious unhappiness with which some key Forum leaders (notably Bärbel Bohley) greeted this historic step and the East German rush to take advantage of it. A final problem was New Forum's highly informal and improvised structure. Until mid-October, it had "contact addresses" but no offices, full-time helpers, or resources to develop a broad network of functioning grassroots organizations. It was only in January 1990, under the threat of the impending Volkskammer election, that a majority of New Forum delegates to its first national convention agreed to a rudimentary organizational structure and electoral program. Their refusal to turn the New Forum into a party, however, prompted many of its initial supporters and activists to join other parties (the SDP as well as the CDU and LDP) or to form their own party (the German Forum Party)[28]

Though far smaller than the New Forum (with at most 3,000 members), Democracy Now played a not inconsiderable role in the revolution and the GDR's subsequent party development. It made its public appearance on 12 September with an "Appeal for Intervening in Your Own Affairs" and its "Theses for the Reconstruction of the GDR's State, Economy, and Society." Democracy Now proved a major force leading to the formation of the Roundtable, and Wolfgang Ullmann, a co-founder of Democracy Now, became one of the Roundtable's central figures.[29] Overcoming the misgivings of the New Forum's East Berlin leadership, Democracy Now ultimately prevailed upon most of the New Forum's regional groups to enter with it and the Initiative for Peace and Human Rights into an electoral alliance, the Alliance 90 (*Bündnis 90*).

Formed by members of the East Berlin human rights, ecological, and peace movements, Democracy Now defined itself as an alliance of Christians and critical Marxists committed to the establishment of a "society based on solidarity, social justice, freedom, human dignity, the rule of law, living pluralism as well as concern for the socially weak (including those exploited in the Third World) and for the protection of the environment." Though Democracy Now, too, saw itself as a citizen movement, its founders never hesitated to advance pragmatic policy recommendations. Many of its demands were subsequently adopted by other opposition groups and even reformers within the bloc parties: an end to the SED's monopoly of power; the separation of state and society; the creation of an independent media with open access by all political groups; the right to form political associations; free elections under United Nations supervision; and independent trade unions. Unlike New Forum, Democracy Now early on understood the revolution's implications for German-German relations. Already in its founding "theses," Democracy Now offered a plan for a gradual unification preceded by internal reforms in both states; it even anticipated Kohl's confederation plan with its own ten-step proposals for gradual unification. Nor did Democracy Now hesitate to offer an economic policy which, while generally committed to socialism, also called for an end to the command economy. It would limit the state to setting general economic guidelines; it also accepted private activities and private property in most areas of the economy.[30]

The third partner in Alliance 90 was the Initiative for Peace and Human Rights. It was founded as early as 1985, in response to the prohibition of a human rights seminar in East Berlin. Thereafter, the Initiative functioned as a cover organization for small peace and human rights groups and as a watchdog over the SED's adherence to the Helsinki agreements. This role made its founders a constant target of harassment, prosecution, and exile. During September and October, when demonstrations were still met with harsh reprisals and violence, the Initiative for Peace and Human Rights kept track of the people arrested by the regime, recorded instances of abuses by police, security and prison authorities, and actively campaigned for the release of demonstrators seized by the regime. Unlike New Forum and Democracy Now, the Initiative for Peace and Human Rights did not view itself as a mass movement (its membership never exceeded 200) but, rather, as a network of policy-oriented project groups in which any citizen could participate on issues of interest to him or her. It was a passionate champion of peace, democracy, individual rights, and a "third way" alternative to the GDR's economic crisis.[31]

Towards the end of November, two new organizations emerged out of the unofficial and clandestine East German environmental and peace movements: the Green Liga and the Green Party. Their respective founders had a long record of opposition activity (as well as persecution and exile) centered on such independent groups as the Green network "Arche," the "Environmental Library," and "Women for Peace." In the wake of the revolution, the East German environmentalists split—as had the West German environmentalists in 1979—between those who favored exclusively citizen actions (Green Liga) and those advocating participation in the electoral and political process (the Green Party). The Green Liga thought of itself primarily as an "action alliance" of all environmentalists in the GDR (including those from the regime-sponsored Society for Nature and Environment) whose task was to coordinate and sponsor grassroots environmental projects and actions.

While the citizen movements represented at the Roundtable generally drew a sharp line between themselves and the SED or its affiliates, this was not true of two participants: the Independent Women's Association (UFV) and the United Left. Formed on 3 December 1989 by 1,000 women, the UFV was open to all women—including those from the SED's women's affiliate, the Democratic Women's Association of Germany (*Demokratischer Frauenbund Deutschlands*, DFD)—who were willing to put aside political differences for the sake of common actions and policies on women rights. It demanded a standing parliamentary committee on women's issues as well as quotas for women in politics. Because of common feminist concerns, the UFV and the Greens formed an electoral alliance prior to the Volkskammer election.[32]

Furthest to the left on the political spectrum among the groups emerging in the fall of 1989 was the United Left. The first step towards its formation on 2 October was the "Böhlen Platform" drawn up by representatives from various left groups in early September 1989. Its founders favored a radically renewed socialism in the GDR along the lines of the *Räterepublik* (Republic of Soviets) established in parts of Germany after World War I. Its membership of about 300-500 came from disaffected SED and FDGB members, various left-leaning opposition groups, self-styled anarchists, and autonomists. They shared with the other opposition groups a common commitment to grassroots democracy.[33]

Among the opposition groups that early on saw the necessity of moving away from spontaneous or conspiratorial activities towards political associations with firm organizational structures and coherent programs were Democratic Awakening and the Social Democratic Party (SDP). Both came out of opposition groups that had functioned under the cover of the church; both began as "pastor parties" in that their founders were theologians and priests; and both sought links to West German parties as soon as it became practicable. But while the SDP ultimately became the strongest of the opposition groups formed during the revolutionary fall of 1989, Democratic Awakening escaped political extinction only by forging an electoral alliance with the East CDU and the German Social Union (DSU).

An initiative to found Democratic Awakening had been announced as early as June 1989. Seven of the original ten signatories were prominent theologians (Bishop Gottfried Forck, Provost Heino Falcke, Pastors Edelbert Richter, Friedrich Schorlemmer, Rudi Pahnke, Wolfram Hülsemann, and Rainer Eppelmann) who since 1988 had called for reforms and a dialogue between the opposition and the regime. Democratic Awakening's formal founding meeting on 30 September 1989 was prevented by the *Stasi* and had to be delayed until 29 October-2 November.[34] At the time of this meeting—the first all-East German assembly by an opposition group—Democratic Awakening had 6,000 members and at least some form of presence in all of the GDR's fifteen administrative districts. During this founding meeting, the delegates voted to have Democratic Awakening become a political party and decided on a program that combined democratic socialism, economic reforms, environmentalism, and some form of confederation with the Federal Republic within the framework of European security. The newly-elected chairman was Wolfgang Schnur, a lawyer known for defending conscientious objectors and dissidents. This choice also reflected the delegates' desire to step out of the shadow of the church and to broaden Democratic Awakening's base of support beyond church-based opposition groups. All three decisions were to be approved by a congress of full members in mid-December.

The October assembly revealed tensions between a right wing (led by Schnur and Eppelmann), who favored a closer alignment of Democratic Awakening with West German parties, and those on the left, who sought democratic renewal within an autonomous, democratic, and socialist GDR. These tensions increased as Schnur and Eppelmann established their own contacts with the West CDU[35] and made frequent appearances on West German television in support of West Germany's economic and political system and Kohl's Ten Point Program. While alienating Democratic Awakening's left-wing, these unauthorized moves also encouraged the influx of new members sympathetic to this westward orientation. By the time of Democratic Awakening's first party congress in mid-December 1989— which was attended by such prominent West German politicians as Rita Süssmuth—a new, more rightist majority approved Schnur's and Eppelmann's shift toward a West German-style social market economy and union with the Federal Republic. Democratic Awakening thus set the pace for the Westernization of East German politics. But the prize was the departure of about one third of its members and most of its prominent founders, losses from which Democratic Awakening never recuperated. Its final blow came with the revelation of Schnur's record as *Stasi* informant and his resignation a day before the Volkskammer election.[36]

By far the most significant of the political parties to emerge from the democratic opposition was the East German Social Democratic Party of Germany. As in the case of Democratic Awakening, the initiative for establishing the SDP came largely from theologians—Markus Meckel, Martin Gutzeit, Arndt Noack, and Helmut Becker. Toward the end of July 1989, they and the historian Ibrahim Böhme drew up a proclamation calling for the (re)creation of a Social Democratic Party that was circulated on 26 August at a human rights seminar in East Berlin. From this resulted the "Initiative for the Establishment of a Social Democratic Party in the GDR."

The party's actual founding came on 7 October 1989, in the tiny village of Schwante. To avoid being tagged an agent of the western SPD, the new party used the initials SDP rather than the West German SPD. Unlike the other opposition groups, the SDP's statement of 7 October demanded the immediate establishment of a parliamentary democracy with full party pluralism and free open elections. Though ready to support more direct modes of citizen participation, the SDP did not see grassroots democracy as a viable alternative to political parties and parliamentary government. The SDP also went further than any other political group at the time in advocating a market economy, though it was to be ecologically oriented, with a mix of private and public property, no excessive concentration of economic power, and strong social policies. The 7 October statement did not address the future of the GDR as a separate state nor of German-German relations.[37]

Unlike New Forum, the SDP refused to register and obtain permission to operate as a party, both because its founders knew this would be denied and because such a request from the SED implied accepting its authority as legitimate. Even more dramatically, the SDP's founders posited their party as the political and legal successor of the pre-1946 East German SPD and as such demanded a return of all its property confiscated by the SED in 1946.[38] At the same time, the SDP initially sought affiliation on 15 October with the Socialist International (i.e., the International Association of Socialist Parties of Europe and Latin America) rather than with the SPD in the Federal Republic. This move was intended both to demonstrate the SDP's independence from the West SPD and to signify its disapproval of the West SPD's previous efforts to seek reforms through the SED rather than through contacts with the opposition.[39]

Contact with the West SPD was finally established at the end of October, after which the relationship became very close.[40] The party announced its change of names and initials to Social Democratic Party of Germany (SPD) on 15 December, largely to head off rumored efforts by the SED to adopt them for its own use. At the SPD's first national party congress, held 15-23 February 1990 in Leipzig, the party approved a new organizational structure, a revised program, and its election platform. Ibrahim Böhme became its leader and principal candidate; former West German Chancellor Willy Brandt its honorary chairman.

Public opinion polls at first indicated widespread support for the SDP, largely because of the enthusiastic embrace by Willy Brandt and the West SPD. Unfortunately, the SDP's founders spend more time on "high politics" than building up the party's organization and membership. They were lulled into a false sense of security by mistaking favorable public opinion responses and requests for information for actual membership and electoral intentions. They also had exaggerated expectations about the SDP's ability to recapture pre-1933 socialist strongholds. The upshot was that at the time the election date was set, the SDP at the most had only 20,000 members (rather than the 100,000 it claimed) who were organized into informal local branches with little coordination. The combination of weak organization, low membership, lack of resources, and the SDP's organizational and political inexperience prompted the West SPD to initiate the massive flow of resources, assistance, and personnel from the West that dominated East German party politics in the second phase.

The final party to emerge from the democratic opposition was the Green Party, formally founded on 24 November 1989. It defined itself as the political arm of the East German environmental movement but also viewed itself as part of the European Greens. Despite the incorporation of the term "party" in its name (in contrast to the West German Greens), the founders favored a loose organization of relatively autonomous local branches as well as grassroots democracy and citizen activism. The Green Party's founding proclamation stressed its commitment not just to the environment, but also to feminism, anti-racism, and non-violence.[41]

Though divided into different and competing groups, the newly formed citizen movements and parties nonetheless shared basic outlooks and programmatic ideas. They all subscribed to the same core values: justice, solidarity, freedom, democracy, non-violence, and tolerance. They also agreed on the key features of a democratic political order: separation of party, state, and society; separation and decentralization of power; full political pluralism through open and free elections, as well as freedom of association, opinions, and information; a state based on the rule of law with guarantees of human and civil rights; a judiciary independent of both party(ies) and the state; protection of the individual against the state; parliamentary or public control over police and security apparatus; and reforms of the existing criminal code, especially the elimination of political crimes. All the new political groups further favored the incorporation of at least some elements of direct democracy: allowing citizens a greater role at work, in education, and in political life; the use of referenda and initiatives; and acceptance of citizen movements in the electoral and political process.

In the economic sphere, most of the opposition groups initially did not want to push the transformation of the economic system as far as had either the Poles or the Hungarians. They generally envisioned reforms that fundamentally departed from "real existing" socialism—but also from the consumerism, excessive competition, monopolies of economic power, and other social injustices they associated with Western capitalism. Instead they envisioned democratically-controlled economic structures, mixed forms of property, a guiding (but not controlling) role for the state, more efficient and varied but also ecologically sound production, and a commitment to economic and social justice. Though far more open to the West German model of the social market, even the SDP and Democratic Awakening shared initially many of the opposition's economic preferences and norms. They moved closer to West German conceptions only in the second phase of party development.

As for German-German relations, most of the opposition groups in the first phase were above all committed to internal democratization. To the extent that unification was considered a possibility (above all by the SDP, Democratic Awakening, and Democracy Now), the consensus was for a gradual process within the framework of European integration and existing treaty obligations that would require changes in both Germanys.[42]

Yet despite a common antipathy toward the regime and a general ideological consensus, three attempts to forge a united front against the regime failed. A coordination meeting of twenty different groups on 24 September could not agree on accepting New Forum as the umbrella organization for all opposition groups. The one instance of a joint opposition action, a common public appeal on 4 October for the democratic restructuring of state and society and democratic elections under UN supervision, was never repeated thereafter. Finally, the electoral alliance of six opposition groups (SDP, Democratic Awakening, New Forum, Democracy Now, the Initiative for Peace and Human Rights, and the United Left) fell apart shortly thereafter when the United Left's members repudiated its leaders for taking this step without consulting them and when the SDP (pressured by the West SPD) decided to withdraw and run on its own.

This inability to work together stemmed in part from the conspiratorial experiences of most opposition figures who found it difficult to make the shift from relying exclusively on a small, clandestine network of trusted friends to working with large numbers of people. Personal rivalries and jealousies were also at work, notably in East Berlin, where the political climate was especially tense and competition for public access and exposure to Western media particularly fierce. In retrospect, however, these tensions may have been created or exacerbated by *Stasi* agents and informants who had successfully infiltrated all major opposition groups and continued to be active through December 1989.[43] But whatever the reasons, the presence of so many competing opposition groups proved highly confusing to a population eager for a clear alternative to the regime and unaccustomed to political pluralism.

Reforming the Bloc Parties

The combined impact of the mass defections and the mass demonstrations also initiated a far-reaching reform process within the bloc parties, most particularly the CDU and LDPD. The leaders of both parties undertook reforms in response to the SED's growing weakness rather than out of personal conviction. Essentially, the transformation of these two bloc parties ensued through three steps: (1) liberalization, or a distancing from the regime; (2) democratization, or the acceptance of the democratic opposition's principal demands for democratic reforms, a new democratic socialism, and the autonomous development of a democratic GDR; and (3) Westernization, or rejection of an East German reform model in favor of full accommodation with West German sister parties.

The reform wave within the bloc parties began with Manfred Gerlach, the LDPD's leader since 1967 and a trusted friend and ally of Honecker and the SED regime.[44] In an article published on 20 September in the LDPD's party paper *Der Morgen*, he called upon the SED to address the reasons for the mass flight, to open itself to the critical, impatient, curious segments of society, and not to confuse argument with resistance. By mid-October, Gerlach, dismayed as well as emboldened by the SED's continued silence, shifted from liberalization to ever more drastic democratic reforms. On 17 October, *Der Morgen* reported the LDPD's decision to initiate a broad democratic dialogue with the opposition and the church on all key political, economic, and social issues. Two weeks later, Gerlach and the LDPD Minister of Justice called for the dissolution of the Democratic Bloc and for multi-party elections with real alternatives. In mid-November, the LDPD came out for full democracy through free and open election as well as fundamental economic changes (albeit without abandoning socialism). Gerlach invited New Forum members to enter the LDPD. He also proposed an electoral law that facilitated the entry of opposition groups into the Volkskammer through joint lists with the bloc parties.[45] When Krenz was elected as head of state by the Volkskammer on 24 October, LDPD members were among those who cast a negative vote and thus in fact withdrew from the governing bloc.[46]

Gerlach had clearly calculated that by adopting a reformist course, he could disassociate himself and his party from the regime and broaden the LDPD's appeal among the newly aroused populace.[47] His public embrace of democratization, however, did not lead to major changes in the LDPD's personnel, program and organization nor to any radical break with the socialist system.[48] It was only under the pressure of the Volkskammer elections and the West German FDP that the LDPD accepted drastic internal reforms. At a special congress held in February 1990, the LDPD renamed itself LDP and created a new organization patterned after that of the West German FDP. The democratically-elected members also replaced all the old leaders (including Gerlach) and chose a new party executive headed by a Rostock academic, Professor Rainer Ortleb. Finally, the LPD's new party program renounced socialism in favor of the social market economy and called for a speedy unification of Germany "within the context of a

European order." Together, these changes completed the LDP's Western conversion.

While the LDPD underwent a "revolution from above," the CDU's transformation was more a "revolution from below." The first step toward liberalization was initiated by reformists within the party who also held prominent positions in the church. On 10 September, they circulated a statement—the "Weimar Letter"—to members of leaders of the CDU (and to the Western press) demanding a critical analysis of the reasons for the mass exodus, more dialogue with the opposition, and reforms in state and society. This statement was rejected by the CDU's then-chair, Gerald Götting, as unwarranted intervention. Nonetheless, the SED's silence in the face of growing public demonstrations finally forced Götting to undertake the first step toward liberalization. On 12 October, he proposed an open discussion on various key questions. At the end of October, he began to urge more substantive reforms such as free and secret elections, fair media, legal protections for emigrants, and a "living" democracy.

This was not enough for the CDU's grassroots members, who were clamoring for drastic programmatic and organizational changes. On 10 November, to head off a full-scale revolt by local branches, the "old guard" executive replaced Götting with Lothar de Maizière. Contrary to their expectation, de Maizière moved quickly to assert control over the CDU and to steer the party toward a more radical course of reform. First he gave "temporary leave" to the senior members of the CDU executive after they tried to fill the post of vice president in the Volkskammer without consulting him. He also called for an extraordinary party congress, which met 15-16 December.[49]

Under de Maizière's leadership, the CDU rejected the SED's leading role at the end of November. On 4 December, prior to the first Roundtable meeting, the party formally withdrew from the Democratic Bloc. The CDU also became the first bloc party to adopt a new program of its own (on 23 November), in which it incorporated most of the political and even economic agenda of the democratic opposition. At this point, de Maizière and the CDU reformers still hoped to "improve" rather than abandon socialism. Friendly intermediaries from the West, however, informed him that socialism in any form was unacceptable—not only to East German voters but also to the West German CDU.

The CDU's December congress confirmed its internal democratization as well as its Westernization. For the first time since 1948, the 800 delegates (about half of whom had only recently joined the party) had been democratically elected by the local branches. The congress supported de Maizière's election as chairman of the party, elected a new party executive to be headed by the forty-year old reformist Martin Kirchner as general secretary, and accepted organizational statutes similar to those of the West German CDU. Most importantly, the East CDU now supported unequivocally the West German social market system and called for a speedy economic, monetary and political union with the Federal Republic.[50]

The two bloc parties created by the SED, the NDPD and DBD, showed little reformist zeal during the fall revolution and never went much beyond liberalization. By the beginning of November, both parties called for democratic renewal but avoided systemic criticisms. In early November, the DBD still accepted the SED's leading position, which the SED rewarded by supporting Günther Maleuda, the DBD's leaders, as president of the Volkskammer. Although subsequently, the DBD claimed equal status with the SED as a "party among other parties," in practice it continued to vote overwhelmingly with the SED. In contrast to the LDPD and the CDU, Maleuda's leadership was never challenged, not even at the party's first free party congress in January 1990. The DBD's only concession to external developments was the establishment of ten commissions to prepare a new party program for the January congress.

The NDPD took the first timid steps towards internal reforms on 7 November 1989 when the party's executive, in a closed meeting, replaced its longtime leader, Heinrich Homann, with Günter Hartmann, the party's deputy chairman and leader of its Volkskammer delegation. In a press conference following his election, Hartmann defined his party's new relationship to the SED as a "real partner, supportive but also critical."[51] No further organizational or programmatic changes were undertaken until the party's first congress in January 1990. At the time of their respective party congresses in January, both the DBD and NPDP finally accepted a Western-style political democracy, a shift to the market, and unification. But they did so with far more qualifications and hesitations than their erstwhile bloc partners.[52]

The Transformation of the SED

For no other party was the change more dramatic and fateful than for the SED. As late as the beginning of October, the SED had absolute power over the East German state and society. Its organization encompassed 2.3 million members, 59,000 local branches, 44,000 fully employed, and 700,000 voluntary functionaries. In 1989 alone, the SED's economic imperium had produced an income of 1.5 billion Ostmark and an additional 100 million West German D-Mark. Four months later, the party was in shambles, its "leading role" stricken from the constitution and forced to share power with an opposition it had previously ignored or persecuted. Yet despite calls from within and without the SED, the party survived—much reduced in size, with a new name, leader, democratic organization, and program. As in the case of its two principal bloc partners, the SED's transformation occurred in three stages: liberalization, democratization, and, if not exactly Westernization, at least grudging accommodation with unification and the West German economic and political model.

The SED's liberalization was initiated with Krenz's ascension on 18 October. During the forty-seven days he was in power, he initiated party reforms, established contact with the opposition, promised constitutional changes, free elections, economic reforms, new media regulations, new laws of association, a new criminal code eliminating political crimes and, most dramatically, opened the East-West borders. On 3 December, having failed to contain the democratic revolution, Krenz and the SED's entire Politburo and Central Committee were forced to resign. A twenty-five member committee was established to prepare for an extraordinary party congress (to be held 8-9 December and 15-16 December) that was to decide the party's future.

With this party congress (only the fourth to be held since the founding of the GDR), the SED entered its democratization phase. As in the case of the CDU, the pressure for radical change had come from below. Evidence of corruption and high living by top party leaders and revelations about the disastrous state of the GDR's economy led to the departure of over a million members between October and November, most of whom were younger functionaries, generally at the low and mid-level of the party apparatus, where party work was extensive but compensation minimal. More importantly, disaffected members and functionaries at the central and local level now began to take the reform process into their own hands. Party cells in factories were dissolved; entrenched local secretaries were forced to resign and give way to newly elected leaders; and enraged members launched a series of anti-SED demonstrations (such as the 8 November mass demonstrations by SED members before the Central Committee building in East Berlin and, on 29 November, before SED offices in Leipzig and Erfurt). The December congress was thus seen as the only way of checking the party's total disintegration.

The 2640 delegates, who were for the first time freely elected by grassroots members, set out to give the party an altogether new character. The SED was renamed the Socialist Unity Party-Party of Democratic Socialism, or SED-PDS. Its newly-elected head was Gregor Gysi, a forty-one year old lawyer who had long defended regime critics and exit visa applicants. The congress also accepted the SED's responsibility for the GDR's economic and political crisis, renounced its adherence to Stalinism, its structure of democratic centralism, and its monopoly of power.

The old Stalinist organization was replaced by an elected, 101-member party executive. Its assigned task was to elect a Presidium consisting of a party chairman and deputy chairman as well as the heads of nine commissions dealing with specific functional areas (such as youth, women, environment, media, etc.). The number of office holders and functionaries was dramatically reduced, and all party positions were to be elective on the basis of secret ballots. The principle of democratic centralism gave way to grassroots participation and control. A Party Umpire Committee was created to deal with grievances of members against party officials.

Programmatically, the congress called for an end of the old command economy, central planning, and excessive state intervention in the management of the economy. While supporting mixed public and private property and elements of the market, the delegates did not renounce socialism as an ideal and reaffirmed the social achievements of the past forty years. Above all, they pledged to prevent the GDR's sell-out to the West and its conversion to "monopoly capitalism." Though opposed to unification, the delegates accepted (with qualifications), Kohl's confederation plan.

Despite these efforts, substantial segments of the public and within the party doubted the sincerity of the SED/PDS's democratization and called for its dissolution. In January, the open conflict between the proponents and opponents of dissolution forced a special meeting of the party's executive on 20 January. The majority voted against the dissolution and limited itself to renaming the former SED the Party of Democratic Socialism (PDS). In protest, thirty-nine prominent reformers (including Wolfgang Berghofer, the former mayor of Dresden) resigned from the party.

The final stage in the SED/PDS's transformation came in the wake of the party's February congress. At this time, the PDS grudgingly accepted the inevitable, namely the shift to a market economy along West German lines and eventual unification. At the same time, the party's program opposed rapid economic and monetary union; it also advocated a market economy that worked for the common good and retained the GDR's social achievements, including the right to work, free education, reasonable housing, child care, and protection of pensioners.[53]

The East German Party System:
From Democratization to Westernization

Together, the emergence of new political groups and the reforms of the old system parties had created an altogether new party structure. Between October and December, "socialist pluralism" had given way to "democratic pluralism." Yet the party system that emerged during this revolutionary phase was short-lived. From December onward, the impending Volkskammer elections, the GDR's mounting economic and political crisis, and a shift in public opinion combined to alter once more the party situation created by the fall revolution. To appreciate the nature and extent of this second transformation, one needs to identify the principal features of the GDR's party system during the revolutionary first phase.

One defining feature of party politics in the first phase was the centrality of the once marginal opposition parties and movements. It was they who initiated the collapse of the old political order and the revolutionary transformations within the five regime parties. The new political forces also initially dictated the political agenda for all the key political actors. Thus, the former ruling parties and systemic mass organizations, the Volkskammer, and the newly-instated Modrow government all accepted and sought to implement the democratic opposition's political and economic principles and reform demands. No less important a feature of the post-revolutionary party system, however, was the weakness of both the opposition groups and the reformed regime parties. For altogether different reasons, they were unable to consolidate their hold over the East German population and hence facilitated the party-political "takeover" by the West German parties.

For the newly formed opposition groups, the key problem was a total lack of the basic resources and skills to create from scratch a national political organization. It was not until 6 January 1990 that they finally forced the SED/PDS and the Modrow government to provide them with space, equipment, financial assistance, and media access. But by then, precious resources and manpower had to be concentrated on governmental work through participation in the Roundtable and Modrow's all-party emergency government and campaigning for the Volkskammer, rather than for organizational development. Though they attracted often large numbers of supporters and sympathizers, only few became members and fewer still were willing to help in the necessary political or organizational work. Hence, with weak organizational links and only haphazard media access, new political groups were ill-prepared to shift from spontaneous protest to effective electoral mobilization.

The tenuous ties between the opposition groups and the population at large derived as well from the predominance of professionals, theologians, artists, university students, and other sectors of the intelligentsia among their founders and core members. Though intent on improving the lot of working people in the GDR, the social background of the founders, in effect, differentiated them from the majority of voters. During the revolutionary upheavals, this social gap did not matter since the opposition groups successfully tapped the strong anti-regime feelings of the population. Subsequently, however, the absence of workers in their midst may have contributed to the oppositions' misreading of the popular mood. Thus, the faith shared by most opposition groups in reforms through broad, open-ended discussion was ill-understood by a population accustomed to guidance from above and eager for concrete plans for the future. More seriously, the distaste for "consumerism" and the West German "elbow society" so often expressed by the leaders of the citizen movements was resented by ordinary East Germans fed up with socialism of any kind, who were eager for material prosperity and imbued with a highly positive image of the Federal Republic—one confirmed by the opening of the Wall.

The difficulties for the old bloc parties and the SED stemmed from the organizational repercussions of the reform process itself. The rapid and dramatic pace of regime change not only forced a revolutionary transformations in their respective central organizations, leaderships, and programs, but also brought turmoil to the local organizational level. Large numbers of old members and functionaries left or else were forced out by reformists. The influx of new members in the wake of internal democratization also created tensions between them and the older functionaries, even those now advocating reform. Under the impact of external and internal pressures, local branches often disintegrated and disbanded altogether, became paper organizations incapable of functioning, or became more or less autonomous from central control.

Even more problematic was the continued distrust and distaste with which the old parties were viewed by much of the population at large. Despite dramatic organizational and programmatic changes, the bloc parties could not overcome on their own the legacy of their past association with and support for the hated regime. As for the SED/PDS, most East Germans demanded dissolution not reform as the SED/PDS's only acceptable course of action.

A problem faced by both the opposition groups and the "reformed" regime parties was that the pace of change during the fall of 1989 far exceeded their respective capacity to direct, much less control it. The rapid disintegration of political authority and structures at all levels, the simultaneous collapse of the economy, the continuation of massive defections to the West, and mass demonstrations in the East all occurred while the new and old political groups were themselves undergoing dramatic changes in their organization, membership, political, and programmatic identities. By late November, something of a stalemate had developed between the opposition groups, the two key reformed and revitalized bloc parties (the CDU and LDPD), and the SED—which though wounded by the revolutionary upheavals within and outside the party—still controlled the security apparatus and massive economic and political resources. The Roundtable was an attempt by the new and old political actors to break this stalemate and thus prevent a total collapse and violence. But as a temporary forum for bringing together disparate regime and opposition forces, it did little to provide the clear directions that an increasingly uneasy population seemed to demand.

Thus, bewildered by the proliferation of new groups and hostile or suspicious toward the now reformed system parties, the ordinary East German lacked a political haven. At a time of rapid political, economic and social change, neither the East German opposition groups nor the reformed system parties had much public credibility. The net result was a political vacuum that was filled by West German parties and politicians during the winter and spring of 1990.

In the first phase of party transformation, the West German parties played but a marginal role. The key actors were East Germany's new and reformed parties. The political agenda still centered on internal democratic reforms. After the opening of the East-West borders, West German politicians initiated contacts with East German reformers and bloc parties. But until the election date was set by the Roundtable, such contacts were personal, informal, and largely at the local or regional level.

Initially the key line of conflict in the restructured East German party system was that between the parties and groups of the democratic opposition on the one side and the old, though now reformed ruling parties on the other. By December 1989, opposition pressures and popular demonstrations forced the Modrow government, reluctantly, to work directly with the opposition within the framework of the Roundtable—a new type of crisis management mechanism first utilized in Poland and Hungary.[54]

With the creation of the Roundtable, the opposition groups had reached their most important objectives: namely to be recognized as legitimate intermediaries for the people and to negotiate as equal partners with the former ruling parties. Contrary to its name, the Roundtable was rectangular, pitting the new groups of the opposition against the old regime parties. From this struggle for power, the opposition groups emerged with major triumphs. Together they had forced the Modrow government to accept a parallel governmental structure, to conduct imminent elections, and, after Modrow's clumsy attempt to revive the Ministry for Security (MfS) or *Stasi* under another guise (the Office for the Protection of the Constitution), to dismantle it altogether, while protecting its vast collection of files. Finally, through the Roundtable, the opposition groups could present their own ideas for change. In record times, they drew up a new constitution and a social charta; an electoral law that permitted the participation of citizen movements as well as parties; and plans for a trust agency (the *Treuhand*) to manage the privatization of state property.

But the Roundtable also heralded the end of the democratic revolution as the opposition groups had envisioned it. Once the date for the Volkskammer election was fixed—initially 6 May but a month later advanced to 18 March 1990—a new struggle commenced, one involving an electoral competition over the GDR's future. This changed the dynamics of the GDR's political development and, with it, the principal features of the party system. The key transformations in the second phase included (1) an open break within the opposition, (2) a restructuring of the competitive party space, (3) the Westernization of party politics, and (4) the emergence of a new political cleavage.

Negotiations over participation in the Roundtable and in the all-party government soon pitted the SDP/SPD against the other opposition groups. Initially, the Social Democrats opposed the Roundtable for fear that it might shore up the regime and force the SDP/SPD into assuming co-responsibility for governmental measures that could backfire electorally.[55] The SDP's prize was agreement to hold elections on 6 May 1990. Party leaders wanted early elections, first, because, as a non-elected body, the Roundtable lacked democratic legitimation and hence could not make major substantive decisions; second, because without a concrete deadline, the opposition would be drawn into lengthy negotiations while the country's crisis deepened; and third, because the earlier the elections were held, the greater their party's own chances for victory.[56] Other opposition groups, however, deeply resented the SDP/SPD's unilateral insistence on early elections since this would give them no time to acquire the resources and organization that would be essential for defeating the still formidable system parties.

When, a month later, Modrow offered genuine participation to the new parties and opposition movements in the "Government of National Responsibility," the by then-renamed SPD had even greater misgivings. To enter directly into a government with communists was too much a reminder of the National Fronts of the 1930s that had invariably benefited communists at the expense of Socialists and Social Democrats. The SPD also feared that cooperation with the discredited SED/PDS in a caretaker crisis government could undermine the electoral edge it had gained as opponent of the regime. The Social Democrats were thus ready to enter the all-party government only under two conditions: that (1) the nine opposition groups would each be given a ministry without portfolio rather than enter the government directly, and (2) the date for the Volkskammer election be advanced to 18 March. The first condition provided the SPD and opposition groups with a check on but no direct responsibility for the formulation of government policy. The second condition would limit the SPD's association with the emergency government and also prevent that government from undertaking major policy initiatives.[57]

Both conditions infuriated the other opposition groups. New Forum was convinced that, given the popular uproar over the government's attempt to revive the *Stasi* under a new guise, Modrow was ready to give the opposition groups virtually anything they asked for. As for the advance of the election, it put the opposition groups under even greater disadvantage than had the already premature 6 May date. They agreed to these conditions only to maintain the unity of the opposition against the old regime parties.

This unity had been formalized in the electoral alliance of 3 January 1990 agreed to by the SPD and five other opposition groups. It was largely a response to the Modrow government's clear reluctance to dismantle the security apparatus as the opposition had repeatedly demanded. Yet, the moment this last confrontation had been resolved in favor of the opposition, the SPD withdrew from the electoral alliance on 27 January, thus shattering once again the precarious unity of the democratic opposition forces. The SPD's readiness to advance its own interests at the expense of the other opposition groups was demonstrated subsequently in Roundtable discussions over the electoral law, when it sought both a 3 percent clause and the exclusion of the citizen movements. In this case, the SPD was overridden in the Volkskammer. Finally, the SPD joined forces with the East CDU and LDP against attempts by opposition groups and the PDS to exclude party financing from the West.[58]

The second major change in East Germany's party system during phase two occurred in the structure of party competition. First, under the pressure of imminent elections, all parties and groups were compelled to institutionalize. The formation of the new parties and the renewal of the system parties had occurred against a background of political upheavals, rapid and uncontrollable changes, and poor communication. Initially, programs and statutes were little more than general statements of principles that often existed only in limited hand- or type-written versions. Committees were subsequently established to work out detailed programs and statutes to be discussed and accepted by membership congresses, most of which were scheduled to take place between December and February. For the most part, these congresses approved earlier reforms and agreements. In some cases, however, such meetings introduced more far-reaching reforms (e.g., in the case of the NDPD and the DBD), leadership changes (such as the LDPD's removal of Gerlach), and organizational or programmatic alterations in preparation for the upcoming electoral campaign. The citizen movements emerged from this process with a more formal structure and program than they had originally desired as embodiments of spontaneous, grassroots, citizen-based politics. For the CDU, LDP, and SPD, the outcome of this institutionalization was essentially to transform themselves into copies of their respective West German sponsors.

A second development was the proliferation of new political groups and parties. This was encouraged by the Volkskammer's electoral law of 20

February. In a self-conscious departure from the Federal Republic's more restrictive electoral rules, this law allowed not only parties but also other forms of political associations such as citizen movements and interest groups to compete. Secondly, the entry rules were lenient. Any group was allowed to compete provided it had an organization and program; its candidates did not belong to or run for other groups and were secretly elected by a majority of the members. The only parties and groups specifically excluded were those with fascist, militarist, anti-humanist, or discriminatory goals or who advocated the use of force or the threat of force. This provision was aimed primarily against East German neo-Nazi groups but also against possible West German imports such as terrorist leftwing groups as the RAF (Red Army Faction) and the *Republikaner*. Third, the electoral law opted for a relatively pure proportional representation system, without a threshold clause so that even groups with 1/400 or .25 percent of the votes cast would receive a mandate. Any party or group with at least .25 percent of vote was to be reimbursed for its election costs at the rate of five DM per vote received. All in all, forty-one new parties registered with the election commission, of which twenty-four appeared on the ballot.[59]

The third development in restructuring party competition was the formation of electoral alliances. This, too, deviated from West German electoral rules that prohibit joint lists and electoral collaboration among competing parties. Two such alliances resulted from pressures by West German parties. The first of these was the Alliance for Germany (*Allianz für Deutschland*), and the second was the League of Free Democrats (*Bund Freier Demokraten*).

The Alliance for Germany consisted of the East CDU, Democratic Awakening, and the German Social Union (*Deutsche Soziale Union*, DSU). The DSU itself was a merger of a dozen or so conservative Christian parties, which, with the help of the Bavarian Christian Social Union (CSU), had formed a new party on 20 January 1990.[60] The Alliance for Germany, officially formed on 5 February 1990, resulted from Kohl's and Volker Rühe's (the West CDU's General Secretary) fears that East German voters might punish the East CDU electorally for its long association with the SED regime. Framing it with two new parties, they hoped, would improve the CDU's electoral chances.

For all three partners, the Alliance was one of convenience not conviction. Democratic Awakening's origins in the opposition made it wary of both the CDU and the conservative DSU, while the DSU worried that its association with the CDU would cost it its own profile and limit its growth—a justified fear, as it turned out. Democratic Awakening joined because it was largely dependent on funding from the West CDU, while the DSU agreed because its late start as a party placed it at a disadvantage.[61] In part to appease their ambivalence toward the Alliance, each of the reluctant partners was allowed to run on its own label rather than as part of a joint list.[62]

The League of Free Democrats was formed on 11 February 1990. Like the Alliance, it was created largely to offset possible voter reactions against the bloc past of the LDP. The West German FDP forced it to enter into a joint list with two newly formed liberal parties, whose respective founders had been part of the opposition. They were the German Forum Party, established on 27 January by former members of New Forum, and the Free Democratic Party, formed on 4 February with the official blessing and participation of such key West FDP leaders as Hans-Dietrich Genscher and Count Lambsdorff. As in the case of the Alliance, there were considerable tensions within the League. The two new parties were highly suspicious of the LDP's old guard, while the LDP resented the equal placement of the two new parties on the League's candidate list. Unlike the Alliance, votes were given to the League rather than to the individual parties.[63]

To pool scarce resources and to run candidates in all of the GDR's fifteen electoral districts, the citizen movements also found it necessary to form electoral agreements but failed to agree on a single, over-arching alliance. Instead several tactical electoral coalitions were formed. The most important of these was Alliance 90 (*Bündnis 90*), which encompassed New Forum, Democracy Now, and the Initiative for Peace and Human Rights. The Green Party and the Independent Women's Association formed a separate electoral alliance (*Grüne/Unabhängige Frauen*), as did the United Left and a new Marxist party, "the Carnations" (*Vereinigte Linke/Nelken*). Finally, a number of leftwing youth groups (including parts of the *Freie Deutsche Jugend*, FDJ) joined together as the Alternative Youth List (*Alternative Jugendliste*). Of the major parties, only the SPD, PDS, DBD, and NDPD ran on their own.

A third major change between the fall of 1989 and the winter and spring of 1990 was the Westernization of East Germany's party political scene. Popular demands for unification and the imminence of the elections galvanized the West German parties to become actively involved in the electoral process. What had begun as a more or less spontaneous and informal process of establishing contacts between East and West German parties after the opening of the Wall ultimately ended with a virtual Western takeover of East German party politics. Between December 1989 and 18 March, the West German parties became the central actors. The result of this intervention was not only to transform the East German into a West German election, but also to turn the East German party system into a virtual copy of the West German one.

The intervention by the principal West German parties assumed several forms. One was to push for organizational and programmatic changes within the key bloc parties, such as the FDP's pressures to replace the LDPD's leader Gerlach with someone less tainted and the West CDU's "suggestions" to de Maizière to drop all support for socialism. Another form of intervention was to sponsor the emergence of new parties. Thus, the Bavarian CSU was responsible for the formation of the DSU, the West German FDP helped found the East German FDP, and the CDU provided critical support for Democratic Awakening.

By far the most important form of intervention was active assistance for and participation in the campaigns of their respective East German "proxy parties."[64] The three principal West German parties helped write the electoral programs of their East German counterparts; taught East German party leaders the basics of modern day campaigning; mobilized and distributed all the requisite financial, material, technical resources; and sent in their own politicians in support of East German candidates.

To facilitate these tasks, the main parties developed a partnership system whereby one or more West German provincial organization (*Landesverband*) would be responsible for assisting their party in one of the East German election districts. (For example, the SPD's South Hesse Verband was responsible for helping the East SPD in Thuringia; the CDU organizations of Bremen, Hamburg, and Schleswig-Holstein assisted the East CDU branches in Mecklenburg and Pomerania.) Coordinating committees were set up in Bonn to prevent duplication of efforts and the equitable distribution of resources, equipment, and campaign helpers. Top politicians from all three parties set up shop in the East for the duration of the campaign to serve as contact persons for Bonn and advisers to the East Germans. In addition, thousands of party workers and functionaries went for shorter periods, especially weekend campaign trips. Party members in the West proved to be extremely generous, with both donations and volunteer work in the East. Finally, the leaders of each of the main Bonn parties appeared at many mass rallies themselves, lending their prestige to candidates largely unknown among East German voters. Rarely in the postwar history of the Bonn parties had their members, functionaries, and politicians been as massively, intensively, and emotionally involved with their party's campaign than during the Volkskammer campaign.[65]

The intervention of the West German parties reduced the opposition groups to marginal players. They could not mobilize resources on the scale of the Western-backed parties. They received some assistance, equipment, information, campaign materials, and speakers from the West German Greens, the trade unions, private individuals, and associations. But essentially those who had made the revolution had to rely on their own wits and grassroots volunteers, the support of the churches, and, by a sad irony, on contributions from the East German government (in terms of finances and equipment) and the PDS (for space).

Finally, the Westernization of party competition during phase two entailed a decisive change in the political agendas of the East German parties and in their political alignment. In contrast to programmatic statements during phase one, the electoral statements in phase two by opposition groups as well as reformed regime parties accepted the shift toward West Germany's social market economy—though with a heavier emphasis on the social part of the West German model than is customarily given by West German parties. Only the Marxist fringe groups—such as the United Left and Carnations—refused to give up their socialist commitments.

Similarly, the dream of an autonomous GDR had given way to acceptance of unification, though with various degrees of enthusiasm and qualifications. Real differences, however, emerged over the speed and mechanisms for merging the two Germanys. On this issue, the East German parties divided into three camps.

The first camp, consisting of the parties of the Alliance for Germany and the League of Free Democrats, unequivocally accepted the Federal Republic's political and economic system, rapid economic and monetary union (based on a 1:1 exchange rate) and a speedy integration of the GDR into the Federal Republic via Article 23 of the Basic Law. The second camp, represented by the SPD, accepted unification but not as merely an eastward extension of the Federal Republic. Rather, it saw in unification an opportunity for long overdue constitutional, political, and economic reforms in the West as in the East. While in favor of monetary and economic union, the Social Democrats also advocated a more gradual, step-by-step plan to manage East Germany's vast and special problems. Finally, the SPD favored Article 146 of the Basic Law as the mechanism by which political integration was to be achieved. This would have entailed both certain constitutional changes and the submission of the revised Basic Law to a popular referendum. Both steps were defended as providing a sounder constitutional basis for united Germany than a simple merger under Article 23. The third camp accepted unification only grudgingly. The parties and groups in this camp (including most of the opposition movements as well as the PDS, the NDPD, the DBD, and the ex-SED women's association (the DFD) argued that unification negotiations must first recognize the "inner sovereignty" and "separateness" of East Germany. They envisioned a transition stage in which East Germany would, for an unspecified time, function as an independent state under its own constitution but would be linked to the West either through a number of association treaties or a confederation (PDS and

NDPD). All rejected Article 23 as a mechanism for integrating the two Germanys in favor of Article 146.

The net effect of the unification issue was to reduce a highly fragmented, pluralistic party spectrum into basically three alternatives. More importantly, the centrality of this issue also altered the previous pattern of party conflict. The confrontation between the former regime parties and the parties and groups of the opposition dominant during the first phase gave way to one between rapid and gradual unifiers. On this issue, the parties and citizen movements of the democratic opposition found themselves unexpectedly aligned with their erstwhile antagonists: the "reformed" SED/PDS against two former bloc parties and a key opposition party, the SPD. More ironically still, having brought down the old communist regime in the first phase, the new opposition parties suddenly defended its cultural and social achievements during the second phase. In doing so, they failed to understand the aspirations of ordinary East German voters and thus emerged from the first free East German election as much the losers as the communists whom they had so effectively challenged in the fall of 1989.

What caused the electoral defeat on 18 March 1990 of those groups and parties championing the internal option—that is, a reformed, democratic socialism within an independent GDR? The losers—among them, the citizen movements largely responsible for the peaceful revolution—have maintained that their poor performance was due to massive intervention and manipulation in the election by the West German parties, especially the Bonn coalition of the CDU and FDP. From their perspective, the victory of the Western-backed former bloc parties amounted to a "hijacking" of the peaceful revolution and with it the end of a dream for a new kind of Germany, one different both from the Stalinist GDR and the capitalist Federal Republic.

While it is impossible to deny the importance of the West German parties, their contribution was a necessary but not sufficient cause of the electoral outcome. External as well as internal conditions beyond the control of the opposition or any other political force almost inevitably dictated a fundamentally different choice than that originally envisioned by those who challenged the SED regime.

One major external influence derived from the GDR's unique geopolitical position. In effect, the GDR had no prior existence to the SED and had never been conceptualized as a system without the SED's monopoly of political and economic power. Hence, reforms that weakened the SED also undermined the survival of the GDR. The displaced Politburo had clearly recognized that moving toward the market, freedom of speech and press, and competitive elections along Polish and Hungarian lines would sooner or later raise the issue of why it was necessary to maintain a separate GDR.

For this reason, it thought it had no choice but to maintain the status quo at all costs.

For Gorbachev, the choice was no less dramatic: maintaining a hardline regime unwilling to accept the necessity of reform and potentially endanger his "new political thinking" vis-à-vis the West or abandoning the regime and hope for the triumph of a reformist communism in East Germany. He ultimately opted for the second course, proclaiming his readiness not only to accept the democratic decision of the East German citizenry but also to enter into the complex international negotiations that eliminated the external hurdles to unification. Once the Soviet Union abandoned its hitherto critical strategic ally and client state, the reason for the GDR's separate existence had disappeared. As East German voters aptly recognized, a democratic alternative to the Federal Republic would be an anomaly, difficult to maintain politically and economically.

No less important was the hold the Federal Republic had achieved over East German voters. This had been forged through ever expanding private contacts, economic ties, and media access over the preceding two decades. Once the borders were opened, the reality of West German prosperity exceeded the expectations of most of those East Germans who had never been to the West. Confronted with what seemed a thriving and democratic society, it became all but impossible to convince East Germans to chose the long, hard, and uncertain path toward an East German model of social democracy.

But there were also reasons internal to the GDR after its revolution that help account for the triumph of those favoring immediate union with the Federal Republic. One was the very pace of political, economic, and social disintegration between October 1989 and March 1990. Against this experience of turmoil, the Federal Republic's image of stability seemed especially comforting and reassuring—a mood that Kohl and Genscher captured and reinforced.

Equally important was the inability of the newly formed opposition groups to develop an alternative to both the system they had successfully toppled and the West German political and economic model. The new democratic groups were unprepared for the speed and extent of political disintegration and economic collapse. They had no experience in creating or managing governments or running complex industrial economies, and the pressure of events precluded any learning period. They also lacked the unity, organization, and manpower to supplant the SED state they helped destroy. Their message of anti-materialism, solidarity, and sacrifice in the name of some unspecified socialist society had little resonance among people fearful for their future and confronted with promises of speedy prosperity by West German parties with a proven record of success.

Could the democratic opposition have won the Volkskammer election without the intervention of the West German parties? This seems doubtful given, on the one side, the SED/PDS's continued control over awesome resources, extensive organization, and the media and, on the other, the opposition's fragmentation, organizational weakness, and financial dependence on the very state it sought to oust. Without the intervention by West Germany's parties, there might have emerged two equally unattractive alternatives. On the one hand, the Volkskammer election could have produced a situation similar to that in Bulgaria or Romania with a victorious "reformed" Communist party confronted by losers unwilling to accept its legitimacy. Or, alternatively, the result might have been a fragmented parliament along Weimar lines with three internally divided and mutually antagonistic camps (the former ruling party, the ex-bloc parties, and the democratic opposition) incapable of working out a viable plan for the country's social, economic, and political restructuring or for unification. It is also unlikely that even in the event of a triumph by the opposition groups, the West German government would have rushed in with substantial amounts of financial assistance. To expect West German tax payers to finance an uncertain economic and political experiment was as unrealistic as the expectation that East Germans might desire to participate in it.

Finally, the sense that the democratic revolution was "hijacked" by West German parties was clearly not shared by most East German voters. During the campaign, West German politicians drew huge crowds, in part out of curiosity, but also because voters were generally both unfamiliar with and wary of East German candidates. Even prior to the revolution, East Germans had at best a precarious identification with the GDR; thereafter this already tenuous bond was destroyed altogether by revelations of official corruption, *Stasi* activities, and the country's disastrous economic conditions. While East Germans disliked certain West German campaign tactics, they generally saw the participation of the "Bonn" parties in the Volkskammer election as a positive step, signifying a commitment by them to ensure a better future for East Germans.

Conclusion

The dual revolution of 1989—by exit and by voice—reshaped the East German party system. A new set of opposition groups and parties brought drastic changes in the power and character of the dominant ruling party and its satellites. These democratic movements produced a new open, genuinely pluralistic, and highly competitive party system. But, in the end, they could not attract voters. Cut loose from the Soviet Union and with unimpeded access to prosperous West Germany, East Germans turned away from their own reformers to the prospect of a new life as part of the Federal Republic. Many did so through emigration, while others shifted their support to those East German parties advocating speedy unification. This dramatic change— the revolution within the revolution—transformed the status of the competing parties, their platforms, and alignments during the GDR's first and only free election. Its outcome—a majority vote for rapid monetary, economic and political union—in effect terminated the GDR's existence as a sovereign state.

This is not to deny the civic courage or political achievements of the democratic opposition. They ended forty years of dictatorship and created conditions for a successful and peaceful transition to democracy. That it was to the Federal Republic's version rather than to their own was as much due to conditions and pressure beyond their control as to their failure to present a common and convincing agenda for citizens desperate to improve their lives. In the end, East German voters made a pragmatic decision. Confronted with the legacies of the "real existing socialism" and tired of yet another social and political experiment, they opted for the proven economic and political record of the Federal Republic.

The obvious beneficiaries of this second transformation were the West German parties and their East German proxies. After the votes had been counted, the East Germans had successfully reproduced the West German party system. The proxies of the three major West German parties drew the overwhelming proportion of East German voters. More to the point, the East German electorate opted for the same structure of political power as in the West, favoring the East German partners of the Bonn coalition, the CDU and FDP, while forcing the East German SPD into the same opposition role it played in the West.

But the West German parties, too, had to pay a price for their efficient (some would say ruthless) incorporation of the East German parties and state. The initial expectation, shared above all by the parties of the Bonn coalition, that unification would entail little more than an eastward extension of the Federal Republic proved unrealistic. The union of East and West German parties has created new intra-party tensions. Unification now forces all-German parties to deal with an East as well as West German electorate with diverging demands and expectations. The challenges of reproducing West Germany's administrative, legal, economic, and political structures and its procedures and norms is proving far more difficult than originally estimated. Ironically, both East German voters and West German parties wanted to avoid experiments, not realizing that unification was precisely that.

East and West German citizens and parties must now adapt themselves to a transformation they did not anticipate or want. In this process, the forces of the peaceful revolution of 1989, represented by the Alliance 90/Greens, may yet come to play a significant role. Among the political parties currently seated in the all-German Bundestag, it is the only party not tainted by the political and financial abuses now associated with the "Bonn" parties. Its parliamentarians, unlike those of the West German Greens in the past, have demonstrated a preference for pragmatic solutions to ideological confrontations. On key issues, such as the asylum law, they have come up with sensible policies that the major parties are now incorporating into their own plans. Assuming that the planned merger with the West German Greens—now dominated by "realists" (*Realos*) rather than ideological fundamentalists—is achieved, the former East German opposition forces could well shape the party and political reforms that were ignored during the Volkskammer election and subsequent unification process.

Notes

1. There is considerable controversy about the applicability of the term "revolution" to the political transformations in Eastern Europe and East Germany during the fall of 1989. Insofar as the term refers to a fundamental change in the political, social, and economic structures of a society, then what happened in the former communist bloc nations certainly amounted to a revolution. This is particularly true of the former GDR where, following the popular vote in favor of unification, the replacement of the previous structures by altogether new ones was especially speedy and radical. For this reason I use the term revolution to describe developments in East Germany during and after the fall of 1989.

2. An excellent source on the formation, organization, programs, and operations of these four parties is Martin Broszat and Hermann Weber, eds., *SBZ-Handbuch. Staatliche Verwaltungen, Parteien, gesellschaftliche Organisationen und ihre Führungskräfte in der Sowjetischen Besatzungszone Deutschlands* (Munich: Oldenbourg, 1990).

3. American and British zonal authorities licensed the same four parties three months later, French authorities not until 1947. For details see Alf Mintzel, "Besatzungspolitik und Entwicklung der bürgerlichen Parteien in den Westzonen," in Dietrich Staritz, ed., *Das Parteiensystem der Bundesrepublik*, 2d ed. (Opladen: Leske Verlag & Budrich, 1980).

4. For details on Soviet restrictions on the parties as well as the origins and role of the bloc in Soviet calculations, see Dietrich Staritz, "Die

130   *Michaela W. Richter*

Entstehung des Parteiensystems der DDR" in Staritz, ed., *Parteiensystem*, 91-94.

5. The leaders of the non-communist parties generally supported the bloc idea as a constructive mechanism for preventing Weimar-style party conflicts and for addressing the critical postwar problems in a non-partisan way. Since most came from the left-wing of their old Weimar parties and had experienced Nazi persecution, they shared the communists' anti-fascist commitments and desire for economic and social reforms. Dietrich Staritz, *Die Gründung der DDR* (Munich: Deutscher Taschenbuch Verlag, 1987), 93ff.

6. Such a merger had first been proposed by the SPD's East Berlin leaders but, for tactical reasons, was rejected by the KPD in favor of a less formal Common Action Agreement signed by both parties on 19 June 1945. At the Wenningsen conference in August 1945, Schumacher forced a split with the East SPD over its cooperation with the communists. In the fall of 1945 the KPD suddenly favored full union and then ruthlessly attacked Social Democrats in the Soviet Zone of Occupation (SBZ) who by now were themselves ambivalent or hostile to such a move. Between December 1945 and April 1946, at least 20,000 Social Democrats were censored, imprisoned, or even killed. Subsequently, 100,000 Social Democrats were forced to flee to the West; 5,000 were condemned by Soviet or East German courts, and some 400 of those who were imprisoned died. See Hermann Weber, "Mit Zwang und Betrug: Der Opfergang der Sozialdemokraten in der Sowjetzone und der DDR," *Die Zeit*, 2 March 1990.

7. Staritz, *Gründung*, 143-46.

8. Ibid., 123-41.

9. More details on internal changes in the SED can be found in Müller, "SED," in *SBZ-Handbuch*, 496-99, and Staritz, *Gründung*, 162-63.

10. Suckut, "CDU," in *SBZ-Handbuch*, 524-56; also in the same volume, Dähn, "LDP," 544-73.

11. For the formation and functions of these two parties, see especially the articles by Dietrich Staritz on the NDPD and by Bernhard Wernet-Tietz on the DBD in the *SBZ-Handbuch*, 574-83 and 584-94.

12. The SED used the People's Congress as the vehicle for achieving separate statehood to prevent the CDU and LDP from derailing the project in the *Länder* parliaments. Following the proclamation of the West German Basic Law on 23 May 1949, elections were held in the SBZ to the Third People's Congress (with an all-party unity list). The Congress proclaimed the German Democratic Republic on 7 October and then asked Otto Grotewohl to form a new all-party government. On 10 October, the Soviet Military Administration (SMAD) formally transferred its authority to the new

GDR government. For details on the formation of the GDR, see especially Staritz, *Gründung*, 165-69.

13. Eventually, the bloc was renamed the Democratic Bloc and was joined by the National Front, a cover organization that encompassed all mass organizations as well as all parties.

14. The largest networks of local branches (*Ortsgruppen*) were those of the CDU (5,750) and the DBD (6,460), followed by the LDPD (3,250) and the NDPD (3,000). The national mouthpiece of the four parties were *Neue Zeit* (CDU, circulation of 90,000); *Der Morgen* (LDPD, circulation 51,000); and *National-Zeitung* (NDPD, circulation 60,000). For organizational details, see Peter Joachim Lapp, *Die 'befreundeten' Parteien der SED. DDR–Blockparteien heute* (Cologne: Verlag Wissenschaft und Politik, 1988), 42-70.

15. The DBD consisted principally of people employed in agriculture. The other bloc parties sought to recruit private artisans and small businessmen as well as certain categories of the professions. About 50 percent of the membership of the CDU, LDPD, and NDPD were in fact white collar workers and professionals. The CDU also attracted religiously affiliated elements of the population. Lapp, *Die 'befreundeten' Parteien*, 33-38.

16. Ibid., 24-25.

17. Excellent analyses of the internal crises of communism include William Griffith, ed., *Central and Eastern Europe: The Opening Curtain?* (Boulder, Col.: Westview Press, 1989) and Zbigniew Brzezinski, *The Grand Failure* (New York: Scribner, 1989). On the role of Gorbachev see especially F. Stephen Larrabee, "The New Soviet Approach to Europe" in Nils H. Wessel, ed., *The New Europe: Revolution in East-West Relations* (New York: Academy of Political Science, 1991), 1-25, and Karen Dawisha, *Eastern Europe, Gorbachev and Reform. The Great Challenge* (New York: Cambridge University Press, 1990).

18. For the GDR's economic crisis and popular reactions, see Rolf Reißig, "Der Umbruch in der DDR und das Scheitern des 'realen Sozialismus'" in Rolf Reißig and Gert-Joachim Glaeßner, eds., *Das Ende eines Experiments. Umbruch in der DDR und deutsche Einheit* (Berlin: Dietz Verlag, 1991), 12-59, and Dietrich Staritz, "Ursachen und Konsequenzen einer Revolution" in *Der Fischer Weltalmanach Sonderband DDR* (Frankfurt a.M: Fischer Taschenbuch Verlag, 1990), 13-44.

19. Reißig, "Umbruch in der DDR," 17-18.

20. The more the SED tried to distance itself from Gorbachev's reforms (reflected in Kurt Hager's notorious remark that the "GDR needn't change its wallpaper merely because its neighbors did"), the more popular support increased for the Soviet Union and its leaders. See Antonia Grunenberg,

"Ich finde mich überhaupt nicht mehr zurecht" in *Die DDR auf dem Weg zur deutschen Einheit. Probleme, Perspektiven, Offene Fragen.* Twenty-third Conference on the State of the GDR Research in the Federal Republic of Germany, 5-8 June 1990 in *Deutschland Archiv*, Special Issue (1990): 47-58.

21. According to Hirschman, "When customers stop buying a firm's products or when individuals leave an organization, they are exercising the exit option." Alternatively, "when a firm's customers or an organization's members express their disaffection directly to management or to some other authority to which management is subordinate, they are using the voice option."A third option is to remain loyal to the firm or organization in the hope that this will give management the flexibility to initiate change without worrying about customer or member defections. Until the end of November, this was essentially the response of SED members, including the reformists. Albert O. Hirschman, *Exit, Voice, and Loyalty. Responses to Decline in Firms, Organizations, and States* (Cambridge, Mass.: Harvard University Press, 1970), 4.

22. Horst Teltschik (former foreign policy adviser to Chancellor Kohl) provides an interesting behind-the-scenes account of the external maneuvers and negotiations in *329 Tage. Innenansichten der Einigung* (Berlin: Siebert, 1991).

23. Good treatments of the political and social concepts of the opposition can be found in Hubertus Knabe, ed., *Aufbruch in eine andere DDR* (Hamburg: Rororo, 1989) and Marlies Menge, *"Ohne uns läuft nichts mehr." Die Revolution in der DDR* (Stuttgart: Deutsche Verlagsanstalt, 1989), 12-126.

24. There were eight Reformed or Calvinist and Lutheran church groups in the League of Protestant Churches. They and the Catholic church were the only organizations in the GDR that were legally independent of state and party and as such endowed with the right of free assembly. For this reason, pastoral work or lay church activities opened a sphere of personal freedom and political experimentation not otherwise available. See Daniel Hamilton, *After the Revolution. The New Political Landscape in East Germany* (Washington, D.C.: American Institute for Contemporary German Studies, 1990), 3-4.

25. For an assessment of opposition activities between 1988 and 1989, see especially Gerhard Rein, *Die protestantische Revolution 1987-1990* (Berlin: Wichern-Verlag, 1991), 57-185.

26. For figures on the opposition, see Armin Müller and Stefan Wolle, eds., *Ich liebe euch doch alle! Befehle und Lageberichte des MfS Januar-November 1989* (Berlin: Basisdruck, 1990), 46-71.

27. The suspected *Stasi* informant had long been active in the oppositional "Church from below" and for this reason was brought in by Rainer Schulte, one of the New Forum's founders. This information was provided the author by Jens Reich on 31 October 1991 in Washington, D.C. On the decision to seek legal recognition, see Jens Reich, *Rückkehr nach Europa* (Munich: Hansa Verlag, 1991), 187.

28. For additional information on the New Forum, see Peter R. Weilemann, et al., *Parteien im Aufbruch: Nichtkommunistische Parteien und politische Vereinigungen in der DDR* (Bonn: Konrad-Adenauer-Stiftung, 1990), 52-59. Also see Gesamtdeutsches Institut, Bundesanstalt für gesamtdeutsche Aufgaben, *Dokumentation zur Entwicklung der neuen Parteien und Bürgerrechtsgruppen in der DDR November 1989-Februar 1990* (Bonn, 1990), 7-48.

29. On Democracy Now's role as initiator of the Roundtable, see Uwe Thaysen, *Der Runde Tisch. Oder: Wo blieb das Volk? Der Weg der DDR in die Demokratie* (Opladen: Westdeutscher Verlag, 1990), 29.

30. For additional information on Democracy Now, see Weilemann, et al., *Parteien*, 59-65, and Gesamtdeutsches Institut, *Neue Parteien und Bürgerrechtsgruppen*, 130-41. Also interview with Konrad Weiß on 14 July 1991 in Bonn.

31. On the Initiative for Peace and Human Rights, see Weilemann, *Parteien*, 65-69, and Gesamtdeutsches Institut, *Neue Parteien und Bürgerrechtsgruppen*, 152-60.

32. Gesamtdeutsches Institut, *Dokumentation zur Entwicklung der neuen Parteien*, 142-47.

33. For information on the United Left, see *Süddeutsche Zeitung*, 21 September 1989: 3; *Tageszeitung*, 23 September 1989; and Gesamtdeutsches Institut, *Analysen, Dokumentationen und Chronik zur Entwicklung in der DDR von September bis Dezember 1989* (Bonn, 1990), 31-35.

34. Tipped off by Wolfgang Schnur, who turned out to be a paid informer, the *Stasi* invaded the apartment where the founding meeting was to be held. The October congress could be held only because of Bishop Forck's intercession with Egon Krenz. Interview with Christiane Ziller, former Democratic Awakening press speaker, on 30 July 1991 in Bonn.

35. These CDU contacts were facilitated by Eppelmann's close relationship with Norbert Blüm, on the one hand, and by the West CDU's own interest in establishing some ties with the democratic opposition (if only to defend itself against SPD charges of refusing to support the new democratic forces in the GDR), on the other. Interview with Hans-Joachim Falenski, deputy head of the West CDU's political office on 24 July 1991 in Bonn.

36. Among the prominent founders who left were Eberhart Richter and Friedrich Schorlemmer who, together with the entire Wittenberg branch,

joined the SPD; Bishop Forck and Provost Falcke, who returned to their church responsibilities; and Sonja Schröder and Christiane Ziller, who went to Democracy Now. For additional information, see Gesamtdeutsches Institut, *Neue Parteien und Bürgerrechtsbewegungen*, 96-129; and Weilemann, et al., *Aufbruch*, 24-32.

37. This became an issue only in the wake of Brandt's stirring speech. Although the sharp rise in the SDP's popularity thereafter resulted largely from its public association with unification, the SDP's founders subsequently made it clear that they did not envision this process as a simple takeover by the Federal Republic. Interview with Markus Meckel, *Das Parlament*, 14 September 1990.

38. Electoral calculations also played a role. The SDP's founders believed a reconstituted Social Democratic party would attract more popular support than an altogether new party, given the old SPD's strength in East Germany prior to the 1946 merger and its historical opposition to the communists.

39. Thus, as late as August 1989, West Berlin's mayor, Momper, still insisted that "nothing could be achieved by forming parties out of small opposition groups." *Der Spiegel*, 3 November 1989: 53.

40. The connection was made by the SDP's press speaker, Steffen Reiche, during an informal visit in Bonn. See *Frankfurter Allgemeine Zeitung*, 28 October 1989, and *Die Zeit*, 3 November 1990.

41. The Green Party demanded not only a strong environmental program but also reductions in the size of the East German army, an end to military education in schools, full equality for men and women, the return of Jewish property seized by the Nazis, and a public education program about the SED's own anti-semitic campaigns of the early 1950s. See Gesamtdeutsches Institut, *Neue Parteien und Bürgerrechtsbewegungen*, 148-52, and *Frankfurter Allgemeine Zeitung*, 27 November 1989: 2.

42. Especially good information on the early programmatic statements of the opposition groups can be found in Gesamtdeutsches Institut, *Analysen, Dokumentation und Chronik*, 131-38, and in the essays on the individual opposition groups in Gesamtdeutsches Institut, *Dokumentation zur Entwicklung der neuen Parteien und Bürgerrechtsgruppen*.

43. The *Stasi's* successful penetration even of the New Forum's secret core of people responsible for creating membership files was described to the author by Jens Reich in an interview on 31 October 1991 in Washington, D.C. Vera Wollenberger, in an interview on 7 April 1992 in Washington, D.C., suggested that *Stasi* informants in opposition groups may have deliberately created or intensified personal differences among opposition figures to prevent the formation of a common opposition front.

44. Gerlach became the LDPD's leader at the age of twenty-six. As founder and executive member (1949-1959) of the communist youth organization, the FDJ (*Freie Deutsche Jugend*), he became Honecker's friend and protégé. He was a deputy chairman of the Council of State, one of the few political positions open to the bloc parties.

45. Gerlach's articles, other reformist statements by LDPD's functionaries, and the November position paper can be found in Gesamtdeutsches Institut, *Dokumentation zur Entwicklung der Blockparteien der DDR von Ende September bis Anfang Dezember 1989* (Bonn, 1989), 7-74.

46. His radical stance cost him the SED's support for Speaker of Parliament on 13 November in favor of the more loyal Günther Maleuda of the DBD. But it also helped his election to acting head-of-state after Krenz's resignation from all SED and governmental posts on 6 December 1989. "Es ist eine Revolution," *Die Zeit*, 3 November 1990.

47. Between October and December, some 8,000 new members joined the LDPD. Weilemann, et al., *Parteien*, 38.

48. Gerlach envisioned a more humane and "fun" socialism rather than the GDR's transformation into a second Federal Republic. See interview with Gerlach in *Der Spiegel*, 6 November 1989.

49. The old guard chose de Maizière for three reasons: as a lawyer with a record for defending regime critics, he would appeal to CDU reformists; as vice president of the Synod of the Protestant Churches, he had the confidence of the church; and never having held a party post before, he was politically unencumbered. For his appointment and conflict with the executive, see his article in *Die Zeit*, 27 September 1991.

50. For additional information, see especially Gesamtdeutsches Institut, *Dokumentation zur Entwicklung der Blockparteien*, 75-115.

51. Gesamtdeutsches Institut, *Dokumentation zur Entwicklung in der DDR vom 7. Oktober - 19 November 1989* (Bonn, 1989), 188.

52. Additional materials on the DBD and NDPD can be found in *Das Parlament*, 9 March 1990: 9, and in Gesamtdeutsches Institut, *Entwicklung in den Blockparteien*, 116-98.

53. An excellent study of the SED's transformation is Thomas Ammer's article, "Von der SED zur PDS—Was bleibt" in *Die DDR auf dem Weg zur deutschen Einheit. Probleme, Perspektiven, Offene Fragen*, 103-16. For additional primary materials, see also Gesamtdeutsches Institut, *Analysen, Dokumentation, Perspektiven*, 78-116.

54. The idea for the Roundtable had come from Democracy Now, but the mechanics of its establishment, rules, and functioning were worked out by representatives from the churches (including the Catholic church) with full agreement from all sides. The first Roundtable meeting was held on 12 December; sessions continued thereafter on a weekly basis until the final

session on 12 March 1990. In addition to the central Roundtable, local ones also met. By far the most comprehensive treatment of the Roundtable's origins, participants, structure, problems, and achievements is provided by Thaysen, *Der Runde Tisch*, 19-39.

55. The New Forum's Berlin leaders also had misgivings about joining the Roundtable. They felt that under continued pressure from mass demonstrations, the SED would have to give way to the opposition. The Roundtable, on the other hand, might end up with the same sort of compromise worked out in Poland under which the communists retained a major share of actual political power. Interview with Jens Reich on 31 October 1991 in Washington, D.C.

56. See especially the interview with Ibrahim Böhme, *TAZ*, 8 December 1989.

57. Serge Schmemann, "The New Politics," *The New York Times*, 30 January 1990. Also, author's interview with Pastor Hans Misselwitz, head of the East SPD's program commission, on 14 March 1990.

58. *Süddeutsche Zeitung*, 22 February 1990.

59. For details of the election law, see *Das Parlament*, 9 March 1990: 9-10.

60. To the Bavarians, the DSU was a means for broadening the CSU's influence beyond its traditional Bavarian base and hence to ensure its political leverage in a unified Germany. For more information on Christian conservative parties that joined the DSU, see Weilemann, et al., *Parteien im Aufbruch*, 31-36; Christian Wernicke, "Spät am Start. DDR Konservative suchen eine neue Heimat," *Die Zeit*, 26 January 1990; and "DSU-Profile," *Das Parlament*, 9 March 1990.

61. For the various motives behind and tensions within the Alliance, see *Das Parlament*, 9 March 1990; *TAZ*, 15 March 1990; Christian Wernecke, "Schatten auf den Schultern der neuen Männer," *Die Zeit*, 16 March 1990; and "Harmonie im konservativen Dreiklang," *Die Zeit*, 2 March 1990.

62. The West CDU recognized too late the risks this involved. Worried that East German voters might actually try to vote for the Alliance or all three parties, which would have rendered their vote invalid, the West CDU had to undertake a last-minute education drive to make it clear to voters that they must support one of the three parties individually. Interview with Hans-Joachim Falenski on 14 July 1991 in Bonn.

63. The West FDP later regretted this as well because it gave the DFP and FDP overrepresentation in the Volkskammer. As part of the agreement, the first three places of the League list were taken by one candidate from each of the three parties. All other places were allocated to LDP candidates. But because of the disappointing showing of the League as a whole, only the first three candidates entered the Volkskammer, thus giving the new

parties more of a voice than their size warranted. Information provided by H. Erkins, head of the FDP's political division, on 12 July 1991 in Bonn.

64. The Volkskammer's electoral law of 20 February 1990 in effect allowed such an active part by West German parties by delaying the date for prohibiting outside assistance until January 1991. At the meeting of the Roundtable on 5 February, the PDS and its affiliates (as well as the citizen movements) had voted against such West German aid over the opposition of the SPD, CDU, LDP, and Democratic Awakening. The latter parties declared the resolution non-binding and made it clear that they would ignore it during the campaign. The meeting on 20 February provided a face-saving compromise. Thaysen, *Der Runde Tisch*, 134-37.

65. On the role of the West German parties in the elections, see Peter Christ, "Start aus dem Nichts," *Die Zeit*, 16 March 1990; *Der Spiegel*, February 1990: 48-50; and *Die Welt*, 22 February 1990. Also interviews with H. Erkins (FDP), K. Hartung (SPD), and H. J. Falenski (CDU) on 14-16 July 1991 in Bonn.

6

Parties and the Problems of Governance During Unification

Gert-Joachim Gloeßner

"We are the people!" was the call raised by hundreds of thousands of demonstrators across the GDR in the autumn of 1989. It was these demonstrators who overthrew the country's communist regime. However, by early 1990 the slogan changed to "We are one people," and so had the composition of the demonstrators. The "people of the GDR" were a single voice only briefly as they swept away the old political order. Then the unified political entity broke up into its various component parts. As Ralf Dahrendorf has aptly pointed out, the slogan "We are the people!" as the maxim of a democratic state and of its constitution is only a mirror image of the totalitarian state which had just been overthrown. "If the monopoly of the party is replaced merely by the victory of the masses, all will be lost before long, for the masses have no structure and no permanence.[1]

Between the autumn of 1989 and the Day of German Unity on 3 October 1990, political events in the GDR reflected three conflicting trends:

- The process of political restructuring and differentiation led to the founding of a variety of political parties, interest groups, and political associations that sought answers to the various problems faced by GDR citizens during this transitional period.[2]
- The transition process was increasingly dominated by the desire to create the prerequisites for the unification of the two German states as quickly as possible. All political groups and members of the East German parliament, the Volkskammer, which had been freely elected on 18 March 1990, attempted to steer a course between the Scylla of a mere annexation of the GDR by the Federal Republic and the Charybdis of ensuring a continuation of the old structures.[3]
- Political forces in the GDR, including both the government and the opposition, lost more and more of their freedom of movement. Their actions were determined by the circumstances accompanying a perma-

nent election campaign and by their superior partners in the West. The latter increasingly decided issues and tactics.

In the weeks following the elections to the Volkskammer, the unification process visibly gathered speed—not only because of the worsening economic and social crisis in the GDR but also because a reassessment of the global situation made the rapid achievement of unity desirable. The intention was to use the window of opportunity that events in Central and Eastern Europe and in the Soviet Union had opened.

The first freely-elected parliament and the first democratically legitimate government of the GDR were confronted by the necessity of finding speedy answers to the fundamentally important questions:

- Which path should the GDR follow in order to reach the goal of unity? Should unification occur according to Article 146 or Article 23 of the Basic Law?
- Should the GDR give itself a new constitution for this period of transition or continue to use the amended old constitution of the GDR?
- Once a decision in favor of Article 23 had been reached, how could the government and parliament best protect the interests of the citizens of the GDR during the process of unification?

Decisions regarding the process of unification, and particularly the debate about the dates of elections and about electoral procedure, led to endless controversies in both German states and ultimately, in the summer of 1990, to the breakdown of the grand coalition in the GDR.

The Establishment of a New Party System

The GDR always described itself officially as a multi-party system. However, the bloc (or "satellite") parties were never anything more than accomplices to SED policies. It is all the more astonishing that they were able, at least superficially, to transform themselves into Western-style parties. They ceased to see themselves as the mouthpieces of ideological concepts or as representatives of certain social groups.

The new party system in the GDR developed in several phases.[4] In the autumn of 1989, the bloc parties cut the umbilical cord to the SED. New political organizations were founded by citizens' movements which, in a second phase in 1990, declared themselves to be parties. The old bloc parties changed leadership and underwent programmatic changes. They abandoned socialism as a political goal. A third phase—leading to March 18 elections to the Volkskammer—was dominated by attempts to create alliances and electoral unions as a means of preventing fragmentation in the infant party system.

Responding to direct influence from the West German Christian Democrats and, in particular from Chancellor Helmut Kohl, the East German CDU, the German Social Union (which was closely associated with the Bavarian CSU), and the Democratic Awakening (*Demokratischer Aufbruch*, initially a citizens' movement) joined forces, in spite of differing views and internal conflicts, to form the Alliance for Germany. The liberal camp founded the League of Free Democrats (*Bund Freier Demokraten*) composed of the East German Liberal Democratic Party (LDP), the FDP of the GDR, and the German Forum Party (*Deutsche Forumpartei*).

A total of twenty-four parties and other organizations, as well as five electoral alliances, competed in the election of 18 March 1990. The unexpected victory of the Christian Democrats added new impetus to the unification process and to the transformation of the party system after the model of the Federal Republic. This development determined the course of political debate in the summer of 1990 but came to an end in the autumn of that same year. East and West German branches of the CDU, SPD, and the FDP merged, while the Party of Democratic Socialism (PDS)—successor to the SED—expanded its political activities into the West. Only the Greens and the citizens' movements of the GDR maintained their autonomy.

From Bloc Party to Catch-all Party?
The Restructuring of the Old Party System

During the elections to the Volkskammer, the former satellite parties of the GDR initiated new programs. While the renewal of former bloc parties such as the CDU and the LDPD was guided by the "classical" ideas of Christian and liberal politics, the German Peasants' Party (DBD) and the National Democrats (NDPD) experienced considerable difficulties of political reorientation, leading ultimately to their demise as autonomous parties. At the end of March, the party leadership of the NDPD, with a membership of 80,000, joined the Liberals. At the end of June, DBD leadership recommended to members a merger with the CDU.

Both parties had been founded in 1948 on the instructions of the SED. Although they never developed independent profiles, they had at their disposal considerable assets which they included in their mergers with the CDU and the LDPD, respectively, in 1990.

The CDU represented itself to the electors as the "people's party of the center," pursuing conservative policies grounded in fundamental ethical values. Initially the CDU found it particularly difficult to develop a new self-image and to abandon established ideological positions:

> The CDU is convinced that the increasingly acute contradictions in today's world can only be resolved if the political necessity of Christian values such as the acknowledgment of guilt, repentance, justice, and solidarity is understood and the possibility of their translation into international politics is ensured. The CDU supports an effective market economy which can be made socially and ecologically responsible. It rejects a centralized planned economy, universal state ownership, and party dictatorship. However, it does not abandon to Marxism those ideals of mankind associated with the word socialism, such as social justice, freedom, equality and brotherhood, but is mindful of their origin in the spirit of Christian ethics.[5]

The Western CDU regarded its GDR sister party with reserve. Their position changed, however, when the results of the elections to the Volkskammer indicated that the voters had "forgiven" the eastern CDU its past affiliation with the SED. The decision to lend full support to the CDU in the East was based on a number of considerations: the CDU in the East contributed a still-considerable number of members, large financial assets, and, above all, a full-fledged party organization of great importance to the upcoming all-German elections in December 1990.

The CDU also benefited from the merger with the DBD (80,000 members) in the summer of 1990, thereby increasing its overall membership gain for the all-German CDU by about 200,000. The successes of the CDU in the GDR did not translate into political power after its merger with the western CDU on October 1, 1990. The former East German CDU was never able to exercise any real influence on the fortunes of the enlarged party—despite the fact that its approximately 200,000 members (compared with 680,000 members in the West) represented about a quarter of the total membership. Indeed, observers of the party conference pointed out that the shift to the left in the CDU which many had feared as a consequence of the merger had not occurred.[6] Neither during the election campaign to the Bundestag nor in the program of the first all-German government was it possible to detect any significant changes in the CDU due to its new eastern members. This holds equally true of the Liberals and the Social Democrats.

The Liberals underwent a development similar to that of the CDU. Early in 1990, the LDPD had renamed itself the Liberal-Democratic Party (LDP). In March 1990, Liberals in the GDR presented themselves as a party with a "liberal attitude of mind and view of the world" for whom the freedom of the individual stood at the center of all political life. "Man is the measure of all things. The state is there for man, not the reverse. State arbitrariness, bureaucracy, and compulsion contradict what we understand by liberalism."[7] The LDP supported the quickest possible unification of Germany within a European peace order, the rule of law, and a free market economy.

The Liberals won only 5.3 percent of the vote in the March 1990 election to the Volkskammer, forcing them to rethink their position. On 28 March, leaders of the LDP, the eastern FDP, and the German Forum Party resolved to merge their three parties, each of which considered themselves liberal. The new party was to be called "Free Democratic Party–the Liberals." But just a few days later the plan foundered due to resistance from rank-and-file members. Members of the German Forum Party (once part of the citizens' movements) particularly rejected an alliance with the LDP because of its past affiliation with the SED. At the end of March, after this failure, the LDP merged with the NDPD and called itself the "League of Free Democrats–the Liberals." In the Volkskammer it entered into a parliamentary alliance with the eastern FDP.

A union of the three liberal parties of the GDR would only be achieved during the merger with the western FDP in August 1990. The approximately 135,000 members of the League of Free Democrats, formed by the fusion of LDP and the NDPD, would have dominated both the small FDP of the GDR (with only 2,000 members) and the Forum Party (estimated membership figures vary between 500 and 3,000). The increase in the number of members created problems for the western FDP, which had only 67,000 members. By use of a complicated delegating procedure, regional branches from the East were denied a majority. The chairman of the League of Free Democrats (previously the LDP), Rainer Ortleb, and of the eastern FDP, Bruno Menzel, were elected vice-chairmen of the FDP at the federal level. The party conference issued a declaration in which the aims of the Liberals were formulated: "The guarantee of inviolable basic rights, the free development of the human personality, the protection of minorities, the division and control of state power, and a free state under the rule of law are the fundamental ideas of liberalism."[8]

Finally, mention must be made of the SED's successor party, the Party of Democratic Socialism (PDS), which is attempting to shake off shadows from the past and to represent itself as a modern socialist party. Within the five months between October and February 1990, the party lost nearly two out of three of its 2.3 million party members, many of whom were reform-minded younger people.

Individual groups within the SED had long attempted to stimulate a reform process. After Mikhail Gorbachev's accession to power in the Soviet

Union in 1985, pressure mounted on the party hierarchy to initiate reforms along Soviet lines. However, the debate never went beyond the stage of informal discussion and was limited to small party circles. It was only in October and November 1989 that reform-oriented members of the SED tried to influence the transformation process of the political party system in the GDR.

At the same time, grassroots discontent mounted. It resulted in the replacement of the party leadership of Egon Krenz, who had taken office in October. Krenz, a long-time member of the Politburo, had been Honecker's "crown prince" and was in charge of state security. In December, further discontent forced the convention of an extraordinary SED party congress—against the wishes of the leadership. This congress agreed to "reform the SED as a modern socialist party" and acknowledged that Stalinist socialism had been unable to respond to the compelling economic, social, defense, ecological and cultural problems; therefore, a radical break with Stalinist structures was unavoidable.

However, the Party congress did not go so far as to dissolve a party so deeply incriminated by its history. Its new name, SED-PDS (Socialist Unity Party–Party of Democratic Socialism) combined two barely reconcilable political views. Despite its radical self-criticism, the SED-PDS was scarcely able to lend credibility to its political transformation. Its influence as the governing party was temporarily secured, albeit at a price: the SED-PDS lost much credibility even with its new, reform-minded leadership. It proved incapable of shedding old-style thinking and dismissing the old structures of the party and state apparatus.

Although in February 1990 the SED-PDS took yet another name—the Party of Democratic Socialism—it still could not shed its reputation. A series of scandals and comprehensive evidence of the complicity of leading PDS members in the old communist system did not, however, destroy the standing of the party in the eyes of long-standing members, as demonstrated by remarkable electoral successes in March 1990. It continued to draw on the support of old-guard communists and of many of those who most feared the social costs of unification with the Federal Republic—first and foremost public servants and members of the security apparatus—but also a large number of intellectuals who had not yet abandoned the socialist ideal.

New Parties and Electoral Pacts

Initially the various attempts to create new parties untainted by the past appeared more important than the reform of the old bloc parties. These attempts were closely associated with the idea that a new political system could be constructed in the GDR which gradually would be unified with the Federal Republic. But even in the period leading up to the Volkskammer elections, it became clear that these new parties were only to be transitional phenomena.

In early autumn 1989, Social Democracy was illegally founded in the GDR. At that time it called itself the Social Democratic Party in the GDR (SDP).[9] On 13 January 1990, at a conference in Berlin, the party renamed itself the SPD and thereby underlined its claim as successor to the old Social Democratic Party, which had been compelled in 1946 in the then-Soviet Zone of Occupation to become part of the SED. Sooner and more rapidly than any of the other parties, the SPD of the GDR developed into part of an all-German party. As early as February, former West German Chancellor Willy Brandt had been elected its honorary chairman. In its program the SPD clearly recognized its duty to its origins while simultaneously describing itself as a new party:

In the revolutionary upheaval of autumn 1989 it stepped into the forefront of the forces for political reform. But our party is not a party of new type. From the outset it consciously placed itself in the long and tested tradition of German and international social democracy. It supports the fundamental idea of the social democratic movement: a democratic order in economy and society which enables every human being to lead a life in freedom, justice and solidarity."[10]

After the Volkskammer election, the SPD faced a serious crisis. As part of the grand coalition with the CDU, the DSU and the Liberals, it was confronted by the problem of developing its own distinctive profile. Claiming to be the party of workers and "little people" did not pay off at the polls; a majority of workers had voted for the CDU. Unlike the former bloc parties, the SPD did not have a functioning party apparatus at its disposal. It was not present in many local communities and districts. The increasingly untenable situation in the GDR made the need for a broad government alliance imperative, and the SPD felt obligated to join the coalition, thereby violating an earlier campaign promise not to enter into a coalition with the right-wing DSU conservatives. This led to considerable tension between the approximately 30,000 rank-and-file members and the party leadership. Driven largely by personal ambitions, Party Chairman Markus Meckel had taken over the foreign ministry even though it was evident that the GDR scarcely had room for maneuvering in this area. In the realm of domestic policy, it had the thankless task of running the ministries of finance and labor and social affairs.

At a party conference held in Halle in June, a new leadership was elected which succeeded in controlling these centrifugal forces without, however, being able to solve the basic problem of developing its own distinctive profile during the difficult phase of transformation. In the months leading up to unification the SPD, too, became prey to West German party tactics.

Oskar Lafontaine, the SPD candidate for federal chancellor, campaigned in East and West focusing on the negative financial and social effects of unification. The western SPD condemned the federal government's policy of interpreting unification to mean only the unification of the two states, while for Social Democrats this term also implied the equalization of living standards.[11] As subsequent developments in the former GDR showed, this was not unjustified criticism. However, this position ignored the general mood in the GDR, where these arguments were understood as criticism of the people's wish to see Germany rapidly unified. The manifesto "Toward a Restoration of the Unity of the Social Democratic Party of Germany" refers to this problem: "The parts of Germany will grow together all the more quickly the more Germans strive for social justice. This is why we cannot allow there to be first- and second-class Germans for years to come."[12]

This appeal had no impact on internal party structures. Although the last chairman of the SPD in the GDR, Wolfgang Thierse, was elected a deputy chairman of the unified SPD, the merger of the two parties was more or less an annexation. Given the disparity in the membership figures (approximately 900,000 in the West and only about 30,000 in the East) it would have been difficult, of course, to secure greater representation for members from the former East Germany.

The German Social Union (DSU), formed on 20 January 1990 from a dozen small Christian and conservative groups and parties, presented itself as the eastern counterpart to the Bavarian CSU. Initially it was highly critical in particular of the CDU as an old bloc party and could be persuaded only with great difficulty to join the "Alliance for Germany." While its founder, Leipzig churchman Hans-Wilhelm Ebeling, viewed the DSU as a partner of its CDU and CSU sister parties in the West, the populist right wing of the party around Hansjoachim Walther (who subsequently became its chairman) preferred a close connection with the CSU. In the election campaign, the DSU presented itself as the party which opposed all forms of socialism. "Freedom instead of socialism" was the message of its program:

> The DSU is a conservative party because it is committed to a lasting system of values. It is a liberal party because it stands for the fundamental rights of the citizen and for his freedom. It is a socially conscious

party because it supports in particular the cause of the weak. Germany needs freedom instead of socialism."[13]

From its very beginning, the "Alliance for Germany" was a marriage of convenience, and immediately after the elections it fell apart. The DSU left the alliance before the coalition negotiations had even been completed. The party leadership including the founding chairman, Hans-Wilhelm Ebeling, and the Secretary General and later Minister for Internal Affairs, Peter-Michael Diestel, were effectively overthrown. The DSU took on right-wing, populist traits. The western CDU had largely broken off contacts with the DSU following the Volkskammer election and concentrated instead on supporting the CDU in the East. Moves in the DSU to establish a permanent presence in all regions of the GDR ruled out a merger with the CSU since it would have violated the principle that the CSU limits its political activities to a certain region. This would have resulted in ending its parliamentary alliance with the CDU in the Bundestag. A variety of scenarios were considered within the DSU, including an alliance with the DBD.

The DSU example demonstrates clearly that the unification of Germany had far-reaching consequences for the constellation of parties in the whole of Germany, not just in the former GDR. In the summer of 1990, bitter disputes raged on the subject of electoral law. In the past, the CSU had been important not only because it was the largest political party in Bavaria but also because it represented an important conservative element within the parliamentary Christian Democratic alliance.[14] Its influence would have been considerably reduced by the expansion to a national constituency. For that reason, the CSU leadership was interested in finding a counterpart in the eastern regions of Germany. Since no firm party alignment existed, the western CDU initially also had a strong interest in channeling potential right-wing votes in the GDR. The DSU appeared to present an attractive proposition to these groups of voters. But, following its poor performance in the March Volkskammer election and an even worse showing in subsequent Landtag elections, it was clear that an autonomous conservative party to the right of the CDU had no prospect for success. In the summer of 1990 the DSU became a bargaining chip for the CSU in its struggle to maintain its influence in federal politics.

At the beginning of 1990, plans to unite all opposition groups in an electoral alliance failed because the Social Democrats did not join. In February, after this failure, New Forum, the Initiative for Peace and Human Rights, and Democracy Now joined to form Alliance 90. Alliance 90 saw itself, and still sees itself, as a coalition of groups which, as a result of their experience of dictatorship, are intent on defending the individual and social rights of all citizens. In their election manifestos, all three groups spoke of the protection of human and civil rights, achieving a society based on solidarity, the maintenance of a state built on the rule of law, and the necessary democratization of state and society. All of them shared the idea that it should be possible to represent the interests of citizens both within and outside of parliament without having to create party structures. The manifesto of Democracy Now thus states:

> More democracy is made possible by citizens' movements which anyone can join without having to became a member of a party. Citizens' movements can work within or outside of parliament. They offer opportunities for direct democracy. They permit the replacement of spectator democracy by one based on active participation.[15]

Disputes between New Forum and the other groups were commonplace. At the heart of these controversies were problems of alignment within the traditional right-left spectrum and of organization. New Forum saw itself as a political group which could not be assigned to the left-wing camp. It exposed a variety of links to conservative ideas and values and rejected any form of organization that might resemble a party. Public forums, functioning as the primary organizational form of the New Forum, were supposed to set in motion social dialogue and discourse about the many and varied problems which had accumulated during the decades of bureaucratic socialism.

Given their origins, various opposition groups were more interested in cultural questions and in grassroots democracy than in achieving power. With the transformation of some groups into parties, the old consensus based on shared values fell away. Yet much that was held in common did survive the campaign and the elections to the Volkskammer.

Despite considerable differences of opinion with the citizens' movements the different groups were largely in agreement that they wished to play a part in shaping political life in the GDR. In July 1990, they called upon "all grassroots groups in the GDR to support our initiative for a common citizens' alliance. It is our aim to form an electable political organization which will then conduct negotiations with the Greens about a common platform for the elections."[16]

In the summer it seemed for a short time as if, given the impact of the discussions about electoral law, the alliance of citizens' movements would be shattered by the problem of its relationship to the Greens in the West. The Greens displayed a demonstrative distaste towards the process of unification. Their enthusiasm for the people—those who in the autumn 1989 had gone on the streets of the GDR—turned into aversion when the demonstrators began to shout "We are one people!" The Greens spoke during the frenzy of unification of a new *Großdeutschland* in the making and the emergence of a Fourth Reich. The slogan "Never again Germany" made the rounds.

The eight Bundestag representatives of the electoral Alliance 90/Greens (which itself had only come into being with considerable difficulty) have found themselves in a dual dilemma following the failure of western Greens in the December 1990 Bundestag election. They alone must represent the young tradition of the ecology movement in the all-German parliament without having any share of its experience. They also see themselves as representatives of former GDR citizens who, for the most part, are primarily concerned with their immediate material interests—including economic growth, secure jobs, consumer durables, and a western way of living—and who are clearly less interested in so-called post-materialist values. Finally, they are regarded with a certain mistrust by the West German electorate of the Greens and by the Green Party because they cannot be pinned down to "left-wing" positions.

A New Regionalism? Party Preferences and Electoral Behavior in 1990

The revolutionary events in the GDR at the end of 1989 and the beginning of 1990 have understandably been seen from one perspective in particular. In this view, a political and social system collapsed which, in spite of obvious signs of crisis, most observers had considered to be relatively stable.[17] When the system fell apart, attention was directed to the contrast between the political system and the citizens themselves. Only gradually did it become clear that social reality was far more complicated. The SED left behind a society which displayed considerable social, cultural and regional differences.

The election results uncovered deep cleavages within the society of the former GDR between north and south, according to class and social stratum, between blue- and white-collar workers, between young and old. Regional variations in the mass exodus of 1989 were already striking.[18] However, the consequences of a centralized party state which had favored the capital and neglected certain regions became even more apparent in the electoral behavior in 1990.

In East Berlin, the CDU received on average less than half the votes and only a third of the share of the vote compared to the region of Erfurt. Only in Berlin and in the neighboring region of Potsdam was the SPD able to exceed the 30 percent mark while, with 30 percent of the votes, the PDS became the second strongest party. In Berlin as a whole, the Liberals performed very poorly while the citizens' movements achieved their best outcome. These results reflect the particular social structure of the former "capital of the GDR" with its large proportion of party functionaries, state employees, academic and cultural institutions, and a traditionally well-organized work force.

In the south of the GDR, on the other hand, in the regions of Dresden, Karl-Marx-Stadt (Chemnitz) and Erfurt, the parties aligned in the Alliance for Germany received about 60 percent of the votes while the SPD achieved only between 10 and 15 percent and was even overtaken by the PDS in the district of Erfurt. Only in Berlin and Potsdam was the SPD able to overtake the CDU. In the northern districts it performed relatively well. The PDS was most successful in Berlin and in the northern part of the country, where the SED had put most industrial investment in recent decades while the traditional industrial areas of the south declined.

Following the Volkskammer election, it was assumed that voter behavior did not indicate firm party preferences. At least the elections of 1990, however, demonstrate a remarkable consistency in voting behavior. Nevertheless, interesting shifts can be observed. A comparison of the March, October, and December 1990 elections reveals a remarkable stability in voting behavior. In particular, the CDU remained the leading political force. Only in Brandenburg, and only in the elections to the regional Landtag, did the SPD become the strongest party. Here, as in Saxony, where the CDU achieved a convincing absolute majority in the Landtag elections, election results for the regional parliament were determined by the strong personalities of those running for the office of prime minister. Manfred Stolpe, a leading churchman in the GDR, was the SPD candidate in Brandenburg, while Kurt Biedenkopf, one of the western CDU's leading programmatic thinkers, ran for the CDU in Saxony.

The PDS consistently lost support in all of the newly-reconstituted eastern *Länder*. Unlike the parties that had emerged from the former bloc parties (namely, the CDU and the FDP), the former communist party is associated with much that stands for the old GDR. This image explains its success in (East) Berlin, where, in the elections to the parliament of the Land Berlin which took place concurrently with elections to the national Bundestag, the PDS was able to secure 23.6 percent of the votes and have several of its members directly elected. In the local elections in May it had received 30 percent. In Berlin it even succeeded in having the party's chairman, Gregor Gysi, directly elected to the Bundestag.

The performance of the DSU, the party founded on the model of and supported by the CSU in Bavaria, is also of interest. In the elections to the Volkskammer it was able to attract 13.9 percent of the votes in Saxony where the CSU had conducted a massive campaign effort. In Thuringia it received a respectable 5.7 percent, while in the other *Länder* it remained insignificant or did not compete at all. In Landtag elections in October, the DSU fell to 3.6 percent in Saxony and in Thuringia to 3.3 percent, losing 237,000 voters overall to the CDU, from which it in turn attracted only 81,000 voters. Of the 6.6 percent the DSU gained in the elections to the Volkskammer in March, a mere 1.0 percent was left by the time of the Bundestag elections in December. The DSU was an experiment that failed.

The failure of the western Greens in the Bundestag elections can be attributed to self-isolation implicit in their political program. There was also considerable skepticism about the process and the speed of unification among members of Alliance 90. In particular, they criticized the way in which decisions were reached without the participation of ordinary citizens. The co-founder of Initiative for Peace and Human Rights, Wolfgang Templin, explained the disastrous showing of the Greens and the poor election results of the citizens' movements with the unfortunate linkage of two irreconcilable political positions: The total rejection of unification and the attempt to introduce their own distinctive approach. To a much greater extent than Alliance 90, Templin believes that the Greens had felt "put out and irritated" by unification and by "the way in which it was executed."[19]

After four elections we can summarize by saying that no dramatic changes in voting behavior have taken place thus far. Conservative-liberal majorities are—for the moment at least—stable. The party system in the eastern *Länder* has largely aligned itself to that in the old Federal Republic.

PDS and Alliance 90 are two exceptions. The PDS will not succeed in shaking off its past; it offers no convincing political program that suggests it might in time be able to establish itself as a socialist party to the left of the SPD. Whether the eight Bundestag representatives of Alliance 90/Greens will be able to anchor a new kind of party in Germany's political system remains questionable.

The Path to Unity

The unexpected result of the 18 March 1990 elections, which indicated the desire for unification and the desperate state of the GDR economy, exerted considerable pressure on the political leadership in East and West. In East Germany, workable majorities in the Volkskammer and a strong government were needed. The "grand coalition" under the leadership of CDU chairman Lothar de Maizière enjoyed productive cooperation for only a few weeks. After that a permanent election campaign was set in motion.

In their coalition pact of April 12, the CDU, the DSU, Democratic Awakening, the Liberals, the German Forum Party, the League of Free Democrats, the FDP, and the SPD had agreed that the GDR should become part of the Federal Republic in accordance with Article 23 of the Basic Law. The coalition saw as its task to promote "the process of German unification with parliamentary participation."

In the spring of 1990 a working party commissioned by the central Roundtable presented its draft of a new constitution for the GDR. All the parties which had taken part in the Roundtable had shared responsibility for this draft, which could also be seen as a possible future all-German constitution or as an improved and modernized Basic Law. The draft constitution included a detailed catalogue of fundamental rights, formulated constitutionally-guaranteed aims such as the right to work and the protection of the environment, and provided provisions for the use of plebiscites.[20] In view of the "peaceful revolution" in the GDR, the overemphasis on the principle of representation in the Basic Law—born of an historical mistrust of the sovereign citizen—seemed out of date. The Roundtable draft emphasized the direct participation of all citizens in the business of government.

The freely-elected Volkskammer faced the question of whether it should adopt this draft. This document reflected the aims of the political groups that had emerged during the fall of 1989. However, the Volkskammer ultimately eschewed a wholesale constitutional reform. In its first session, it symbolically deleted the preamble to the old constitution of the GDR, in which reference was made to a "developed socialist society," but subsequently it could not agree either on the Roundtable's draft constitution or on a new draft. The coalition pact had left open the possibility of working out a new constitution for the GDR in which fundamental social rights—above all, the right to work, housing, and education—were to be anchored. If no new constitution could be devised, these aspects were to be incorporated in the Federal Republic's Basic Law. The coalition called for the unification process to be organized "rapidly and in a responsible manner" and according to the rule of law. Transitional legal arrangements were supposed to take into account elements of the old GDR constitution of 1949 as well as of the Roundtable's constitutional draft.[21] Time never permitted such arrangements.

At its fifteenth meeting on 17 June 1990, the Volkskammer approved new constitutional principles. These canceled all legal provisions in the GDR which placed the individual citizen or state institutions under an obligation to socialism, "socialist law," and "democratic centralism." In order to make monetary, economic, and social union with the Federal Republic possible, they also determined that the GDR could transfer its sovereign rights to international institutions as well as institutions of the Federal Republic. The GDR was described as a "free, democratic, federal, socially-conscious, and ecologically-oriented state governed by the rule of law" in which local self-government was guaranteed. The principles provided for free collective bargaining, economic freedom, private ownership, an independent judiciary, and the protection of the environment.[22] They created the framework for producing the two most important documents that were to determine how the unification of the two German states was to be implemented: the "State Treaty on Monetary, Economic, and Social Union" of 18 May 1990 and the "Unification Treaty" of 31 August 1990.

The State Treaty on Monetary, Economic, and Social Union

Control of the budget is the prerequisite for autonomous action by any political community. In the early summer of 1990 the economic and social situation in the GDR had become so dismal that politicians saw no alternative than ending the sovereignty of the GDR by handing over responsibility for financial policy to the Federal Republic. By approving new constitutional principles, the Volkskammer had created the necessary legal framework for concluding a "State Treaty" between the Federal Republic and the GDR that resulted in a monetary, economic, and social union on 1 July 1990.[23] At the urging of the federal government, discussions had been conducted with the Modrow government since 20 February. At the time of union, discussions about possible methods of monetary union and confederation were still in progress.

Later, however, tens of thousands had left the GDR for the Federal Republic each month, attracted by better economic circumstances and social opportunities. The abolition of the GDR's currency and the introduction of the D-Mark were intended to bring the flow of emigrants to a standstill and create the right conditions for the recovery of the GDR economy. But it was also a signal that the unification of Germany was to be completed quickly. It also meant the end of the GDR, and this is how it was seen by the majority of the population. As the GDR Minister of Finance, Walter Romberg, stated in the Volkskammer, the end of monetary sovereignty meant the loss of a fundamental part of "economic sovereignty and therefore also of political sovereignty."[24] The introduction of the D-Mark thus became the "brand label of the unification process."[25]

Many of the Federal Republic's laws immediately applied in the GDR. Former GDR laws were rescinded, and the Volkskammer was obliged to pass new laws to ensure an orderly transition.[26] Even before formal unification was completed, cooperation between authorities took place "in accordance with international law," the possibility of legal protection was created, and a mutual government commission was formed for the implementation of the State Treaty. The State Treaty was explicitly conceived as the first step on the path leading to the unification of the two German states. Its preamble declares that the parties to the treaty are determined "to achieve immediately and in freedom the unification of Germany within a European peace order."[27]

The Treaty ended all discussion about whether certain elements of the GDR's socioeconomic system should be retained. It described the "social market economy" as the economic system common to both states and even provided a definition: "It is characterized in particular by private ownership, competition, the free setting of prices, and as a matter of principle the free movement of labor, capital, goods, and services." Only after the GDR government intervened was it stipulated that this did "not exclude the legal authorization of certain forms of ownership which would allow the participation of government or of other bodies in economic affairs as long as this does not discriminate against private bodies."[28]

The GDR representatives also argued successfully for the inclusion in the treaty of the statement that "social union forms an integrated whole with monetary and economic union." The original formulation had specified that the "social community" "supplemented" monetary and economic union.[29] These statements were of concrete significance only to the extent that a series of measures were envisaged which were to soften the impact of a direct transition to a market economy. In particular special provisions were made in the field of industrial law, and these remained in force in the eastern part of Germany even after unification had formally taken place.

Volkskammer delegates conducted a controversial debate about the State Treaty. In particular members of Alliance 90 and the PDS reproached the government for not having guaranteed through the Treaty the equal participation of GDR citizens and for simply taking over the political and social system of the Federal Republic. In a particularly animated session of the Volkskammer, an Alliance 90 representative maintained that the GDR was being transferred to the Federal Republic "under the domination of the social system which has developed there."[30] By contrast, the government coalition painted a positive picture of the opportunities presented by the Treaty. Against the background of the catastrophic economic situation in the *Länder* of the former GDR, the expectations of the de Maizière government's chief negotiator, Günter Krause, appear unduly optimistic: "The State Treaty creates the necessary framework for a rapid transition from a socialist command economy to a social market economy in all spheres of the economy. . . . The restructuring of the economy and of agriculture will rapidly improve productivity at the workplace and in the future create modern, secure jobs which are above all not a danger to health."[31]

At the signing of the Treaty, Prime Minister de Maizière proclaimed: "No one will be worse off than before. On the contrary!" Later it was often quoted as an example of the hope and naiveté with which the introduction of the market economy was awaited. Similarly, Federal Chancellor Helmut Kohl stressed that no one would be expected to suffer "unreasonable hardships."[32]

The parties involved in the de Maizière government agreed that there was no political alternative to monetary union. But there were serious differences about how to ensure that there were no negative social consequences. The minister of finance, a member of the SPD, pointed repeatedly to the ominous state of public finances, while the minister of social affairs warned about mass unemployment. The SPD party whip believed that there was a prospect not of long-term mass unemployment but only of a "lengthy search for work."[33]

Opposition spokesmen in the Volkskammer and Bundestag were not the only critics of optimistic expectations. Leading economists—for example, those representing the German Bundesbank—had also expressed reservations about whether the economy of the GDR could cope with the shock of the sudden impact of the laws of the market and believed that the consequences for the Federal Republic's economic competitiveness were unpredictable.[34] That these reservations were justified became apparent very shortly after economic and monetary union: The expected investment by western firms did not take place. GDR companies, which had been previously represented in western markets because their prices were politically supported, were no longer competitive. In Eastern Europe, Comecon's market collapsed.

An objective discussion of these problems was rendered more difficult by the fact that the question of the social consequences of monetary union and the "costs of unification" started to dominate the election campaign. Not until the end of February 1991, when the GDR had become history and the smoke of several election campaigns had dissipated, was it possible to perceive the economic and social misery in what had once been the GDR. Only now did government and opposition begin seriously to consider what it would mean if the division of Germany into two states were replaced by a long-term economic and social division. In a statement to the Bundestag, Chancellor Helmut Kohl demanded the achievement of equal living standards in the immediate years ahead—a demand which the SPD opposition had placed at the focus of its electoral campaign in 1990.[35]

The State Treaty was seen by Germany's neighbors as containing more than certain economic and social provisions. They perceived it as the first decisive step toward the restoration of Germany as one state. Not surprisingly, even prior to the unification of the two German states, the question of

Germany's border with Poland become part of the political agenda. While in the Federal Republic this led to a lively controversy and the federal government lost much of its credibility by a lengthy silence on the matter, political forces in the GDR were of the unanimous view that the western border of Poland was inviolable. The Volkskammer and the Bundestag approved, alongside with the State Treaty, a resolution on the German-Polish border guaranteeing that the border will remain inviolable in the future and that no territorial claims will be raised.

Unification Treaty

How fragile political circumstances in the GDR were in the summer of 1990 is documented by one day in the Volkskammer. On the symbolic date of 17 June, the anniversary of the 1953 uprising in the GDR, the DSU formally moved the immediate accession of the GDR to the Federal Republic. For very different reasons—namely to bring to an end a "lawless situation"—a representative of Alliance 90 submitted a similar argument.[36]

Although the State Treaty had de facto rescinded the sovereignty of the GDR, it continued to exist in international law. In a formal sense the Treaty was one between the Federal Republic and the GDR, but in real terms it was a constitutional treaty which nullified large parts of GDR law.[37] If the planned accession of the GDR to the Federal Republic was not to be tantamount to an *Anschluß*, then the proper basis for an ordered accession would have to be created in a second State Treaty.

On 23 August, after long and agonizing public discussions about methods and timetable of the process, the Volkskammer announced the accession of the GDR to the Federal Republic. Accession was based on the following conditions: that the planned second State Treaty (the "Unification Treaty") was concluded; that the "Two-Plus-Four" Talks had reached the stage of finalizing the foreign and security policies and preconditions of German unity; and that work on reestablishing the *Länder* was sufficiently advanced to enable Landtag elections to take place on 14 October. The Unification Treaty was signed on 31 August. On 23 September, both the Bundestag (with 440 votes in favor, 47 against, and 3 abstentions) and the Volkskammer (with 299 in favor, 80 opposed, and 1 abstention) approved the Unification Treaty. The upper house of the Federal Republic, the Bundesrat, had already given its unanimous approval on 21 September.[38]

While the first State Treaty was concerned above all with the reform of the economic system, the Unification Treaty embraces all other areas of the law—including constitutional, administrative, criminal, European Community and international law. On approximately nine hundred typed pages, almost everything was sorted out—from party law to provisions dealing with the files of the State Security Service (*Stasi*), to the provisions of the law on the transport of seeds, to the decision that the registrar in Registry Office I in Berlin (West) is now the registrar in Registry Office I in Berlin.

The ambitious treaty, however, was not without considerable gaps. For instance, local authorities were scarcely mentioned in the Treaty, and this subsequently led to considerable problems. At the beginning of 1991, most local authorities in the new *Länder* were faced with bankruptcy. The Unification Treaty also did not ensure the rapid installment of an efficient administration. The combination of a lack of finances and of qualified personnel proved a considerable obstacle to the unification process. To some extent administrations are having to work with the same people as before but are now guided and controlled by Western advisers. Given the much less satisfactory remuneration and the poorer quality of life in the towns and communities of the eastern *Länder*, administration experts from the old Federal Republic initially showed little interest in changing their places of work. The training of new experts in administration will take time.

Since the federal government believed it would be able to finance the cost of unification through a special fund called "German Unity,"[39] it made special provisions until the end of 1994 for financing the *Länder* of the former GDR. This means that the new federal states were excluded from horizontal equalization, the so-called *Länderfinanzausgleich*, the system of financial redistribution which is meant to ensure that no major disparities are to be found between the poorer and the more wealthy parts of Germany's federal system.[40] It was hoped that citizens of the old Federal Republic could be spared additional burdens and that former citizens of the GDR would be satisfied with a gradual improvement in their standard of living.

In the view of Minister President Manfred Stolpe of Brandenburg, the Unification Treaty has one cardinal defect: "the conscious or unconscious underestimation of the financial requirements of the new *Länder* and local authorities." It had lasted a very long time, Stolpe added, before this was realized.[41]

Moreover, it became apparent that it was unrealistic to assume the economy in the new *Länder* would very quickly experience a boom. The opposite was true. The transition from a centrally-run economy to a market economy is proving so difficult that at the beginning of 1991 the federal government had to subject its previous policy to radical change. Major economic provisions of the Unification Treaty had proven to be illusory. The political success story which saw the realization of Germany's unity into one state has yet to be followed by economic and above all social unity— that is, by the equality of living conditions that is guaranteed by the Basic Law.

If the division of Germany is not to be replaced by a long-lasting social division, policies are required which do not kow-tow to the interests of particular electorates or party clients. These decisions will also fundamentally change life in the old Federal Republic. The unity of Germany as one state has been completed. The process of unifying two very different German societies has just begun.

Conclusion

The short time during which the GDR pursued its own democratic form of government was shaped by the conflicts surrounding the accession to the Federal Republic of Germany and the continuing electoral campaign. The process, the turnout, and the outcome of the elections in 1990 proved a clear affirmation of Western-style democracy. In March 1990, the electorate voted for a quick change. The vote signified a radical break with the GDR's political, economic, social, and cultural past and expressed the hope that life would soon be like that in the West—that is, a life in political freedom and economic prosperity. Having grown up in a society that took care of its citizens from the "cradle to the grave," most citizens in the GDR were unfamiliar with the risks associated with this new kind of life. Grassroots citizens' movements, which had opposed quick unification, and the SPD, which had favored it, both emphasized the need for policies that would cushion the rough transition to a market economy in the GDR. Christian Democratic and Liberal politicians, in contrast, gave the impression that monetary union, based on the introduction of the West German mark, would automatically guarantee an economic improvement. Initial optimism turned to deep resignation when the economic situation worsened in the summer and early fall of 1990.

Political forces recognized the shift in opinion. The SPD tried to use the shift to its favor during the election campaign in the fall of 1990 by emphasizing the negative social consequences of unification. The CDU succeeded in pushing for an early election date in order to avoid being victimized by the economic disaster that was in the offing.

Conflicts surrounding the date of the election and the electoral procedures led to the collapse of the grand coalition in the GDR in late summer. Initially the GDR government had favored unification after all-German elections, claiming that this would ensure a truly democratic transition. Despite these assurances, the date of unification was moved up to a date before the all-German election. The new GDR political elite's actions seemed ever more driven by electoral tactics of western origin than by the intention to act as interest representatives of its citizens.

The population in the GDR recognized this. However, they still voted for political parties that were either modeled after those in the West or had joined forces with parties in the West. It was expected that this would create a party system similar to the one that had proven successful in the West, thereby alleviating the difficult transition process. At the same time, this development created a variety of problems.

The new political order was not one that had evolved; it had simply been adopted. The representatives of the West were and are still not sufficiently familiar with the circumstances and conditions in the former GDR. The adoption of the legal system, institutions, modes of behavior, and routinized procedures from the West will confirm the inequality between East and West for the foreseeable future. For a long time to come, new institutions will be perceived as "alien," in particular since their executive positions are largely staffed with people from the West.

One needs to remember that the citizens of the Federal Republic needed about twenty years to shed their authority-oriented behavior of the more distant past and to become accustomed to democratic norms and forms of behavior. It is an advantage of the former GDR, in particular when compared with its neighbors in Central and Eastern Europe, that a system of democratic institutions is already in place and is not seriously questioned.

Notes

1. Ralf Dahrendorf, *Reflections on the Revolution in Europe in a Letter to have been sent to a Gentleman in Warsaw* (New York: Random House, 1990), 105.

2. Cf. Juan Linz, "Transition to Democracy," *Washington Quarterly*, 13 (1990): 143-64.

3. The first position was adopted above all by the German Social Union *(Deutsche Soziale Union/DSU)* and the second by the successor party of the SED, the Party of Democratic Socialism *(Partei des Demokratischen Sozialismus/PDS)*.

4. For a more detailed discussion of the initial development of political groups and parties, see chapter 5 by Michaela W. Richter.

5. *Politische Parteien und Bewegungen der DDR über sich selbst. Handbuch* (Berlin: Staatsverlag, 1990), 12.

6. Peter Schmidt, "Erster Parteitag der CDU Deutschlands in Hamburg," *Deutschland Archiv*, 22 (1990): 1662-64.

7. *Politische Parteien und Bewegungen*, 55.

8. "Für ein liberales Deutschland," *Das Parlament*, 17-24 August 1990.

9. Gerhard Rein, ed., *Die Opposition in der DDR. Entwürfe für einen anderen Sozialismus* (Berlin: Wichern-Verlag, 1989), 84-90.

10. Cited in Helmut Müller-Enbergs, "Volkskammerwahlen in der DDR 1990–Synopse von (Wahl-)Programmen 15 kandidierender Parteien," *Berliner Arbeitshefte und Berichte zur sozialwissenschaftlichen Forschung,* 28: 11.

11. "Eine eminente Fehlentscheidung." Interview with Oskar Lafontaine, *Der Spiegel,* 28 May 1990: 26-29.

12. "Zur Wiederherstellung der Einheit der Sozialdemokratischen Partei Deutschlands," *Vorwärts,* 10 (1990).

13. Cited in Müller-Enbergs, "Volkskammerwahlen," 6.

14. See Alf Mintzel, *Die CSU. Anatomie einer konservativen Partei* (Opladen: Westdeutscher Verlag, 1975).

15. *Politische Parteien und Bewegungen,* 18.

16. "Offener Brief an alle Bürgerbewegten," *Die Tageszeitung,* 23 July 1990.

17. See Gert-Joachim Glaeßner, ed., *Die DDR in der Ära Honecker. Politik–Gesellschaft–Kultur* (Opladen: Westdeutscher Verlag, 1989).

18. Siegfried Grundmann, "Außen- und Binnenmigration der DDR 1989. Versuch einer Bilanz," *Deutschland Archiv* 22 (1990): 1422-32; Siegfried Grundmann and Ines Schmidt, "Wanderungsbewegungen in der DDR 1989," *Berliner Arbeitshefte und Berichte zur sozialwissenschaftlichen Forschung,* 30 (1990).

19. Wolfgang Templin, "Eine bittere Lektion," in *Bündnis 2000. Forum für Demokratie, Ökologie und Menschenrechte,* 1 (1990): 7.

20. *Entwurf. Verfassung der Deutschen Demokratischen Republik. Arbeitsgruppe "Neue Verfassung der DDR" des Runden Tisches* (Berlin: Staatsverlag, 1990).

21. Bundesminister für innerdeutsche Beziehungen, ed., *Informationen, Beilage,* 8 (1990).

22. *Frankfurter Rundschau,* 18 May 1990.

23. *Vertrag über die Schaffung einer Währungs-, Wirtschafts- und Sozialunion zwischen der Bundesrepublik Deutschland und der Deutschen Demokratischen Republik vom 18.5.1990* (BGBl. II, 537).

24. Volkskammer der Deutschen Demokratischen Republik, 10. Wahlperiode, Special Session (8th Session, 21 May 1990): 211.

25. Karl Otto Pöhl, "Das Diktat der Stunde ließ längeres Warten nicht zu. Zwei Währungsunionen–Die Sicht der Bundesbank," *Frankfurter Rundschau,* 4 July 1990.

26. Appendixes to the State Treaty.

27. Treaty on Monetary, Economic, and Social Union; see Appendix 3.

28. State Treaty, Art.1, 3.

29. State Treaty, Art.1,4; "Wie die Bundesrepublik sich einen Vertrag mit der DDR vorstellt. Das 'Arbeitspapier' über die Währungsunion, Wirtschafts- und Sozialgemeinschaft," *Frankfurter Rundschau,* 26 April 1990.

30. Volkskammer der Deutschen Demokratischen Republik, 10. Wahlperiode, 16th Session (21 June 1990): 576.

31. Volkskammer der Deutschen Demokratischen Republik, 10. Wahlperiode, 16th Session (21 June 1990): 568.

32. *Frankfurter Rundschau,* 19 May 1990.

33. Volkskammer der Deutschen Demokratischen Republik, 10. Wahlperiode, Special Session (8th Session, 21 May 1989): 218.

34. Karl Otto Pöhl, quoted in *Frankfurter Rundschau,* 4 July 1990.

35. "Regierungserklärung und Bundestagsdebatte," *Das Parlament,* 41 (1991); "Eine eminente Fehlentscheidung," *Der Spiegel,* 28 May 1990: 26-29.

36. Volkskammer der Deutschen Demokratischen Republik, 10. Wahlperiode, 15. Session (Special Session, 17 June 1989): 536.

37. Ingo von Münch, ed., *Die Verträge zur deutschen Einheit* (Munich: Beck, 1990), xv-xvi.

38. "Vertrag zwischen der Bundesrepublik Deutschland und der Deutschen Demokratischen Republik über die Herstellung der Einheit Deutschlands—Einigungsvertrag vom 31.8.1990, BGBl. II, 889," in *Die Verträge zur deutschen Einheit,* 43-569.

39. Gesetz über die Errichtung eines Fonds "Deutsche Einheit" vom 25. Juni 1990, BGBl. 1990 II, 518.

40. Unification Treaty; see Appendix 4.

41. Manfred Stolpe, "Wir fordern nur das Notwendigste zum Überleben," *Frankfurter Allgemeine Zeitung,* 18 February 1991.

7

An Unwelcome Enlargement?
The European Community and
German Unification

Andreas Falke

The integration of the former GDR into the European Community (EC) has been an unusually smooth process. It did not stir many waves and never really held the headlines for long. It thus bore little resemblance to the contentious enlargement of the EC in the 1970s when Britain, Ireland and Denmark joined. Even before actual completion of German unification on 3 October 1990, the GDR was made a nominal part of the EC. This occurred on 1 July 1990 with the signing of the State Treaty establishing German monetary, economic, and social union between the two German states. Given that the GDR had been one of the most devoted members of the communist bloc, with a very rigid political structure and command economy, this outcome is quite surprising.

Considering the unusual acceleration of political time in 1990, characterized by Werner Weidenfeld as "a movie in fast motion,"[1] it is important to remember that each step in the unification process might not have proceeded with such speed and with so few traps and obstacles. This is also true for the EC's reaction (especially that of the principal member states) to the unification process, as specific steps of GDR integration had considerable potential for a variety of risks and conflicts. From the view of the European Community, four issues might have given cause to protracted conflict and discussion:

- For the EC, the GDR was something of a nondescript entity. The EC had no direct relationship with the GDR but, rather, a relationship that worked indirectly through West Germany's ties to the GDR. The basis of this relationship was the privileged "intra-German trade" (IGT) arrangement. The IGT was actually a source of irritation to West Germany's EC partners, who tended to view the GDR with disfavor.

- Another potential problem could have been the projection of British and French uneasiness into Community decisionmaking. A political-psychological resistance to unification was likely, and such attitudes were expressed more or less openly by political leaders and commentators from the two World War II victors.
- Equally plausible was a long and tortuous debate about the costs and burdens of integrating a structurally-obsolete and inflexible economy into the EC economy. During the adjustment process it could be anticipated that, in all likelihood, the GDR economy would evolve into one of the major crisis regions of the EC and thus compete with economically weaker countries for scarce EC aid funds. Reluctance, if not resistance, was to be expected from countries such as Greece, Portugal, Spain, and Ireland.
- As long as continuing, independent statehood of the GDR was a possibility, formal membership would have been the principal option.[2] This option would have been subject to much debate, complicating negotiations and violating the commitment not to burden the creation of the Single Market by accepting new members.[3]

In short, a significant potential existed in the EC context for blocking a constructive German unification process and avoiding the challenges that the GDR posed. It is also conceivable that these four isolated factors could have coalesced to generate a united front of rejection. Even temporary resistance would have burdened the Federal Republic's relationship with its EC partners and would have subjected European Community institutions to serious conflicting pressures. Any attempt to block GDR integration or to slow down the pace of unification through mobilizing EC resistance would actually have led to a situation in which Germany might have been forced to choose between unification or preserving and deepening the ties with its European partners. Should unification ever become a real possibility, according to many observers, this was a likely scenario. The underlying thesis was that German unification and European integration were incompatible processes and that any prospect of unification would draw the Germans inevitably toward a nationalist path of separatism. Given the existence of the communist bloc, some commentators assumed that unification and European integration were exclusionary and incompatible processes.[4] On the basis of that assumption, the prospect of German unification should have had an explosive potential for the European Community.

By historical standards, the fear that Germany would loosen its attachment to the EC when given an opportunity for unification was not altogether unfounded. During the negotiations of the Treaty of Rome in 1957, the West German government had declared that Germany would reserve its right to review the treaties concerning the Common Market and Euratom in the event of unification. The Adenauer government assumed that German unification would be compatible with Community membership but at the same time wanted to keep all options open. The assumption was that a reunited Germany would be part of the EC, as Foreign Ministry Undersecretary Hallstein explained before the West German parliament in March 1957.[5] But he stipulated that it would have to request a renegotiation of the treaty.

In retrospect, the obstacles to integration were not insurmountable, nor did German unification prove incompatible with German membership in the European Community or even a deepening of European integration. The integration of the GDR into the EC was pushed forward by the seeming inevitability of the unification process, and it benefited from the favorable East-West foreign policy environment. One of the preconditions for its acceptance by the international community at large was that unification actually became a process of "dual integration."[6] In the end, the EC's enlargement through German economic and monetary union and the final integration of the GDR upon unification was a smooth and non-controversial act of unspectacular administrative ratification.[7]

This chapter will analyze the discussion and decisionmaking processes leading to GDR integration into the European Community. The implementation of the most important administrative and regulatory steps will be described and the risks and liabilities of these steps evaluated. In a final section, I will highlight the role of the unified Germany in the European Community. The starting point will be an account of EC relations under communism.

European Community Relations Before the Collapse of the Communist Regime

Prior to 1990, relations between the EC and the GDR had been defined indirectly through West Germany's trading relationship with the GDR. Due to Soviet hostility toward European integration, the European Community did not maintain diplomatic relations with the GDR or with Comecon. Although the Soviet Union began to accept the EC as a political reality in the early 1970s, many problems prevented the establishment of formal relations between the EC and Comecon. One obstacle was the inclusion of West Berlin in any formal agreement, as part of the Community under the Treaty of Rome. Another obstacle rested with the legal power of Comecon. Since Comecon had no jurisdiction over foreign trade, the feasibility of bilateral treaties seemed questionable. Finally, the deteriorating

East-West climate after the Soviet invasion of Afghanistan brought any formal contacts between the European Community and Comecon to a halt.[8] It took a Gorbachev initiative in May 1985 and the thaw in East-West relations to restart the negotiations, leading on 25 June 1988 to a joint declaration on cooperation between the EC and Comecon and an agreement to establish formal diplomatic relations. The Berlin problem was solved by not mentioning the city in the text; instead, the agreement was valid for the entire area under EC jurisdiction. The lack of Comecon jurisdiction in foreign trade was circumvented by a "parallel approach," i.e., bilateral trade agreements with individual Comecon countries were to be negotiated. Following the declaration, the EC established official diplomatic relations with the GDR in August 1988, and the GDR announced its intention to conclude a trade agreement with the European Community.[9] This trade and cooperation agreement was negotiated during the political upheavals that led to the downfall of the communist regime. The agreement was signed in May 1990, when the end of the GDR was already in sight, but was overshadowed by events and never took effect. Thus, there never was a formal framework for the EC-GDR relationship.[10]

Through all the years before unification, intra-German trade (IGT) shaped the EC-GDR relationship. From the inception of the Federal Republic, the West German government had insisted the GDR could not be considered a foreign country. Therefore the trade between them could not be treated as foreign trade. Consequently, commercial relations between the two German states were handled as domestic commerce—that is, no tariffs, quotas or other barriers existed for GDR goods and services. Technically, with a few exceptions, the GDR had free access to the largest market in the Community and was frequently called the thirteenth member state.[11] This situation was in clear contradiction to Article 227 of the Treaty of Rome, which stipulates that every country not a signatory to the Treaty be considered a third party to which the common foreign trade powers to the European Community apply.[12] However, the West German government viewed IGT as the most important tie between the two Germanys. Having finally accepted the GDR as a sovereign state in the Basic Treaty between the two Germanys (*Grundlagenvertrag*), IGT remained as one of the clearest expressions of German togetherness. It proved to be a stabilizing element in the relationship, and the economic benefits of this arrangement for the GDR were evident. Therefore, in 1957, the West German government insisted upon the inclusion of a protocol to the Treaty of Rome which legitimized the IGT system. As such, the protocol was primary EC law, i.e., akin to constitutional quality and not amendable by unilateral declaration of members states or any provisions in the Single European Act. Paragraph one of the protocol states that no change is necessary in the trading relationship after the signing of the Treaty of Rome and that IGT will be considered domestic trade. Paragraph two allows bilateral trade agreements with non-German EC member states and obliges members to avoid injuries and damages to the economies of member states that might arise from their trade with the GDR. This passage called for particular circumspection and restraint on part of the West German government. Finally, paragraph three allows the implementation of safeguard measures by member governments for possible injuries as a result of IGT.[13]

Under the protocol, the West German government maintained that goods from East Germany could be traded freely within the entire Community without extra levies imposed on them.[14] But this arrangement was a sore point for West Germany's EC partners. Particularly after the Basic Treaty between the two Germanys was signed, critics from these countries viewed the domestic trading relationship as a black hole in the EC's external front. In particular, they feared market disruption through the illegal export of goods from other Comecon countries in the guise of IGT. Other targets of criticism were the "swing"—an interest-free line of credit (800 million DM in 1988)—which the GDR enjoyed for the short-term financing of its imports, the absence of all tariffs, and a value-added tax rebate for German importers. It was noted that 75 percent of all EC trade with the GDR was between the GDR and West Germany.[15] The criticism, however, was hardly justified. The West German government itself took stringent measures to contain damage, as mandated by paragraph two of the protocol. Measures were taken to guarantee that only goods of German origin were part of the trade between the two Germanys. At times, six-month bans on certain goods were instituted. The re-export of agricultural products was banned altogether. In the case of re-exports, the value-added tax had to be paid. For certain goods, quotas were introduced to protect German as well as other EC producers. Moreover, EC anti-dumping laws were applicable to IGT. Yet these protective measures did not satisfy neighboring EC states such as France, Denmark and the Benelux countries, which eventually provided no import licenses for any goods originating from IGT.[16]

In retrospect, the discussion about the special relationship between the two Germanys appears like much ado about nothing. Only 0.02-0.8 percent of East German goods were re-exported, and IGT made up only 1.5 percent of all West German trade. Also, of the DM 800 million line of credit, the GDR only used DM 265 million in 1988, since it wanted to avoid financial dependence on the West.[17] The true problem of IGT at the end of the 1980s was its stagnation. IGT was, to say the least, a reflection of the decreasing competitiveness of the GDR and a precursor of its economic collapse. In its trading relationships, the GDR increasingly resembled a developing country which exchanged raw materials and unfinished goods as well as standard mass consumer goods against sophisticated investment goods. The trading relationship was complementary and contained little inter-industry trade. Particularly in the traditional mass consumer goods markets (e.g., furniture, textiles, and apparel), the GDR experienced severe setbacks. Poor quality, untimely delivery of desired quantities, and an absence of marketing skills, distribution channels, and proper advertising typified the problems. The GDR economy was losing its ability to produce marketable products at competitive prices.[18]

It is interesting to note that few experts properly read the signals emanating from the development of IGT. Experiencing immense structural problems in the economy, the GDR was faced with the prospect that it would be unable to meet the increased competitive pressures after the completion of the Single Market in 1993. Germany's EC partners feared that—with the elimination of border controls under the Single Market—the safeguard measures would no longer be effective. But, considering the weakness of the GDR economy,[19] these fears seemed unwarranted. Even without unification, the coming of the Single Market and the East German economy's severe structural problems would have required assistance programs that dwarfed the problems IGT posed for Germany's EC partners. Even before unification, West Germany initiated a massive multi-billion DM program of environmental and infrastructural modernization in East Germany.[20] This would have been the only way for East Germany to survive in the Single Market. Speculation about consequences is difficult, but the outcome most likely would have been increased GDR dependence on West Germany.

National Interests and GDR Integration

With the impending collapse of the communist regime in the GDR and the prospect of German unification in 1989, perceptions of divergent national interests dominated the agenda in Europe. This development was primarily fueled by a belief that German unification would tip the political balance in Europe—and therefore inevitably within the EC. The prospect of unification initially caused great uneasiness not only in France and Great Britain but also among smaller EC partners such as the Netherlands. Memories of Germany's imperial aspirations gave rise to fears of a return of a German Reich. For France and Great Britain, the continued existence of two German states was the best way to safeguard their national interests. Great Britain's reluctance was vividly expressed in Prime Minister

Margaret Thatcher's skeptical attitude toward German unification, culminating in her meeting with various British German experts during which somber scenarios were forecast. This attitude was typified in a newspaper interview with British Minister of Trade and Industry Nicholas Ridley, in which he called the proposed European Monetary Union "a German racket designed to take over the whole of Europe."[21] Margaret Thatcher indicated publicly that the upheavals in the GDR would negatively affect the functioning of the EC and that slowing of the integration process was called for. Without stating it publicly, she feared that German unification would accelerate the process of European integration. Indeed, that was precisely what happened. Aside from initially hoping to retain some of the allied powers' residual rights, Thatcher preferred to rely on NATO as an instrument to be used jointly with the Americans to control a united Germany. Thatcher's inability to play the EC card left her in an awkward situation in which she had less influence over the process than might have been expected.

France, in particular its political elite, was also caught off-guard by the prospect of German unification. France's displeasure about German unification came to the fore in the angry reaction to Chancellor Helmut Kohl's failure to inform President Mitterrand in advance of his Ten-Point Program of November 1989. The plan outlined a basis for intensified cooperation between the two Germanys, but it also contained references to future confederate structures or a federation, i.e., a federal government system.[22] Chancellor Kohl's vague allusion to German unification, which was carefully couched in terms of adherence to the firm commitments to supranational structures, prompted President Mitterrand to take the bold step of a state visit to the GDR on 20 December 1989 as if to confirm his wish for the continued existence of that state. Contrary to British concerns regarding the effects of integration on the EC, France feared a slowdown of the process, particularly the formation of a monetary union. Events also revived French concerns about a disproportionate German economic influence in the EC, which would be reflected in greater German political power in EC decisionmaking.[23] When emotional reactions to German unification had subsided, Mitterrand embarked on a course of committing Germany to a deepening of European integration, i.e., to political and monetary union. France came to see the EC as an instrument to contain Germany within a European framework, an approach that Britain initially did not consider as an option.[24] There was considerable likelihood of intense nationalistic debate over EC-GDR integration, given the responses of Germany's major western partners to prospects of unification following the revolution in the GDR. The projection of national interests into the EC debate on integrating East Germany was a real possibility until the first few months of 1990.

National interests also shaped the policy of many smaller member states. The economically weaker EC countries such as Greece, Portugal, Spain and Ireland had strong misgivings about GDR integration into the EC framework. Whatever mode of EC-GDR relationship developed, they feared West Germany would concentrate all of its resources on the economic reconstruction of the GDR, leaving fewer resources for West German investment in their economies. Such investment would bring substantial benefits subsequent to the removal of all barriers for investment and services under the Single Market program. Even greater were their concerns that integration of the GDR into the EC system of financial transfers and aid programs would burden these systems to their own disadvantage. On the budgetary side, for instance, Germany is a net payer into the EC budget, contributing, for example, 11,110 million ecu in 1989 but only receiving 4,580 million ecu in return, most of which is for agriculture.[25] Spain, in contrast, has an even balance (3,575 vs. 3,544), while Portugal (458 vs. 946), Greece (566 vs. 2,565), and Ireland (371 vs. 1,712) are all net receivers. However, while fiscal balances are heavily dependent on the size of agricultural sectors in the member states (60 percent of the EC budget under the Common Agricultural Policy went to agriculture in the early 1990s) and therefore are somewhat distorted,[26] the situation with respect to the structural aid funds—consisting of the EC's Regional Fund, Social Fund, and Agricultural Fund—is much clearer. Spain, for instance, receives almost a quarter of the $75 billion allocated to the structural funds until 1993, which had been doubled in 1988 as a way to induce the weaker states to agree to the Single Market program.[27] Economically weaker states feared that with the GDR's integration into the EC, Germany would cease to be the greatest single net-contributor and that substantial portions of the structural funds would be diverted to East Germany.[28] This imminent development affected the weaker member states even more as they already felt increasingly marginalized by the "big four" (Germany, Great Britain, France, and Italy) which participate in the G-7 economic summits and other G-7 decisionmaking forums that appear to have more impact on the world economy than EC policy initiatives.[29]

Any form of integration of the GDR also seemed like a stumbling block for a reform of the EC budgetary and fiscal system. Weaker countries such as Spain called for establishing an equalizing budgetary fund of transfers to those countries whose GNP is below 90 percent of the average and a progressive taxation system with contributions by member states measured by their relative economic strength, a system actually modeled after *Finanzausgleich* (fiscal equalization) between the German *Länder*.[30]

The costs of a formal EC-GDR relationship were clearly on the minds of Germany's other EC partners, as such a move would affect their positions on the economic ladder of the Community. For this reason the Netherlands and Belgium opposed formal EC membership for the GDR and France showed strong reservations. As long as the GDR continued to exist as a sovereign state, these members preferred an "association" with the GDR, even if a monetary and economic union between West Germany and the GDR was on the horizon. The standard rationale for this position was that other countries such as Austria and Turkey, which had already applied for membership, deserved preference.[31]

EC Debate About GDR Integration:
The Role of the European Commission

Integrating the GDR into the EC has to be understood within the institutional context of EC decisionmaking. The right to initiate legislation lies with the European Commission, which accords the Commission a prominent policymaking role. However, the effective legislature of the EC is the Council of Ministers, which represents the single member states. When substantial issues like treaty changes are at stake, representation is through the heads-of-government via the European Council. The Council of Ministers, in which each member state has voting strength nominally proportional to its size, adopts measures, except for cases of existential importance to a member state, by qualified majority vote.[32] The European Parliament is the third actor in the legislative process. Previously it had only an advisory role, but since the adoption of the Single European Act in 1986 it has increased its clout. In particular, it has the right to veto and amend Council positions on issues of Single Market and structural policy. The veto, however, can be overruled by the Council of Ministers by unanimous vote, and amendments can be disregarded by the Commission or the Council in the final stages of the legislative process. The Parliament plays an important and equal role in approving countries' formal membership or association applications. Although the decisionmaking process has become much more complex, the old adage is still true that the Commission proposes and the Council disposes. However, all too frequently the Council of Ministers acted as a brake, delaying or not making decisions at all.[33]

Final decisionmaking in the EC lies with the European Council (representing the European governments), and any important decision is an intergovernmental bargain between national member governments.[34] A debate influenced by diverse national interests was thus expected in the EC decision concerning the integration of East Germany. But this is not what happened. One reason was that—before national debates could begin—the Commission took the lead in formulating a response to the collapse of the GDR and began to prepare for its eventual integration into the EC system. Above all, the French President of the Commission, Jacques Delors, showed enormous foresight in dealing with the situation, spearheading and facilitating the integration of the GDR into the EC. Delors chose an offensive approach to the issue, an approach that was not supported by all of the Commissioners. Immediately after the Berlin Wall fell in November 1989, the Commission under Delors' leadership began deliberating about how to interact with a non-communist East Germany.[35] From the beginning, the discussion focused on future arrangements sought with the GDR. The debate within the Commission thus bypassed foreign policy apprehensions of the new German power status. To a large extent, this was due to Jacques Delors' leadership and alacrity. A Frenchman became a leading promoter of German unity.

In contrast to the Commission, national concerns were voiced more forcefully in the European Council. Here again, Kohl's "Ten-Point Plan" and the lack of consultation with Mitterrand about it, as well as the absence of any German statement recognizing the Polish border, were all major considerations. And while the German question was not explicitly on the agenda during the special EC summit in Paris on 18 November 1989, the Strasbourg summit of 8-9 December 1989 revealed the uneasiness of Germany's EC partners, particularly France. It appeared as if this summit's central issue, the decision about European political and monetary union, would become entangled in questions concerning German unification. In the end, however, the European Council faced reality and, in a declaration on European political cooperation, it confirmed the German people's right to self-determination within existing treaties and obligations and announced the EC's intention to execute a cooperation and trade agreement with the GDR.[36] In principle, German unity had the blessing of the European Council. The statement, however, gave no indication how the Council would approach the integration of the GDR which still existed as a separate state.

The principal question then was how to integrate the GDR. This, of course, depended on a rapidly-changing political environment. Once again, the initiative came from Jacques Delors. Early on, Delors and the Commission perceived that changes in Germany would work toward German monetary and economic social union. As early as January 1990, in a speech before the European Parliament introducing the Commission's 1990 program, Delors pleaded for consideration of East Germany as a special case that should be granted membership if it so desired. Thus, he deviated from the official stance that no new membership should be considered until the Single Market was completed,[37] a position that was still held by the Council of European Foreign Ministers. In this assessment Delors was certainly helped by good contacts with the Bonn bureaucracy and by the smooth flow of information between the Bonn government and the Commission. The Commission knew that since late January 1990 experts in the Bonn finance ministry had been preparing the necessary steps for monetary, economic, and social union. Four possible scenarios existed for dealing with the GDR:

- Closer relations through a cooperation and trade agreement.
- Associate status with the EC which would extend some EC privileges to the GDR.
- Formal East German membership in the European Comunity.
- The automatic integration of the GDR through the unification of the two Germanys.[38]

Only a month later, in another speech before the European Parliament, Delors stated that the latter option was the most realistic and that it was time to think about steps to implement such an approach.[39] Delors read the situation correctly, as events that followed proved—including the formal announcement and initiation of negotiations on economic and monetary union, the outcome of the 18 March elections in the GDR, and Moscow's signals that it would accept a unified Germany. Proper evaluation of events in early February 1990 prompted the Commission to establish a "working group on German unity." This coincided with preparations for German economic and monetary union.[40] Thus, the negotiations—a milestone and the core of domestic aspects of the unification process[41]—and EC preparation for GDR integration proceeded in tandem. They actually amounted to a highly coordinated process. Senior German government officials informed the "working group" about the state of negotiations, and EC officials participated in the West German delegation's negotiation of the German economic and monetary union.[42] Close cooperation between the Commission and the West German government at the working level was buttressed by Delors' close personal relationships with Chancellor Kohl and West German Foreign Minister Hans-Dietrich Genscher.[43] Cooperation also meant that the State Treaty establishing German monetary, economic, and social union, as well as the subsequent State Treaty on German constitutional and political unity, reflected the needs and imperatives of EC law—and, conversely, that the package which the EC developed took the terms of the two German treaties fully into account.[44] In short, the EC—represented by the Commission—was not a secondary partner which could only ratify the outcomes of the German unification process but instead was an involved actor. This demonstrated how closely national and EC laws and political processes are intertwined.

Close coordination between EC and German negotiations was necessary because the compatibility of German laws with EC laws and regulations was a precondition of successful German economic and monetary union. The new union created a customs union between the GDR and the entire European Community, and the unity treaty made secondary EC law immediately applicable to all respective areas of law in East Germany, subject only to those exceptions allowed by the EC.

One crucial issue of the unification process was whether the GDR would simply accede to West Germany through Article 23 of the Basic Law or whether Germany would unify on the basis of a new constitution according to Article 146. This was of great significance for the EC, because had the latter option been chosen, the Federal Republic's EC membership would have ended and membership of a new Germany would have had to be renegotiated. Early in the process, the Commission endorsed procedures under Article 23, which meant that unification would simply extend the territory of the Federal Republic and thus of the EC. A treaty renegotiation would therefore not be necessary. In the domestic debate with the SPD about the route to unification, the Commission sided with the CDU/CSU-FDP coalition government.[45] For the EC, the procedure through Article 23 was preferable on all accounts, although, ultimately, this was a German decision.

Taking another initiative, the European Parliament established a nonpermanent committee on German unity. This committee took special interest in procedures by which the GDR would accede to the Federal Republic since, in the case of the renegotiation of the Treaty of Rome, the Parliament would have had an enhanced role in approving treaty changes on membership by absolute majority and would have had considerable procedural powers such as delay of a final decision. There was, however, no indication that the Parliament was planning to interfere with GDR integration and unification.[46] Parliament was also concerned about demands the GDR (or the new German state) could make on the structural funds after unification. For example, the research service of the European Parliament estimated that the GDR would be entitled to receive three billion DM in regional aid (one category of structural funds) annually.[47] But this problem was to be shelved since statistical indicators for calculating aid were not available and because all the funds were already committed to qualifying regions under a five-year plan.[48]

Any change in the distribution of structural funds would have required action by the Commission and the Council. Again, close cooperation of the Commission with the German government worked well in dispelling fears that GDR accession would come at the expense of structurally-weaker countries. Critics from weaker countries were silenced by West Germany's rejection of the Commission's offer of a "special GDR fund."[49] This position was confirmed in July 1990 when West German Chancellor Helmut Kohl reaffirmed that GDR accession should not diminish any existing claims.[50] The intention of both the Commission and the German government was "to keep the unification process free of all quarrels with the European Community."[51] German unification was not to disrupt the financial status quo. A formal, separate membership of the GDR in the EC probably would have been much more expensive for the EC. That is, a greater part of the burden for East German adjustments to market capitalism would have been shifted to the EC had the GDR made its claims as a sovereign country. However, as unification progressed, concerns of EC members seemed to be dealt with satisfactorily.

With the clear but unexpected victory of the CDU in the first free elections in the GDR in March 1990, the entire EC debate concerning GDR-EC relationships became subject to the dynamics of German unification and accession under Article 23 of the Basic Law. Internally, the EC was well-prepared for this development by the consistent approach of the Commission and its close cooperation with the German government. At the special European summit in Dublin in April 1990, heads of EC governments "welcomed most warmly and without reservations that German unity is enacted under a European roof."[52] The Commission presented a report outlining the major problems and steps for GDR integration.[53] As Christine Holeschovsky has pointed out,

> the core thesis of the Commission was that the integration of the GDR into the EC by way of Germany's unification will be enacted according to Art. 23. Formally, this integration of the GDR was not be understood as membership accession. For a transition period until the complete integration, technical procedures analogous to a formal accession should be operative. This construction solved two problems in one stroke: On the one hand, time-consuming treaty negotiations could be avoided, on the other, the chosen framework was so flexible as to leave sufficient leeway for negotiating transition rules.[54]

Under Delors' leadership, the Commission anticipated the course of German unification and paved the way for appropriate EC responses. By supporting the Article 23 route, the Commission took the smoothest and least complicated approach and avoided a situation whereby Germany could have been forced into choosing between unification and EC membership. In the end, unification and GDR integration were one and the same thing. All that remained was technocratic ratification of the inevitable.

Of crucial importance was Jacques Delors' role in shaping the attitude of the Commission. Early on, Delors actively promoted speedy accommodation of the GDR's needs within the EC system as a means to clear the hurdles to German unity. On French television he asked for support and understanding from his fellow countrymen for the unification process and was, in many ways, more cooperative than the French government. Based on his staunch support for the unification process, it was unlikely that the more national concerns of France and Britain could spill over into the EC decisionmaking process. Thus, the EC never became a panel debating whether or not final unification of the two German states was desirable. Such a debate would have represented a major burden for the EC and its relationship with Germany. Delors responded with foresight to historical forces, although his reaction might also have been influenced by calculations that he could later be rewarded with German support for the Commission's conception of European economic and monetary union.

Even if EC integration of the GDR ratified the dynamics of German unification, the Commission's perceptive approach allowed these dynamics to drive the EC response. Potential national barriers did not appear during the EC process, a remarkable result for an institution whose decisionmaking is frequently subject to severely-conflicting national pressures. In its approach to German unification the EC displayed considerable pragmatism as well as surprising autonomy, making it possible to isolate itself from national pressures and sentiments in order to react to dynamics of the unification process and to prepare the necessary steps. It is, therefore, no exaggeration to claim that the Commission—in cooperation with the German government—became a major (if silent) actor in the unification process. As proven in promoting the Single Market, the Commission is more than the sum of the parts of the EC. It is capable of integrative processes which nationally-influenced political decisionmaking cannot achieve as easily. In individual member states, skeptics toward German unification were forced to concede that smooth integration of a united Germany into the EC makes a substantial contribution to fitting Germany into a European framework. Even Margaret Thatcher began to see the virtues of closely coordinating German unification within an EC context.[55]

As for economic consequences of unification for other EC members, concerns and opportunities were balanced. Initial fears that German monetary union would unleash inflationary pressures in Germany because of possibly rapid reductions in East German savings accounts did not materialize. More urgent were concerns that the Bundesbank would adopt a policy of tight money and high interest rates to hold down an emerging wage-price spiral, fueled by the extra demand from East Germany. It was feared that such a policy would force higher interest rates on other European countries, thereby increasing the cost of capital.[56] But positive macroeconomic effects were also anticipated, because German unification would increase demand and growth in the entire Community and would also contribute to a reduction of the high current account surplus of Germany's EC partners. France, for example, was able to reduce its trade deficit by DM 1.5 billion in the first half of 1990. A more realistic assessment of investment effects on weaker EC countries was now possible. Countries like Spain and Portugal were hoping to benefit from investment from Germany and the other more industrialized EC countries. The EC Commission pointed out that such investment is determined by opportunities for high returns, and this situation would not necessarily change through opening up the GDR for Western investment, as investment conditions might quickly come to resemble those in West Germany.[57] In the short run, and particularly in 1990 when decisions on EC-GDR integration were made, the unification process stimulated continental European economies and shielded them from recessionary pressures coming from the United States. Germany was the locomotive for European growth and, for the first time in July 1991, the inflation rate in Germany was higher than that in France—leading to a convergence crucial for the establishment of European monetary union.[58]

Implementing GDR Integration

The route chosen to unification via Article 23 made a change of the Treaty of Rome and a formal German accession to the EC as a third party superfluous. The area of East Germany, now organized as five German states, would automatically become part of the European Community. EC primary law (the treaties), secondary law (the body of regulations and directives passed by the Council of Ministers and the Parliament), and deduced law (regulations issued by the Commission) became immediately applicable to the accession territory.[59] Application of the laws actually started several months before formal unification when Germany achieved economic and monetary union. However, because of drastically different circumstances in East Germany (and later the five federal states formed within its boundaries), it was clear that compliance with EC law was not immediately possible. The EC Commission consequently insisted on the need to achieve GDR integration in phases. In this respect, the process resembled the formal accession of other new EC members like Portugal and

Spain, where transitional periods were allowed for particularly burdensome regulations. In the case of the GDR, the Commission proposed that integration would consist of (1) an interim phase between economic and monetary union and formal unification, when a few EC norms—particularly those relating to foreign trade—would apply; (2) a transitional phase (after unification), during which the bulk of EC law would be introduced but certain exceptions would be allowed; and (3) a final phase, beginning in 1993, when, with very few exceptions, all EC law would be applicable. From the outset, the Commission urged the German government to make the unification process compatible with EC law in order to avoid the erosion of EC law.[60] The Commission's central intention was to allow for a short period of transitional rules without endangering the joint legal framework. Above all, the Single Market project was not to be compromised as a result of GDR integration. The State Treaty on Monetary, Economic, and Social Union between West Germany and the GDR took this into account; the preamble stated that the State Treaty was to facilitate the application of EC law after unification. In practice, this meant that no clause in the treaty was to compromise West Germany's obligations to the EC and that, until unification, GDR law was to take account of EC law wherever relevant.[61]

On 28 August 1990, the European Commission ratified the integration of the GDR into the EC. After passage by the Council of Ministers and the East German parliament, approximately 80 percent of EC law was effective in the five *Länder* at the moment of formal East and West German unification. For 20 percent of EC law, there were exceptions and transitional rules which were terminated at the end of 1992. In principle, EC law was to be fully applicable in the five *Länder* by 1993, except in the area of environment where different air and water standards are allowed until at least 1995.[62] The Commission acted pragmatically, allowing the necessary exceptions without endangering the basic applicability of EC law. The EC Commission also made preliminary estimates of budgetary effects for the fiscal year 1991. It concluded that additional expenditures would amount to 2 billion ecu (approximately four billion DM), but that the net effect would only be 500 million ecu, as revenues would increase by 1.5 billion ecu.[63] The Council of Ministers and the European Parliament agreed to the package on 12 and 13 September, respectively, and granted the Commission and the German government extraordinary authority to adopt certain rules until the end of 1991 without parliamentary approval.[64]

Assessing the GDR Economy

The Commission cautiously assessed the state of the GDR economy; attempts to compare basic parameters such as GNP of the GDR to other EC members would not have yielded reliable conclusions due to unreliable GDR data. The Commission admitted—on the basis of raw quantitative data—that the GDR's gross national product (GNP) may be far ahead of other Comecon states and may come close to the EC average. However, the Commission insisted such an assessment would have to be qualified by qualitative aspects such as structural obsoleteness and grave technological deficiencies of capital stock, especially a collapsing infrastructure (roads, transportation, and communication systems), and severe environmental damage. On the other hand, the Commission estimated that the per capita income of the GDR before unification was higher than that in Portugal, Greece, and Ireland—but lower than that in Spain.[65] Grim realism dominated assessments of individual industrial sectors. From steel to microelectronics, no sector was judged competitive by Western standards, and this judgment was implicitly a prediction of an industrial collapse which became evident by the summer of 1991. The Commission was also pessimistic with regard to the role of trade with ex-Comecon countries and predicted massive reductions of exports from the GDR. However, the Commission did not warn of any impending disaster, and was more concerned with macroeconomic consequences for the West German economy and the EC as a whole.[66]

Agricultural Policy

The Commission analyzed in detail the situation of the agricultural sector in the GDR, and it noted unusual structural features such as a large proportion of the workforce employed in agriculture (10 percent compared to 5 percent in West Germany); the large size of farms (averaging 4500 ha as opposed to 16 ha in West Germany and 65.1 ha in Great Britain, whose farms are the largest farms in the EC); and grave deficits in food processing, marketing, environmental safety, and product quality.[67]

Upon unification, the East German agricultural system was fully integrated into the EC's Common Agricultural Policy (CAP). Price supports (including intervention prices and producer subsidies) as well as production quotas (primarily for milk and sugar) were gradually introduced. Export refunds and variable levies, assessed to assure that imports do not undercut EC price levels, were adopted in farm trade—thereby integrating the new *Länder* into the protectionist CAP. The Commission approved special national aid schemes to accelerate structural change and to assure that the burden of integration did not fall on the EC alone. Because the food processing industry, and some agricultural products were not up to EC standards, these standards were not applicable in the new federal states until 1993. However, such products could only be marketed in the five *Länder* to avoid EC dumping of non-standard products. It was questionable whether this could be guaranteed.[68] Costs for supporting GDR agriculture were not included in the 1990-91 budget, and the Commission was silent about burdens it would create for the budget. For 1991-92, the extra costs were estimated to exceed 1.7 billion ecu, and the ex-GDR was scheduled to receive approximately 500 million ecu in agricultural aid funds.[69] However, serious conflicts have already arisen over Germany's enhanced sugar quotas and the export of East German pork to member states at dumping prices.[70] Given the grave problems of the GDR economy, with its large agricultural production cooperatives and the controversial nature of agricultural policy in the EC, integration of the new *Länder* into the CAP will remain a touchy issue.

Environmental Issues

East Germany's environmental disaster is one of the most depressing legacies of the communist regime. Air pollution is about four times the EC average. Sulfur dioxide emissions are the highest of all European countries. Almost half of the water supply is unusable as drinking water. Sixty percent of all industrial refuse is dumped without any controls.[71] In view of the seriousness of the problems, the Commission felt compelled to grant the longest transition periods in the environmental area (for water, air, and ground pollution until 1996), and even this deadline may be overly optimistic. No grace period was given to atomic power plants of the old GDR, which posed a serious security risk and had to be discontinued with unification. The German government and the Commission shared the same position on this issue. Still, one can assume that the new *Länder* will deviate from EC environmental norms for a long time to come.

Trade with Comecon States

The state of trading relationships with Comecon countries was seen as one of the most complicated and volatile issues of integration. Before 1990, the GDR was fully integrated into the Comecon trading system, which was governed by an array of treaties. Most important, the GDR conducted 40 percent of its trade with the Soviet Union. Thus, a core area of the future Soviet-German relationship was affected by unification. However, the issue became inconsequential as trade with the Soviet Union collapsed. The Soviet Union was no longer willing to buy obsolete equipment with hard currency, particularly since its currency reserves were dwindling. The adaptation process was partially alleviated by the fact that some old GDR trade treaties were expiring. The Commission agreed to grandfather on-going treaties which served as the basis for GDR economic ties with Eastern Europe, but in most cases it limited the validity to the area of East Germany. As a consequence, no levies were imposed on goods from Eastern Europe until 1991, with the possibility of a one-year extension. Imported goods have to be consumed or processed in the five *Länder*, and after two years EC quality and products norms would apply. With regard to the former Soviet Union, the future introduction of EC tariffs and quotas will not be as great an issue, since most of its exports to the GDR have been raw materials and energy resources which are only subject to low duties.[72] In contrast, Poland faces steep EC barriers to steel, textiles, coal, and agricultural products. Exports to Russia and other republics in the former Soviet Union from East Germany will only be possible with export guarantees or loans provided by the German government.

Subsidies and Competition Policy

Since the implementation of the Single Market, the Commission has taken a very critical stance toward national subsidies for ailing industries or regions. Theoretically, the flexibility of the Commission regarding subsidy and competition issues seemed limited. It did acknowledge that considerable subsidies are necessary for restructuring, revitalizing, and modernizing GDR industry and was therefore willing to consider "the sensitive and adaptive handling of EC regulations regarding subsidies."[73] At the same time, the Commission insisted that such regulations be applied as soon as possible to avoid unfair competition. Special regulations were considered inappropriate, as existing law was deemed sufficiently flexible for dealing with different economic and regional situations.[74] It was evident that the Commission did not want to establish exceptions that would endanger the Single Market project. It is also interesting that the Commission pressured the Bonn government to terminate regional aid to the former border areas (*Zonenrandförderung*) and western Berlin. The German government agreed to reduce the area receiving aid from a territory where 39 percent of the West German population lived to 27 percent and to phase out all Berlin aid by 1994.[75] This pressure may have been welcome to the German government, as it provided a rationale for budgetary cuts.

In the area of competition, the Commission is confronted with a special challenge, as East German industry was highly concentrated in a few industrial conglomerates (*Kombinate*) which impeded the introduction of competitive structures. Above all, it was feared that joint ventures with market-dominating West German companies and the various cooperation agreements between large West German firms and Eastern industrial conglomerates would lead to monopolistic structures. The Commission's interest in the effects of unification on competition policy was enhanced by the fact that the Commission now has jurisdiction over cross-border mergers in the EC. British competition commissioner, Sir Leon Brittan, judged the situation serious enough to warrant Commission intervention even before unification.[76] The Commission was particularly concerned that non-German companies would not have equal opportunities to acquire more promising GDR companies from the Trust Agency (*Treuhandanstalt*) charged with the privatization of East German companies. The failed purchase of Interflug, the GDR airline, by British Airways seemed to confirm this view. However, the Commission has not yet intervened in any transaction.

Structural Aids Funds

Participation of the *Länder* in the three structural aid funds was probably the most explosive issue of integration since it is easily recognized as an emergency area in need of substantial funds. Fortunately, the West German government renounced any claims on existing fund allocations. If Germany had insisted on immediate inclusion, it would have created a serious situation within the EC because in the European Regional Fund (the largest fund), 85 percent of the allocations were already committed to other member countries until 1993. Only the Agricultural Fund and the Social Fund, which are much smaller, allowed the Commission any flexibility. The Commission remained vague on issues regarding East German participation in the funds, claiming that the statistical bases (per capita income determining regional aid and unemployment figures for the Social Fund) were not available for allocation of funds under existing formulas. This way, no binding commitment had to be made while discussing GDR integration.[77]

It was clear to more realistic observers, however, that if current EC rules applied to the East German area, it could make heavy demands on the EC budget. As regions with a per capita income of less than three-quarters of the EC average qualify for Regional Fund aid,[78] it followed that based on an average per capita income of DM 16,000 - 17,000, the entire newly-integrated portion of Germany would be eligible to receive regional aid. This meant that the population in such areas would automatically grow by 15 percent and would conceivably lead to lower per capita payments in the future. As early as 1990, the research service of the European Parliament estimated the additional annual burden at 1.5 billion ecu (= DM 3.0 billion).[79] As unemployment figures to that point in 1990 were not dramatic, no clear statements were forthcoming on the disposition of the Social Funds.

In its position paper, the Commission—with the consent of the German government—dropped the idea of a special GDR aid fund and gave only one specific assurance: that steel-producing regions of East Germany would receive adjustment assistance under the regional aid fund. As most monies under the Regional Fund were committed until 1993, the Commission proposed additional allocations of 3 billion ecu from 1991-1993, which meant that any regional assistance for the new area would have to come from extra allocations. A conservative estimate was that these areas were eligible for about two billion DM in regional aid money, although methods of financing were not then specified. The Commission's stated intention was to finance the bulk of extra assistance from increased revenues.[80] During the visit of Commission President Delors to the five new *Länder* in early June 1991, it was clear that the entire GDR area would be eligible for assistance from the Regional Fund and would also receive agricultural adjustment funds of approximately one billion DM.[81] The precise implementation of a regional aid package was still unclear in the summer of 1991, as the German government had not come up with a comprehensive assistance package—which is a precondition for EC assistance. For a transitional period, the questions of structural assistance for the GDR area did not pose a problem. Some observers predicted the true challenge would come in the summer of 1992 when East German economic activity, particularly in industry, would reach the bottom line and unemployment could rise to 50 percent. Hopes that an economic upturn would reduce the level of assistance needed to as little as 900 million DM seem to be unrealistic.[82]

Assessing the Integration Package

How is the integration package to be judged? One prime objective of the Commission—not to compromise creation of the Single Market in the legal sphere—was certainly achieved. There were only a few special rules, and the transition period was deliberately kept short. Integrity of the Single Market project had preference over any exceptional status for Germany as a whole or the former GDR territory. The best evidence of this is that exceptions (e.g., deviations from European Community standards and the rules for trade with former Comecon countries) were subject to strict territorial and temporal limitations.

The package also underscores attempts to shield Germany's EC partners, at least in the short run, from any financial burdens and regulatory
adjustments precipitating from integration. This is particularly evident
with regard to the weaker EC states whose shares in various assistance
schemes remained intact. Attempts to ask them for contributions to GDR
reconstruction would have aroused emotional, nationalistic conflicts that,
from the beginning, the Commission and the German government wanted
to avoid. In addition, the task of reconstructing the former GDR economy
is so immense, and monies available through the structural funds are so
limited, that their contribution to economic revitalization of the GDR—
even if used to the full extent—must be considered minor. Had Germany
requested massive help from the structural funds, it would have seriously
overburdened them and even jeopardized the European Community. For
this reason, some German observers suggested that Germany voluntarily
forego all assistance from the funds for the five new *Länder* in order to
win complete leeway from the EC for reconstruction of the East.[83]

The package devised by the Commission was balanced and pragmatic,
and it sought to assuage European fears of German unification. This, however, is only true in the short run. For very good reasons, the medium-term
risks inherent in German unification for the EC were not stressed by the
Commission. This is particularly true for the long-term budgetary implications and specific programs such as structural assistance and common
agricultural policies. In light of the German approach to the structural fund
issue thus far, one can assume that the German government will not make
excessive claims, i.e., it will continue to maintain the status quo for
weaker member states and only request for the five *Länder* what is available through new revenues. Evidence suggests that this includes plans by
the German government and the EC to target regional EC funds in the new
Länder to the most needy regions, such as the coastal north and the decay-
ing industrial areas.[84] Whatever the approach to the structural funds, unification has clearly increased strains on the German budget.[85] Germany will
be less willing to finance further expansion of the EC budget through net
contributions. Thus, the end of German alimentation of Community policies is in sight. Additional monies for structural funds will not be available
or will have to come from agricultural budgets, which is most unlikely
given the strength of the farm lobby. This means that there will be little
movement with regard to the "policies of cohesion," which are supposed
to balance differences between developed states and technologically- and
economically-backward ones. If it is true that cohesion policy is a one
central task of accomplishing the integration process after the Single Market has been created, then German unification bodes ill for its prospects.[86]

German Unification and the Future
of European Integration

Did German unification and the integration of East Germany into the EC result in an unwelcome enlargement? The question must be answered with an emphatic no. Indeed, the question was actually never raised in EC circles. This was due to three factors: (1) the coordinated, farsighted strategy of the Commission, which was basically an *administrative* strategy that managed to keep the process free from possible psychological irritations; (2) German willingness to forego major claims on the EC budget to finance reconstruction in the five new *Länder* and not to insist on a special regulatory treatment there; and (3) close coordination of every step between the Commission and the German government. This approach ensured that unification and GDR-integration were basically two concomitant and parallel processes. Thus, GDR integration proceeded with little friction, and it can be termed one of the most successful aspects of the unification process.

The approach taken by the Commission and the German government embedded unification in the European integration process and legitimized it from a European perspective. German unification and European integration evolved compatibly, and the opposite scenario of mutual exclusivity—an absolute certainty according to some observers—did not occur.[87] With the Maastricht summit approaching, there was no sign that Germany, beset by the internal problems of unification, would attempt to stop the acceleration of the European integration process leading to European monetary and political union. "Europhoria" pervaded the attitudes and speeches of Chancellor Kohl and Foreign Minister Genscher. After unification, their rhetoric became even more pro-European. European union seemed clearly slated as their next "historic project." The crucial point in the German strategy was a linkage between monetary and political union. Germany would only agree to giving up the DM and its privileged status as a reserve currency if substantial progress on political union could be achieved in terms of increasing the power of the European Parliament. The German government (represented by the finance ministry and supported by the Bundesbank), however, set tough terms for European monetary union: full independence of the European Central Bank; no member government deficit financing; no guidance of exchange rate settings by finance ministers; and, most importantly, a timetable presupposing economic and monetary convergence among the member states. The latter point effectively meant that monetary union would only include those member states that conformed to German-style stability requirements. Yet, while these terms may be seen as delaying the achievement of European monetary union, both Kohl and Genscher pushed for political and monetary union at the Maastricht European Council summit of December 1991. Prior to the Maastricht meeting, they even gave the impression at times that they would be willing to give up the cherished hard DM and possibly even compromise on terms for establishing the European Federal Reserve System in exchange for political union and greatly increased powers for the European Parliament—and in particular a common foreign policy.[88]

The Maastricht outcome, however, did not meet the expectations of the German government. While the Treaty on European Union committed member governments to monetary union by 1997 if a majority of member states fulfill the convergence criteria with regard to public debt, the annual budget deficit, and inflation rates, it failed to expand the powers of the European Parliament to the degree desired by the Germans as fulfilling the terms for political union. The Parliament did not obtain co-legislation rights but merely a veto in the form of the so-called "Negative Assent Procedure," which allows Parliament equal say with the Council of Ministers.[89] Unexpected to the German government, which carried on the negotiations on such fundamental issues without seeking the public's consent or conducting a broad public debate, the results of Maastricht—particularly the decision to give up the DM—met with strong disapproval on the part of the public and the media. Germany seemed to have given away the store with too little in return.[90] Economists and the German banking community feared that the convergence criteria would be watered down by political compromise and that Germany would be asked to pay for the economic discipline imposed on the weaker countries.[91]

The latter concern became even more pronounced when seen in connection with the newly-established Cohesion Fund for Spain, Portugal, Greece, and Ireland and the intermediate budgetary plans of the Commission. According to a Commission proposal submitted in February 1992, the EC budget is expected to increase from 133 billion DM to 175 billion DM from 1993 to 1997 (in 1993 prices). Aside from industrial policy and aid to Eastern Europe, the bulk of the money is to be used for a massive redistribution of wealth from the northern states to the south (and to Ireland). The total subsidies for infrastructure development will grow from 40 billion DM to 70 billion DM in nominal terms. The German contributions will increase in real terms from 37 billion DM to almost 50 billion DM by 1997; Germany's net contribution to the Community (i.e., German payments minus EC expenditures for Germany) will grow from 18 billion DM to 26 billion DM during the same period.[92] The five new *Bundesländer* will also receive higher EC subsidies (three billion DM instead of two billion annually), but these increases fall far behind the increases allotted the southern member states. Germany as a whole will continue to contribute two-thirds of the entire net transfer volume. Given concern about the German budget deficit (which constituted 3.3 percent of gross national product in 1991),[93] one can expect tacit but tenacious resistance among German policymakers against the Commission's proposal.

German critics see this as intolerable in light of the decline of unified Germany's per capita GNP within the Community in 1991 to eighth place—ahead only of Spain, Ireland, Portugal, and Greece. Concurrently, the per capita GNP in the five new *Bundesländer* was a mere 40 percent of Spain's in 1991.[94] Some critics have argued that Germany, by giving up its greatest competitive asset (the DM), is relinquishing its greatest competitive asset and, at the same time, is even being asked to pay for it. In addition, there is no sign that Germany could expect to receive any effective help in dealing with the economic problems of the new *Länder* nor that Germany will encounter any willingness on the part of the EC to commit significant new resources to help the former Eastern bloc countries, Russia, and the successor states.[95]

In the aftermath of Maastricht and the budgetary plans of the European Commission, enthusiasm for Europe has waned considerably among the German public and many informed observers. Even the ratification of the Maastricht treaty seemed, for a while, to be in doubt.[96] The Kohl government now pays the price for not stimulating a public debate about the aims and purposes of the Maastricht treaty and seeking public support for its strategies. In addition, it now seems that the relentless Europe mystique propagated by the German political elite will no longer suffice for plastering over the fundamental conflicts of interests that separate Germany and its partners with regard to shouldering the economic burdens of the historic changes in Europe. It should be noted that one of the factors encouraging increased popular support for right-wing parties in state elections in Baden-Württemberg and Schleswig-Holstein in April 1992 was not only the asylum question but also the issue of giving up the DM. While the German government and the public-at-large will undoubtedly affirm their European orientation in the long run, Germany may prove less willing and able to finance the continuation of the integration process in the intermediate run. Beset by the financial burdens of integration with the former GDR and confronted by threats emanating from its attendant economic dislocation, German politics as well as the German public will weigh much more carefully the costs and benefits of EC integration.[97] In this sense, Germany will become a more normal member, but it will lose some of its moral authority as a catalyst for European integration. One victim, then, of German unification may well be the unconditional commitment to European integration that has been a hallmark of postwar German politics.

German unification inevitably raised the issue of German weight and power in the Community. After all, with almost 80 million people, Germany is now the most populous member state. French leaders confirmed this apprehension by making catching up with Germany one of their top priorities. The issue has surfaced with concrete implications in connection with representation of the five new German *Länder* in the European Parliament and discussion about the number of deputies that a united Germany can claim in the next legislative session. Eighty-one seats are reserved for each of the four larger member states (Germany, France, Italy, and Britain), and this equilibrium was not to be disrupted by German unification. French, British, Italian, and even Spanish representatives resisted the enlargement of the German delegation. The solution was to give the new *Länder* eighteen representatives with observer status (i.e., without a vote and without the right of speech). This kept the total German number below the symbolic 100, although it should have been 110 under the current distribution formula. But even the eighteen East German representatives with no power were objectionable to many parliamentarians, as the representatives' presence could conceivably prejudice the number of legislative seats in the next session.[98] The principle of one-man-one-vote will be even more compromised with German unification. If no change is made for the next legislative session, a German representative will represent close to 1 million citizens, while his French and Luxembourg counterparts will each represent 672,000 and 20,000, respectively.[99] Discussion about East German representation has demonstrated again how sensitive the issue of relative German weight is. It may have explosive power, if the European Parliament has its powers increased under any move toward political union—a strategy that the German government clearly favors. The issue of German weight is not immediately relevant after unification, but it may be one of the most controversial issues on the road to true European political union. As a matter of fact, at the Maastricht summit in December 1991 the question of East German representation was not solved but postponed to a later date.[100]

Last, but not least, it should be noted that integration of the GDR into the EC was a unique process and cannot serve as a model for integration of other East European countries. It could have been a model only if the GDR had joined the EC as the thirteenth member state. In this case, as was discussed above, the process would have been much more difficult and contentious as it would have required substantial sacrifices from all EC member states. Formal GDR membership would have imposed much higher costs on the EC and would have required a much longer period of transitional rules. The EC was forced to be accommodating because GDR integration happened concomitant with the movement to German unification and the Federal Republic was a strong partner available to shoulder the burdens of the legacy of communist rule. This is not the case with most East European countries, as the EC relationship with Poland demonstrates. The Community is extremely hesitant to make any concessions on Polish imports of agricultural products, steel, textiles, and clothing to help in the transition to a market economy and to bear any costs of this process.[101]

Moreover, German monetary union cannot be a model for European monetary union. Its impetus was short-term and primarily political, and it did not aim at creating a permanent and stable framework for major European currencies. If there is a lesson, it is that the so-called "crowning theory"—according to which countries seeking currency union must first have a stable currency before they can be merged—has not been refuted. Rather, the case of the GDR proves that a weak economy must be kept alive with massive fiscal transfers if a hard currency is introduced.[102] For these reasons, there is little to learn for future Community development from GDR integration into the EC. Integration was a unique process, under unique historical circumstances, and it will be a hard act to follow.

Notes

1. Werner Weidenfeld, "Die gesamteuropäische Dimension der deutschen Einheit," in Weidenfeld, et al., *Die doppelte Integration: Europa und das größere Deutschland* (Gütersloh: Bertelsmann, 1991), 9.

2. The crucial variable here was the Soviet position. Although it was undergoing constant changes until the unification of Germany within the Two-Plus-Four talks was assured, the first clear indication that the Soviet Union would give its approval to German unification came with GDR Ministerpresident Modrow's visit to Moscow. Up to this point, only formal membership or association seemed to be feasible options for redefining the GDR's relationship to the European Community. See Elizabeth Pond, *After the Wall: American Policy Toward Germany* (New York: Priority Press Publications, 1990), 41-54. Also see Karl Kaiser, *Deutschlands Vereinigung. Die internationalen Aspekte* (Bergisch Gladbach: Bastei Lübbe, 1991), 60.

3. In addition, other countries such as Austria and Turkey had made entry bids before and were thought to have priority.

4. Weidenfeld, "Die gesamteuropäische Dimension," 9.

5. "Erklärung der Bundesregierung zum Vertrag über die Europäische Wirtschaftsgemeinschaft, abgegeben vom Staatssekretär des Auswärtigen Amtes, Walter Hallstein, vor dem Deutschen Bundestag am 21. März 1957," reprinted in Kaiser, *Deutschlands Vereinigung*, 139-40.

6. Thus the title of the book by Weidenfeld, et al., *Die doppelte Integration.*

7. When in August 1990 the EC Commission presented its final plan for the integration of the GDR, the EC public relations office in Bonn had problems in interesting any journalists for this process. Interview with Gerd Langguth, Director of the EC office in Bonn, 9 September 1990.

8. Bernhard May, "Normalisierung der Beziehungen zwischen der EG und dem RGW," in *Aus Politik und Zeitgeschichte*, B 3 (1989): 44 ff.

9. Ibid., 46-48, 53.

10. Jürgen Klose, "Die wirtschaftliche Integration der DDR in die EG: Bedingungen für den Übergang," in Weidenfeld et al., 65 ff.

11. May, "Normalisierung der Beziehungen," Fn. 33, 53.

12. The legal aspects of the relationship between the EC and the GDR are discussed by Peter Scharpf, "Die Bedeutung des innerdeutschen Handels für die Beziehungen der EWG zur DDR," in *Deutschland Archiv*, 7 (1973): 261 ff.

13. Ibid., 260 ff., and Fritz Homann, "Innerdeutscher Handel und EG-Binnenmarkt," in *Deutschland Archiv*, 19 (1989): 305 ff.

14. Homann, 106.

15. Ibid., 305 ff., and Scharpf, "Die Bedeutung des innerdeutschen Handels," 264 ff.

16. Homann, 306.

17. See Deutsches Institut für Wirtschaftsforschung, "Innerdeutscher Handel: Expansionsmöglichkeiten wirklich nutzen!" in *Wochenbericht*, No. 9-10 (1989): 95-97, 104 ff.

18. Ibid., 97-101, and Homann, "Innerdeutscher Handel," 303 ff.

19. Homann, 306-8.

20. Horst Lambrecht, "Die deutsch-deutschen Wirtschaftsbeziehungen zum Ende der achtziger Jahre," in *Aus Politik und Zeitgeschichte*, B 10 (1989): 24-27.

21. See Pond, *After the Wall*, 58.

22. "Zehn-Punkte-Programm zur Überwindung der Teilung Deutschlands und Europas, vorgelegt von Bundeskanzler Helmut Kohl in der Haushaltsdebatte des Deutschen Bundestages am 28. November 1989," reprinted in Kaiser, *Deutschlands Vereinigung*, 158-68. Confederate or federal structures are addressed in particular on 164-65. Also see Appendix 2.

23. Horst Werner, "Ökonomische Probleme der deutschen Einheit und der europäischen Einigung," in *Aus Politik und Zeitgeschichte*, B 28 (1990): 17.

24. For Britain's and France's attitude toward unification and their assessment of the role ascribed to the EC, see Pond, *After the Wall*, 24-26;

Kaiser, *Deutschlands Vereinigung,* 64-68; and Stefan Fröhlich, "Umbruch in Europa," in *Aus Politik und Zeitgeschichte,* B 29 (1990): 39-43.

25. The ecu, or European Currency Unit, is used for accounting and budgetary purposes within the EC. Its value is based on an adjusted weight of each of the currencies of the twelve member states; in 1992, one ecu was worth approximately $1.60.

26. For instance, Denmark and the Netherlands are also net-beneficiaries, receiving 83 percent and 90 percent, respectively, of their allocations from the agricultural budget.

27. For the budget and aid figures, see "Southern Discomfort," *Financial Times,* 18 June 1991.

28. Gerd Langguth, "Die deutsche Frage und die Europäische Gemeinschaft," in *Aus Politik und Zeitgeschichte,* B 29 (1990): 19.

29. See "A Strong Center, a Worried Periphery," in *Financial Times,* 6 August 1990.

30. The average per capita GNP of the four poorest member states (Greece, Portugal, Ireland, and Spain) is 69 percent of the EC average. See "Southern Discomfort," 16.

31. Langguth, "Die deutsche Frage," 19.

32. The twelve governments have seventy-six votes in the EC's Council of Ministers; fifty-six votes are required for a qualified majority

33. See Juliet Lodge, "European Community Policy-Making: Institutional Consideration," in Juliet Lodge, ed., *The European Community and the Challenge of the Future* (London: Frances Pinter, 1989), 42-50; and Lodge, "The European Parliament—From Assembly to Co-legislature: Changing the Institutional Dynamics," in ibid., 58-79.

34. See Andrew Moravcsik, "Negotiating the Single European Act. National Interests and Conventional Statecraft in the European Community," in *International Organization,* 45 (1991): 19-56.

35. The internal European Community discussion is assessed by Christine Holeschovsky, "Der innergemeinschaftliche Abstimmungsprozeß zur Deutschen Einheit," in Weidenfeld, et al., *Die doppelte Integration,* 17-29.

36. Ibid., 18 ff.

37. Langguth, "Die deutsche Frage," 19.

38. According to this scenario, it still would have made a difference which procedure was used for unification; i.e., accession according to Article 23 of the German Basic Law, or through negotiating a new constitution according to Art. 146.

39. Holeschovsky, "Der innergemeinschaftliche Abstimmungsprozeß," 21.

40. The West German government proposed talks on monetary union on 7 February 1990. The announcement of the formation of the European Community commission working group on German unity came on 8 February, and the agreement to start the talks between the two German states followed on 13 February. The actual negotiations between the two German states began on 20 February. See the chronology of events by Christoph Jung in Weidenfeld, et al., *Die doppelte Integration*, 80 ff., and Appendix 1 to this volume.

41. One can also argue that the collapse of political authority in the GDR and the rapprochement of the two German states evident already during the Modrow government contributed to the pace of problem solving in the international arena. The agreement to start the Two-Plus-Four talks also occurred during that period, i.e., on 13 February. See Pond, *After the Wall*, 41 ff.

42. See Commission of the European Communities, "The Community and German unification," presented by the Commission to the Council on 22 August 1990, reprinted in *The European Community and German unification*, Bulletin of the European Communities, Supplement 4 (Luxembourg, 1990), 27-193, 42. In following references this document is cited as COM (90) 400.

43. Interview with Gerd Langguth, Director of the European Community office in Bonn, 13 September 1990.

44. The role of the working group and the close coordination with the West German side is discussed by Holeschovsky, "Der innergemeinschaftliche Abstimmungsprozeß," 22 ff.

45. COM (90) 400, 28.

46. See Holeschovsky, "Der innergemeinschaftliche Abstimmungsprozeß," 24, and Elmar Brok, "Europäisches Parlament und Deutsche Einheit," in Weidenfeld, et al., *Die doppelte Integration*, 30-40.

47. European Parliament, Directorate General for Research, *The Impact of German Unification on the European Community*, Working Document No. 1 (Luxembourg 1990), 147.

48. Fritz Franzmeyer and Dieter Schumacher, "EG-Aspekte der deutschen Einheit," in Weidenfeld et al., 45.

49. Brok, "Europäisches Parlament," 32.

50. "Kohl gegen höhere EG-Beiträge," in *Süddeutsche Zeitung*, 31 July 1990.

51. "Die EG zahlt doch," in *Süddeutsche Zeitung*, 22 August 1990.

52. The quote is from "Brückenschlag für neue Beziehungen," in *Das Parlament*, 17/24 August 1990.

53. "The European Community and German unification," Communication from the Commission to the special session of the European Coun-

cil in Dublin on 28 April 1990, reprinted in *The European Community and German unification*, Bulletin of the European Communities, Supplement 4 (Luxembourg, 1990), 9-16.

54. Holeschovsky, "Der innergemeinschaftliche Abstimmungsprozeß," 25 (author's translation).

55 "Thatcher says curbing Bonn is up to European Community," in *Financial Times*, 3 September 1990.

56. Franzmeyer and Schumacher, "EG-Aspekte," 43.

57. COM (90) 400, 35.

58. See "French Inflation falls below German level," in *Financial Times*, 17 July 1991.

59. This is a translation of the term *Beitrittsgebiet* used by the Bonn bureaucracy to refer to the GDR.

60. Commission of the European Communities, "The Community and German unification," reprinted in *Bulletin of the European Communities*, Supplement 4 (Luxembourg, 1990), 9-16. This source is cited in following references as SEC (90) 751. See also Christine Holeschovsky, "Deutsche Einheit und europäische Integration. EG-Kompatibilität sichern," in Werner Weidenfeld, ed., *Die Deutschen und die Architektur des Europäischen Hauses* (Cologne: Verlag Wissenschaft und Politik, 1990), 175-84.

61. Kommission der europäischen Gemeinschaften, "Die Gemeinschaft und die deutsche Vereinigung," SEK (90) 1138, reprinted in *Bulletin der Europäischen Gemeinschaften*, Beilage 4/90 (Luxembourg 1990), 21-23. This source is cited in following references as SEK (90) 1138.

62. See Kommission der Europäischen Gemeinschaften, Vertretung in der Bundesrepublik Deutschland, *Pressemitteilung*, Bonn, 22 August 1990.

63. Commission, COM (90) 400, 109-111.

64. "Im Eilverfahren durch Institutionen," in *Das Parlament*, 12 October 1990.

65. COM (90) 400, 30.

66. Ibid., 32-40.

67. Ibid., 87 ff. For the figures on the EC, see Gerhard Maier, *Agrarpolitik Kontrovers* (Bonn: Bundeszentrale für politische Bildung, 1989), 32.

68. For the measures, see ibid., 92-96.

69. "EG-Etat übersteigt 100 Milliarden," in *Süddeutsche Zeitung*, 30 July 1990; "Bauern sollen Einkommenseinbußen erspart bleiben," in *Süddeutsche Zeitung*, 4 March 1991.

70. "European Community Row Builds Up Over Sugar Quota for East Germany," in *Financial Times*, 24 September 1990.

71. COM (90) 400, 97-100.

72. Ibid., 53-55.

73. See Sir Leon Brittan, "Wettbewerbspolitik in einem vereinigten Deutschland—die europäische Dimension," in *Europäische Gespräche*, ed. by the Kommission der Europäischen Gemeinschaft, Vertretung in der Bundesrepublik Deutschland (Bonn, 1990), 11.

74. Ibid., 11-14.

75. "Regionalhilfen werden drastisch abgebaut," in *Süddeutsche Zeitung*, 2 May 1991.

76. Brittan, "Wettbewerbspolitik," 11.

77. COM (90) 400, 94-95.

78. Harvey Armstrong, "Community Regional Policy," in Lodge, *The European Community*, 178-81.

79. Franzmeyer and Schumacher, "EG-Aspekte," 45 ff., and European Parliament, *Impact*, 147.

80. Ibid., 47.

81. "Mit Sorgen im Eiltempo nach Europa," in *Süddeutsche Zeitung*, 6 June 1991.

82. Franzmeyer and Schumacher, "EG-Aspekte," 48.

83. For instance, Franzmeyer and Schumacher (ibid., 48), who echoed concerns by the prestigious Rheinisch-Westfälische Institute for Economic Research (RWI) in Essen.

84. Ibid., 47 ff.

85. In May 1991, the German budget deficit was estimated at DM 150 billion, roughly 5 percent of the GNP. See "A Nation Unified, and Yet Apart," in *Financial Times*, 1 July 1991.

86. On the role of cohesion policies, see Manfred Schäfers and Joachim Strabatty, "Das Instrumentarium zur Förderung innergemeinschaftlicher Kohäsion," in *Aus Politik und Zeitgeschichte*, B 28 (1990): 1-15.

87. After the collapse of the Wall in late 1989, this feeling was particularly pronounced in France among observers like Alan Mink who predicted the disintegration of the EC. See "Basic Principles Bolstered," in *Financial Times Survey France*, 17 June 1991.

88. As few other European countries share the German intensity for political union, the Germans may not get what they want on political union and therefore will not have to give up the DM. Germany may thus be able to hide behind this position on political union. For a good analysis, see "Horse-trading before high noon" in *Financial Times*, 28 June 1991.

89. See"Bonn agrees to surrender the D-Mark," in *Financial Times*, 12 December 1991; and "Strasbourg MPs straining to flex their new muscles," ibid.

90. See "German nerves at loss of D-Mark," *Financial Times*, 12 December 1991.

91. See "European business endorses move on monetary union," ibid.

92. See "Brüssel will mehr Geld in den Süden verteilen," *Süddeutsche Zeitung*, 13 February 1992; and "Streit in der EG ums Geld," ibid., 6 April 1992.

93. The 3.3 percent represents only general budget deficits. When off-budget deficies of public bodies such as the railway system and the *Treuhand* are included, the deficit is closer to 6 percent of GNP. See "IMF urges Germany to reduce its fiscal deficit," in *Financial Times*, 23 April 1992.

94. "Arm und Reich in der EG," in *Süddeutsche Zeitung*, 13 February 1992.

95. "Der Norden muß zahlen," *Süddeutsche Zeitung*, 15/16 February 1992.

96. "Kohl struggles to land his catch," *Financial Times*, 17 March 1992.

97. See "Die EG hält weitere Enttäuschungen bereit," *Süddeutsche Zeitung*, 10 February 1992.

98. See "Europa Parlament steuert Lex Germania an," in *Süddeutsche Zeitung*, 20 September 1990; "Zusätzliche Abgeordnete nicht erwünscht" in ibid., 23 October 1990; and "Zuschauer, enttäuscht von den Tribünenplätzen" in ibid., 1 February 1991.

99. Thomas Läufer, *Die Europäische Gemeinschaft* (Bonn, 1989), 84.

100. "German nerves at loss of D-Mark."

101. "Beating on the European Community's doors," in *Financial Times*, Country Survey Poland, 3 May 1991.

102. "Kampf um stabiles Geld. Nationalinteressen dominieren den Disput um EG-Währungsunion," in *Süddeutsche Zeitung*, 8/9 September 1990; and Werner, "Ökonomische Probleme," 18, 23.

PART THREE
Consequences and Problematics

8

An Impossible Dream?
Privatizing Collective Property in
Eastern Germany

Peter H. Merkl

Advocates of the free market both inside Eastern European countries and in the West have dreamed for decades of a shift of power from states to private firms in the wake of the collapse of communist regimes. Yet the stubborn realities of property relations, technological backwardness, and inexperienced entrepreneurs[1]—to name only some of the obstacles found in ex-communist economies—have tended to frustrate the fulfillment of their ideological aspirations of economic transformation and recovery. In this chapter, I will concentrate on the so far not very successful efforts of the Trust Agency for the People's Property (*Treuhandanstalt*) to privatize the industrial and agricultural collective enterprises that made up the bulk of the economy of former East Germany. I shall attempt to assess and compare the significance of this quasi-statal method of privatization with the experience of other East European countries and its likely consequences in unified Germany.

The Changing Property Constitution

At the heart of the communist economy is a concept of property and governmental powers over private property in the hands of a state planning commission and party agencies that amounts to a profoundly different order of property (or *Eigentumsverfassung*) than that prevailing in the Federal Republic and other Western capitalistic states. We need to examine these changing concepts of property, including the transfer from collective to private ownership, and the work of the Trust Agency for the People's Property to understand this important aspect of constitutional change in East Germany. Nearly all productive enterprises in the GDR were "people's own firms" (VEBs, or *Volkseigene Betriebe*), often grouped into large *Kombi-*

nate. Privatization—which encompasses a return of property to former owners, the sale of such enterprises, and "joint ventures" with foreign firms—involves disentangling the complexities of the old forms of collective property in the ex-GDR. Since the vast majority of capital assets like factories, cooperative farms, and apartment houses in the GDR belonged to the state and other public bodies, it was only logical to look to this large reserve as a source of capital to bail out the failing economy, settle debts, and provide collateral for credits. As it turned out, however, things were not that simple. To begin with, different categories of ownership existed prior to the East German election in March 1990. State and semi-statal property dominated with 80.7 percent of total assets, followed by cooperative property with 14.7 percent. Private property made up a mere 4.7 percent of economic resources. "Socialist property," as defined by the GDR constitution, also included the considerable property of the communist SED,[2] other "bloc parties," and vacation homes and printing facilities maintained by state-controlled mass organizations such as the Free German Trade Union Federation (FDGB) and the communist youth association (FDJ). State or "people's property"—the GDR always preferred juristically dubious or hazy definitions—included mines, power plants, factories, industrial land sites, banks and insurance companies, whole estates, and the transport and communications equipment of the railroads and postal service. Cooperative property belonged mostly to agricultural (LPGs), handicraft (PGMs), or housing cooperatives (AWGs); it included tools, machinery, livestock, buildings, and the yield of these operations.

This left little private property and few people independently employed. In 1988, only 2 percent of the gainfully employed were independent workers (down from 20 percent in 1955). They included 81,700 employed in trades, 39,200 in commerce, and 27,000 service operators.[3] Their property consisted of shops, business lots, retail stores, and some manufacturing equipment; the members' land used by agricultural and other cooperatives (which was originally contributed when a person joined the cooperative); as well as church property and the assets of refugees who had fled the GDR in earlier years and whose property was then taken over by trustees. Cooperatives did not permit their members to withdraw their assets, nor could members sell their assets except within the cooperative. GDR law also spoke of "personal property" such as family residences, weekend dachas, residential lots, and garages, with the state reserving a first right of purchase and approval of all property transactions.

The Soviet occupation had begun the first round of expropriations when it took away the property of "war criminals" and Nazi activists. Soviet expropriations included houses, furniture, and real estate as well as industrial plants, all of which were placed under communal trusteeship.[4] By 1948,

3,843 firms had been expropriated without compensation. Of these, 676 (including 213 large enterprises) were dismantled and transported as reparations to the Soviet Union. This left 61 percent of East German industrial capacity in state (or Soviet) hands.[5]

Under the authority of East German state constitutions, coal, and metals mining, iron and steel production, energy supply monopolies, natural resources, and banks and insurance firms were also turned over to the state. This time, however, local counties (*Kreise*) determined without further recourse a compensation to the previous owners. A "democratic land reform" in 1946 also expropriated all estates over 1∞ hectares (250 acres) for the purpose of "punishing and taking away the power of Junkers and large landowners." Their land was confiscated without compensation and without any regard to the past political conduct of the owners. The expropriated land was transferred to a Land Fund and, in large part, distributed in lots of 20-22 acres to small peasants and landless agricultural workers, tradesmen, and German ethnic refugees from Eastern Europe. The new owners were not allowed to sell or lease their properties. A total area of about eight million acres was expropriated in this fashion, not including estates in former German territories in Poland and East Prussia. About 2.5 million acres were eventually turned into state farms.[6]

After long discussions between government officials and parliamentary deputies, the East German cabinet decided in 1990 not to reopen the question of returning or offering compensation for property that had been expropriated during the Soviet occupation (1945-1949). Plaintiffs representing more than 10,000 expropriated parties challenged this decree before the Federal Constitutional Court in the Federal Republic, but the court ruled that international agreements with the Soviet Union in the course of the Two-Plus-Four negotiations in 1990 on German unification took precedence over legal claims to compensation based on constitutional principles. "An assessment of what could be gotten out of the negotiations," the court said with remarkable judicial self-restraint, "was up to the judgment of the federal government and cannot be reassessed by a constitutional court." The plaintiffs' claim was reduced to a theoretical right to compensation commensurate to "the desolate situation of the new *Länder*" at the time of unification. Like territory ceded to Poland and the Soviet Union as a result of wartime defeat, the loss was not to be treated like similar losses after 1949 (to the great relief of East German farmers).

Once the GDR was established in 1949, it acquired the legal authority to determine its own policy of nationalization. Deliberate economic discrimination—for example, in allocating skilled labor and supplies—had already reduced the share of private industrial enterprises between 1948 and 1952 from 60 percent to a mere 19 percent. In 1955-1956, the SED Central Committee began to "offer" state participation to some of the remaining private firms, and in 1959 a wave of semi-public enterprises resulted whose partial private owners were made chief managers but were also liable along with their own property for the firms' debts or failure. In 1972, the GDR Council of Ministers transferred all remaining industrial and construction firms and cooperatives to "people's property" and froze compensation for confiscation in a form that permitted only limited annual withdrawals. This action resulted in the creation of 11,000 new VEBs.[7]

In agriculture, the great wave of collectivization began in 1952-1953 when "abandoned or improperly maintained farms" (meaning mostly those belonging to GDR refugees to the West) were given to the counties to administer. Refugees from the GDR were promised they could have their property back if they returned. In practice, however, they could not extract their land from the agricultural LPGs that were created during the massive campaigns of the mid-1950s to force farmers under great pressure to join the "voluntary" LPG cooperatives.[8] Some farmers also lost their farms because they happened to be located along the boundary with western Germany. Their complaints were ignored while they were hauled away against their will to a grim factory job. LPG members retained property rights to their land, but they could sell it only to the LPG or other LPG members. By 1967, 9,000 LPGs had been formed with an average size of 1,500 acres. The cooperatives encompassed 95 percent of the GDR's agricultural production. I shall return below to the resulting agrifactories and their problems.

The GDR constitutions of 1949 and 1968 did set forth a legal procedure for expropriations, but formal preference for "socialist" over private property offered little hope for the individual property owner. Expropriation was permissible in "barred areas" and border zones and in cases when buildings in bad repair needed to be torn down. These rules could be applied easily to three-fourths of the country in 1990. Providing housing, urban renewal, or the need for workers or large families to build their own homes was considered sufficient reason to nationalize a house. Today, very few East German families own their houses or condominiums: only 25 percent, compared to 39 percent in western Germany and 64 percent in the United States. Those who do often owe this privilege to past political favoritism or clout.

East Germans who retained ownership of rental housing found themselves beset by the double impact of incredibly low rents and the obligation to pay for repairs. Most of them ended up donating their apartment house to municipal housing authorities for nothing, and they often had to pay the authorities to accept it. But following unification, a wave of expropriated persons has begun to return with a vengeance. Half a million former East German refugees have demanded either the return of their property or, alternatively, compensation for it if in the meantime their property has become too transformed or entangled in common institutions to be returned.[9] Compensation will cost more than 100 billion marks even if, as currently estimated, payments are limited to 5 to 20 percent of today's market value of the property.

After March 1990, the new GDR government insisted that the present renters, users, and cooperative partners should also have certain protected rights. Unfortunately in 1990, the entire GDR had only about 700 "independent" attorneys—West Berlin alone had 2,000—and almost no trained assessors of property or land registry personnel to straighten out all the legal complications. The courts will be busy for many years to come. West German law is quite different and recognizes neither "people's property" nor the ins and outs of users' rights governing, for example, the one million private dachas that were built on people's property. Outside investors and joint venture partners have a right to know the property status of what they wish to acquire and are, in fact, kept from investing by clouded property titles. The decision to give preference to restitution of property to the previous owners over compensation is widely blamed for slowing economic redevelopment.

Expropriating the Expropriators

A growing number of court cases has already revealed weak areas in resolving disputes over the properties of refugees. Thousands of cases involve former SED or People's Army (NVA) functionaries, perhaps even *Stasi* operatives who acquired attractive properties at low cost before the currency union. Such functionaries sometimes managed to destroy or remove all public records of the previous ownership, presumably with the assistance of the same friends who had facilitated the dubious acquisition of a refugee's property in the first place. Present-day local officials who belong to the SED's successor organization, the Party of Democratic Soialism (PDS), often did their best to interfere with efforts to reestablish the claim of the refugee. All the while the PDS daily newspaper, *Neues Deutschland*, trumpeted headlines about the "great raid" of the rich West Germans on East German real estate.

The Unification Treaty of 3 October 1990 contains numerous formulations inviting claims for restitution—even from those who donated their apartment houses to local authorities—but it is also full of loopholes that set up hurdles for the claimants. It is rarely easy after forty years of communist rule to demonstrate the chicanery of corrupt officials and their party friends. Moreover, public use of property for building residential housing, parks, or sports facilities revives old GDR laws regarding the priority of public property over its restoration to a previous owner. Compensation depends on the "value at the point of expropriation," and there is bound to be controversy about real estate values of years ago (especially in the absence of a market economy). Many properties were also overloaded with mortgages by the GDR government that now have to be serviced. In addition, they are likely to be woefully rundown, polluted, and neglected.[10] Title records are so poor that even East German cities and towns have difficulties documenting their own property titles. Since private ownership of land was undesirable in the GDR, some land registry records were lost, destroyed, or not maintained from the late 1940s onward. Whatever new records ensued often did not match the old ones and were not based on accurate measurements or boundaries. The new land registry personnel can hardly keep up with new transactions, not to mention clearing up the old ones.

Participants in the Roundtable discussions during the winter of 1989-1990 addressed the extraordinary complexity of these questions. A prominent member of the Roundtable, Wolfgang Ullmann (a leader of Democracy Now and later a Minister without portfolio in the de Maizière government), proposed the creation of a Trust Agency (*Treuhandanstalt*) for maintaining partial ownership by GDR citizens in people's property. Ullmann's initiative constituted a daring attempt to make average citizens shareholders in "GDR, Incorporated."[11] Thanks to his efforts—though probably many years down the road—the average GDR citizen may yet receive such a share, albeit small compensation for decades of repression.

Meanwhile, the Democratic Peasants' Party (DBD) sponsored a bill in the Volkskammer prior to the March 1990 election seeking to transform land owned by the LPG cooperatives from "people's property" into private property to be sold or leased by LPG members if desired.[12] Ullmann succeeded in stopping this proposed raid on people's property, just as he headed off attempts by trust agencies of various *Kombinate* and housing authorities that sought to sell public assets as if they were theirs alone.

The legal tangles resulting from cold expropriations under pressure and the corrupt shenanigans of individual former power-holders and profiteers, however, must not be confused with earlier legal enactments—including the democratic land reform and legal expropriation procedures against individuals—during the years of Soviet occupation. On the other hand, the victims of such measures and the government in Bonn may hesitate to accept the "socialist legality" of these transactions. In March 1991, a law was passed facilitating at least the process of determining ownership, compensation, and transfer to new owners. In spite of some flaws, it was a milestone on the way to a clearer "property constitution" in the ex-GDR.

The State Treaty on Monetary, Economic, and Social Union contains special provisions ensuring that new enterprises could acquire full title to property and committed the GDR to making suitable commercial and manufacturing sites available to the firms. Even the "people's land" under the VEBs that were being transformed into privately owned firms was to be deeded to them as their own property, with the proviso that a purchase price could be settled later when a functioning market would allow its de-termination. Once the purchase prices have been collected, the resulting sum will be the basis for the shares of the GDR citizens. There is considerable doubt, however, whether this solution is sufficiently reassuring to new buyers, investors, or entrepreneurs. The end of communist economic management on 1 July 1990 also brought an end to the recurrent annual bleeding of some 200 billion Marks from the VEB's production for the benefit of the state, promised new investment subsidies, and exchanged both the credits and the liabilities of the VEBs at an exchange rate of 2:1. All of these provisions constituted a notable advantage for enterprises embarking on the formation of a market economy.[13]

The Trust Agency for the People's Property

The problems of reconciling collective property and privatization were finally placed in the hands of a Trust Agency for the People's Property (the *Treuhandgesellschaft*). Established as a public holding company by the Law for the Privatization and Reorganization of People's Own Property of 1 July 1990, the *Treuhandanstalt* was authorized to administer eastern Germany's 8,000 VEBs and *Kombinate* as well as the "people's own" estates and forests. The Trust Agency was to decide which GDR firms would be bailed out and with how much money, which firms could invite outside partners and under what conditions, conditions for the outright sale of VEB firms, the future of the *Kombinate* and the people's own estates and forests, and the use of the profits generated by these firms.

Popularly called the *Treuhand*, the Trust Agency was inauspiciously housed in Nazi Air Force Minister Hermann Göring's old aviation ministry building in East Berlin. In terms of the assets and number of employees under its control, the agency is the largest enterprise of the world. It has also attracted never-ending criticism, attacks, and public demonstrations because of the painful nature of its decisions. The most spectacular expression of hostility to the *Treuhand* was the assassination on 1 April 1991 of its activist first president, Detlev Karsten Rohwedder, by the terrorist Red Army Faction.

The Trust Agency was originally responsible to the GDR's prime minister and cabinet, who in turn were accountable to the Volkskammer. Together, the cabinet and parliament appointed an administrative council. The council was composed of West German business leaders and experts and East German CEOs, but it included no representatives of small or medium-sized business or the trade unions. At the beginning of its operations, the Trust Agency established five trust stock companies (*Treuhand-AGs*)—one for the people's forests and estates and the others for all the VEBs—to oversee their transformation into private joint stock companies. Each VEB was required to produce a plan for this purpose and a certified opening balance by 13 October 1990. Failure to comply would mean automatic dissolution on 1 July 1991. For the first three months the Trust Agency provided liquidity loans to VEBs so that they could meet their payrolls and other obligations after the currency reform of 1 July 1990.[14]

The evolution of its difficult task can be followed by a perusal of relevant enactments between 17 June (the date on which the treaty on the currency union was completed) and mid-September 1990. Upon the insistence of the SPD in the Volkskammer, residential properties were allocated to municipal authorities that also controlled people's own property that was required for local services. The organic law for the privatization and reorganization of people's own property of 17 June set the following goals for the Trust Agency: (1) the speedy reduction of state entrepreneurial activity through privatization, (2) the establishment of competitive principles as quickly as possible, (3) the availability of real estate for economic purposes, and (4) the allocation of certified shares in people's property (which can be redeemed later) to holders of savings accounts that were exchanged on 2 July at exchange rates lower than 1:1. Such shares can be determined only after a survey of the people's own property and its productivity and other priorities have been set for its use in restructuring the economy and consolidating the state budget.[15]

The Trust Agency became the holder of the capital shares of the VEBs that were restructured or were in the process of reorganization until the creation of the trust joint stock companies. This was clarified further with a resolution of the de Maizière cabinet that provided the Trust Agency with a statute in mid-July and added further specifics about its legal rights in an executive ordinance in mid-August.[16] A second ordinance, enacted a week later, regulated the privatization of the considerable land, buildings, and other assets of the East German military and the Ministry for Disarmament and Defense. A third ordinance gave the Trust Agency control over the people's own estates, fisheries, fish ponds, horse ranches, state-owned forestry operations, and the *Kombinat* Animal Products. A fourth and fifth ordinance, on 12 September 1990, turned over the considerable property of the *Stasi* Ministry to the agency and determined the specifics of its takeover of *Stasi* commercial real estate.[17] In a report to the Volkskammer a day later, Trust Agency President Rohwedder announced that regional trust agencies should be established in place of the trust joint stock companies that had been decided earlier. Each would supervise about 250 to 350 small and medium-sized VEB enterprises. Rohwedder hoped that the decentralization of the mammoth responsibilities of the Trust Agency would benefit the growth of the East German market economy.

By this time, the text of the treaty on political union, which determined details of the Trust Agency's organization and capital, was already firm. The treaty subordinated the agency to the Federal Minister of Finance together with the Economics Ministry and whatever other ministries might be involved in particular cases. Henceforth, the statute of the Trust Agency could be changed only with the consent of the federal cabinet. Article 25 added representatives of each of the new *Länder* to the administrative council, eliminated representatives from the Volkskammer, and increased the number of council members to twenty. All members (including the chair) were to be appointed by the federal cabinet. The treaty pledged that the people's own property would only be used and sold for the benefit of the eastern areas. It authorized the Trust Agency to assist with clearing the debts of agricultural LPGs and to issue guarantees and other pledges. It raised its capital from 17 billion DM to 25 billion and specified that credits granted by it should be repaid "as a rule" by the end of 1995. Finally, the treaty on political union repeated the cabinet's earlier promise to indemnify the holders of savings accounts that exceeded the ceilings for the exchange rate of 1:1 at some future date.

A preliminary balance sheet in April 1991 revealed that only 300 VEBs had been privatized. Sales had secured approximately 300,000 jobs and generated 55 billion DM in promised investment by the new owners. Only 4 billion DM had been collected for these sales, while the *Treuhand* already expected to exceed its 1991 budget by 21 billion DM. This amount included 12 billion DM in assumed VEB interest payments, 4 billion for environmental clean-ups, 9 billion for rehabilitating run-down or inefficient VEBs, 2.5 billion to aid exports to Eastern Europe, 3.5 billion to assure liquidity, and 2 billion to close down some 330 VEBs (causing a loss of 80,000 jobs). In the end, the *Treuhand* expected to expend some 35 billion DM while gaining only 14 billion DM in sales—a substantial deficit to add to the cost of German unification. At the time of Rohwedder's assassination, East German unemployment was at a peak of 837,000 (representing 12 percent of the work force) plus another two million who were employed on shorter hours. The latter figure dropped by nearly one half by the end of the year, but the number of unemployed rose to over a million.[18]

Toward the end of 1991, in a November talk in Washington, D.C., Rohwedder's successor as *Treuhand* president, Birgit Breuel, claimed that the sale of 4,000 of 10,500 firms had generated revenues of $5 billion and yielded pledges of $55 billion in investments by the new owners. Two hundred enterprises had been acquired by foreign companies, mostly European,[19] and the *Treuhand* hoped to raise the share of foreign businesses to the 15 percent level typical of the western German "open economy." Branch-offices had been established in New York, Tokyo, and other cities abroad to promote such sales. Mrs. Breuel also cited the privatization of 24,000 retail stores, restaurants, and similar consumer outlets and the liquidation of 800 companies. Prospective buyers had to promise substantial future investments and plans for the modernization of their acquisitions. The German government promised investment grants of up to 23 percent of the total costs of acquisition, including real estate, and up to 20 percent of the costs associated with the expansion of an existing business. On purchases of vital capital equipment, the government offered grants up to 12 percent. Extraordinary tax incentives and depreciation allowances were also available for the first three years, and the *Treuhand* absorbed 85 percent of the old debts of privatized businesses.[20] Finally, prospective buyers were told that economic growth in East Germany was expected to exceed 10 percent in 1992 and 1993 and that public investment in the East German economy would continue at about $100 billion a year.

According to President Breuel, the speed of privatization accelerated in late 1991. Companies were sold, she said, at a rate of fifteen to twenty a day. If this rate could be maintained—and for March 1992, for example, a sales total of 511 firms was reported[21]—the *Treuhand* would complete its task by the end of 1993 or shortly thereafter. An underlying assumption—buttressed by demands by the trade unions and the eastern CDU—was that the unsalable remainder of large firms should be sold at any price. Many observers obviously expect that some of the biggest industrial white elephants or leftovers of VEBs, which remain after the profitable parts have been sold off, cannot possibly find buyers (even in the form of a management buyout). Reasons include the fact that they no longer have a market or are incapable of becoming competitive—given their low productivity, hugely redundant labor force, and/or rust-belt industry character. The death of such enterprises would not only increase mass unemployment but condemn whole regions to economic atrophy. The *Treuhand* would thus indeed become an industrial holding company but with the power to enforce modernization, trim the work force, and implement other measures to promote improved economic health of firms and the surrounding economic environment.

Privatize, Rehabilitate, or Shut Down?

Problems of personnel and leadership confronted the Trust Agency from the beginning. Rohwedder, who was appointed president followed a management shake-up in the wake of the resignation of the agency's first director, Reiner Gohlke (a railroad executive), set the agenda for a series of privatization measures.[22] Premier de Maizière's candidates for the administrative council of the agency were not only inexperienced in questions of market economics and capital but were also all former SED activists; some were possibly even *Stasi* agents.

In the first month after Germany's currency union, the Trust Agency's subsidy program for the 8,000 VEBs in its care became the target of requests totalling 20 billion DM. Rather than investigating each claim on its own merits, the agency simply decided to give each of the applicants 40 percent of what they had requested. Rohwedder's council proved to be a strong and prudent management team. After all of the East German regional trust directors had been replaced with West Germans or East German refugees with Western experience, the council stood up to West German takeover schemes such as those attempted by the luxury Steigenberger Hotel chain, which sought to buy all thirty-four Interhotel branches in eastern Germany. Nonetheless, the agency confronted numerous critics, ranging from workers facing unemployment to Western business managers complaining about bureaucratic complications and slow pace of the agency. Its biggest problem by far was its inability to attract the thousands of top Western executives Rohwedder had hoped to enlist to help manage the difficult task of transition.[23] Estimated needs included 12,000 CEOs and 30,000 members of boards for all the VEBs.

Differences of opinion also arose concerning the best policy for the difficult journey towards a market economy. The last communist government, headed by Hans Modrow, had only planned to turn the 8,000 VEBs into public stock companies that would operate within a market context—not to privatize them, as the *Treuhand* intended to do. Should the agency try to sell the old VEBs as quickly as possible, or should it attempt to help rehabilitate the East German enterprises regardless of the mounting costs? After lengthy deliberations, the agency dispatched a new set of guidelines opting for the second policy choice to the regional trust offices in late October 1990. The *Treuhand* considered most VEBs capable of successful restructuring, and it particularly favored those that continued to export to their former East European markets (such as the Trabant factory in Zwickau and the truck factory in Ludwigsfelde), even though such exports were heavily in need of subsidies.[24] This course of action at least bought time for the transition and, according to the opposition SPD, also bought CDU/CSU votes in the all-German elections on 2 December 1990.

The agency also became the object of bitter criticisms from such political heavyweights as the director of the Kiel Institute for World Economics, Saxony's Minister-President Kurt Biedenkopf (CDU), and former CDU General Secretary Heiner Geissler. Some critics considered the restructuring of communist enterprises by the agency, rather than by a new owner, an impossibility; others picked on Rohwedder himself; and a third line of attack aimed at the agency's alleged centralism. The president offered his critics a self-confident answer: "The Trust Agency is a machinery that has barely started, for the purpose of decommunizing forty years of communist economics. This is a unique undertaking that cannot be found in any of the other former socialist countries in the process of reform. There are no models for our task."[25]

Eventually, Biedenkopf joined the administrative council of the Trust Agency, and Rohwedder received the nomination of "Manager of the Year 1990" by *Industriemagazin,* a prominent business journal. Business organizations such as the National Chamber of Commerce (DIHT) and German employers associations began to endorse the agency and its desire for more autonomy in deciding the privatization of particular VEBs and for less interference by the new *Länder* governments. A spin-off organization, the Trust Agency for the Privatization of Retail Business, offered 8,500 retail stores and 2,500 restaurants for sale in November 1990. Economics Minister Haussmann (FDP) wanted to speed up the disassembly and reassembly of the *Kombinate* to make the new pieces more attractive for buyers. Haussmann considered the remuneration of VEB employees on short hours (who received 90 percent of salary) not low enough to encourage their looking for another job. At the same time, everyone feared that the East-West drain of qualified labor, caused by wage differentials in the two parts of Germany, would undermine the viability of the VEBs.

The claim of uniqueness for the Trust Agency is true enough. In Eastern Europe, the process of privatizing a communist economy has been compared to trying to turn fish soup into an aquarium of live fish—a process of change that is more easily accomplished in the opposite direction. Friedmanesque economic preferences would militate against the adoption of a public super agency like the *Treuhand,* which to Eastern Europeans has overtones of the old state planning commissions. But their choice is not free from criticism, either. In Hungary, which has been at privatization the longest, charges have been made that public enterprises are being sold too cheaply. The newly-elected government of July 1990 took firm control of the privatization process and prepared a major sale of state shops, restaurants, and retail businesses in 1991. In Poland, in contrast, the finance ministry handles privatization at a snail's pace. Among its early successes were sales of large enterprises to their workers for cash and "citizens' vouchers" issued as shares in the enterprises to be privatized. This idea enjoys the backing of both Lech Walesa and then Czechoslovak President Václav Havel. Polish state monopolies are frequently accused of exploiting their position to increase prices, cut output, and fuel inflation. A "shock privatization plan" was launched in the winter of 1990-1991 that would turn several hundred state enterprises into joint stock companies for provincial and local governments to sell off so they can raise revenues for the benefit of hospitals and other local services. Czechoslovakia passed a law on "small company privatization" in October 1990 but faces considerable difficulties with large factories and enterprises which, like the East German *Kombinate*, have to prepare their own plans for privatization. The country had a separate Ministry of Privatization, but its staff consisted of only a dozen officials.[26]

Why do Eastern Europeans shy away from the *Treuhand* approach to privatizing publicly-owned enterprises? Aside from its resemblance to the old state planning commissions, financial and socioeconomic costs are an important reason. A June 1991 symposium at the Eastern Europe Institute of the Free University of Berlin addressed this question and obtained some answers. As an economist from Hungary pointed out, Hungary's first privatization law initially applied only to 200 large state-owned companies and relied on Western consultants. Employing thousands of bureaucrats, as the Trust Agency does, seems extravagant to the Hungarian government. A second stage aimed at the Hungarian service sector, especially hotels and restaurants. The third stage, involving small and medium enterprises with fewer than 300 employees, was just beginning in mid-1991, again with consultants (who are entitled to a commission on each sale). The annual *Treuhand* budget of 17-25 billion DM or the vast sums flowing from Bonn into the five new *Länder* are far beyond the financial capacity of the Eastern European states, and they clearly prefer a gradual changeover of the legal framework to a market economy to the East German plunge. East Europeans particularly prefer joint ventures and arrangements limiting liability and offering tax breaks. Partnerships for manufacturing usually pair the Western investor's role of supplying technical know-how and marketability with the Eastern partner's ability to get along with the local authorities. Multinational investors even contract with the appropriate native ministries in order to operate and plan on a large-scale basis. In this fashion, Hungary and Poland have already traversed three-fourths of the way towards free market institutions—including private property rights and contract, commercial, tax, and social security law—and a free market in goods and labor. Hungary, moreover, has developed its capital market (banking and stock exchange systems) half the way, a step barely begun in Poland and all the other East European countries in 1991. The Commonwealth of Independent States has progressed a quarter of the way towards a market economy in its institutions and in the exchange of goods, as have the the then unified Czech and Slovak Republics. But the Russian labor market was also half emancipated in 1991, a process that had only just begun in the Czechoslovak federation. The rest of the East Europeans still confronts nearly all of the great changes required of a transition to a market economy.[27]

Preceding the establishment of the Trust Agency (and as a necessary precondition of its subsequent work), the first unification treaty of July 1990 already provided for a single currency, a common system of economic management, and a merger of the two welfare states. Joint committees of experts representing both governments had been at work since January. Bonn had formed a cabinet committee on German unity in early February. A first proposal for the currency union became a matter of public knowledge, and an object of heated debates, a mere two weeks after the March 1990 election. From 25 April onward, the East-West German groups of experts once again opened negotiations that resulted in a political showdown in which the Bonn government rejected a series of East and West German SPD demands for modifying the agreements (3 May). The resulting Treaty on Monetary, Economic, and Social union authorized the Bundesbank to exercise sweeping currency powers normally associated with a central bank. Pledging both parties to a common economic and legal order, the Treaty also established an arbitration tribunal for disputes and a common governing committee composed of representatives of both governments.[28] The governing committee was authorized to resolve disputes in the first instance, after which a dissatisfied party could appeal to the arbiters. Other articles spelt out details of the economic and social order that was to obtain following unification: trade, restructuring of GDR economic enterprises, agriculture, environmental protection, labor law, and social insurance. It also pledged Bonn to provide initial financing of unemployment insurance and pension benefits and extended the West German system of public insurance and budgetary law to the new states.

At the same time, the German-German treaty was remarkably vague about the problems of privatizing property, although it did mention "people's own property," economic restructuring, and the sale of "property held in trust" (*Treuhandvermögen*) in a cursory way. It also gave the West German finance minister special powers to limit the amount of credit given to public bodies in the GDR.[29]

An Evaluation of *Treuhand* Activities

East German workers have called the *Treuhand* the "job killer," even though the agency has labored mightily to save at least some of their jobs and had obliged VEBs to work out "social plans" for them in case they are left unemployed. Trade unionists have called it worse names ("butcher of East Berlin"), and at least one commentator has dubbed the agency "the former GDR's revenge" on the West Germans who have to pay about 30 billion DM a year for its operation while its sales generate only modest revenue. Without question, the Trust Agency performs an almost impossible mission against enormous odds.[30]

The herculean tasks confronting the *Treuhand* were enormously complicated by circumstances of German economic unification. However robust the East German economy may have seemed to foreign (and West German) observers before the collapse of the GDR, conditions had in fact become desolate even before the mass flight of workers in 1989-1990.[31] The economy suffered a knockout blow when, in response to passionate East German popular insistence, the East German mark was made equivalent to the West German DM at an exchange rate of 1:1.[32] Once implemented, the currency union significantly undermined the ability of most East German firms to survive in a free market. After 1 July 1990, the VEBs were compelled to meet their payrolls and other recurrent obligations at an inflated level priced in DM. Simultaneously, they faced a crushing debt load from what used to be normal transactions with the East German State Bank.[33] Low labor productivity—which was less than half of that of comparable West German enterprises—and antiquated production methods and facilities cried out for modernization credits in DM. Yet credit proved difficult to obtain, given the diminished value of company assets[34] and possible liens against enterprises for environmental cleanup.

Economic performance promptly faltered as East German consumers (at least initially) revealed their preference for West German products. Prices rose precipitously as government subsidies for basic goods and services were progressively eliminated. Sharply compounding the GDR's economic difficulties was the loss of postwar East German export markets in Eastern Europe. Former trading partners in Russia, Poland, Czechoslovakia, and elsewhere proved unwilling and unable to spend scarce hard currency for what used to be bartered goods at frequently discounted rates. The cumulative result of these circumstances was a basket case of a modern economy.

To be sure, the unifiers on both sides really had little choice in the currency question. Except for some protesting bankers (including Bundesbank President Karl-Otto Pöhl) and a jittery Frankfurt stock exchange, the advocates of rapid monetary and economic union may not have fully understood the magnitude of the step they were undertaking. If they had not given in to the thunderous demand of the East German populace and politicians for 1:1 exchange rate, the migration of the East Germans to the West would have become a torrent. Once they had done so, they found it almost impossible to overcome the pressure from unionized East German workers for wage increases that further reduced the expected attraction of a "low-wage area" for West German businesses. If only East Germany had remained a separate country with its own currency, like Poland—and without the discouraging compulsion to compare itself only with West Germany—it would have had an easier time putting its economic house in order.

There is no lack of critical literature on most aspects of West German economic unification policy and, in particular, the actions of the *Treuhand*. One former SPD member of parliament, Heinz Suhr, has cited a long list of improper decisions involving various VEBs, *Kombinate*, and buyers ranging from Siemens to Brown-Boveri. He blames in particular huge frauds and misrepresentations perpetrated by the old communist leadership and conspiracies on the part of the remaining functionaries. In his view, the *Treuhand* was a dubious construction from the outset, and its balance sheet from mid-1990 to mid-1991 constitutes a thinly disguised attempt to hide its obvious failures and political mismanagement. Suhr contends: "This approach to leave the transition from a planned economy to a market economy to the forces of the free market, was a failure."[35] According to Suhr, the *Treuhand* agency deserves the same fate as awaited many East German officials and agencies: to be *abgewickelt* (fired or shut down).

Two economically-trained journalists, Peter Christ (*Die Zeit*) and Ralf Neubauer (*Stuttgarter Zeitung*), depict the former GDR as an "internal colony" and criticize the paucity of industrial policy ideas within the *Treuhand*. In their view, the emphasis on privatization at, literally, any price creates anything but a stable new economic order, while the exorbitant costs of rehabilitating arbitrarily chosen enterprises does not make up for the absence of an industrial-political concept.[36] Neither Rohwedder, the "viceroy of Bonn colonialism" in East Berlin, nor Breuel escape accusations of serving as prime agents in the great "sell-out" of East German assets.

In a third critical book, economists Jan Priewe and Rudolf Hickel refer to the *Treuhand* as the "motor of East German de-industrialization."[37] They assail its "one-sided" emphasis on privatization and centralistic-bureaucratic structure, which has not even enabled the Trust Agency to prevail over state and local resistance.They also criticize the neglect in both the unity treaty and the *Treuhand* statute of labor market, regional, and environmental policy to buttress its decisions. The agency's personnel also comes in for criticisms directed at both old communist holdovers and the conflicts of interest among the West German CEOs on loan—some of whom may be tempted to hobble rather than develop their future East German competition.

Priewe and Hickel are well aware of the enormity of the *Treuhand's* mission, but they fault its conduct on several grounds. First, rehabilitation and orientation to the market of firms that were sold during the initial phase of the agency's existence were left entirely to the whims of the new owners. No attempt was made to harmonize privatization with the remaining mixed economic structures. Second, few foreign buyers appeared, and the rash of management buyouts (approximately 500 by the fall of 1991) virtually handed large firms over to the old communist managers rather than creating cooperatives made up of rank-and-file employees.[38] Third, they criticize the prevalence of smaller enterprises that were privatized through the fall of 1991 (51 percent employed fewer than 500 workers and 35 percent had only 150 employees or less) and the large number of layoffs that ensued. Forty-six percent of the workers were dismissed, 14 percent resigned, 11 percent retired early, and a similar percentage is being retrained. About a third of the firms unsold by late 1991 seems incapable of rehabilitation. Priewe and Hickel also note the unexpectedly large number of applications by local governments (33,000) for the acquisition of enterprises, which the unification treaties invited.[39]

Priewe and Hickel conclude that the currency and economic policies of unification have largely destroyed the East German network of suppliers and markets, such as they were, and replaced them with dependence on West German firms. Little remains of the autonomy of the East German industrial complex, and the high indebtedness and cost of salvaging the firms are making it doubtful whether the *Treuhand* will continue to receive the huge sums from Bonn envisaged thus far (30 billion DM annually and possibly as much as 400 billion DM to cover the debts by the year 2000).[40] The authors fear that after the initial unification boom, the East German burden will slow down West German growth as well and bring united Germany into a chronic crisis determined by the presence of the East German mezzogiorno. In combination, the Kohl government's policy of tax increases at the expense of workers and the lower classes and the danger that massive East German unemployment might create leverage to "deregulate" all labor markets in Germany indicate possible sources of destabilizing change within the unified nation.

So, in conclusion, what is the significance and what are the conceivable consequences of the ongoing transfer of power from the state to private enterprise in the former GDR? The *Treuhand* is obviously both an étatist stand-in for the deposed communist state and a harbinger of future economic change because of its penetration by private firms in the West. A considerable part of the East German economy will remain in public owner-

ship: the now communally-owned VEBs transferred from *Treuhand* control
to local governments, the unsalable white elephants that may be held as federal property or by a *Treuhand* industrial holding company, and enterprises
that receive temporary *Treuhand* guidance and subventions while they are
still in the process of privatization. On the other hand, a lion's share of former state enterprises—including some of the best firms and pieces of VEBs,
as well as spin-offs and new ventures—is solidly in the hands of West
German companies, including banks and insurance firms. Only a relatively
small part of privatized businesses, especially small and medium-sized *Mit-
telstand* enterprises (in keeping with Bonn ideological preferences), belongs
to East German entrepreneurs, including East German refugees who have
returned to the new states. Many such firms are dependent for their survival
on public or West German financial support and cooperation.

What is clearly emerging is a mixed economy containing both strong
pluralist (mainly West German) and decentralized public (local and *Länder*
government) elements. Even though this outcome hardly resembles unrealistic expectations of an aquarium of East German fish, monistic communist
antecedents are undeniably yielding to economic and institutional pluralism.
Despite many transitional problems in the wake of unification, the result
provides a basis for democratic government not unlike the one that prevailed
in the Federal Republic before 1990.

Notes

1. East Europeans like to use the simile of the aquarium full of fish
turned into fish soup. Easy as it has been to turn the live fish into soup, it is
well-nigh impossible to turn the fish soup back into an aquarium of live
fish, or profit-maximizing entrepreneurs.

2. Some SED/PDS functionaries obviously had their own idea of socialist property when they attempted to flee to the Soviet Union with 107
million DM ($70 million) of party property in cash in October 1990 and
were caught. Secret bank accounts of the state party have been subsequently
found, and the issue of such dubious wealth in a poor country—SED property alone is believed to total 3 billion DM—loomed large in the public
mind. PDS leaders, in particular Gregor Gysi, denied knowledge of the financial shenanigans of party functionaries.

3. *Die Zeit*, 16 March 1990.

4. Order no. 124 of the Soviet Military Administration in Germany
(SMAD) decreed this pursuant to the Potsdam Agreements and Allied
Control Council Law no. 10. See Gregory W. Sandford, *From Hitler to*

Ulbricht: The Communist Reconstruction of Eastern Germany, 1945-46 (Princeton, New Jersey: Princeton University Press, 1983), esp. chapter 3.

5. A plebiscite in 1946 in Saxony ostensibly sanctioned the seizure of expropriated assets without compensation and their transfer to state ownership. SMAD Order no. 64 of 17 April 1948 completed this phase and declared the "people's property" to be inviolable.

6. Sandford, 85-118, provides an account of the land reform campaign and its implementation. The Modrow government and the Soviet Union insisted in 1990 that the 1945-49 expropriations not be undone but simply accepted.

7. The Modrow government, in early 1990, for the first time reversed the trend and encouraged the creation of new private enterprises. It also permitted the repurchase of firms expropriated since 1972.

8. There were three types of these cooperative farms: one involving only arable land, a second involving arable land as well as machinery and draft animals, and a third encompassing everything. In 1957, the share of refugee properties among the LPGs amount to 57 percent of the arable acreage. At that time, nearly a million farmers had been collectivized, and a similar number followed by 1960.

9. Prime Minister de Maizière and others resisted returning the property itself, if at all possible. They favored compensation in all cases but were overruled. The government decision to favor restitution over compensation is now considered a major mistake because it hindered rapid privatization. See *Stuttgarter Zeitung*, 18 June 1990. Observers also feared that windfall appreciation of some properties would unduly favor some owners.

10. For details of the unification treaty, see the *Bulletin*, 6 September 1990, and the Basic Law, arts. 14 and 135a. Also see *Der Spiegel*, 8 October 1990: 46-77, and Appendix 4 to this volume. By 1991, experts estimated over one million claimants. Among them are various victims of expropriation by the Third Reich. Some of those who lost their property by action under the Soviet occupation (1945-1949) are also suing to overturn the clauses of the treaty that have legalized those expropriations.

11. Wolfgang Ullmann, a theologian and church historian, viewed the privatization campaign and refugee claims with some misgivings and proposed a periodization that would separate claims from pre-Wall flight from the post-1961 properties in question. *Die Zeit*, 16 March 1990.

12. Many of the LPG members showed little desire to pull out of their respective cooperative agribusinesses because their original farms and the conditions that had made them viable had long disappeared. Similarly, many refugees saw little point in reclaiming their farms whose soil had been depleted and polluted and whose other assets had been ruined by the longtime operations of the LPGs' monoculture.

13. The inalienability of about 50 percent of the land had also been a major obstacle for the 600 joint ventures established by June 1990. Moreover, there was no lack of West German speculators and real estate agents with few scruples who were travelling up and down the GDR looking for bargains and opportunities in the midst of all the legal confusion. See *Der Spiegel*, 26 March 1990: 140-42. On the property questions, see *Rheinischer Merkur/Christ und Welt*, 11 May 1990; *Göttinger Tageszeitung*, 10 May 1990; and *Stuttgarter Zeitung*, 18 June 1990. For an account of incidents of massive fraud and racketeering, see *Der Spiegel*, 29 October 1990: 16-27.

14. See Heinz Suhr, *Was kostet uns die DDR?* (Frankfurt: Eichborn, 1990), 14-21; and *Die Zeit*, 13 July 1990.

15. *Gesetz zur Privatisierung und Reorganisierung des volkseigenen Vermögens (Treuhandgesetz) vom 17. Juni 1990*, effective 1 July 1990. Also see art. 25 of the Unification Treaty of 3 October 1990 and Federal Ministry of Finance, *Die Tätigkeit der Treuhandanstalt* (31 October 1991): 8-13.

16. *Beschluß des Ministerrates über die Satzung der Treuhandanstalt vom 18. Juli 1990 und Erste Durchführungsverordnung zum Treuhandgesetz vom 15. August 1990*.

17. *Vierte und Fünfte Durchführungsverordnung zum Treuhandgesetz vom 12. September 1990*. The *Stasi* alone owned over 2,000 buildings, apartments, and recreation facilities, not to mention its vast military arsenal. The considerable property of the SED/PDS and the other bloc parties also became part of the assets at the disposal of the Trust Agency.

18. Hans Luft, "Die Treuhandanstalt," in *Deutschland Archiv*, 24 (December 1991): 1270-76. The "shorter hours" ranged from zero to most of the working day.

19. According to *The Economist* (14 September 1991), the list of foreign buyers by 1 July 1991 was headed by Switzerland (with twenty-one), followed by France (fourteen), Austria (ten), Sweden (nine), and the United Kingdom (eight). The United States followed with seven. Well over 3,000 firms had been sold by that date.

20. See Federal Ministry of Economics, *Investing in the Future: Germany's New Federal States* (Bonn, 1991) and *Investment Incentives in Eastern Germany* (New York: Treuhand Office, 1991). For a running tally of privatizations, see also the monthly *Treuhandanstalt Informationen*.

21. *The Week in Germany* (24 April 1992). At that time, about 5,000 companies were said to be still for sale, but there was no mention of an unsalable remainder. In December 1991, the eastern CDU spoke of ten to fifteen "structure-determining" larger enterprises that were to become federally-owned. At about the same time, Metal Workers Union President

Franz Steinkühler repeated his suggestion to turn the *Treuhand* into an industrial holding company to be supported by a public investment trust that
would finance one-fourth of the capital of *Treuhand* and the privatized enterprises. See *Der Tagesspiegel*, 10 December 1991, and *Handelsblatt*, 1
December 1991. Also see Federal Ministry of Finance, *Economic Assistance in the New German Länder* (Bonn: May 1991).

22. Rohwedder, who at one time had served as state secretary of the
Economics Ministry in the Helmut Schmidt administration, was the very
successful chair of the Hösch steel group that had required rescue from the
brink of oblivion earlier. One of his East German privatizations involved
Pentacon, the makers of Praktica cameras, three-fourths of which used to be
exported at sizable discounts to attract foreign currency. With a workforce
of 5,600, Pentacon was considered unsalvageable unless the agency would
pump 160 million DM into its operations, even after dismissing two-thirds
of its employees. Rohwedder decided to liquidate the firm. See *The Economist*, 25 August and 20 October 1990.

23. *Der Spiegel*, 15 October 1990: 40-45. Rohwedder served as head
of the Trust Agency at a considerable loss in salary and had signed a four-
year renewal contract.

24. *Der Spiegel*, 29 October 1990: 146-49. There are conflicting esti-
mates of the market value of the East German industrial enterprises.
Modrow's government had estimated them at 750 billion East Marks;
Rohwedder casually mentioned the figure of 600 billion DM.

25. *Der Spiegel*, 12 November 1990: 154-55 and *Die Zeit*, 16 November 1990. As a result of substantial decentralization, regional offices had
taken over some 3,500 of the 8,000 VEBs. Municipalities were expected to
run another 2,000, which would leave only 1,000-1,500 VEBs under the
central office. About 1,000 were expected to fold. Some 500 agricultural
processing firms were to become municipal as well.

26. *The Economist*, 17 November 1990: 88.

27. *Tagesspiegel*, 11 and 25 June 1991.

28. The independent arbitral tribunal (*Schiedsgericht*) consisted of a
president and four members to be appointed for two-year terms, with each
government proposing candidates and alternates. If the appointments were
not completed within a month following the treaty's implementation, the
president of the EC court was authorized to make the appropriate appointments.

29. For authoritative texts, see "Vertrag über die Schaffung einer
Währungs-, Wirtschafts- und Sozialunion," *Bulletin* (New York: German
Press and Information Office, 18 May 1990), and *Treaty Between the FRG
and the GDR Establishing a Monetary, Economic and Social Union* (New
York: German Information Center, nd). Also see Appendix 3.

30. Among its trials and tribulations, there have been a number of scandals involving particular cases of privatization such as that of the Henningsdorf steelworks, which were occupied by the workers to keep them from being sold to an Italian bidder.

31. See especially the accounts in "The European Community and German Unification," *Bulletin of the European Communities*, supplement 4/90: 30-33, and Leslie Lipschitz and Donogh McDonald, eds., *German Unification: Economic Issues* (Washington, D.C.: International Monetary Fund, December 1990). The GDP level for all employed persons in the GDR was estimated at 40 percent of its equivalent in West Germany prior to the collapse of the East German regime. See Deutsches Institut für Wirtschaftsforschung, *DIW Wochenbericht* (28 June 1990).

32. The 1:1 ratio was to apply to wages, pensions, rents, and savings up to a level of 4,000 East Marks, after which an exchange rate of 2:1 prevailed. Persons over fifty-nine were allowed a higher savings threshold (DM 6,000), and those under fifteen a lower level (DM 2,000) before their money came under the 2:1 rate. The view that the currency reform had a major negative impact on the future of the GDR economy is widely shared. See, for example, Wolfram Engels, "Kein Aufschwung Ost," in *Wirtschaftswoche* (1991).

33. Under the communist system, the East German State Bank collected all the profits of firms and returned some of the money to selected enterprises for expansion and development. These were not true debts and credits, but a mechanism for central planning and direction. At the time of the currency reform, the State Bank held some 200 billion East marks for this purpose.

34. According to a survey of the *EC Bulletin* in late 1990, East German steel production was inefficient and expensive, the chemical industries of pre-1939 vintage, and machinery devoid of the electronic control mechanisms barred by the Western Cocom list. *Bulletin of the European Communities*, supplement 4/90: 30-33. The entire infrastructure of roads, transport, and communications was likewise in a dismal state, and energy supplies depended heavily on pollution-generating lignite coal as well as on a string of Chernobyl-style nuclear plants.

35. Heinz Suhr, *Der Treuhandskandal. Wie Ostdeutschland geschlachtet wurde* (Frankfurt: Eichborn, 1991), esp. 149-208. The author criticizes in particular the centralistic and bureaucratic nature of the *Treuhand*, its neglect of structural measures to encourage competition and curb mass unemployment, and its personal conflicts of interest and frequent partisan interference in economic decisions.

36. Peter Christ and Ralf Neubauer, *Kolonie im eigenen Land. Die Treuhand, Bonn und die Wirtschaftskatastrophe der fünf neuen Länder* (Berlin: Rowohlt, 1991), esp. 113-54.

37. Jan Priewe and Rudolf Hickel, *Der Preis der Einheit. Bilanz und Perspektiven der deutschen Vereinigung* (Frankfurt: Fischer, 1991): 164.

38. Ibid., 173.

39. Ibid., 164-78.

40. Ibid., 179-84, and chapters 8-10.

9

Social Policies at a Crossroads

Gunnar Winkler

As a result of the defeat of German fascism in World War II, two German states emerged with a common historical past but with different economic, political, and social systems. In the West, the Federal Republic's "social market system" combined market-oriented economics with socialist German traditions.[1] At the same time, a system developed in the East that closely followed the Soviet Union's interpretation of socialism. The East German system, however, was no mere copy of the Soviet system. Instead, it combined elements of traditional socialist policy with new elements of social justice which had been ignored in the past. Among them were the right to work, receive equitable monetary compensation, obtain guaranteed access to housing and leisure, and access to a system of social benefits that would provide for illness and social security at old age based on gender equality. Most workers, in particular, associated these guarantees with socialist ideals in general rather than prior achievements of the Soviet Union.

After forty years of "real existing socialism" in the German Democratic Republic (GDR), the social goals of equality, and equal treatment of persons regardless of gender, race, nationality, and age had not been attained in practice. This is not to deny real progress. The population of the former GDR regarded many accomplishments in education, social provisions governing pregnancy and maternity leave, maternal obligations, and uniform social security arrangements as worthwhile—and assumed they would have lasting value even after German unification.[2] The social goals and achievements in themselves were neither unrealistic nor overly ambitious. Instead, the reasons such goals had not been fully achieved lie in political and economic structures that caused a myriad of social problems, tensions, and conflicts. A policy of substantial income equalization within the framework of a centrally-directed state economy which was based exclusively on public ownership restricted inducements for economic development and production. In particular, limitations imposed on private businesses reduced performance, and the absence of self-motivating incentives discouraged economic development as a requisite for improvements in the general standard of living. Lingering income inequalities between blue collar and white collar workers, members of the intelligentsia and functionaries in the Party and state apparatus, between young and old, and men and women intensified the discussion about social equality and ultimately resulted in lowering professional motivations. In the area of social policy, the decline in production capabilities had serious consequences for the maintenance of an increasingly expensive social security network.

Incomes generally increased during the 1980s, but money in private hands could not be effectively utilized because of the lack of consumer goods and services. Consumption stagnated or declined. Inconsistencies in the economic development of the two German states became ever more evident and—coupled with extremely limited travel opportunities—led to increased emigration to West Germany and other Western countries. In turn, this contributed to heightened pressure by state security institutions on individual citizens.

The exaggerated concern for domestic stability—or at least the appearance thereof—distorted economic and social developments in the former GDR. The right to work resulted in unlimited job security which detrimentally affected production performance. Inflated conceptions and expectations of social protection led to widespread misuse of social regulations in the areas of sick leave and working hours.

The achievements of social policy increasingly became subject to the threat of economic failure. Growing production inefficiencies threatened the maintenance of guaranteed social rights. Special social programs such as the provision of public housing could be realized only by reducing the quality of construction.

Social policy planning became more and more centralized, and the rights and opportunities of communes and factories were subject to ever increasing central restrictions. The participatory role of citizens and officially sanctioned mass organizations such as the Free German Federation of Trade Unions (*Freier Deutscher Gewerkschaftsbund*, or FDGB) was limited to the ideological legitimation of the political system. Decisionmaking in the area of social policy excluded cooperation and participation as well as a willingness to consider new scientific, theoretical, and empirical findings.

Social Policy and German Unification

The unification process offered a historical opportunity to realize a comprehensive social reform, at the end of which an improved system of social security could have emerged in the unified German state.[3] Combining the two systems created possibilities for social innovation, including new organizational forms, new regulations, and new ways of problem solving. Unlike a social union reduced to a uniform welfare system providing equal benefits for all citizens, a comprehensive social reform in both parts of Germany which would have aimed at higher levels of social security, minimized unwarranted social differences, and fostered an environment of dialogue could have set an example of social innovation for all of Europe. However, the current social union falls short of such expectations..

Germany's social union is a social and economic experiment in two important respects.[4] First, the former GDR's social system—which was rooted in a centrally-planned economy—has rapidly been displaced by an established system of social security based on market principles. The new all-German system does not reflect the fact that different social systems are based on different political and economic conditions as well as contrasting autobiographical circumstances, ways of life, mentalities, values, and behavior patterns which cannot be changed within a short period of time. Social union is not only the adoption of a legal system such as social law; instead, it mainly represents an assimilation of living conditions—a process which will inevitably prove time-consuming. Finally, it is apparent that social union will lead to social changes in all of the German *Länder*, albeit with different foci and results.

Second, the realization of social union in unified Germany can contribute to the fusion of social systems within the context of a European union. In the long run, different social models from Eastern Europe will merge with those in the West. More progressive solutions for a higher standard of social security are at least a possibility.

Social union in Germany is based on assimilation. The final policy objective is to standardize the system of social security throughout both parts of the country. In contrast, the Commission of the European Community favors a system of "social convergence" which "fosters cooperation in order to achieve certain social and political aims, but the paths taken to realize those aims are left to the individual states."[5] European conceptions should not be ignored in the process of social union in Germany. Time pressure should not lead to changes that will later hinder the European integration process and contradict the basic conceptions of the 1989 European Community Charter of Fundamental Social Rights.[6]

The specific conditions in the new federal states that have influenced and continue to influence the implementation of social union include the following:

- Since the mid-1980s, deficient supplies of luxury goods and services were accompanied by deficits in products and services of even basic needs. Contradictions between income and consumption became a factor of social insecurity in the GDR. Stagnation and dissatisfaction finally led to political instability and the loss of political power by the ruling Socialist Unity Party.[7] The obvious decline in the standard of living and the gap between living conditions of the general population and the political elite, on the one hand, and between the population in the GDR and in the Federal Republic of Germany, on the other hand, contributed to political unrest in East Germany in the late 1980s.

- The transition to a market economy has created unavoidable social conflicts in that former problems of the socialist planned economy are supposed to be resolved by an economically efficient market-oriented system which manifests, however, totally different social structures than those in the former GDR.[8] Since unification, the existing contradictions inherent in the legal social system of the Federal Republic of Germany have been imposed on the five new federal states. That is, shortcomings, deficiencies, and injustices inherent in the West German social system have been exported to the East German setting.[9]
- A different appreciation of social security and social equality which was deeply implanted in the minds of the East German citizens impedes faster progress toward the standardization of social policy. Recognized rights to work and governmental assistance have caused a "comprehensive insurance mentality."[10] Already in the past, high expectations concerning social policy had proven to be a demotivating and hindering factor in the GDR. Today, East Germans are ill prepared to deal with new circumstances such as mass unemployment.
- The German social union is not a model for Europe since the character of the unification process reflects the adaptation and adoption of social laws and services already in existence in the western part of the nation. Many of the citizens in the new eastern states resent the fact that they could not contribute to the Unification Treaty because they were not invited to enter into a social dialogue regarding the issue of unification. Only those with a grasp of the legislation of the Federal Republic of Germany are able to comprehend the content of the state treaties on monetary, economic, social, and political union. Confronted with a new and alien legal system, most East German citizens share a sense of powerlessness and insecurity.

The Implementation of Social Union: Three Phases

Immediately preceding and following unification, the concepts regarding a pending social union have undergone a series of modifications. So far, three main phases can be distinguished. The first phase, which lasted from early 1990 to mid-1990, involved the conception of a new social policy. Initially, the concept of a new social policy based on the principles of market economy sought to link features of the social systems in the East and the West that were considered worth preserving. Prior to unification, only politicians of the major parties had commented sporadically on issues of social policy; now, for the first time, the public began to involve itself in the discussion.[11] During the so-called Roundtable discussions and later in the Volkskammer, a Social Charter for Germany was developed which was based on the EC's draft of a European Social Charter.[12] Scientists and practitioners in the various fields of social policy initiated a lively debate regarding different aspects of the social union. In particular, general pension adjustments, issues related to women's pensions, and policies that would facilitate combining work and family duties for women were discussed.[13]

It became quickly evident that social union involved more than just a social cushion during the transition process of the GDR.[14] Instead, it implied a fundamental change of social structures and living conditions. However, public pressure in East Germany and the interests of leading politicians in both parts of the country did not allow sufficient time for the development of new concepts. With the introduction of monetary union on 1 July 1990, hitherto unknown consumption and travel possibilities became a reality for millions of people.

A second phase in the modification of concepts regarding a pending social union ensued with the conclusion of the Unification Treaty during the summer and fall of 1990. The Treaty assumes that the adaptation of the political and economic structure of the Federal Republic of Germany by East Germany would be accompanied by the mandatory introduction of social legislation in the West.

The third phase spans the implementation of social union from the winter of 1990 to the present. Unprecedented social problems in both parts of Germany have led to necessary adaptation processes which became known as *"Nachbesserungen"* ("touch up measures"). Errors in conceptualization and in judgment about the nature and the magnitude of economic and social problems have demanded continuous adjustments, in particular with regard to the following issues:

- A growing unemployment rate, which seems impervious to traditional policy measures such as employment subsidies and therefore causes social and political conflicts.
- Impoverishment of social groups, especially retirees, can be expected and will eventually lead to a growing number of citizens who will depend on welfare or other public assistance to avoid becoming home-

less. Within the German retirement system, women are particularly disadvantaged.
• Growing discrimination against women in professional career situations and their displacement into the role of housewives.

The first two years of the social union not only raised expectations and hopes but also induced fears and feelings of resignation. East Germans do not long for the old system of the former GDR, but most are disappointed about social inequalities and polarization between East and West. A comparison between socialist and capitalist systems has become a regional comparison between East and West, at least for citizens in the new federal states.

Illusions about the social union are widespread. Especially in the former GDR, principles of a market economy have been reduced to the availability of goods and services. The market economy is not yet understood as a system that combines economic strength with unemployment, homelessness, poverty, and discrimination. Many East Germans still rely on orders from authorities ("those up there"). To take responsibility is a learning process that is still under way. The realization that the advantages of socialism and a social market economy are not available at the same time and that the accompanying disadvantages are also a fact of life is only slowly being accepted.

Illusions also existed in the western part of Germany. Social problems which have not been solved in the past forty years cannot be solved via unification with East Germany. Many planned social reforms, such as basic security and opportunities for women in their professional as well as their family life, have been put on hold. A joint solution for unresolved social questions in East and West Germany has been postponed to a later date and will have to be dealt with within the framework of a common social policy devised by the European Community.

In the remaining sections, I will concentrate on the topics and problems that will remain of central importance in the development of social issues in unified Germany. These include

• Changes in the social structure and associated labor market problems.
• Changes in the standard of living for all social groups and increasing levels of inequality.
• Social problems for women and senior citizens which result from the adoption of West German social laws and social instruments to the region of East Germany.

Changes in the Social Structure

As has been mentioned earlier, social union is more than just a social cushion accompanying economic and political change. More fundamentally, it is a process of social transformation which is in no way inferior to qualitative changes in the economy. It does not entail a simple integration of East German citizen into an existing system comparable to a person's joining a club. Instead, it constitutes a change in social structures caused by basic economic reconstruction as well as changes in patterns of thinking and behavior.

It is often ascertained that many problems, such as the high rate of unemployment in the new federal states, could not have been predicted because of the lack of accurate empirical data regarding the economy of the former GDR. This is true to some extent, but such assertions certainly should not be generalized.

A number of reasons account for the precipitous increase in the number of unemployed workers in eastern Germany.[15] First, the GDR's economic system produced predominantly for purposes of its own consumption. Once confronted with the unified German market, many goods were not competitive. Many of the industries have been and will be eliminated because of the superior production conditions in western Germany.

In addition, East German industrial productivity at the time of unification was only about half of that in the West. Exports to the Federal Republic were subsidized in order to obtain convertible currency. Moreover, the East German economy was closely linked to the economies of Eastern Europe. Following unification, traditional markets in Russia, the Ukraine, Poland, and Czechoslovakia—to name only the most important trading partners in the East—virtually disappeared. Thus, employment for export-oriented businesses was no longer available, while the reorientation of trade from the East to the competitive West failed. Overall, East German productive capabilities could not survive in a market-driven economy.

Finally, the former GDR had nurtured a system that secured employment for women by providing, among other things, an extensive network of child care facilities but neglected technical infrastructure and health care. A necessary improvement of the technical infrastructure can only be accomplished in connection with a complete change of the former employment structures.

Economic changes will significantly affect class and group structures. The privatization of the economy will encourage the creation of a middle class, and cooperatives in agriculture and trade will disappear. The percentage of white collar workers will increase as the number of blue collar workers declines. Large sectors of the former intelligentsia will retire early, become unemployed, or will have to work in completely different professional areas since most of them are considered to be too closely aligned with the former communist system. The emergence of a new intellectual elite will take decades.

Existing professional and educational arrangements are adjusted to the new economic structures. The level of education was high in the former GDR, even in international comparison. For example, mandatory education encompassed ten years of schooling; more than 90 percent of the workforce had some form of professional training. However, this system had limitations as well. Not everyone was allowed to work in his or her desired profession or to study one's area of choice at the university. The right to work and to an education was achieved by matching the number of trainees and students with the number and the kinds of available jobs. Current changes imply a completely new employment structure with uncertain future contours. The results are high unemployment rates and uncertainties regarding professional training and retraining. In the past, 75 percent of the job-related training in the former GDR was pursued directly at the enterprise level. Since such firms are now being closed, new private and municipal institutions will have to take their place.

New employment structures increase the variety of individual employment patterns, but they also imply changes in demographic structures. The percentage of employed women already has been reduced drastically in favor of their male counterparts. The number of unskilled workers is likely to increase.

The birth rate in the former GDR was relatively high compared to other Central European countries. The majority of women gave birth very early, i.e., between the age of twenty and twenty-four, and about 90 percent of women had at least one child. About 30 percent of the parents were single parents. The divorce rate and the number of singles in the GDR were comparatively high as well. Demographers predict that the birth rate will decline, women will have children at a later age, and the divorce rate will fall because women will tend to stay with their husbands to be financially secure. Thus, the traditional family pattern in western Germany will become dominant in the new federal states because of changed employment and income conditions.

All of these changes are associated with a considerable increase in unemployment. Instead of the earlier GDR pattern of subsidized underemployment, unemployment is now subsidized by the public sector. As indicated in Table 10.1, the number of registered unemployed workers and persons who participated in short-time work (*Kurzarbeit*) and work-creating measures or chose early retirement toaled more than 3.5 million by April 1992.

Table 10.1
Development of the Labor Market in Eastern Germany, 1990-1992
(average numbers in thousands)

	1990	1991	1992 (April)
Employees	8,844	7,054	7,014
Registered Unemployed	240	1,180	1,150
Short-time Workers	758	1,700	437
Early retirement	165	483	779
Participants in Work-Creating Measures	18	290	1,156

Source: Federal Labor Agency, Institute for Labor Market and Job-Related Research.

At first glance, the risk of becoming unemployed is similar among men, women, the old and the young, and different occupational groups. Chances for reemployment, however, are much lower for women, older citizens, handicapped people, and single parents. For the present, the problems of the past still influence the pattern of unemployment and the chances for reemployment. These affect primarily

- The reduction of high employment rates in inefficient industrial sectors (e.g., the energy sector) and lay-offs of employees in ecologically outdated factories.
- The elimination of institutions associated with the centralized Party and state apparatus of the previous GDR regime.
- The decrease in the number of jobs in the consumer goods industry through the import of goods instead of import of capital.
- The elimination of jobs caused by the decay or the liquidation of social infrastructure previously provided by companies (such as child care and health care facilities) and municipal institutions (including out-patient clinics, public health care centers). The reduction of these institutions limits the possibilities of women to find employment and to coordinate family duties and professional careers.

Unemployment in eastern Germany is not the result of technological advances but is caused instead by economic stagnation which contributes in turn to a further decline in industrial efficiency. Possibilities for creating new jobs are restricted by the inadequate utilization of industrial capacity, which both lessens incentives by private entrepreneurs to invest and restricts the financial resources of local and regional political communities. Persisting wage differentials between the new and the "old" federal states exacerbate the unemployment situation by encouraging many East German workers to commute to better-paying jobs in the West.

The extension of private enterprises has led in eastern Germany to a "renaissance of entrepreneurship," resulting at least in the short run in a "high rate of losers" because of a lack of experience and investment capital.[16] Solutions are hard to come by since a certain level of unemployment is characteristic of all market economies.[17] In addition, the adaptation of West German regulations seems problematic. In the Federal Republic, a second market in the form of work-providing measures, retraining, and occupational institutions was created in the early 1980s. Long-term unemployed and persons subject to welfare were provided with work for two to three years, which had the added advantage of improving public services in the communal and social areas. In the eastern part of Germany, however, such measures are presently being utilized in all areas and industrial branches in order to ensure normal economic processes, maintain social services, and minimize the risk of conflict among certain occupational groups (e.g., scientists). However, long-term unemployment of women and certain professionals already became evident by the end of 1991.

Unemployment among women is a special problem. In the past, a high rate of employment among women was characteristic for the former GDR. On the average, 4.2 million out of a total of approximately 5.5 million women between the age of 15 and 65 were employed in 1989. This corresponds to 48.9 percent of the total workforce. At the beginning of 1990, 90 percent of all women between the age of 15 and 60 were either still employed, apprentices, or students.

It was not only the acute lack of labor after World War II that created new employment possibilities for women but also the idea that the personal development and the economic independence of women could only be secured through their integration into the labor force. The right to work, which was guaranteed in the constitution of the former GDR, and its corresponding legal regulations created conditions which allowed life-long employment. At the same time, the underemployment of men and women limited their efficient use and their competitiveness.

Since 1990, the unemployment rate of women has exceeded the share of women in general employment. In April 1992, 62.3 percent of all unemployed workers were female. At 19.9 percent, the female unemployment rate was higher than the male unemployment rate of 10.8 percent. Often women with children and single parents are the first to lose their jobs. Their chances of reentering the job market are slim since men are accorded preference in even traditional female jobs. Few economists or politicians have addressed the issue of how to secure future employment of women. Indeed, the decline of female employment to the level of the "old" federal states is often declared as "normal." Concomitant implications are being accepted throughout East German society—for example, in the area of child care—as traditional patriarchal mentalities once again come to the fore.

The Development of the Standard of Living

The different initial levels of the economy and of the standard of living in both parts of Germany will have long-term consequences for the social system. A relatively low but rather equalized standard of living was characteristic of the former GDR.[18] At the same time, retired people in particular lived well below the average standard of living. The sources of poverty common in Western societies[19]—such as unemployment, a large number of children, and single parents supporting two or more children—were much less evident in East Germany, since support for single parents and families with children was especially well developed.

Poverty in East Germany is presently being caused by a variety of factors. Among them are general economic development, which combines growing unemployment with a longer duration of unemployment; changing employment conditions, which increase short- and part-time work, change permanent work contracts into temporary work contracts, and often result in reduced wages and salaries; and structural changes in jobs and professions due to changes in the economic and political structures. In certain job categories, this will result in the displacement of East Germans (and not only those who supported the old regime) by West Germans. Despite positive individual background verification, every civil servant is considered to be newly employed and past years of service are only partially counted toward income and retirement. For example, after thirty-five years of service, a fifty-one year old nurse is employed and paid as if she were only forty-one years of age. These policies result in lifelong reductions in incomes and pensions which will never be completely recouped. Fewer women, handicapped people, and retirees will be employed. Finally, the emergence of an all-German social system oriented toward families will discriminate against single persons and single parents.

As the new federal states continue to develop economically and socially, poverty will depend not only on one's position in life but also on existing resources. The living conditions of the entire region will be influenced by a lack of individual provisions for the future, small savings, and capital. In addition, income differentials between East and West will continue to exist for a number of years while consumer goods, rents, and services will cost nearly the same as in western Germany (and to some extent have already reached that level).[20] Citizens of the former GDR measure poverty less and less in relation to their situation in 1989 but compare instead their standard of living with that in western Germany. That is, East Germans are more concerned today with the "relative discrimination of a group of citizens within a given society."[21]

The material standard of living in the former GDR has increased, in particular when measured in terms of consumption levels, the availability of products, and unlimited travel opportunities. At the same time, social insecurity and fear have increased. Sociological surveys reveal that 50 percent of respondents express dissatisfaction with the perceived lack of social security, 70 percent with environmental problems, and fully 80 percent with the relation between prices and wages. High expectations about consumption and the future development of income levels and improvements in the environment are tempered by apprehension concerning work and the possibilities of linking jobs and motherhood.[22]

The Role of Women

The employment rate of women in the former GDR was one of the highest in the industrialized world. For many women, work was no longer considered an obligation or a pure economic necessity but had become an expression of individual freedom reflecting the desire to be economically independent. In other words, women increasingly had rejected the idea of being only housewives, economically dependent on their husbands and relying on their families for social interaction.

From the very beginning of the GDR's existence, policies toward women tended to concentrate on provisions that would allow the incorporation of the female sector of society into the workforce while allowing them to have families as well. The freedom of choice, to decide between work and motherhood, never existed in the GDR. Party and government officials confidently asserted that the problem of combining work and motherhood had been solved by the early 1970s.

The state, municipalities, and industrial enterprises had organized a comprehensive day care system in the GDR. In 1989, 802 of 1,000 children three years and younger were taken care of in day care nurseries, 951 between the ages of three and six attended nursery schools, and 812 school-age children utilized childcare facilities. Generally speaking, women consider the public day care system well worth maintaining.

Official sanctioning of work and motherhood led to special social privileges at work. For example, women with two children were entitled to work only forty hours a week instead of the normal load of forty-three hours. Almost all women could take one paid day of absence per month to tend to housework. Pension calculations incorporated the birth of children. Although many of these measures were born of necessity to increase the declining birth rate in the GDR, their effect on women was considered positive.

In the GDR, women enjoyed special status in social and family politics and in social and family law. Social security provisions (including health insurance and pension plans) took employment patterns into consideration. Marital status played a minor role since almost all women worked. Only a few family-related political measures reflected marital status. Even when a husband provided for the material and social security of his non-working wife, the independent social protection of the spouse was usually guaranteed. The material security of the woman did not depend on her husband's income.

Family law in the former GDR assumed the ideal case of life-long marriage and did not encompass other family units, such as unmarried couples living together, single parents, and foster families. Changes in living patterns were officially ignored, and the family—based on marriage—remained the legal standard.

Abortions were legal during the first twelve weeks after conception. West German law governing abortions, in contrast, was far more restrictive. Following unification, the Bundestag adopted a uniform abortion law based largely on the more liberal East German provisions. In response to a legal challenge by the Bavarian state government and dissident Christian Democratic parliamentarians, the Federal Constitutional Court declared the all-German law unconstitutional in May 1993. Pending passage of a new abortion bill by the Bundestag, however, women seeking an abortion will not be subject to legal prosecution.

Despite achievements in the level of education among women and the provision of day care facilities, a number of problems remained. While motherhood and family obligations permitted full time employment and continued professional training, possibilities for professional development were limited and were feasible only at high physical and psychological costs. To combine family and work often turned out to be a "double burden." In addition, gender inequalities persisted and were more pronounced than inequalities between other social groups despite legal achievements aimed at guaranteeing the equality of men and women. Many policy measures reinforced the maintenance of social differences and strengthened traditional role patterns. During the 1980s, in particular, policies aimed at women were made by men for women. Moreover, political measures were almost always limited to the working population—and increasingly to working mothers. Policymakers did not accord attention to non-working groups such as female retirees; indeed, the latter became victims of official policies.

Since unification, many of the social benefits that women in eastern Germany once considered essential for their own development have been eliminated or drastically curtailed. These include an extensive network of day care facilities, paid leaves of absence when children are sick, special protection regarding termination of employment, and a social security system based on one's own work and not that of the husband. While most East German women realize that these provisions did not guarantee social equality under the previous regime, they are now experiencing increasing social inequality due to the deterioration of conditions that once supported female work and economic independence. Many women in eastern Germany regret that social changes which were part of unification were not used to improve their situation, and most still believe in a career outside of the home.[23] In March 1991, 81 percent of women affirmed that job and family were equally important parts of their lives. Being "only" a housewife is hardly an alternative for most women, and employment is considered to be of central importance.

Those seriously seeking to combine family obligations with work must reconsider established West German social policy norms and practices. Their concerns must necessarily address the entry or reentry of women on the job market, the maintenance of day care facilities in the East and their development in the West, the separation of the role of women from marital status, a flexible acceptance of house work and child rearing duties for purposes of calculating social security benefits, and possibilities for family planning which include abortion as the final choice.[24]

Social Security

One of the major changes associated with unification involves the adoption of the West German social security law for all of Germany.[25] Although based on a common tradition, two very different social security systems developed in the two Germanys. The major problems associated with the transition can be summarized as follows:

- Instead of a highly centralized system with only two underwriters, a number of insurance companies whose programs differ only in minor fee differences and coverage policies compete for customers. Attempts to overcome the distinction between separate insurance schemes for blue collar and white collar workers insurance failed. Nor was it possible to establish a mandatory insurance system for everybody.

• The standardized fee of 10 percent for all employees was substituted by a system of premiums consisting of 6.4 per cent for health insurance, 8.35 percent for pension plans, and 3.4 percent for unemployment insurance. Thus, significantly higher insurance premiums have to be paid.

• Special services for mothers and single parents, such as extensive benefits in case of a child's illness, were eliminated. Free medication and out-patient and in-patient treatments will also gradually be adjusted to the West German system.[26]

A related problem involves the extension of the West German system of health care and out-patient services provided by private physicians in place of the previous state system administered by polyclinics on behalf of local government and industrial firms. On the one hand, this substitution will guarantee that health care accompanied by a low level of medical technology is a thing of the past. On the other hand, the cost-intensive monopoly of private doctors characteristic of western Germany was adopted in the new federal states without any modification. Out-patient and inpatient care were separated and partially inefficient organizational forms of health care were introduced. The total elimination of existing structures was faster than the short- and medium-term adjustments which might have been more desirable.[27]

Unification brought the inclusion of approximately 2.7 million retirees and more than 1.1 million men and women between the ages of fifty-five and sixty-five into the all-German population. In the past, inequalities in the standard of living were confined to the group of older versus younger retirees in western Germany. Today, a new dimension has been added: almost three million retirees differ significantly in their general standard of living, values, expectations, and patterns of behavior from their counterparts in the "old" states of the Federal Republic.[28]

Due to their shared past, pensioners in the new federal states share a number of social characteristics:

• Virtually all retirees, especially women, have worked all their lives.
• Almost all pensions are at a uniformly low level.
• Retirees are accustomed to a secure, although not always qualitatively high system of health care and social benefits.
• Retirees are accustomed to a system of basic security that is based on minimal pensions and subsidies of goods for basic needs and services.

Although a minimum level of existence was secured, the standard of living of retirees worsened, especially during the 1980s. The concerns of the older population were increasingly ignored, and many felt that they lived at the social fringe of society.

The developments surrounding the unification of the two Germanys led to a number of pension adaptations. From July 1990 through July 1991, pensions were increased for nearly 2.3 million retirees; 440,000 did not get the benefits of the adjustments because of their already high level of pension; and an additional 220,000 recipients of special pensions were not affected.[29] Increases in the amount of pension payments from June 1990 through January 1992 are shown in Table 10.2.

Another major change involves the acceptance of a dynamic system of pensions which guarantees yearly adjustments, a reduction of the retirement age to sixty for women and to sixty-three for men, and the adaptation of pensions for surviving dependents.[30] Thus, the ratio between pensions in the new and old states was approximately 1:2 in 1991. Men receive about 45 percent and women receive 83 percent of their counterparts in the West.

Economic and monetary union created new possibilities for consumption, services, recreation, and tourism for all retired people. Whereas consumer goods already reached prices equivalent to those in the West in 1990, major changes in tariffs, rents, and other fees took effect only in 1991. As a result, rent increased four to six times, the cost of energy three times, tariffs three to four times and fees three to five times. In the long run, these changes will lead to a significant differentiation in thematerial and financial living conditions for East German pensioners as compared to those living in the West.

Savings worth more than DM 6,000, life insurance, and individual old age insurance were decreased by 50 percent, effective 1 July 1990. In general, one can assume that retirees in the former GDR only had limited savings for retirement since the pension system provided basic security. In the West, social security provided only 58 percent of pensioners' income. This compares to 90 to 95 percent of the income of retirees in the East.

Major changes have also occurred in the work area. It was not only for financial reasons that approximately 10 percent of all retirees in the former GDR continued to work after they had reached retirement age; possibilities for early retirement were simply not available. Since unification, in contrast, forced early retirement has affected some 400,000 East German workers.

Women, in particular, have been affected by the pension adjustments. Their low level of pensions had to be raised disproportionately in order to guarantee a minimum pension of DM 545 (which was increased to DM 610 in January 1991). Of those receiving special assistance, 95 percent were

Table 10.2
Pension Development in the New Federal States, 1990-1992
(in DM)

	June 1990	July 1990	January 1991[a]	July 1991[a]	January 1992[a]
		Mandatory Social Insurance			
Total	555	638	737	890	n/a
Men	502	654	752	865	1,157
Women	511	588	676	773	n/a
Widow's pension	336	414	476	547	1,156

[a] Author's calculations.

Source: Federal Government, *Rentenanpassungsbericht der Bundesregierung* (Bonn, 1990), and *Statistik der deutschen gesetzlichen Rentenversicherung. VDR-Statistik-Rentenbestand*, 100 (Frankfurt am Main: 1992), table 2.1.R.

women needed additional support between DM 150 and DM 170 monthly in order to maintain their basic pensions. Many women did not receive an increase in their retirement benefits because their pensions were higher before monetary union than afterwards. Even though women in the former GDR had worked significantly longer than female retirees in western Germany, the number of women who are eligible for welfare is considerable higher today in the new federal states.[31] Contrasting patterns of years of employment and years of insurance among women in eastern and western Germany are shown in Table 10.3.

The pension adaptation law, which became effective on 1 January 1992, discriminates especially against women. An independent pension based on employment and child care was replaced by a pension law that makes retired women dependent on their husbands' pensions and assumes a longer period of non-employment. This adaptation caused noticeable reductions in retirement benefits for those who will retire in the next several years.

Despite noticeable improvements in the standard of living in eastern Germany since unification, policymakers have not yet devised an appropriate conception for decreasing existing inequalities among retirees in the unified nation. This omission includes issues of basic security, social security for women, as well as questions concerning a flexible retirement age.[32]

Table 10.3
Female Retirees in Eastern and Western Germany
According to Years of Insurance and Years of Employment (1991)
(in percentages)

Years of Employment Years of Insurance	Eastern Germany	Western Germany
0-10	4.8	10.7
11-20	7.8	33.1
21-30	15.6	32.7
31-40	23.8	13.0
Over 40	46.9	10.4

Source: Calculated from *Statistik der deutschen gesetzlichen Rentenversicherung. VDR-Statistik-Rentenbestand 1.1.91*, 95 (Frankfurt am Main, 1991), 150 and 237.

Unification has changed life dramatically in the former GDR, in both a positive and negative sense. The material standard of living has undeniably increased, yet certain social groups are adversely affected by unemployment and changing social policies.

Notes

1. See Dieter Grosser, et al., *Soziale Marktwirtschaft. Geschichte - Konzept - Leistung* (Stuttgart: W. Kohlhammer, 1988), and Fritz U. Fack and Peter Hort, *Soziale Marktwirtschaft. Stationen einer freiheitlichen Ordnung* (Freiburg and Würzburg: Ploetz, 1990).
2. In the past, official censorship in the GDR established strict limits on what could be published. A critical evaluation of social policies in the former GDR is therefore still absent. However, a number of publications have appeared in recent years that provide a good overview of social policies in East Germany. Among them are Günter Manz and Gunnar Winkler, eds., *Sozialpolitik* (Berlin: Die Wirtschaft, 1988); Gunnar Winkler, ed.,*Geschichte der Sozialpolitik der DDR. 1945-1985* (Berlin: Akademie-Verlag, 1989); Heinz Lampert, "Theorie und Praxis der Sozialpolitik in der DDR," *Arbeitsberichte zum Systemvergleich*, 13 (Marburg: Philipps-Universität Marburg, 1989); Gunnar Winkler, ed., *Sozialreport '90. Daten und Fakten zur sozialen Lage in der DDR* (Berlin: Die Wirtschaft, 1990); "Alten-

report '90," *Blätter der Wohlfahrtspflege*, 137 (1990): 262-305; and Institut für Soziologie und Sozialpolitik, ed., *Sozialpolitik Konkret*, 1-9 (1990).

3. Walter Hanesch, Statement at the press conference of the Paritätischer Wohlfahrtsverband regarding the social development in both German states (Bonn, 13 September 1990).

4. Cf. Gunnar Winkler, "Sozialunion - Sozialpolitik," in *WSI-Mitteilungen*, 43 (1990): 528-35; Gerhard Bäcker and Johannes Steffen, "Reichtum im Westen - Armut im Osten?" *WSI-Mitteilungen*, 44 (1991): 292-307; and Gerhard Bäcker and Johannes Steffen, "Sozialunion: Was soll wie vereinigt werden?" *WSI-Mitteilungen*, 43 (1990): 265-81.

5. *Sozialraum Europa* (Berlin: Paritätisches Bildungswerk, 1990).

6. Commission of the European Community, "Mitteilung der Kommission über ihr Aktionsprogramm zur Anwendung der Gemeinschaftscharta der sozialen Grundrechte," *COM* (89)568 (Brussels, 1989).

7. Winkler, ed., *Sozialpolitik*, 21, 30.

8. Manfred Lötsch, "Sozialunion aus soziologischer Sicht," in ibid., 27.

9. "Über das Soziale in der sozialen Marktwirtschaft," *Blätter der Wohlfahrtspflege*, 137 (1990): 254-61.

10. Grosser, et al., *Soziale Marktwirtschaft*, 21.

11. Rudolf Dreßler (Deputy Chairman of the SPD faction in the Bundestag), "Erste Schritte zur Sozialunion Bundesrepublik - DDR," Diskussionspapier (Bonn: 5 March 1990); and Ulf Fink (Federal Chairman of the Christian Democratic Workers' Union), "10 Punkte für die Sozialgemeinschaft in der DDR" (Bonn: March 1990). Cf. *WSI-Mitteilungen* (Düsseldorf: Bund Verlag, 1990).

12. *Social Charter of the GDR. Resolution of the Volkskammer of the GDR* (7 March 1990).

13. Heinz Lampert, "Die soziale Komponente in einem vereinten Deutschland. Überlegungen zur künftigen gesamtdeutschen Sozialpolitik," *Zeitschrift für Bevölkerungswissenschaft*, 16 (1990); Johannes Neumann, "Probleme der Sozialunion," *Der Bürger im Staat*, 40 (1990): 102-9; Wolfgang Heinrichs and Heinz Lampert, "Soziale Flankierung der Reformprozesse in der DDR," *Zeitschrift für Wirtschaftspolitik*, 39 (1990): 365 and 375; and Winfried Schmähl, ed., *Sozialpolitik im Prozeß der deutschen Vereinigung* (Frankfurt am Main: Campus, 1992).

14. Cf. Lampert and Heinrichs, 365 ff.

15. Cf. Christa Luft, "Ein Jahr Währungsunion," *Neues Deutschland* (29/30 June 1991).

16. Walter Hanesch, *Armutspolitik in der Beschäftigungskrise. Bestandsaufnahme und Alternativen* (Wiesbaden: Deutscher Universitäts-Verlag, 1988), 70.

17. Doris Cornelsen and Günther Schmid, eds., *Ost-West Öffnung. Folgen und Herausforderungen für die deutschen Arbeitsmärkte* (Berlin: Forschungshefte des Wissenschaftszentrums Berlin für Sozialforschung, 1990).

18. Winkler, ed., *Sozialreport '90*, 111 ff.

19. Cf. "Polarisierungstendenzen in der Einkommensentwicklung," *Informationsdienst Soziale Indikatoren. Mitteilungen*, 3 (1990); "Armutsbericht des Paritätischen Wohlfahrtsverbandes Deutschland für die Bundesrepublik Deutschland," *Blätter der Wohlfahrtspflege*, 136, nos. 11 and 12 (1989); and Hanesch, *Armutspolitik*, 70.

20. Cf. Heinz Vortmann, "Bestandsaufnahme: Die Wirtschafts- und Währungsunion nach drei Monaten," *Von der Einigung zur Einheit - Probleme und Perspektiven des deutschen Einigungsprozesses* (Düsseldorf: Landeszentrale für politische Bildung Nordrhein-Westfalen, 1991), 91-114; and Bäcker and Steffen, "Reichtum im Westen - Armut im Osten?": 292-307.

21. Klaus Lompe, ed., *Die Realität der neuen Armut. Analyse der Beziehungen zwischen Arbeitslosigkeit und Armut in einer Problemregion* (Regensburg: Transfer-Verlag GmbH, 1987), 25.

22. Institut für Soziologie und Sozialpolitik, "Leben 91" (internal survey).

23. These findings are based on research conducted by the research unit "Family" of the Institute of Sociology and Social Policy. Cf. "Ein einig Volk von Schwestern, die deutsche Einigung und die Zukunft der Frauenpolitik und -emanzipation," in *Von der Einigung zur Einheit*, 285-306; "Vereintes Deutschland - geteilte Frauengesellschaft," *DIW-Wochenbericht*, 41 (1990); and Rainer Geißler, "Soziale Ungleichheiten zwischen Frauen und Männern im geteilten und im vereinten Deutschland," *Aus Politik und Zeitgeschichte*, B 14/15 (1991): 13-24.

24. Cf. Max Wingen, "Familien im gesellschaftlichen Wandel: Herausforderungen an eine künftige Familienpolitik im geeinten Deutschland," *Aus Politik und Zeitgeschichte*, B 14/15 (1991): 3-12.

25. *Harmonisierungsprobleme zwischen den Sozialversicherungen beider deutscher Staaten. Forum des Verbandes der Kriegs- und Wehrdienstopfer (VdK)* (Unterhachingen: Helmut Gerber GmbH, 1990).

26. Deductible payment for medication: 5 percent from 1 July 1991; 10 percent from 1 July 1992; denture: 20 percent until 30 June 1992, from then on 50 percent; hospitalization and spa treatment: DM 5.00 per day beginning 1 July 1991, from 1 July 1992, DM 10.00.

27. Arbeitsgruppe des Wirtschafts- und Sozialwissenschaftlichen Instituts des DGB, "Zur wirtschaftlichen und sozialen Entwicklung in den ostdeutschen Ländern," *WSI-Mitteilungen*, 44 (1991): 276-92, 285.

28. Margret Dieck and Gerhard Naegele, *Die "neuen Alten." Soziale Ungleichheiten vertiefen sich* (unpublished manuscript, Kassel, 1989).
29. Cf. *Statistik Rentenbestand vom 1.1.1991* (Frankfurt am Main: Verband Deutscher Rentenversicherungsträger, 1991), 249 ff.; and *Rentenanpassungsbericht der Bundesregierung* (Bonn, 1990), 47-54.
30. Gerhard Bäcker and Johannes Steffen, *Sozialunion: Das Beispiel Rentenversicherung. Die Duplizierung bundesdeutscher Verhältnisse auf DDR-Sozialstrukturen* (unpublished manuscript, Düsseldorf/Bremen, 1990).
31. Mechthild Veil, "Frauen in der Rentenversicherung," *WSI-Mitteilungen*, 44 (1991): 315-22; and Mechthild Veil, *Am modernen Frauenleben vorbei. Verliererinnen und Gewinnerinnen der Rentenreform 1992* (Berlin: Edition Sigma, 1992).
32. Cf. Winfried Schmähl, *Alterssicherung in der DDR und ihre Umgestaltung im Zuge des deutschen Einigungsprozesses. Einige verteilungspolitische Aspekte* (Bremen: Schriften des Zentrums für Sozial-politik, 1990).

10

Economic and Political Performance: Patterns and Prospects

M. Donald Hancock

Following unabashed public euphoria in the immediate aftermath of the opening of the German-German border in 1989 and a short-term economic boom in the western part of the country in 1991, Germany has embarked on disquieting patterns of economic and political performance which raise fundamental questions about the future of the unified nation. There are ample reasons for short-term pessimism. In 1993 government officials formally declared Germany in economic recession, with the projected annual rate of economic growth to be only 1 percent. Since unification, unemployment has increased in both western and especially eastern Germany. Unified Germany confronts a tarnished international image because of an increase in electoral support for right wing political parties and murderous assaults against foreign residents and asylum-seekers. Externally, Germany and other members of the European Community (EC) face uncertainty about the further course of European integration due to domestic political and regional economic challenges to the December 1991 Maastricht Treaty on European Union.

Many of the problems confronting Germany in the mid-1990s are the consequence of an unprecedented legal-institutional merger of two highly disparate industrial societies. Mass expectations concerning the anticipated benefits of unification have proved unrealistic, at least in the short run. Exacerbating domestic problems of integration are destabilizing external economic factors and political upheavals in Central and Eastern Europe. Whether Germany can cope with these simultaneous demands on its economic and social resources is primarily a function of adequate policy response and elite cohesion comparable to achievements during the formative years of regime consolidation and legitimation in the "old" Federal Republic.

This chapter will assess Germany's economic and political prospects on the basis of empirical trends since 1990 and necessary conditions for successful regime transition. I will focus on three central problematics of system change in unified Germany: (1) economic reconstruction in the former German Democratic Republic; (2) the emergence of new conflictual issues which have resulted in incipient electoral dealignment and the erosion of labor peace; and (3) renewed uncertainty about the course of European integration. My thesis argument is that long-term prospects of economic renewal and successful democratization will depend on responsible leadership choices and behavior in the decisive years ahead.

Requisites of Successful Modernity

The attainment of national unity in 1990 significantly enhanced Germany's material, human, and political requisites of modernity. Both its territory and population expanded by nearly a third, such that unified German now ranks fourth in size in Western Europe after France, Spain, and Sweden and first in population (nearly 80 million citizens compared to approximately 58 million Italians, 57 million Britons, and 56 million French men and women). Western Germany brought to unified Germany one of Europe's highest standards of living—as measured by a per capita income in 1988 of $12,604 compared to $12,190 in France and $11,982 in the United Kingdom.[1] It also contributed a highly institutionalized, stable, and effective system of parliamentary democracy and political federalism

These requisites of successful modernity were the products of a postwar confluence of international and domestic factors that facilitated West Germany's decisive break with historical patterns of recurrent economic and political crises which had led to the downfall of the Weimar Republic and Hitler's rise to power as the architect of Nazi totalitarianism and chief instigator of World War II. Among them were decartelization during the occupation regime of 1945-49; far-reaching democratic consensus among the leaders of the principal political parties; the political irrelevance of extremist movements on both the right and the left; Germany's impressive "economic miracle" during the 1950s and most of the 1960s; the emergence of a unified trade union movement committed to a strategy of cooperation rather than confrontation with industrial managers; and demonstrated policy successes on the part of Chancellors Konrad Adenauer, Ludwig Erhard, Willy Brandt, and other executive leaders which facilitated social integration on the basis of shared prosperity and integration with the West.

In contrast, the forced pace of communization in the former Soviet Zone of Occupation had yielded an inefficient command economy and a highly authoritarian political system in the GDR. The abject failure of that system—which became increasingly acknowledged by both counter-elites within the political class and the mass of East German citizens in the course of Mikhail Gorbachev's efforts to promote comprehensive socialist reform during the second half of the 1980s—sparked the "people's revolution" that resulted in the downfall of the GDR by the early spring of 1990.

As other contributors to this volume have recounted,[2] Chancellor Helmut Kohl of the CDU and Foreign Minister Hans-Dietrich Genscher of the FDP acted to stem a rising tide of economic refugees after GDR officials opened the German-German border in November 1989 (as well as to seek Soviet concurrence in resolving the historic "German question" while Gorbachev was still in power) by pressing for the rapid unification of the two German states. Leaders of the opposition Social Democrats, notably Oskar Lafontaine (the party's chancellor-candidate in the December 1990 parliamentary election), called for a more gradual course of economic and political integration on the basis of a federative political system. In the event, Kohl's and Genscher's campaign vision of immediate (and financially painless) prosperity among East Germany's 16.5 million citizens carried the day. In Germany's first free national election since 1932, the Christian Democrats and the Free Democrats won early 44 percent and 11 percent of the vote, respectively, while the Social Democrats amassed a dismal 33.5 percent.[3]

Kohl's election as head of an all-German CDU/CSU-FDP coalition government in January 1991 proved the high water mark in Germany's rush to unity. During the nearly three years since unification, multiple domestic difficulties and unsettling political and economic problems within the European Community have inordinately complicated the task of extending western Germany's successful pattern of modernity to the nation as a whole.

Economic Reconstruction and Performance

A fundamental challenge confronting both the federal government in Bonn and regional governments in the five newly reconstituted *Bundesländer* in the East is the wholesale reconstruction of the former GDR's economy. This has involved a concerted effort to privatize industry and collective farms while maintaining as many jobs as possible during a difficult and unprecedented transition from socialism to capitalism. Parallel with the transition to a market economy in eastern Germany, an all-German system of industrial relations was established with the reconstitution of democratic trade unions and employer associations modeled after those in the West.[4]

Entrusted with legal and administrative responsibility for privatization was the Trust Agency for the People's Property (the *Treuhandanstalt*, or *"Treuhand"*), which was established by the GDR's last government in July 1990.[5] Following political union on 3 October 1990, political authority over the Trust Agency was transferred to the Federal Ministry of Finance and the Ministry of Economics in Bonn. The *Treuhand* assumed interim ownership of some 16,933 "people's own firms" (*Volkseigene Betriebe*) and collective farms while it sought previous owners of the property or suitable buyers either in western Germany or abroad. The Trust Agency was empowered to liquidate economically marginal enterprises and services or, alternatively, to maintain selected firms in operation through government subsidies. To execute these duties, the Trust Agency recruited a veritable army of administrative officials and outside consultants to serve at its headquarters in Berlin and fifteen regional offices throughout the new federal states.

From the outset, the *Treuhand* confronted a number of formidable technological, structural, and market obstacles to its work. Much eastern German industry was technologically obsolete, and the existing economic infrastructure—including telecommunication facilities, highways, and the rail system—required fundamental renewal.[6] The virtual collapse of traditional export markets in Central and Eastern Europe after 1989 forced even potentially viable high-tech industries such as electronics to curtail production and sales drastically. Eastern Germany's steel, mining and ship-building industries faced a grave structural crisis because of their sudden exposure to a highly competitive international market priced almost exclusively in hard currency.

Despite these difficulties, *Treuhand* officials pursued a relentless pace of privatization that resulted in the sale of an overwhelming majority of the previously state-owned enterprises within less than three years following unification. By July 1993, the Trust Agency reported it had sold 12,360 firms and had liquidated 2,702 companies for which it could find no buyers. Only 1,871 firms—representing 11 percent of the original total—remained in *Treuhand* hands.[7] Most of the new owners were West German companies or individual entrepreneurs.[8] In light of the ostensible success of the privatization effort, *Treuhand* officials announced in February 1992 that they hoped the Trust Agency would be able to close its doors by the end of the following year.

Yet appearances deceived. Influential critics have faulted the *Treuhand* for proceeding far too quickly with the privatization process, often without regard for the prospective survival of individual firms. In addition, numerous West German owners have been accused of fraudulent purchasing procedures and/or "plundering" the capital resources of their new acquisitions in the East. Contrary to the Trust Agency's declared intent to view sales as final, a number of investors have sought to renegotiate the contractual price of enterprises and land. Others have attempted to return ownership of their firms to the Trust Agency.[9] Predictably, the *Treuhand* has become a target of deep resentment and political protests throughout the eastern states. Many Germans have questioned whether it can cease operations on schedule, thereby leaving open the question of whether unsold enterprises might remain public property.

More ominously, from a macroeconomic perspective, privatization has been accompanied by a sharp reduction in the eastern German workforce and a corresponding surge in unemployment. From the attainment of monetary, economic, and social union on 1 July 1990 through November 1992, the size of the workforce in the former GDR shrank from 9.2 million workers to approximately 6 million. The number of farmers was reduced by half (to 160,000). Because of plant liquidations and rationalizing measures at those still in operation, nearly 1.1 million workers (representing 13.4 percent of the labor force) were unemployed. A hidden unemployed contingent consisted of nearly 2 million workers who participated in job-training and job creation programs or worked fewer hours. Women were among those most adversely affected by the loss of jobs; they comprised nearly two-thirds of the registered unemployed.

While eastern Germany's transition to capitalism promises greater prosperity in the region, it has also brought burdensome economic and social costs. Hourly wages remain significantly lower in the new eastern states than in the West because of the region's lower economic productivity. Phasing out the previous regime's subsidies for basic commodities such as rent and food meant an 11.2 percent increase in 1992 in the cost-of-living for citizens in the new federal states (compared to a 4 percent increase in the "old" federal states). Average rental expenses jumped fully 400 percent.[10] Many basic social services such as child care have been curtailed, and the provision of health care—while technologically more effective since unification—has become both more complicated and more expensive.[11]

Structural dislocations in eastern Germany were temporarily eclipsed by rapid economic expansion in the western states. In the immediate aftermath of unification, West German firms swiftly expanded their production of consumer goods to meet market demands in the former GDR. During 1991 the annual growth rate in western Germany jumped to 4.5 percent (its highest level in fourteen years). Economic expansion was stimulated by increased private investments in plants and equipment, the construction of new office buildings and retail outlets in Berlin and other major cities in the East, and the modernization of eastern Germany's antiquated infrastructure.

By 1992, however, Germany's economic performance began to falter. Contributing causes included a one-year 7.5 percent surcharge on personal income taxes (which was implemented on 1 July 1991) to help finance economic reconstruction in the new federal states, a policy of high interest rates charged by the Bundesbank in an effort to curtail domestic inflationary pressures, and a general downturn in the international economy. As a result, the annual growth rate slowed to 2 percent. Economic experts projected an increase in the gross national product (GNP) in 1993 of only .5 percent in the old federal states and 1 percent in the country as a whole. The unemployment rate continued to inch upward in eastern Germany through most of 1992; in western Germany, it rose steadily from 6.3 percent in March 1992 to 7.8 percent twelve months later. By June 1993, nearly 2.2 million West Germans were without work.

Germany's economic malaise has led to serious domestic and international repercussions. The public mood darkened appreciably from 1991 onward in tandem with an erosion of electoral support for the major political parties, escalating attacks against asylum-seekers and other foreigners, and successive political scandals.

Destabilizing Political and Social Trends

Dawning public awareness of the difficulties of economic integration prompted an electoral backlash against all of the mainstream parties. The Social Democrats—under the new leadership of Björn Engholm, who was elected SPD chair at a special party congress in May 1991— were the initial beneficiaries of voter discontent directed against the governing Christian Democrats and Free Democrats. Engholm, the prime minister of Schleswig-Holstein, exemplified qualities of pragmatic but visionary economic and social reform reminiscent of Social Democratic achievements in neighboring Denmark and Sweden, and he quickly came to outpoll Kohl in public opinion surveys.

Capitalizing on growing public discontent with the unexpectedly high costs of unification, the SPD gained votes in state elections in Hesse, Rheinland-Pfalz, and Hamburg during the first half of 1991 while both the CDU and the FDP lost support. In a remarkable swing in public opinion during the first half of 1991, fully 44 percent of German voters endorsed the Social Democrats, compared to 38 percent who favored the Christian Democrats.[12]

Subsequent electoral trends, however, proved unsettling for even the SPD. A continuing influx of asylum-seekers and other immigrants from Central and Eastern Europe—who numbered 256,000 in 1991 and 438,000 in 1992 (most of them from Romania and war-ravaged former Yugoslavia)—deepened social tensions throughout unified Germany. The electoral result was an increase in support for regional right wing parties at the expense of both the CDU and the SPD. Radical right parties mobilized nearly 11 percent and more than 6 percent of the vote in regional elections in Baden-Württemberg and Schleswig-Holstein, respectively, in April 1992. The erosion of electoral support for Germany's two largest parties continued through the March 1993 local elections in Hesse (albeit more for the Social Democrats than the Christian Democrats) when the right wing *Republikaner* garnered over 8 percent of the popular vote.[13] Contributing to electoral dealignment at the expense of the two major parties was a decline in the rate of voter participation from an average of 79.1 percent in various Landtag elections held in 1987 (and 84.3 percent in that year's Bundestag election) to an average of just over 70 percent in Landtag elections from 1991 through 1992.[14]

On the street level of anti-system violence, gangs of alienated "skinheads" and avowed neo-Nazis instigated direct (sometimes fatal) attacks against foreigners—both individually and at crowded refugee centers. Federal officials reported that 2,285 such attacks occurred in 1992 (an increase of 54 percent over the preceding year), resulting in seventeen deaths. The most dramatic confrontation occurred in late August 1992 in the Baltic coastal city of Rostock, where youthful protesters staged a four-day rampage against Romanian asylum-seekers and Vietnamese guest workers while the local police looked helplessly on. Attacks against foreigners have subsequently occurred in a number of cities in eastern and western German cities, including the heinous murder of five Turkish residents by right wing arsonists in Solingen in late May 1993.

Scandals involving prominent political and group officials intensified a growing sense of public cynicism toward the German establishment. Two members of Chancellor Kohl's national cabinet (including Minister of Economics Jürgen Möllemann) were forced to resign in January 1993 because they allegedly exploited their office for personal advantage. In May 1993, Bavarian Prime Minister Max Streibl stepped down when he was accused of accepting free travel from an industrialist. That same month, Björn Engholm abruptly submitted his resignation as chairman of the SPD and prime minister of Schleswig-Holstein after admitting he had withheld knowledge from an investigative committee about under-the-counter payments to a CDU informant for damaging information about his Christian Democratic opponent during the 1987 state election campaign. Another prominent Social Democrat—Franz Steinkühler, chairman of the Metal Workers' Union (*IG Metall*)—also resigned under pressure in May when he was charged with using insider information for personal profit on the stock market.

The Erosion of Labor Peace

Recurrent conflicts have also characterized relations since unification on Germany's normally tranquil labor market. Postal, automotive, and metal workers staged successive warning strikes in eastern Germany in early 1991 to protest the threatened loss of jobs and to demand wages commensurate with those in the West. *Treuhand* officials ignored the workers' protests while proceeding with a number of plant closures—including the Wartburg automobile factory in Eisenach—but agreed to rescind their original decision to shut down shipbuilding facilities in Rostock. In the private sector, employer associations granted substantial wage increases to East German metal and steel workers and pledged to achieve wage equalization in the two parts of Germany by the end of 1994.

In early 1992, incipient labor unrest spread to the old federal states as well. Union leaders demanded wage hikes averaging 10 percent to compensate workers for their loss of purchasing power due to inflation and the tax hike the preceding July. The employer associations balked, and warning strikes ensued in the banking and other private service sectors in March. The conflict was resolved with a compromise settlement in April, but collective bargaining subsequently stalled over wages in the public sector. When government representatives rejected a compromise proposal submitted by an arbitration commission, the Public Employees Union (*ÖTV*) authorized its members to go on strike the last week in April. Some 250,000 workers took part, disrupting rail service, postal deliveries, some air traffic, and garbage collection throughout most of western Germany. The strike ended in early May when government negotiators reluctantly accepted the arbitration commission's proposed compromise of a 5.4 percent increase in wages. A potential strike in the manufacturing sector was narrowly averted a week later when the Metal Workers' Union (*IG Metall*) and the engineering association representing private employers agreed on similar terms.

A new round of industrial conflict followed in eastern Germany in early 1993. Claiming that increased competition from steel imports from Central Europe and lower industrial productivity in the former GDR made it impossible for them to honor their 1991 agreement to equalize wage levels in the two parts of Germany by 1994, employer associations rejected union demands for a compensatory wage increase of 26 percent for East German metal workers. After a preliminary series of warning skirmishes failed to budge the employers, a majority of *IG Metall* members in the new federal states voted to go on strike in late April. More than 40,000 workers walked off their jobs in the first legal strike in eastern Germany since 1933. Due to mediation efforts by state government officials, the metal workers' union and the engineering association agreed after twelve days of conflict to a compromise formula calling for an average wage increase of 18 percent and a two-year postponement in wage equalization. Significantly, the accord permits individual firms to negotiate lower wage levels with workers at their plants in cases of demonstrated economic hardship—subject to the joint concurrence of *IG Metall* and the engineering association.[15]

The Uncertain Course of European Integration

Accompanying unified Germany's domestic economic, social, and political upheavals was a discernible slowdown in the momentum of European integration after 1991. From the beginning of the integration movement in the early 1950s, West German political and industrial leaders have consistently endorsed regional cooperation and long-term progress toward a regional West European market for the free movement of goods, services, capital, and labor. Chancellor Kohl and other members of the CDU/CSU-FDP governing coalition played a crucial supportive role in inter-governmental negotiations which commenced in 1990 within the European Community to achieve regional economic, monetary, and political union by the end of the decade. These efforts culminated in the historic endorsement by the EC's twelve member states of the Treaty on European Union in December 1991 in Maastricht. Despite subsequent public unease in Germany about the prospective disappearance of the D-Mark with the creation of a common West European currency, all of the major political parties, business associations, and the German Confederation of Trade Unions (*Deutscher Gewerkschaftsbund*, DGB) have declared their support of the Treaty.

Denmark's narrow rejection of the Maastricht accord in a popular referendum in June 1992 and a ground swell of public opposition in France in the weeks preceding a crucial national referendum on the Treaty in September abruptly slowed the integration momentum. Simultaneously, a European currency crises during the early fall of 1992 prompted dormant national animosities to resurface among key members of the Community. British officials faulted the high interest rate policy of Germany's Bundesbank for causing a run against the British pound, thereby forcing the pound's devaluation and a British withdrawal from the EC's European Monetary System (EMS) and its cornerstone European Exchange Rate Mechanism.[16] German spokesmen responded that the real cause of the crisis was the United Kingdom's weak economic performance.

French popular endorsement of the Treaty on European Union in the September 1992 referendum—albeit by a scant majority of 50 percent—and the willingness of the other eleven Community members to allow Denmark to opt-out of Treaty provisions for a European currency and a common security policy restored muted elite and public confidence in the Treaty's basic objectives. The Danish electorate reversed its judgment of the preceding year by endorsing the Maastricht agreement with its attached qualifying protocols in a second national referendum in May 1993, and—after an intensely acrimonious debate that nearly toppled the Conservative government—a majority in the British House of Commons followed suit in July. Constitutional challenges by individual opponents to the Treaty temporarily delayed the Treaty's implementation, but most observers expected it to go into effect by late 1993.

The attainment of economic, monetary, and political union by the end of the decade—as formally stipulated in the Treaty on European Union—is increasingly doubtful. Sluggish growth and a persistently high rate of unemployment within the Community as a whole will likely delay the attainment of economic "convergence" among member states required for the creation of a common European currency and a new supranational European Bank. A renewed currency crisis during the summer of 1993 involving speculation against the French franc—fueled in part by the Bundesbank's continuing refusal to jeopardize its domestic anti-inflationary policy by significantly lowering interest rates—even called the existence of the European Monetary System into serious question. According to pessimistic predictions at the height of the crisis, the demise of the EMS would "make a mockery of Europe's plans for further integration."[17]

Germany's domestic difficulties in the aftermath of unification are thus painfully reflected in renewed uncertainty about prospective European economic and political union. Despite such uncertainty, the EC—as both a political institution and an established regional market—remains an immutable reality for Germany and other members of the Community. Accordingly, the EC's role in facilitating the internationalization of production, capital, and labor within Europe will affect future economic performance and organizational innovation in Germany (as well as other member states)—just as restored growth and a renewed sense of political purpose in the expanded Federal Republic will affect the future of the European Community. The remainder of the 1990s clearly constitute a decisive turning point in the further development of both the expanded Federal Republic and the European Community.

Interim Responses

In the short run, German unification has resulted in erratic patterns of economic performance, new social and industrial conflicts, a loss of electoral support for the mainstream democratic parties, and a growing mood of public cynicism. Unexpected difficulties of privatization in the new federal states have slowed economic growth in both Germany and the European Community. Unified Germany—like the EC itself—remains far from integrated.

Germany's longer-term prospects for the attainment of a viable national economy and successful democratization will require resolute action by political and economic elites in dealing constructively with pressing national problems. These include the laggard pace of economic reconstruction in the former GDR, the asylum issue, and threats to political stability posed by increased electoral support for right wing parties. Political leaders have already addressed each of these issues through a series of important policy and constitutional initiatives.

During the spring of 1993, federal and state officials and opposition leaders reached a comprehensive policy agreement on a new "Solidarity Pact" designed to accelerate economic reconstruction and growth in the East. Originally proposed in January by the CDU/CSU-FDP coalition as a program of economic assistance that would be funded through the reinstitution of a 7.5 percent surcharge on personal income taxes and extensive reductions in social services, the plan at first elicited intense criticism from the Social Democrats and the trade unions. The SPD countered with an economic plan of its own which rejected social cuts in favor of new taxes on wealthy taxpayers and reduced expenditures on the military and Germany's space program. After three days of intensive bargaining in March, members of the government coalition, the Social Democrats, and the prime ministers of the sixteen federal states agreed to a compromise package that includes the 7.5 percent tax surcharge but omits any cutbacks in social services. The consensual Solidarity Pact will entail an annual transfer from West to East—beginning in 1995—of 56 billion DM ($34.5 billion) in public funds (plus additional grants and credits) to help finance infrastructure modernization, housing construction, and environmental cleanup in the new federal states.

More controversial, especially in the eyes of parliamentary dissidents and social activists, was a parallel agreement among the major parties to restrict Germany's constitutional guarantee of political asylum. To help make restitution for the brutal suppression of human rights under the Third Reich, the Basic Law of 1949 categorically granted the right of asylum to all persons who were subject to political persecution.[18] This constitutional provision invited (coupled with German prosperity and generous social benefits) the vast influx of refugees from Central and Eastern Europe during the early 1990s which had indirectly elicited the escalation of violent attacks against foreigners and had contributed to the growing appeal of right wing parties in state elections. Hesitant at first to change the constitution for moral reasons, the Social Democrats reluctantly agreed with the Christian Democrats and the Free Democrats to amend the Basic Law to deny the right of asylum to persons entering the Federal Republic from countries that adhere to the Geneva Convention on Human Rights (which include all the EC member states as well as Germany's Central European neighbors). The practical effect of the amendment would be to close Germany's borders to most future asylum-seekers.

German politicians justified the proposed restrictions on practical, financial, and sociopolitical grounds. Administrative review of individual cases proved inordinately slow and cumbersome because of the overwhelming number of applicants. Moreover, in recent years federal officials had ruled that only about 2 percent of the refugees could actually prove political persecution in their native country and were therefore entitled to remain in the Federal Republic as registered aliens. In the meantime, refugee camps and social service agencies were strained virtually beyond capacity, and social resentment at the mounting number of asylum-seekers had escalated to politically dangerous proportions.[19]

Members of the Greens/Alliance 90, the Party of Democratic Socialism, some Social Democrats, and grassroots dissidents sharply criticized the inter-party agreement for tactical as well as idealistic reasons. During the final vote on the amendment on 26 May 1993, Bonn was besieged by thousands of protesters who sought to prevent parliamentarians from reaching the plenary hall in the Bundeshaus—but to no avail. The measure passed by a margin of 521 to 132 (with one abstention), and went into effect on 1 July.

Supportive elite-mass behavior toward Germany's 6.5 million foreigner residents has partially diffused the controversy surrounding the asylum issue. Responsible politicians have repeatedly condemned acts of right wing violence, and concerned citizens have staged massive rallies and candle light demonstrations in numerous cities throughout Germany in defense of the civil rights of asylum-seekers and other foreigners. Chancellor Kohl and other cabinet officials have urged that naturalization procedures be simplified and have suggested the possibility of dual citizenship for long-term residents and their families.[20] Members of the Greens/Alliance 90 are even more radical in demanding public recognition that "Germany is not homogeneous but a nation of immigrants."[21]

Parallel with executive-legislative initiatives on expanded economic investments in the new federal states and constitutional restrictions on future immigration, administrative officials have also instigated legal measures to curtail the activities of some of the right wing parties. Mindful of the constitutional prohibition against "[p]arties which, by reason of their aims or the behavior of their adherents, seek to impair or abolish the free democratic basic order, . . ."[22] the Ministry of the Interior declared four neo-Nazi organizations illegal in late 1992.[23] The ministry also petitioned the Federal Constitutional Court to forbid leaders of one of the banned parties from publicly disseminating their xenophobic and politically inflammable views. In addition, the Ministry of the Interior and the sixteen *Länder* have jointly concurred in placing the *Republikaner*—Germany's largest and best-known radical right party—under close surveillance because of allegations that it is in violation of the Basic Law.

Future Prospects

While elite unity and decisive action are undeniably essential conditions for unified Germany's successful transition to a market economy and stable democracy, the quality of leadership is equally important. Recent political scandals have contributed to an erosion of public trust in the political establishment. Yet, the departure of officials tainted by controversy may well have a redemptive effect. Engholm's resignation from public office in Schleswig-Holstein meant the elevation of Heide Simonis as regional prime minister—the first female to hold such an executive position in Germany's history. Succeeding Engholm as Social Democratic chair and designated chancellor-candidate in the 1994 Bundestag election is Rudolf Scharping, prime minister of Rheinland-Pfalz and a respected younger party moderate. Scharping's election at a special party conference in May 1993 promises to re-energize the SPD's programmatic commitment to the "modernization" of both party and state. Klaus Zwickel—another pragmatist—has taken Steinkühler's place as head of the powerful Metal Workers' Union. Zwickel has already announced a shift in *IG Metall*'s collective bargaining strategy away from confrontation over higher wages in favor of greater emphasis on improved working conditions, job security, and expanded rights of co-determination.[24]

Leadership renewal also characterizes the Free Democrats. Otto Graf Lambsdorff's resignation after five years of service as chair of the FDP paved the way for the election of Klaus Kinkel as his successor in June 1993. Kinkel, who also succeeded Hans-Dietrich Genscher in 1992 as foreign minister, exemplifies core German liberal values of constitutionalism, humanism, and compassion. His public statements emphasize the importance of "honest patriotism," Germany's European identity, and human rights in the conduct of foreign policy. Kinkel, more than his immediate predecessor, projects an image of independence (despite his somewhat opaque personality) which suggests a greater receptivity to political and social innovation.

Whether leadership changes within the SPD, the FDP, and Germany's largest and most important union will encourage the emergence of a broad executive consensus in favor of more active industrial and labor market policies—perhaps accompanied by the restoration of either a social-liberal or a grand coalition government—remains to be seen. Imponderable factors in any such calculation include the choice of Kohl's successor within the CDU and the future electoral performance of the Greens/Alliance 90. Continued electoral dealignment at the expense of the major parties in forthcoming elections on the state and federal levels will almost certainly signal a change in the composition of the national cabinet.

The contrasting experience of the early years of the Weimar and Federal republics underscores the importance of economic performance for successful democratization. Elite cohesion and effective policies greatly facilitate both processes. Ultimately, however, a viable democracy requires civic virtues of tolerance and political trust on the part of elites and citizens alike. "A new political regime," Dankwart A. Rustow observes, "is a novel prescription for taking joint chances on the unknown. With its basic practice of multilateral debate, democracy . . . involves a process of trial and error, a joint learning experience."[25] Unified Germany is no exception.

Notes

1. Robert Summers and Alan Heston, "The Penn World Table. An Expanded Set of International Comparisons, 1950-1988," *Quarterly Journal of Economics*, May 1991: 327-68.

2. See in particular the chapters by Michael G. Huelshoff and Arthur M. Hanhardt, Jr., and Michaela W. Richter.

3. It was the worst defeat for the Social Democrats since the 1957 Bundestag election. See Appendix 5.

4. For an account of the internal democratization of the former socialist trade unions in the GDR and the re-establishment of employer associations from mid-1990 into 1991, see my chapter on "Reinventing Trade Unionism in Unified Germany: The Domestic and European Challenge," in Peter H. Merkl, ed., *The Federal Republic at Forty-Five* (New York: New York University Press, forthcoming in 1994).

5. Peter H. Merkl provides a detailed account of the origins and activities of the Treuhand in Chapter 8 in this volume.

6. Federal Press Office, *The State of Economic Integration in Germany* (New York: German Information Center, September 1992).

7. The figures are reported in "Treuhand. Chaos und ein Böses Ende," *Der Spiegel*, 12 July 1993: 85.

8. West Germans purchased more than 90 percent of the firms. Nearly 2,000 were privatized through management buyouts, while foreign investors (primarily British, Swiss, Austrians, and Americans) bought the remainder. *The Week in Germany*, 4 December 1992; and 18 June 1993.

9. "Treuhand. Chaos und ein Böses Ende," *Der Spiegel*, 12 July 1993: 84-86.

10. *The Week in Germany*, 29 January 1993.

11. For details on the benefits and costs of social union in Germany, see Gunnar Winkler's chapter in this volume on "Social Policy at the Crossroads."

12. *Der Spiegel*, 16 September 1991: 45.

13. SPD support fell in the state-wide local elections from an average of 44.1 percent in 1989 to 36.4 percent, while the CDU declined from 34.3 percent to 32.0 percent. The Greens advanced from 9.1 percent to 11 percent, and the FDP increased its share of the popular vote from 4.8 percent to 5.1 percent.

14. The rate of electoral participation in postwar West German national elections peaked at 91.1 percent in 1972. Since then, the tendency—except for a marginal increase in 1983—has been steadily downward.

15. This "opt-out" provision constitutes an important departure from the established postwar German practice of industry-wide collective agreements and poses a potential risk to both unions and employer associations. As Dieter Sadowski has observed, the opt-out clause may reduce incentives for individual workers to remain in unions or join them in the first place. Similarly, if employer associations lose their "capacity to negotiate industry-wide agreements, [they], too, will lose membership." Sadowski, "The Effects of European Integration on National Industrial Relations Systems: The Ambiguous Case of Germany." Paper presented at the Third Biennial Conference of the European Community Studies Association on 27-29 May 1993 in Washington, D.C., 21.

16. France, Germany, and other core members of the European Community established the Exchange Rate Mechanism (ERM) in 1979 as a means to promote regional economic stability. The ERM restricted allowable fluctuations in the currency exchange rates of participating nations to 2.25 percent in either direction of each currency's nominal exchange value.

17. "European System Linking Currency Faces a Rupture," *The New York Times*, 31 July 1993. The financial crisis subsequently abated, at least temporarily, when the members of the ERM widened the permissable fluctuation band to 15 percent.

18. Article 16, Section 2 of the Basic Law.

19. Negative citizen attitudes toward the new immigrants of the 1990s are by no mean restricted to the Germans. A recent *Newsweek* poll reveals

that 60 percent of Americans consider immigration "a bad thing for [the United States] today." *Newsweek*, 9 August 1993: 19.

20. *The Week in Germany*, 18 June 1993.

21. *The Week in Germany*, 20 November 1992.

22. Article 21 of the Basic Law. Ultimate authority to rule on the question of constitutionality of political parties is vested in the Federal Constitutional Court.

23. The banned organizations included the *Nationalistische Front*, the *Demokratische Alternative*, the *Deutscher Kameradschaftsbund*, and the *Nationale Offensive*. All four were small, claiming only between 130 and 200 members, but their influence was greater than their numbers would indicate. See German Information Center, *Focus on Rightwing Radicalism in Germany* (New York, February 1993).

24. *The Week in Germany*, 2 July 1993.

25. Dankwart A. Rustow, "Transitions to Democracy: Toward a Dynamic Model," *Comparative Politics*, 2 (April 1970): 358.

11

German Security Policy
In Post-Yalta Europe

James Sperling

The defining characteristics of the postwar European security system have either vanished or are undergoing a fundamental reordering. Ideological antipathy has been replaced by a pan-European embrace of liberal democracy and the free market system. Europe may no longer be discussed or described in terms of "East" and "West." The former Soviet Union has splintered into any number of independent states, the Warsaw Pact has dissolved while NATO searches for a military and political mission consistent with the changed European security environment, and a unified Germany occupies the geographical and political center of Europe. Europe's dominance by the two extra-European powers has come to an end. Military-political bipolarity has given way to economic multipolarity.

A unified Germany is poised to play a leading—if not the preponderant—role in shaping the future European security order. Germany's role raises a number of significant questions: How do the Germans define security in post-Yalta Europe? What are the elements of continuity and change in German security policy? What are the institutions of German security policy? What is the German security architecture for the post-Yalta system? What are the likely contours of the post-Yalta European security system?

The Redefinition of German Security

The turbulence of alliance relations and the uncertainties of the East-West conflict between 1949 and 1989 now appear, in retrospect, to encompass a long period of continuity, certainty, and stability. The content and direction of German security policy were narrowly circumscribed by the Federal Republic's membership in NATO and dependence upon the

United States, and they were defined by the need to contain Soviet power in Europe. But the changes that have taken place in the European state system, particularly the unseemly and hasty Soviet retreat from empire and consequent internal disintegration; the prospect of an unwelcome American retreat from its empire, driven by frustration with European demands compounded by severe domestic disabilities; and the process of West European political and economic integration have pushed into the background the traditional security concern over Germany's territorial integrity. The question has therefore arisen: From whom and for what reason should the Germans prepare to defend themselves militarily?

At the same time, the Germans have refined and broadened their concept of security to conform with the pressures generated—and to exploit the opportunities offered—by the evolution of the European state system. Today, German security is threatened not by an invasion of the Soviet army but instead by diverse external and domestic uncertainties. These include ethnic implosions in Eastern, Central, and Southern Europe and the former Soviet Union which could draw the Germans into civil wars as mediators or as protectors of a threatened German minority; the inability of Germany to control its borders in the event of mass migrations from Eastern and Southern Europe driven by political chaos (particularly in the former Soviet Union) and/or economic deprivation; the proliferation of terrorist groups operating in Germany, both indigenous and foreign; and threats to German economic security defined not only in traditional terms of access to foreign markets or assured supply to raw materials but also in terms of protecting Germany's social market economy, its preference for price stability and fiscal rectitude, and its environment.

This broadened and evolving redefinition of German security interests also reflects a redefinition of the German state.[1] The Germans have seized upon the idea that Germany must play the role of a "civilian" power in Europe,[2] since the role of a great or middle power defined militarily has been proscribed by history, conscience, treaty obligations, and self-interest. The Germans are unwilling (and unable) to contribute to the military requirements of global stability;[3] it is acceded that these tasks are best left to the United States, France, and the United Kingdom. Nonetheless, the German role in the future European order, although militarily circumscribed, is expansively defined economically, technologically, environmentally, and politically. Germany desires full participation in the political and economic reconstruction of Eastern Europe, the creation of European political and economic union, the restoration of the European environment, and the construction of a functioning security structure encompassing the whole of Europe and based on the twin principles of democracy and the market economy. Germany remains satisfied to contribute to the economic requirements of security and to accelerate the demilitarization of interstate relations, particularly in Europe—a development that plays to Germany's economic capacity and not coincidentally enhances German influence in the reconstruction and recasting of the European order.

The Institutions of European Security: The German Perspective

The redefinition of Germany security and the changed (and changing) European state system have shaped and reshaped the role and promise of the existing institutions of European security. Germany, the key continental European partner of the United States in NATO, now faces a choice in the procurement of its security. Whereas NATO had the character of an automatic alliance over the course of the postwar period (the Germans had little choice but to support NATO in exchange for an extended American deterrent), the collapse of the Warsaw Pact and the absence of a countervailing order in the eastern portion of the European continent has had the unsettling affect of providing Germany with choice.[4] While NATO remains the essential institutional guarantor of security and stability in Europe and for Germany, it faces a longer term challenge from the Conference on Security and Cooperation in Europe (CSCE), the European Community (EC), and the Western European Union (WEU).

The German security strategy envisions specific roles for NATO, the CSCE, and the EC-WEU, but that strategy remains contingent upon the evolution of the European state system and the evolving redefinition of German interests, both of which will be influenced by the paths taken by the erstwhile republics of the former Soviet Union and the unfolding relationships among the major European powers and between Europe and America in post-Yalta Europe.

NATO and the NACC: Military Alliance or Half-Way House to the CSCE?

NATO, and the extended American nuclear deterrent, guaranteed German security in the postwar period, supported the German effort to achieve Western European political and economic integration, and was considered essential to the eventual unification of the two Germanys. Prior to unification, the German adherence to NATO derived from the structure of power in the international system and the geo-strategic position of Germany in Europe. It was not surprising, therefore, to find Chancellor Kohl stating in 1988 that "the western alliance is a part of our *Staats-*

raison" and that NATO is "the cornerstone of [German] security policy."[5] The German-American security link within NATO has been and remains essential for German security and European stability.[6] A continued American presence in Germany is required not only for military reasons but also for reasons of political stability in Europe.[7] But the sources of cohesion in the alliance have undergone a subtle but significant change. NATO member states, to be sure, share common security interests, but the Germans argue that common values are the glue that holds the alliance together.[8] For the Germans, the American role in Europe has evolved into the explicit role of night watchman.[9] The necessity of NATO for the success of the EC-WEU in forging a European defense identity or the CSCE in providing the basis of a pan-European security system has forced the Germans to argue against the proposition that NATO, the EC-WEU, and the CSCE have conflicting purposes or conflicting logics. Hence, the Germans have adopted the slogan "*sowohl-als auch*" (this as well as that) and the emphatic rejection of "*entweder-oder*" (either this or that) in their discussions of the future institutional constellation of the future European security order.[10] The Germans desire to have it three ways: NATO and the American security guarantee, the EC-WEU and a single European security identity, and the CSCE and a pan-European security order. The German preference for a set of "interlocking institutions" has become a key component of the alliance's lexicon[11] as has the need for the complementarity of those institutions.[12] The Germans have consistently assigned NATO a preeminent role in the future European security architecture.[13] One question remains open: What is the relationship of those institutions to one another and what purposes will those institutions serve?

NATO has changed in three important respects since 1989: NATO membership has been effectively expanded to include the former member states of the Warsaw Pact with the creation of the North Atlantic Cooperation Council (NACC); NATO has acknowledged that political, economic, and even environmental concerns are displacing the military mission of the alliance; and NATO has redefined its military mission and has jettisoned "flexible response" as alliance military doctrine. The NATO London Declaration of July 1990 cited the need for the establishment of a closer relationship with the nations of Central and Eastern Europe.[14] At the June 1991 Copenhagen NATO meeting, the alliance proposed the "further development of a network of interlocking institutions and relationships" with the former Warsaw Pact nations, including the Soviet Union,[15] and the November 1991 Rome Declaration proposed the creation of the North Atlantic Cooperation Council.[16]

The NACC has been described by both former Foreign Minister Hans-Dietrich Genscher and former Secretary of State James Baker as a new pillar of the emerging European security order. It will play specific and unique functions. Among them, it will serve as a forum for consultation with the "liaison states" on issues such as civilian control of the military and the conversion of defense industries to civilian purposes; it may also serve as a forum for negotiating further conventional arms control and confidence and security building measures; and it has been suggested that the NACC can play a peacekeeping role in Nagorno-Karabakh and other contested areas in the former Soviet Union and Eastern Europe.[17]

The military purpose of the alliance has been irrevocably altered by the changed context of the European state system. In response to those changes, the alliance enumerated four principles of security policy:

- Providing the "indispensable" foundation for a stable European security order and the prevention of hegemony by any single nation.
- Serving as the primary forum for resolving disputes between alliance members on any issue of vital national interest.
- Deterring and defending any possible threat of aggression against a member-state of NATO.
- Preserving the Euro-strategic balance.[18]

These so-called Copenhagen principles now define the "fundamental tasks of the alliance."[19] These military principles are reinforced by an updated and reformulated Harmel doctrine, which was the prior touchstone of alliance policy. The dyad of détente and defense has been replaced with the triad of dialogue, cooperation, and collective defense capability within the alliance[20] and the triad of dialogue, partnership, and cooperation among the member states of the NACC.[21]

NATO remains attractive to the Germans because it provides them with a number of positive externalities. First, the stability afforded by the alliance "reach(es) beyond the immediate circle of its member states" and contributes to the stability of the reforming nations of Eastern and Central Europe.[22] Second, NATO and the NACC provide an institutional mechanism to integrate all the nations of Europe into a pan-European security system, reinforcing (and possibly usurping) the role of the CSCE. Third, the changes in NATO strategy promise a more secure Germany with a lessened exposure to nuclear war. Fourth, NATO serves as a hedge against neo-isolationism in the United States.[23] Finally, as former Defense Minister Stoltenberg noted, NATO is "the single functioning security structure in Europe" and serves as a yardstick against "fair-weathered security structures" that are pretenders to NATO's role.[24]

Within the German government there is general agreement that NATO, as the sole functioning security structure in Europe, is necessary for the foreseeable future. It is also clear that the Germans believe that without NATO (and to a lesser extent the NACC), the CSCE and probably European political union would be nonstarters.[25] This position answers in the affirmative the question of whether NATO is a key element of the German security strategy. But it also raises a number of other significant questions: Is NATO important simply because it is the only realistic alternative facing the Germans? Is NATO important because it remains part and parcel of a unified Germany's *Staatsraison*? Is NATO important because it is the foundation upon which a collective security system spanning the Atlantic to the Urals can be safely constructed? Or has NATO merely become, in the words of former Foreign Minister Genscher, "a transatlantic security bridge for the whole of Europe, for the democracies of Eastern and Western Europe."[26] Answers to these questions turn upon the future (and indeterminate) relationship between the NACC and the CSCE and upon the expectations that the Germans have for the CSCE and the EC-WEU in the future European security order.

CSCE: The Security Institution of the Future?

The CSCE promises the institutionalization of a pan-European peace order based upon the principle of collective security. The Germans still agree with former Soviet President Mikhail Gorbachev that the security concerns of Germany's neighbors can only be resolved in a "common European house." Yet, the German government's attitude towards the CSCE remains somewhat ambivalent. In repeated policy statements, Chancellor Kohl first expresses German dependence upon NATO for German security, then discusses the prospects for a European security identity that would serve as the second pillar of the Atlantic security system, and only then mentions the CSCE, normally highlighting the institution's future promise as the framework for a pan-European peace order. But even then, Chancellor Kohl (and former Foreign Minister Genscher) carefully note that any European security arrangement dominated by the CSCE cannot exclude the two North American powers.[27] Nonetheless, the CSCE frames Germany's security (and economic) aspirations in Eastern and Central Europe.[28]

From the perspective of the German government, the CSCE process and its nascent security institutions complement NATO without threatening to displace it or make it redundant. Whereas NATO provides insurance against any military threat to German territorial integrity, the CSCE makes a positive contribution to European security by integrating the former Warsaw Pact member states—including the former republics of the Soviet Union—into the Western economic and political orbit and by providing a potential mechanism for resolving disputes and managing crises in Europe, particularly in the eastern portion of the continent.

At the Prague meeting of the CSCE in January 1992, the Germans, along with the Czechs, advocated the expansion of the CSCE's role in the area of security. Foreign Minister Genscher proposed that the CSCE should "provide the opportunity of creating CSCE 'blue helmet' and CSCE 'green helmet' missions to safeguard peace and to secure our natural environment."[29] The Americans, French, and British considered the creation of CSCE peacekeeping forces redundant. This issue was not settled and was therefore left on the agenda for the March foreign ministers meeting in Helsinki. The Nagorno-Karabakh dispute, which provided the backdrop for the meeting, helped produce a broad agreement on the creation of CSCE peacekeeping forces. Once again, the Germans found themselves opposed to the United States and the United Kingdom. The Americans and British position remained that such peacekeeping forces should be supplied by NATO, the WEU, or the United Nations rather than by the CSCE.[30] The eventual outcome—and the success or failure of the German position—hinges on both the ability of the CSCE to negotiate political solutions to disputes in the former Soviet Union and elsewhere and the ability of the CSCE to draw successfully and, when necessary, on peacekeeping forces from other security institutions. The Germans are painfully aware that a broader role for the CSCE in the emerging European security architecture remains dependent on the United States; the success of the CSCE requires an American imprimatur to lend it legitimacy and effectiveness in an expanded peacekeeping role.[31]

The CSCE plays an important function for the Germans that NATO cannot play and the EC is unlikely to play, now or in the future: CSCE provides an institutional mechanism for integrating the successor states of the Soviet Union into a pan-European security and economic space without necessarily compromising or threatening the geopolitical and military logic of NATO or undermining further progress toward European political union within the framework of the EC. The meaning and importance of the CSCE for the Germans may be located as well in Genscher's assertion in early 1991 that "the German-Soviet relationship possesses a central importance for the stability of Europe."[32] The fragmentation of the former Soviet Union and the uncertain future of the Commonwealth of Independent States makes it uncertain whether Germany will have a lone partner or a number of partners in the place of the Soviet Union. But if the Commonwealth of Independent States survives (or is replaced by a loose confederation of states conducting a common foreign policy), then only the CSCE provides a ready-made mechanism for ordering that relationship within a multilateral framework. The CSCE also unburdens Russo-German cooperation by diminishing the specter of a second Rapallo, because the relationship between a Russian-dominated Commonwealth of Independent States and Germany will be conducted within and sanctioned by an established multilateral framework.[33]

The CSCE also offers an additional mechanism for continuing Germany's economic agenda in Europe and more specifically for overcoming the "prosperity barrier" (*Wohlstandsgrenze*) between the nations of Western and Eastern Europe with the establishment of a free market regime throughout Europe. The Germans argue that economic envy (*Wirtschaftsneid*) on the part of the immiserated nations of Europe, rather than the exercise or exploitation of Germany's economic power (*Wirtschaftsmacht*), is an important and very real threat to the stability of Europe and consequently to German security.[34] Although the EC plays the dominant role in securing the economic dimension of German security, the CSCE provides an important mechanism for constructing a stable and prosperous European economic space. Towards that end, the Germans proposed and hosted the 1990 CSCE Bonn conference on economic cooperation in Europe.[35]

The Bonn CSCE document obligated the non-market economies of Europe to institute price reform, implement policies that would lead to currency convertibility, and adopt the principles of the market economy. The Germans believe that the Bonn CSCE document on economic cooperation provides a stable framework for the creation of a single, integrated European economic space spanning the Atlantic to the Urals—in effect, the establishment of a European economic regime favoring the principles of the market economy.[36] The emphasis on the economic aspect of interstate relations among the nations of Europe reflects the German redefinition of security, and it has the practical consequence of altering the calculus of power in the European area. It shifts attention away from the military potential of a state to its productive capability and rate of technological innovation, thereby further strengthening German diplomacy at the expense of France and Britain. Moreover, the German government views pan-European economic cooperation as an essential aspect of the CSCE process because the basis for social stability—and therefore national security—is economic welfare.[37] For the Germans, security cooperation is contingent on economic cooperation.[38] This assumption goes a long way in explaining German enthusiasm for the Bonn CSCE document as well as European economic and eventual monetary union.

The European Community and the Western European Union: What Kind of European Security Identity?

The political unification of Europe—a foreign policy objective mandated by the German Basic Law—was intended initially as a method of burying European animosities which had built up during seven decades of intermittent war as well as eradicating its source: Franco-German competition for European hegemony. For the Germans, European integration also served the larger political purpose of reintegrating Germany into the society of western states after World War II, and it eventually became the idiom in which German interests, particularly in the economic sphere, were expressed and identified. Today, leading German politicians describe the European Community as "the sheet anchor of Europe," "the stable anchor in a stormy sea," and "the cornerstone of European stability and an essential component of the future European political structure."[39] Moreover, the Germans claim that since the EC is the only "area of stability" (*Stabilitätsraum*) in Europe, it demonstrates that stability on the European continent need not reflect or depend upon military power.[40] The combination of historical escape, tactical necessity, and strategic realism has left a legacy of a genuine German dedication to European political and economic integration, albeit on German terms.

The EC plays a quintuple role in the German security strategy. First, it provides a mechanism for ensuring German predominance in Europe on economic affairs. Second, the progress towards political union and economic and monetary union provides a magnet for the reforming states of Central and Eastern Europe that will contribute to the erasure of the *"Wohlstandsgrenze"* (prosperity border) between capitalist and proto-capitalist Europe.[41] Third, the trend toward the creation of a common security and foreign policy will contribute to the creation of a European security identity and enable "Europe" to function as a second pillar within NATO and assume responsibilities commensurate with Europe's economic and military power. Fourth, the European Community (along with NATO and the CSCE) assures Germany's neighbors and partners that Germany is cognizant of and will respect the "security needs and the feelings of all Europeans, understandably and above-all our neighbors."[42] Finally, German enthusiasm for the EC demonstrates, at least from the German perspective, that Germany has renounced, once and for all, the "national unilateralism and the Sonderweg" that has shaped modern European history.[43] But, the creation of a European security identity remains problematic because it must strike a delicate balance between the competing demands of the NATO alliance (and the United States), progress toward European political and economic union, and the creation of a pan-European security order.

The Germans view the process of European political union and the absorption of the WEU by the EC as a major contribution to the stabilization of Europe and the creation of an effective second pillar in the Atlantic Alliance. The benefits of a European security identity flow from the "enormous economic, social, and ecological problems facing the world" for which NATO is ill-equipped to deal.[44] Thus, German dependence on NATO—as reinsurance against the unraveling of the reform process in Eastern Europe and the former Soviet Union and as the nexus for the coordination of policy on a broad array of issues ranging from security to the environment to debt relief—has not precluded a European option for Germany, an option seen as complementary to rather than competitive with continued German membership in NATO or partnership with the United States.[45]

The prospect of a constitutional relationship between the European Community and the Western European Union did not gain momentum until 1990, but the contemporary "prehistory" of the WEU is instructive.[46] When former French Prime Minister Jacques Chirac suggested the revitalization of the WEU and the creation of a European security identity in December 1986, the European member states responded in October 1987 with a "Platform on European Security Interests." This platform drew in varying degrees from the Atlanticist, Gaullist, and Europeanist catechisms. American and European security was indivisible and the Alliance required a credible European pillar. But, at the same time, the protection of European interests in the Atlantic area required the creation of a European security identity independent of the United States. Moreover, the Europeans agreed that "the construction of an integrated Europe will remain incomplete as long as it does not include security and defense."[47] In addition, they linked the revitalization of the WEU to the process of European political union.

Two ambiguities arose from the envisaged role of the WEU. First, would it become the second pillar of the Atlantic Alliance or the security and defense policy arm of the European Community? Second, would it promise intensified security cooperation or, conversely, competition and potential conflict between the United States and Europe not only on security issues that were "out of area" but also on security issues within the purview of NATO as well?

In 1990, French President Mitterrand and Chancellor Kohl agreed that both NATO and the WEU were essential to the continued stability and cooperation in Europe. They also declared that both institutions occupied the same "security area" and therefore needed to intensify their cooperation.[48]

President Mitterrand and Chancellor Kohl later proposed that the EC inter-governmental conference on political union consider how the WEU could be strengthened and how it could become merged with the European Community.[49] Their purpose was two-fold. First, the WEU could serve as a transitional institution prior to the creation of a federal Europe and would thus enable the Europeans to jump-start their security cooperation by grafting an existing institution onto the EC. Second, it would enable France and Germany to cooperate on security policy without compelling France to choose between an ever ephemeral (and pointless) security independence and, simultaneously, without forcing the Germans to make (an increasingly irrelevant) choice between the United States and France, between NATO and Europe. The importance vested in the WEU reflects the German calculation that European political union has made the concept (and practice) of national military autonomy outmoded.[50]

The June 1991 Viaden communiqué of the WEU did not clarify the ultimate shape of the institutional linkages between the WEU, the EC, and NATO. In fact, the WEU ministers settled to have it both ways: the communiqué described the WEU as an important component of the process of European union, the basis for expanding defense cooperation between the member states of the WEU and the EC, and the institutional vehicle for strengthening the European pillar of the Atlantic Alliance.[51] This policy position was common to the communiqués issued by the European Council at the June 1991 Luxembourg meeting and the NATO Council at the June 1991 Copenhagen meeting, and was even included in the August 1991 Franco-German-Polish Weimar declaration.[52]

The German policy position shifted perceptibly in favor of subordinating the WEU to the EC beginning in July 1991.[53] By October 1991, the institutional relationship between the WEU, NATO, and the EC became a highly charged affair when France and Germany responded to an Anglo-Italian proposal outlining the future goals and institutional relationships of the WEU to NATO and the EC. The Anglo-Italian declaration proposed that the WEU should be guided by the common foreign and security policy of the EC and NATO policy; that there be a complementarity in decisionmaking between the alliance and WEU; that NATO remain the "essential forum for agreement on policies bearing on the security and defence commitments of its members . . ."; that decisions "out of area" be taken in close consultation with "other allies"—meaning the United States; that the WEU develop a European Reaction Force and participate in peacekeeping operations "out of area"; and that a European security identity be independent of the EC and remain subordinated to NATO.[54]

The Franco-German counterproposal identified a number of overarching objectives for the WEU: strengthening the WEU as an essential component of the process of European integration; creating a European security and defense identity; (3) progressively expanding the WEU as the defense component of a European union; and (4) offering membership to EC states not a part of the WEU and observer status to European states not a part of the EC. The proposal underlined the need for an "organic" relationship between the EC and WEU. It suggested closer institutional cooperation between the EC and the WEU and the creation of a European corps that would serve as the military arm of a future European security identity. The proposed European corps would be based on the preexisting Franco-German brigade stationed in the Federal Republic. It would be open to any member of the WEU, and would be jointly assigned to the WEU and NATO. The Franco-German proposal also addressed the need for cooperation between NATO and the WEU, the need to ensure transparency and complementarity between NATO and the WEU in accordance with the Copenhagen principles, the need for expanded cooperation between the WEU and NATO, and the need for common WEU positions within the Alliance.[55]

The Anglo-Italian and Franco-German declarations exhibited a fundamental schism. Whereas the British and Italians preferred a WEU that continued to operate in an intergovernmental framework, protected the privileged position of the United States within the Alliance, preserved the intergovernmental character of defense cooperation, and facilitated cooperation "out of area," the French and Germans clearly preferred a WEU that cooperated with NATO within Europe and "out of area" but sought closer institutional ties between the EC and the WEU. In contrast to the British and the Italians, the French and the Germans viewed the WEU as the core of the future defense identity of a European union. The Franco-German proposal, if realized, could limit American influence in Europe on security matters by providing a politically coherent European pillar for the alliance. In contrast, the Anglo-Italian proposals—by retaining American dominance and an intergovernmental framework—provide the Americans with a ready mechanism for pressing the Europeans into "out of area" duties. The Americans clearly favored the Anglo-Italian position. Former President George Bush, at the Rome NATO summit, stated that the WEU was not an alternative to the alliance. Since neither the Anglo-Italian nor the Franco-German proposal suggested that the WEU could displace NATO, it appears the American government suspected that the substance of the Franco-German proposal could lead to the prospect of a Europe independent enough to resist American leadership but too weak to act independently.[56]

At the Maastricht summit in December 1991, the Europeans agreed to the Franco-German position in substance but employed language allowing the British to claim that the WEU will remain subordinated to NATO. The EC Treaty on European Union commits the member states to "the eventual framing of a common defense policy, which might in time lead to a common defense . . ." and identified the WEU as an "integral part of the development of the European Union." The treaty also provided that the WEU could be requested to "elaborate and implement decisions and actions of the Union which have defence implications."[57] Although language in the treaty provided that the evolution of this relationship between the WEU and the EC be compatible with NATO, it is also clear that the Franco-German design for a separate security identity won the day.[58]

Chancellor Kohl, speaking before the Bundestag after the Maastricht summit, stated that the WEU would be an "integral component" of European Union and would strengthen its role as a "bridge between the Atlantic Alliance and the European Union."[59] The Germans have held tightly to the critical elements of the October proposal. In January 1992, Chancellor Kohl restated the German expectation that the joint Franco-German brigade would serve as the core of a future European army. The following month, the Germans invited those member states of the WEU "seriously interested" in creating an integrated European defense corps to attend a seminar in Bonn in mid-February to flesh out the operational dimension of the Franco-German proposal of October 1991. In April 1992, the Germans and French announced the establishment of a joint Franco-German naval squadron.[60] Although the exact institutional relationship between the WEU and the EC to NATO remains uncertain, it seems clear that the relationship will be determined as much by the foreign policy calculations of France and Germany as by the internal dynamics of European union.[61]

The German Security Architecture

The Germans increasingly view NATO as a short- to medium-term vehicle for addressing the symptoms of the security dilemma facing the Europeans and Germans and for reinsuring Germany against the possible failure of the CSCE—in short, as the institution best suited to the task of resolving the conflicting demands of Germany's security interests. The Germans view the EC as the economic and political magnet for North Central and Nordic Europe, as the "stability anchor" for all of Europe, as the core of a future European (con)federation, and as the vehicle for ensuring Germany's economic security. The Germans consider the WEU the most promising European security institution because it will allow a uniting Europe to forge a single foreign and defense policy without requiring the Europeans to jettison NATO prematurely.[62] The fortunes of the WEU, however, are dependent upon the process of European political unification.

The institutional solution to Germany's security dilemma—retaining the American extended deterrent, building an independent Europe, and creating an inclusive pan-European security system—cannot be found in a simple choice between NATO, CSCE, and the EC-WEU. The Germans, in fact, reject the notion that a choice must be made. For the Germans, all of these security institutions are compatible and mutually reinforcing. Each serves specific and interrelated tasks for the Germans. NATO reinsures against the unraveling of post-Yalta Europe as the Germans (and other Europeans) construct a (con)federal Europe and a European security identity. The CSCE is inclusive (both the United States and Russia are members), provides a framework for the continued demilitarization of European foreign affairs with accelerated arms control and disarmament, and furnishes Europe with embryonic regimes that lend support to the embrace of the market economy and democracy in Eastern Europe and the erstwhile republics of the former Soviet Union. And the EC and the WEU provide the Germans with a mechanism for ensuring a German voice in the evolution of the European order, providing the Germans with the consummation of the constitutionally dictated objective of European unification, creating a European security identity capable of contesting American pretensions in Europe, and constructing a political entity capable of withstanding pressures from a renascent Russia. Despite the seeming compatibility of these institutions, the logic of the German security strategy leads inexorably to the conclusion that the CSCE and the EC will inevitably become the preferred institutions of European security.

Yet, paradoxically, NATO remains the key institution in the German strategy. NATO is considered essential to the creation of a European political and security identity. It is considered the only credible guarantor of European (and German) security, and serves as reinsurance against the misfiring of political and economic liberalization in Eastern Europe and the political disintegration of the successor republics of the former Soviet Union. Moreover, only NATO can support the transition to a CSCE dominated pan-European security system by providing a stable international environment.

The Germans refuse to make an unambiguous choice between these institutions, partly because there is no compelling reason to make such a choice at this juncture and partly because these institutions are in fact complementary rather than competitive, at least for now. The German preoccupation with the institutional character of the post-Yalta order and the mutual dependence of these institutions reflect, no doubt, two lessons of history: first, peace and stability in Europe are only possible if Germany is closely tied to its neighbors in a manner that benefits each reciprocally; and second, NATO provided Germany and the other European democracies with the longest period of peace in contemporary history.[63]

Conclusion

Post-Yalta Europe is in the process of rapid demilitarization. Both NATO and the former member states of the Warsaw Pact have adopted the common strategic language of "defensive defense." Yet the primary challenges facing the nations of Western Europe are economic in nature. At home, the objective is sustained economic growth and a protected standard of living; in Central and Eastern Europe, the objective is finding sufficient capital to underwrite the construction of functioning capitalist and liberal democratic states that will enhance the economic welfare and political security of all. It is clear that issues of economy now have a much greater salience than the issue of territorial defense; it is also clear that the German strategy for Europe, by deemphasizing the military dimension of interstate relations, will enhance German influence on all issues European. Nonetheless, the prerequisite for the demilitarization of foreign policy is a pan-European security architecture that removes the prospect of a European war.

The Germans seek the creation of a European order congenial to the instruments, concerns, and calculations of power and interest of a "civilian power." It is questionable whether the final contours of the post-Yalta European order will conform to the cooperative security system anticipated by the Germans. A German-inspired Europe would require, at a minimum, the continued and permanent demilitarization of European affairs; an economic, social, and environmental definition of security by the major players of the European system; and the acknowledgment and internalization by national elites of the linkage between economic stability and political security. Put simply, the contours of the European state system will depend on the ability of the Germans, Americans, and other Europeans to overcome the ingrained habits of the postwar order and on the acceptance of the German definition of security and economic probity as well as the success of the German strategy for demilitarizing the political space occupied by Europe. These conditions require the transformation of the European state system from a system driven by the competitive logic of power and *Staatsraison* to a system ordered by the cooperative logic of economics and transnationality. Moreover, it requires that the dynamics of economic bipolarity differ fundamentally from those of military-political bipolarity.

The German architecture for Europe has three primary elements: (1) the self-containment of German military power in order that Germany may use its economic power to influence its European neighbors to effect German policy objectives; (2) the creation of an independent Europe capable of negotiating on an equal basis with the United States on economic issues; and (3) the continued demilitarization of Europe, which depends in turn on the sustained growth of democracy and the free market in the former member states of the Warsaw Pact. German security policy in post-Yalta Europe has four objectives: (1) to create a pan-European security structure that integrates Germany into Europe as an equal if not a leading state; (2) to accelerate the demilitarization of the European area in order to create an environment favoring German economic interests, a development that would increase German leverage with the other European states and minimize Germany's historically dictated disadvantage in the military realm; (3) to retain the American presence in Europe as reinsurance against the failure of a demilitarized pan-European security structure; and (4) to ensure the integration of the republics of the former Soviet Union, especially Russia, Ukraine, and Belarus in that pan-European order. This set of policy objectives indicates a continuation of the postwar strategy of self-containment, which had complemented the American security strategy of double-containment[64] and has had the (retrospectively beneficial) consequence of producing foreign and security policies that reflexively expressed German interests in the language of Europe or the Atlantic Alliance. Germany has offered to entrap itself in integrative and constraining political and military structures, despite a legitimate claim to European leadership by virtue of geography, demography, economic capacity, and latent military power.

Germany only seeks a leadership role in defining the critical framework conditions of the post-Yalta European security order. In the end, this German leadership role will be paid for in the coin of diminished national prerogative in the fashioning of its foreign policy on military and political issues. But the payoff for Germany and Europe will be the resolution of the "German problem": Germany will be integrated into a pan-European security structure, Germany will emerge as a "satisfied" power, and Germany will threaten neither European stability nor the long postwar peace.

Notes

1. For a discussion of the redefinition of state and nation in Germany, see Ole Wæver, "Three Competing Europes: German, French, and Russian," *International Affairs*, 66 (July 1990): 477-94.

2. See Theo Sommer, "Die Deutschen an die Front?" *Die Zeit*, 29 March 1991; Hanns W. Maull, "Germany and Japan: The New Civilian Powers," *Foreign Affairs*, 65 (Winter 1990/91): 92-93; and Stephen Szabo, *The Changing Politics of Germany Security* (New York: St. Martin's Press, 1990). John Mearsheimer, in "Back to the Future: Instability in Europe after the Cold War," *International Security*, 15 (Summer 1990): 5-56, and David Garnham, in "Extending Deterrence with German Nuclear Weapons," *International Security*, 10 (Summer 1985): 96-110, advocate the acquisition of nuclear weapons by Germany. I agree with Thomas Kielinger that Germany is an unlikely candidate for nuclear proliferation because "(f)or the German people this is a matter of holy writ as they have once and for all renounced production or possession of nuclear weapons. Any office holder attempting even to mention a change in this policy would be committing suicide." Thomas Kielinger, "Waking Up in the New Europe—With a Headache," *International Affairs*, 66 (April 1990): 261.

3. It appears that the Basic Law does not prohibit the Bundeswehr from participating in United Nations peacekeeping missions. See Peter Bardehle, "'Blue Helmets' from Germany? Opportunities and Limits of UN Peacekeeping," *Aussenpolitik*, 40 (1989): 381 ff.; and Christoph Bertram, "Wo nicht hin mit der Bundeswehr?" *Die Zeit*, 7 June 1991.

4. For an extended discussion of NATO as a "fated community" (*Schicksalsgemeinschaft*), see Emil J. Kirchner and James Sperling, "The Future Germany and the Future of NATO," *German Politics*, 1 (April 1992): 50-77; and "From Success to Uncertainty" in Emil J. Kirchner and James Sperling, eds., *The Federal Republic of Germany and NATO. 40 Years After* (London: Macmillan, 1992), 252-66.

5. Helmut Kohl, "Die Streitkräfte als wichtigstes Instrument der Sicherheitspolitik," 13 December 1988, in Presse- and Informationsamt der Bundesregierung, *Bulletin*, 175 (16 December 1988): 1550-51.

6. On this issue there is little disagreement. See Michael Broer and Ole Diehl, "Die Sicherheit der neuen Demokratien in Europa und die NATO," *Europa Archiv*, 46, (15 June 1991): 372-76; Joseph Joffe, "The Security Implications of a United Germany: Paper I," *America's Role in a Changing World*, Part II. Adelphi Paper 257 (Winter 1990/91): 84-91; Robert D. Blackwill, "The Security Implications of a United Germany: Paper II," *America's Role in a Changing World*, Part II. Adelphi Paper 257 (Winter 1990/91): 92-95; Gerhard Wettig, "German Unification and European Security," *Aussenpolitik*, 42 (1991): 13-19; Rupert Scholz, "Deutsche Frage und europäische Sicherheit. Sicherheitspolitik in einem sich einigenden Deutschland und Europa," *Europa Archiv*, 45 (April 1990): 239-46; Michael Howard, "The Remaking of Europe," *Survival*,

XXII (March/April 1990): 99-106; and Stanley Hoffmann, "The Case for Leadership," *Foreign Policy*, 81 (Winter 1990/91): 20-38. Contrary views are found in Earl C. Ravenal, "The Case for Adjustment," *Foreign Policy*, 81 (Winter 1990-91): 3-19; and Christopher Layne, "Superpower Disengagement," *Foreign Policy*, 77 (Winter 1989/90): 17-40. A skeptical view of NATO's future, written before the collapse of the postwar order, is found in David P. Calleo, "NATO's Middle Course," *Foreign Policy*, 69 (Winter 1987-88): 135-47.

7. Helmut Kohl, "Erklärung der Bundesregierung," 6 November 1991, *Bulletin*, 124 (7 November 1991): 986.

8. Helmut Kohl, for example, stated that "NATO must always be understood as a community of values . . . and this means that we neither can replace nor desire the replacement of NATO." See his remarks in "Die Rolle Deutschlands in Europa," 13 March 1991, *Bulletin*, 33 (22 March 1991): 244. See also Kohl, "Aufgaben deutscher Politik in den neunziger Jahren," 20 May 1991, *Bulletin*, 56 (22 May 1991): 443

9. In Chancellor Kohl's estimation, the American role and responsibility "in and for Europe remains of critical meaning for the peace and security of our continent and above all for the unified Germany in the middle of that continent." Kohl, "Regierungserklärung des Bundeskanzlers vor dem Deutschen Bundestag: Unsere Verantwortung für die Freiheit," 30 January 1991, *Bulletin*, 11 (31 January 1991): 73-74.

10. See Kohl, "Die Rolle Deutschlands in Europa," 245; and "Aufgaben deutscher Politik in den neunziger Jahren," 441. This formula is endorsed by Jiri Dienstbier, former Foreign Minister of the Czech and Slovak Federal Republic, in "Central Europe's Security," *Foreign Policy*, 83 (Summer 1991): 125-27.

11. The December 1991 Rome NATO summit produced a Declaration on Peace and Cooperation that speaks of the need for a "framework of interlocking institutions tying together the countries of Europe and North America" and notes the importance of NATO, the CSCE, WEU, and the EC. See "Rome Declaration on Peace and Cooperation," *NATO Review*, 39 (December 1991): 19. See also remarks by former Secretary of State James A. Baker, III, "US Commitment to Strengthening Euro-Atlantic Cooperation," *US Department of State Dispatch*, 2 (23 December 1991): 903.

12. North Atlantic Council, "Communiqué," 19 December 1991, reprinted in *NATO Review*, 40 (February 1991): 27.

13. Helmut Kohl, "Verantwortung für das Zusammenwachsen Deutschlands und Europas," 6 June 1991, *Bulletin*, 64 (7 June 1991): 513. See also Theodor Waigel, "Haushaltsgesetz vor dem Deutschen Bundestag," 3 September 1991, *Bulletin*, 93 (4 September 1991): 747. Waigel,

in response to SPD criticism that he ignored the CSCE, argues that NATO and the CSCE are not in opposition to one another and that "both are necessary instruments for peace in Europe and the world."

14. Manfred Wörner, "NATO transformed: the significance of the Rome Summit," *NATO Review*, 39 (December 1991): 3.

15. *New York Times*, 7 June 1991.

16. North Atlantic Council, "Rome Declaration on Peace and Cooperation," 7-8 November 1991, reprinted in *NATO Review*, 39 (December 1991): 20. The Rome meeting fulfilled the intentions expressed at the July 1990 London meeting. Perhaps more importantly, the NACC was proposed jointly by Genscher and Baker in accordance with the "liaison concept" for forging closer links between the nations of the alliance and Central and Eastern Europe. See Kohl, "Erklärung der Bundesregierung," 986.

17. "Rome Declaration," 21; James A. Baker, III, "US Commitment," 903; Hans-Dietrich Genscher, "Ansprache des Bundesaußenministers," 10 March 1992, *Bulletin*, 27 (12 March 1992): 264; Robert Mauthner, "NATO, CIS peace plan for Nagorno-Karabakh," *Financial Times*, 11 March 1992; Edward Mortimer, "Europe's Security Surplus," *Financial Times*, 4 March 1992.

18. These principles have been complemented by a new force structure and strategy that emphasizes smaller forces, enhanced flexibility and mobility, and a substantially reduced reliance upon nuclear weapons, and is accompanied by an abandonment of the linear defense posture in central Europe and a major reduction of the NATO stockpile of sub-strategic weapons in Europe. See ibid., 27, 29-32, and Marc Rogers, "NATO shapes up for new role," *Jane's Defence Weekly*, 16 (November 1991): 926.

19. See North Atlantic Council, "The Alliance's New Strategic Concept," 7-8 November 1991, reprinted in *NATO Review*, 39 (December 1991): 25.

20. "Rome Declaration," 19.

21. North Atlantic Cooperation Council, "Statement on Dialogue, Partnership and Cooperation," 20 December 1991, reprinted in *NATO Review*, 40 (February 1992): 29-30.

22. Helmut Kohl, "Erstes Treffen des Rates der Außenminister der Teilnehmerstaaten der KSZE," 19 June 1991, *Bulletin*, 72 (22 June 1991): 579. This position reflected the outcome of the Copenhagen NATO summit on 6 June 1991 where the allies made an effort to reassure the nations of the former Warsaw Pact with language that stopped short of offering a unilateral security guarantee. *New York Times*, 7 June 1991.

23. Hans-Dietrich Genscher, "Eine Vision für das ganze Europa," 3 February 1991, *Bulletin*, 14 (February 1991): 92.

24. Gerhard Stoltenberg, "Zukunftsaufgaben der Bundeswehr im vereinten Deutschland," 13 March 1991, *Bulletin*, 29 (15 March 1991): 215. See also Stoltenberg, "Der Selbstverständnis des Soldaten in der Bundeswehr von morgen," 17 June 1991, *Bulletin*, 70 (19 June 1991): 566.

25. Gerhard Stoltenberg, "Deutsche Einheit und europäische Sicherheit," 1 May 1990, *Bulletin*, 52 (5 May 1990): 406.

26. Hans-Dietrich Genscher, "Eine Vision für das ganze Europa," 3 February 1991, *Bulletin*, 14 (February 1991): 92.

27. See Kohl, "Regierungserklärung," 72-75, and Kohl, "Verantwortung für das Zusammenwachsen Deutschlands und Europas," 513. See also Genscher, "Rede des Bundesaußenministers vor den Vereinten Nationen," 25 September 1991, *Bulletin*, 104 (26 September 1991): 825. For an analysis of Genscher's foreign policy strategy, see Emil J. Kirchner, "Genscher and What Lies Behind 'Genscherism'," *West European Politics*, 13 (April 1990): 159-77.

28. The German-Polish Treaty of June 1991, for example, is littered with references to the various CSCE meetings and documents. Article three of the Treaty commits the contracting parties to "seek peace through the elaboration of 24 cooperative structures of security for the whole of Europe . . . [including the full implementation of] the Helsinki Final Accords, the Charter of Paris [as well as other documents relating to the CSCE process]." "Vertrag zwischen der Bundesrepublik Deutschland und der Republik Polen über gute Nachbarschaft und freundschaftliche Zusammenarbeit," 18 June 1991, *Bulletin*, 68 (18 June 1991): 542. More generally, the Germans consider the CSCE to be "the stability framework for the enlarged Europe" and "the bracket for the emerging pan-European order in all spheres." The Paris Charter is viewed as the quasi constitutional framework for a pan-European system ordered by the principles of democracy, human rights, and the market economy. See Genscher, "Eine Vision für das ganze Europa," 3 February 1991, *Bulletin*, 14 (6 February 1991): 92-93, and "The Future of Europe," 12 July 1991, *Statements and Speeches*, XIV: 3-4.

29. Hans-Dietrich Genscher, "Zweites Treffen des Rates der Außenminister der Teilnehmerstaaten der KSZE," 30 January 1992, *Bulletin*, 12 (4 February 1992): 83,

30. Robert Mauthner, "New world watchdog in search of bark and bite," *Financial Times*, 24 March 1992, and *Financial Times*, 27 March 1992.

31. Helmut Kohl, "Deutsch-amerikanischer Beitrag zur Stabilität und Sicherheit," 21 May 1991, *Bulletin*, 58 (28 May 1991): 458. This argument is also made by Stanley Sloan, "NATO's Future in a New Europe: An American Perspective," *International Affairs*, 66, (July 1990): 504 ff.

32. Genscher, "Eine Vision für das ganze Europa," 93.

33. Less relaxed appraisals of the new German-Russian relationship can be found in W.R. Smyser, "USSR-Germany: A Link Restored," *Foreign Policy*, 84 (Fall 1991): 125-141, and Marian Leighton and Robert Rudney, "Non-Offensive Defense: Toward a Soviet-German Security Partnership?" *Orbis*, 35 (Summer 1991): 377-94.

34. Kohl, "Die Rolle Deutschlands in Europa": 245.

35. For an analysis of the Bonn conference, see Hans-Christian Reichel, "Die Bonner Wirtschaftskonferenz und die Zukunft der KSZE," *Europa Archiv*, 45 (10 August 1990): 461-70, and *Task Force on German Unification, The United States and United Germany* (Washington, D.C.: The Atlantic Council of the United States, October 1990), 22.

36. See "KSZE-Konferenz über wirtschaftliche Zusammenarbeit in Europa. Dokument der Bonner Konferenz," 11 April 1990, *Bulletin*, 46 (19 April 1990): 357-62. The role of economic cooperation in the creation of a pan-European security system were acknowledged in the Paris Charter of the CSCE. See "Charta von Paris für ein neues Europa. Erklärung des Pariser KSZE-Treffens der Staats- und Regierungschefs," 24 November 1990, *Bulletin*, 137 (24 November 1990): 1412-13; Helmut Haussmann, "Neue Chancen und Impulse der West-Ost-Zusammenarbeit," 31 January 1990, *Bulletin*, 20 (2 February 1990): 162; "Rede des Bundesministers des Auswärtigen der Bundesrepublik Deutschland, Hans-Dietrich Genscher, auf der Konferenz über wirtschaftliche Zusammenarbeit in Europa im Rahmen der KSZE in Bonn am 11. April 1990," *Europa Archiv*, 45 (10 May 1990): D218-24.

37. Helmut Kohl, "Ein geeintes Deutschland als Gewinn für Stabilität und Sicherheit in Europa," 25 May 1990, *Bulletin*, 68 (29 May 1990): 587. See also Kohl, "Regierungserklärung des Bundeskanzlers," 63, and Richard von Weizsäcker, "Ansprache des Bundespräsidenten," 9 April 1990, *Bulletin*, 46 (19 April 1990): 362-3. Similar sentiments were expressed by Helmut Haussmann, "Abschlußerklärung des Bundeswirtschaftsminister," 9 April 1990, ibid.: 363; Hans-Dietrich Genscher, "Rede des Bundesaußenministers," 11 April 1990, ibid.: 365; and Gerhard Stoltenberg, "Deutsche Einheit und europäische Sicherheit," 1 May 1990, *Bulletin*, 52 (5 May 1990): 408.

38. Helmut Kohl, "KSZE-Wirtschaftskonferenz in Bonn," 19 March 1990, *Bulletin*, 37 (20 March 1990): 287; and Kohl, "Ein geeintes Deutschland als Gewinn für Stabilität und Sicherheit in Europa," 589.

39. Helmut Kohl, "Regierungserklärung," 72; Hans-Dietrich Genscher, "Eine Vision für das ganze Europa," 91; Gerhard Stoltenberg, "Das Selbstverständnis des Soldaten," 566.

40. Helmut Kohl, "Erstes Treffen des Rates der Außenminister der Teilnehmerstaaten der KSZE," 19 June 1991, *Bulletin*, 72 (22 June 1991): 578.

41. Hans-Dietrich Genscher, "Bewertung des Ratsvorsitzenden," 20 June 1991, *Bulletin*, 72 (22 June 1991): 584; "Deutschland, Frankreich und Polen in der Verantwortung für Europas Zukunft. Gemeinsame Erklärung der Außenminister von Deutschland, Frankreich und Polen in Weimar," 29 August 1991, *Bulletin*, 92 (3 September 1991): 735. The European Community embraced the German position. The Luxembourg European Council Meeting communiqué of June 1991 stated that "The European Council considers the creation of a European economic space to be an essential element of the future architecture of Europe." See "Europäischer Rat in Luxembourg," 29 June 1991, *Bulletin*, 78 (9 July 1991): 625.

42. Gerhard Stoltenberg, "Künftige Perspektiven deutscher Sicherheitspolitik," 13 June 1990, *Bulletin*, 76 (14 June 1990): 655.

43. Gerhard Stoltenberg and Hans-Dietrich Genscher, "Sicherheitspolitische Fragen eines künftigen geeinten Deutschland," 19 February 1990, *Bulletin*, 28 (21 February 1990): 218.

44. See Gerhard Stoltenberg, "Das Selbstverständnis des Soldaten," 566. Finance Minister Theodor Waigel has stated the need for European union in starker terms: "The world needs a single Europe as a world economic and world political stability factor." See Waigel, "Haushaltsgesetz 1992," 747.

45. Helmut Kohl, "Verantwortung für das Zusammenwachsen Deutschlands und Europa," 513.

46. For an historical overview of the WEU, see Alfred Cahan, *The Western European Union and NATO: Building a European Defence Identity within the Context of Atlantic Solidarity* (London: Brassey's, 1989), and K.E. Jorgensen, "The Western European Union and the Imbroglio of European Security," *Cooperation and Conflict*, XXV (1990): 135-52. On the future roles of the WEU, see Günther van Well, "Zur Europa-Politik eines vereinigten Deutschland," *Europa Archiv*, 45 (10 May 1990): 35.

47. Western European Union, *Platform on European Security Interests* (The Hague, 27 October 1987, mimeo.).

48. "Gemeinsame Erklärung anläßlich der 56. deutsch-französischen Konsultationen am 17. und 18. September 1990 in München," 18 September 1990, *Bulletin*, 111 (19 September 1990): 1170.

49. Helmut Kohl, "Regierungserklärung," 73. The logic of the Franco-German position is presented in Jacques Delors, "European Integration and Security," *Survival*, XXXIII (March/April 1991): 99-110.

50. Gerhard Stoltenberg, "Das Selbstverständnis des Soldaten," 566.

51. "Kommunique des Ministerrates der Westeuropäischen Union," 27 June 1991, *Bulletin* (5 July 1991): 621.

52. "Europäischer Rat in Luxembourg," 29 June 1991, *Bulletin*, 78 (9 June 1991): 625; "Kommunique der Ministertagung des Nordatlantikrats," 7 June 1991, *Bulletin*, 66 (11 June 1991): 527; "Deutschland, Frankreich und Polen in der Verantwortung für Europas Zukunft," 29 August 1991, *Bulletin*, 92 (3 September 1991): 734; and "Kommunique des Ministerrates der Westeuropäischen Union," ibid.

53. Hans-Dietrich Genscher, speech before the WEU, 8 July 1991, *Statements and Speeches*, XIV: 1.

54. "European Security: Anglo-Italian Declaration," 5 October 1991, 2.

55. The French and Germans also proposed an expansion of the Franco-German brigade from 5,000 to over 30,000 troops. *New York Times*, October 17, 1991. For a detailed statement of the Franco-German proposal, see "Botschaft zur gemeinsamen europäischen Außen- und Sicherheitspolitik," 14 October 1991, *Bulletin*, 117 (18 October 1991): 929-31. For American objections to the proposal, see Jenonne Walker, "Keeping American in Europe," *Foreign Policy*, 83 (Summer 1991): 141. For Italian objections, see Marta Dassú, "The Future of Europe: The View from Rome," *International Affairs*, 66 (April 1990): 302-03.

56. George Bush, "A Time of Decision for the NATO Alliance," 7 November 1992, *US Department of State Dispatch*, 2 (11 November 1991): 823, and *New York Times*, 8 November 1991.

57. *The Economist*, 14 December 1991: 52. For post-Maastricht statement on the WEU and the EC, see Helmut Kohl, "Erklärung der Bundesregierung," 986.

58. Nonetheless, German public support for an independent European army remains lukewarm at best. A public opinion survey conducted by the Sozialwissenschaftliches Institut der Bundeswehr found that 66 percent of the respondents believed that any European army should remain within the NATO framework and only 22 percent believed that it should operate outside it. Poll cited in Hans-Joachim Veen, "Die Westbindung der Deutschen in einer Phase der Neuorientierung," *Europa Archiv*, 46 (25 January 1991): 35.

59. Helmut Kohl, "Erklärung der Bundesregierung," 1156. The declaration of the EC member states of the WEU identified the WEU as "the defence component of the European Union and as the instrument for strengthening the European pillar of the Atlantic alliance . . . ." Chancellor Kohl took this statement as an unqualified endorsement of the Franco-German position. Ibid.

60. Helmut Kohl, "Die Bedeutung der Westeuropäischen Union für die gemeinsame Sicherheitspolitik, " 27 January 1992, *Bulletin*, 11 (31 January 1992): 78; Quentin Peel, "Bonn presses Euro force plan," *Financial Times*, 6 February 1992; and *Financial Times*, 23 April 1992.

61. Urs Leimbacher, in *Die unverzichtbare Allianz: Deutschfranzösische sicherheitspolitische Zusammenarbeit, 1982-1989* (Baden-Baden: Nomos Verlag, 1992), argues that the German and French interest in defense cooperation has been contingent upon domestic coalition politics and coalescent, but different, national interests.

62. It is also the case, that the WEU allows the Europeans to sidestep the immediate problems associated with Irish (and Austrian and Swedish) neutrality and the longer-term problems associated with the EC membership of former member states of the Warsaw Pact, particularly Poland, Hungary, and the Czech Republic.

63. Helmut Kohl, "Ein geeintes Deutschland als Gewinn für Stabilität und Sicherheit in Europa," 586; Seiters, "Perspektiven der Deutschlandpolitik im geeinten Europa," 1485; and Helmut Kohl, "Besuch des Bundeskanzlers in den Vereinigten Staaten von Amerika," 5 June 1990, *Bulletin*, 74 (13 June 1990): 638.

64. On the strategy of double-containment, see Wolfram F. Hanrieder, *Germany, America, Europe. Forty Years of German Foreign Policy* (New Haven: Yale, 1989).

12

Germany in Transition:
The Challenge of Coping
with Unification

Petra Bauer-Kaase

During the 1970s Western European social scientists repeatedly posed the question of whether liberal democracy might be in a grave structural crisis.[1] At the same time, voices were occasionally heard that postulated the waning of alternatives to liberal democracy.[2] However, only the political transitions in Central and Eastern Europe seem to have created a consensus that Soviet-style communism as a political and economic political order has exhausted its potential.[3] Whether the breakdown of communism automatically implies that liberal democracy and capitalism per se are the sole surviving options for the organization of the state and the economy is still an open question.[4] This only time will tell.

In some parts of Central and Eastern Europe, tentative efforts toward democratization were under way at the beginning of the 1980s. These early developments had little impact on the German Democratic Republic, but processes of political transition in Poland and Hungary at the end of the decade compelled GDR leaders to confront acute pressures of reform. Once these processes gained momentum, it became apparent that the debate no longer could be restricted to the implementation of limited reforms, as some Soviet and East European reformers had initially thought. Instead, reform efforts were aborted and full-fledged system transformations to liberal democracy and a competitive market-oriented economy were launched.

In the autumn of 1989, pressures created by the exodus of its citizens to the West jolted the usually tranquil GDR. At that time, many members of the intellectual opposition which had crystallized around the Protestant churches still hoped for and believed in an alternative path between capitalism and socialism, the so-called "third way" (*der dritte Weg*). Encouraged by the growing number of participants in the "Monday demonstrations" in Leipzig and elsewhere, the opposition movements in the GDR continued to gain ground. But this turned out to be only a brief interlude. The dynamics of the mass protest changed when the slogan of "We are the people" was replaced by "We are *one* people," thereby signaling that most citizens were beginning to understand and grasp the historical chance of German unification. Thus dreams of the third way, which had been a major topic of debate in the Roundtable discussions, vanished into the blue.

The speed of unification came as a surprise to everybody. From the creation of the Federal Republic in 1949 until the late 1950s, unification had been one of the most important issues in West German politics. Only the construction of the Berlin Wall on 13 August 1961 made it clear that the provisional solution of a divided country was to last for some time to come. Much more so than before, both the GDR and the Federal Republic of Germany took on a life of their own. At least two factors facilitated this process. One was the relentless and systematic effort by the government of the GDR—strongly supported by the Soviet Union—to obtain an independent political and diplomatic identity in the international community. Second, the shift from a conservative government to a social-liberal coalition in 1969 in the Federal Republic changed the parameters of German foreign policy. Chancellor Willy Brandt developed his "*Ost- und Deutschland-politik*," which resulted in the acknowledgment of existing German borders in the East, in particular regarding Poland. The Basic Treaty between the Federal Republic and the GDR in 1972 was the most obvious expression of these new policy initiatives.[5]

The recognition of the GDR as a separate state reduced the importance of the unification issue in West German public opinion,[6] but, as Erwin Scheuch points out, it remained latent and could be revitalized at any time.[7] In addition, West German citizens and opinion leaders regarded the probability of unification as extremely remote. However, the famous speech by Chancellor Helmut Kohl in November 1989 in which he outlined "Ten Points on the Road to German Unity" changed the direction of the discourse: Once again the unification issue became a topic of utmost importance and remained so until unification was effected on 3 October 1990.[8]

The surprise victory of the conservative Alliance for Germany in the Volkskammer election on 18 March 1990 was interpreted by most observers as a plebiscite for quick unification.[9] Between 23 August and 20 September 1990, all legal steps necessary for the formal unification were taken and on 2 December 1990, the unified German people elected the first all-German parliament.

This chapter analyzes the political orientations of East and West German citizens as they emerged and crystallized during the process of unification. West Germany will be used as a reference point for comparison. I will emphasize in particular the following problems:

- What were the expectations of East and West Germans regarding unification? How important were economic considerations in the process of unification?
- After 45 years of communist indoctrination, what are the concepts East Germans have developed toward the way society should be organized? How do they define democracy and what do they expect from democracy? How are their views different from those of West Germans?
- Viewed against the backdrop of the peaceful mass upheaval in the former GDR, are East Germans more interested in different modes of participation as compared to West Germans?
- Unification has had such far-reaching economic, social, and political implications for all of Germany that major political conflicts are possible. What is the impact of unification on the stability of the political system in Germany?

To answer these questions, data will be utilized that were collected in East and West Germany in 1990, 1991, and 1992 by the Institut für praxisorientierte Sozialforschung (IPOS) for the Federal Ministry of the Interior. Other data sources include the monthly national surveys of the Forschungsgruppe Wahlen, conducted on behalf of the Second German Television Network (ZDF); data from the German National Social Survey (Allbus) for 1990 and 1991 (Allbus-Basisumfrage);[10] and data from a 1990 survey in East Germany (ISSP-Plus survey) which was conducted as part of the International Social Survey Program.[11]

Already when the GDR was still a sovereign state, German market research institutes spread into East Germany to speedily set up the infrastructure to conduct nationally representative survey studies. Such an infrastructure had not existed before. German social scientists quickly became engaged in a debate about whether two populations, even if they had continued to speak the same language during separation, could be questioned on social and political orientations with instruments that had been developed and used in studies of the West German population. Although there continues to be a certain uneasiness about the matter,[12] so far no findings have emerged clearly indicating that this has been a major problem.

Expectations and Hopes

It was not until the demise of the GDR that any systematic information on political orientations of the GDR citizenry became available in the West. The identification of East Germans with their political system had begun to falter in the early 1980s when East Germans began to experience the consequences of decreasing economic outputs and infrastructure problems.[13] These developments coincided with a larger permeability of the political borders between East and West, and—coupled with unrestricted access to West German television—increased the visibility of West German achievements. Thus, for many East Germans unification became an early code-word for high expectations in all areas of life.

By 1993, almost three years after unification, it has become common wisdom that the reigning German political elites underestimated the difficulties of unification. By contrast and in retrospect, East and West German citizens from the outset had assessed the likely consequences of unification more realistically. Although it remains an open question whether respondents had the same time perspective in mind when they made a distinction between short- and long-term implications of unification, skepticism regarding the short-term consequences clearly dominated whereas the future was seen in much more optimistic terms. (See Table 12.1.)

As previously mentioned, East Germans viewed unification as the opportunity to overcome their economic problems which had accumulated during the 1980s. This does not imply that they were naive in the sense that they expected the economic situation to turn abruptly to the better once unification would be effected. Once unification was achieved, however, its economic dimension became the overarching topic of debate. (See Table 12.2.)

Initially, the political agenda in the two Germanys differed in important respects, and it is only recently that issues of right-wing extremism and asylum policy have become problems of controversy in eastern Germany. In contrast to the western part of Germany, the problem of political asylum had assumed top priority already in 1992. In addition, it is only recently that concern over the economic implications of unification has assumed greater importance among West Germans as well. It seems that unified Germany is at least beginning to move toward a common political agenda. (See Table 12.2.) Most likely this process will continue into 1994 when Germany will be politicized by a general national election, eight state elections, the election to the European parliament, and a series of communal elections.

Table 12.1
Perceived Advantages and Disadvantages of German
Unification in 1990 East and West Germany (in percentages)

	February		March		April		May		June	
	East	West	East	West	East	West	East	West	East	West
Short-term										
Advantages	–	10	21	12	14	14	17	12	23	12
Disadvantages	–	55	27	52	35	49	41	56	30	48
Both	–	33	46	34	43	36	37	30	45	38
No answer	–	2	6	2	8	1	4	2	2	2
Long-term										
Advantages	–	44	58	47	56	46	56	48	62	46
Disadvantages	–	7	4	9	5	8	5	7	9	11
Both	–	43	38	40	38	41	38	39	29	38
No answer	–	6	–	4	1	5	1	6	1	5

Source: Various Politbarometers: Forschungsgruppe Wahlen e.V.

Merging Two Worlds:
Social Values in East and West Germany

As East and West German citizens are slowly beginning to learn to live together, the consequences of unification—which will influence the landscape of German political culture for many years to come—are a matter of controversial discourse.[14] Viewed against the background of forty-five years of communist indoctrination, the question how East German citizens envisioned an "ideal society" and how these perceptions have changed since 1990 is of obvious interest.[15]

In 1990, the comparison of preferred social values between East and West Germans yielded surprising similarities. Having said this, one might have expected that whatever differences were prevalent in 1990 would diminish or disappear in the following years. However, quite the contrary is true. While the data for West Germany are almost unchanged between 1990 and 1992, the grave economic and social problems in East Germany

Table 12.2
Most Important Problems, 1990-93 in East and West Germany
(multiple responses - in percentages)

East Germany

Problems concerning. . .	Nov. 1990	Feb. 1991	May 1991	Feb. 1992	April 1992	Jan. 1993
unification	–	6	6	11	13	10
economy	76	106	123	120	113	96
social security	16	17	22	23	28	32
aliens/asylum seekers	1	–	–	8	10	19
domestic security	1	–	7	9	13	11
environment	4	6	7	9	8	4
right-wing extremism	–	–	–	–	–	12

West Germany

Problems concerning. . .	Nov. 1990	Feb. 1991	May 1991	Feb. 1992	April 1992	Jan. 1993
unification	55	40	64	33	26	18
economy	26	31	27	42	28	44
social security	18	11	15	17	25	14
aliens/asylum seekers	16	5	8	40	64	55
domestic security	2	1	3	–	–	–
environment	28	13	26	20	12	8
right-wing extremism	–	–	–	–	–	12

The individual issues were categorized into main topics.

Source: Various Politbarometers: Forschungsgruppe Wahlen e.V.

have greatly influenced East German thinking. Disappointment centers in particular around the economy; apparently the concrete experiences East Germans have made since 1990 have been negative enough to nurture increasing skepticism toward a market economy and the principle of performance. (See Table 12.3.)

A number of surveys indicate that former GDR citizens appear much more welfare-state oriented (or even state-oriented in general) than those of the neighboring Central and East European countries. This is confirmed once again in the IPOS data. However, the largest change of all can be observed regarding the desire for law and order, as operationalized by the need to have a strong police force. This new emphasis reflects a large and growing concern over a phenomenon that seemingly had played a rather minor role in the former GDR: crime. Problems associated with rising crime rates and with the economy constitute the greatest concerns for East Germans. It is interesting that this set of disappointments has created at least traces of a socialist backlash up to the point that the "socialist welfare state" has become the focus of myth building.[16]

Attitudes Toward Democracy

Whereas notions of an "ideal society" pertain to many different aspects of socio-political organization, the analysis of attitudes toward democracy are at the core of every debate regarding the implications of unification. Citizen attitudes by themselves are, of course, not enough to make for a democratic political system; political institutions matter as much, if not more. Nevertheless, there is an obvious relationship between the support for certain values, norms, and institutions of democracy and the stability of a democratic political system as such. If one considers the political history of Germany with one authoritarian, one democratic, and one totalitarian period before the Federal Republic came into existence, it is easily understood why the study of democratic orientations in Germany has a long tradition.[17]

There is reliable evidence that for a considerable length of time the new democratic political order imposed upon West Germany by the three Western Allies and some German elite groups after the Second World War was without broad public acceptance.[18] Only after two decades the support for a democratic political order was considered sound and political support no longer was based predominantly on outcome-oriented criteria. In addition, the transfer of power from a conservative to a social-liberal government in 1969 seemed to underscore findings that West Germany has joined the ranks of "normal" Western democracies.[19]

While the political orientations of West Germans have been traced over a long period of time, at the time of unification little was known about those of East Germans. Is it possible that the peaceful revolution of 1989 and the active protest of hundreds of thousands of East German citizens against the SED regime has prepared the ground for a level of democratic consciousness that West Germans without this kind of experience had to wait for over a period of two decades? At the time of unification, to

Table 12.3
Preferred Social Values in 1990, 1991, and 1992
in East and West Germany on a Seven-Point-Scale (Means)

Scale Point 1	East	West	Scale Point 7
Limitations in economic growth	6.2[a]	5.3[a]	Economic growth
promoted	6.1[b]	5.2[b]	promoted
	5.8[c]	5.3[c]	
As small a police force as	3.9	3.7	Strong police
possible	5.0	3.9	force
	5.1	4.2	
Guaranteed standard of	5.6	5.0	Standard of living
living independent of	5.0	4.9	based on individual
individual achievement	4.7	4.9	achievement
Centrally-planned	5.8	5.5	Free market
economy	5.4	5.4	economy
	5.0	5.3	
Equal income	5.6	5.2	Unequal income
	5.2	5.2	
	5.0	5.1	
Environment over	2.8	2.9	Economy over
economy	2.9	2.9	environment
	3.0	3.0	
Decisions made	2.4	3.1	Decisions made
by public	2.6	3.1	by elites
	2.5	3.1	
Government responsible	2.6	2.9	Individual responsible
for social security	2.2	3.1	for social security
	2.2	3.0	
Skepticism toward	5.7	4.4	Technological progress
technology	5.5	4.4	promoted
	5.4	4.4	

[a] 1990
[b] 1991
[c] 1992

Source: IPOS surveys 1990, 1991, 1992.

what extent did East Germans display democratic orientations? How have they changed over time, in particular in view of the dismal economic situation in East Germany?

To answer these questions a scale of democratic attitudes developed by Max Kaase and Rudolf Wildenmann in the late 1960s was applied.[20] Based on works by Seymour M. Lipset[21] and Ralf Dahrendorf,[22] they singled out five dimensions of democratic orientations which were transformed into a 9-item Likert scale.[23] Kaase and Wildenmann constructed this battery of items so that several items tap what might be termed consensual democratic values (items 1, 2, 3, 4 in Table 12.4); they are phrased such that agreement implies a democratic response. Another set of items contrasts values of participation and social order and are phrased such that disagreement signifies a democratic response (items 5, 6, 7, 8 and 9 in Table 12.4).[24] The battery has been replicated several times over the past two decades in West Germany, and in the spring of 1990 it was included in a survey of East Germans.[25]

In 1968 these items were presented for the first time to representative samples of the West German population, students and non-academic youth. Citizens already expressed broad support for general democratic values; this support was even more prominent among the youth and particularly among students. At the same time it became clear that the conflict dimension of democracy was much less accepted by West Germans than the consensus dimension.

Over the years West Germany has witnessed a gradual increase both in the support of democratic values and in the acceptance of political conflict, although the idea of protest as a threat to political order still looms large. These findings are characteristic of political values changes which were triggered by the student movement, the challenge to established political institutions, an extension of political participation,[26] and an increasing tendency for individual self-fulfillment.[27] But they are also indicative of the length of time it took to implant democratic orientations in West Germany.

When East Germans were first interviewed, there was a remarkable convergence of orientations between the East and the West. However, democratic norms which related to the conflict potential of social groups and individual citizens and to the role of the political opposition were even more strongly accepted in the East than in the West.[28] For East Germans the suppression of any political opposition in the former GDR had sharpened the perception of the importance of political opposition in the democratic process. In addition, in early 1990 the peaceful transition in East Germany still seemed to have been very much on the people's mind: 50 percent of the respondents rejected the statement that a citizen loses his or her right to demonstrate when endangering the public order, as opposed to 28 percent of West Germans. (See Table 12.4.)

However, it seems that the recollection of those conflictual days soon gave way to everyday problems that emerged from unification. In December 1990, half of the respondents disagreed that conflicts between interest groups are detrimental to public welfare; earlier in the year the level of disagreement was much stronger (74 percent). The rejection of the statement that a citizen forfeits the right to protest if he threatens the public order has declined as well and is now approaching the level of the West Germans. The rising need for political harmony is also transformed into a growing expectation that the political opposition should support the government. In 1991 this attitude was shared by two-thirds of East Germans. If such an attitude were put into political effect it would imply a grand coalition between the two major parties. Frederick D. Weil argues that the rejection of a grand coalition is an important notion in a democratic political system because such coalitions are acceptable only under extremely critical circumstances.[29] To ingrain this democratic principle into the political belief system of citizens in newly emerging democracies, the argument continues, will require a long period of time.

In principle, Weil's point seems to be well taken. How it applies concretely, however, depends on what is regarded as a critical situation. In early 1993, even many members of the political elite seemed to think that Germany is quickly moving in the direction of a grand coalition because of severe economic strains. Under these circumstances it is not surprising that even the citizens follow suit. In 1993 surveys, a grand coalition government emerged as the most preferred form of government.

One particularly interesting finding relates to the attitudes of East Germans toward violence. While the increase in the rejection of political violence in December 1990 appeared to indicate a process of normalization, the 10 percent decrease in 1991 seems to show that citizens in eastern Germany are beginning to wonder whether peaceful means are sufficient to solve their problems.[30] Undoubtedly, any increase in the acceptance of political violence is reason for concern.

In sum, the analysis of democratic attitudes has provided some interesting results. Unfortunately, comparable data for Eastern Europe are presently not available; hence, the East Germans' democratic attitudes can only be compared to those in the western part of Germany. Here, one cannot help but being impressed by the fact that the distribution of attitudes in the two populations is very similar and sometimes, in particular in early 1990, more on the democratic side in eastern Germany than in western

Table 12.4

Scale of Democratic Values 1968-91 in East and West Germany

(in percentages)

	East Germany			West Germany					
	1990[a]	1990[b]	1991	1968	1979	1982	1988	1990	1991
A. Consensual democratic values				Percentage Agreeing					
1. Every citizen has the right to demonstrate	90	92	96	74	86	87	91	90	94
2. Everyone should have the right to express his/her opinion freely	90	98	97	93	95	94	91	92	97
3. A living democracy requires a political opposition	95	95	96	89	93	92	94	93	95
4. Every democratic party should have the chance to govern	88	91	95	86	93	93	92	91	92
B. Conflict versus Order				Percentage Disagreeing					
5. Conflicts between interests are adverse to the public interest	74	51	50	27	26	21	48	47	56
6. A citizen forfeits the right to protest if he/she threatens the order	50	32	33	30	26	21	30	28	31
7. In a democratic society, some conflicts require violence to be solved	81	88	78	73	81	83	86	79	86
8. The political opposition should support the government	53	42	33	26	31	34	46	39	41
9. Public interests should have priority over individual interests	15	8	7	6	5	8	11	11	11

[a]April/May 1990.
[b]December 1990.

Source: Kaase 1971; *Allbus surveys* 1979, 1982, 1988; *German Identity Survey Wildenmann* (April/May 1990); *ISSP-Plus Survey* 1990 (December); Weil 1993.

Germany. There are two possible explanations for this phenomenon. The first is based on the observation that East Germans for well over a decade have been regularly exposed to West German television which, as public television, traditionally has placed high emphasis on political reporting. In a sense one could speak of a virtual learning process via West German media. The second explanation relates to the potentially positive effect of the peaceful revolution of 1989 in which substantial segments of the population were actively involved. On the other hand, the lessening of support for some elements of democratic orientations since 1990 also hints at the possibility that political orientations in East Germany are still quite fluid and can be substantially influenced by political events and the mass media.

Attitudes Toward Political Participation

Until the late 1960s empirical research on political participation concentrated on conventional institutionalized modes. Emphasis was given to the analysis of electoral behavior and all activities related to elections, such as support for political parties during election campaigns.[31] In the mid-1960s, when the period of economic and political reconstruction after World War II in the advanced Western Democracies had come to an end, the interaction of structural changes (that is, the growth of higher education and the spread of television) and specific mobilizing events like the civil rights movement in the United States and the Vietnam war stimulated a development toward increasing engagement in so-called unconventional modes of political participation.

Initially, "unconventional" forms of political participation were analyzed in the context of protest movements and were therefore not perceived as a structural development. As comparative and nationally representative information on these forms of participation began to accumulate, however, it became increasingly clear that these developments embraced not only special segments but large parts of the population. They reflected processes of cognitive political mobilization and were in part fed by changes from materialist to postmaterialist values which Ronald Inglehart has described in detail.[32] All studies in this field have consistently reported a positive correlation between engagement in institutionalized and non-institutionalized political participation. These findings stimulated Barnes, Kaase, et al., to speak of a "widened political repertory."[33] Given the general nature of this phenomenon, one can no longer conceptualize it as a threat to pluralist democracy. Rather, it is a challenge to pluralist democracy in that systems of indirect, parliamentary democracy must now consider means for including more plebiscitary elements into their institutional framework.[34]

These changes in the nature of political participation evolved over a period of thirty years. This makes it particularly interesting to analyze the status of participatory orientations in a society such as eastern Germany where citizens had been denied the right of free expression for more than four decades. In the following section, I will examine (1) modes of political participation in the former GDR, (2) whether and how East and West Germans differ in this respect, and (3) some of the factors that make individual participation more or less likely.

Before considering individual orientations toward political participation, I shall first address the "legitimacy" of certain legal and illegal modes of "uninstitutionalized" modes of political participation in East and West Germany as early as 1990. As Table 12.5 indicates, there were similarities as well as differences. With respect to the former, the absolute magnitude of the respective figures does not hint at principal differences in attitudes between the two populations. In eastern Germany, however, there seem to belingering effects of the peaceful revolution on political attitudes. This shows up particularly in the +15 percentage point difference in the propensity to organize a nationwide strike but also in the +4 percentage point difference when it comes to organizing a demonstration or an official hearing. In contrast, the two illegal modes (occupying buildings and damaging public properties) clearly find less support among East Germans.

Table 12.5
Permissible Actions as Means of Political Protest
Against the Government in 1990 in East and West Germany
(in percentages)

Action which should be permitted	East	West
To organize an official hearing	88	84
To organize a demonstration	84	80
To publish handbills	62	74
To organize a nation-wide strike	59	44
To paralyze an administrative authority by occupying buildings	11	17
To damage public properties	1	3

Source: ISSP-Plus Survey East Germany 1990; Allbus 1990.

The data presented in Table 12.5 are pertinent for the analysis of political participation in the sense that a positive attitude toward a given action enhances the probability of participation in such an action.[35] Unfortunately, existing research does not contain information on whether certain actions are regarded as socially permissible. Instead, respondents were only asked whether they would be willing to engage in various political actions "with certainty," "perhaps" or "not at all." Nine actions were included in the IPOS surveys of 1991 and 1992, as inciated below. The actions cited tap different dimensions of uninstitutionalized political involvement—including the conceptual and empirical contrast between legal forms and illegal forms of political participation as well as the potential for political violence against persons and objects in the second of these categories.

To evaluate the dimensional structure of participatory acts as studied in the 1991 IPOS survey, a separate factor analysis was performed with data from the eastern and western parts of Germany. In the West, a two-dimensional structure resulted which nicely differentiates between the legal and the illegal modes of action. In the East, a similar picture emerged, although the two dimensions are not as clearly separated as in the West. This is probably due to the lack of public debate and expertise regarding acts such as "potentially violent demonstrations," "occupying construction sites," and "boycotts."

A. Legal modes of Political Participation:

1. Signing a petition
2. Taking part in a lawful political demonstration
3. Taking part in a citizens' action group
4. Taking part in a boycott

B. Illegal modes of Political Participation:

5. Hindering military transports through sit-ins
6. Taking part in a demonstration even if there could be violent actions
7. Occupying construction sites
8. Spraying political slogans on walls
9. Damaging property

In order to penetrate more deeply into these findings, an analysis was performed which examined the inter-item correlations within each of the two dimensions and the way in which the whole set of items was related to each other (see Table 12.6).[36] When one compares the average within cor-

Table 12.6
Average Correlations Within and Between Two Subdmensions
Of Unconventional Political Participation in 1991
in East and West Germany
(Correlation Coefficients - Pearson r)

Subdimensions	Number of Correlations	Average Correlation	
		East	West
Within the Dimensions			
Legal unconventional political participation (4 items)	(6)[a]	.36	.52
Illegal unconventional political participation (5 items)	(10)	.29	.49
Between the Dimensions			
Legal and illegal political participation (9 items)	(36)	.18	.28

[a]The entries are the number of pairs of correlations, based on the following formula: (number of items) x (n-1/2) (See Kaase and Neidhardt, 1990).

Source: IPOS Survey 1991.

relations across dimensions, the values for the two dimensions are about equal and substantially higher than the average correlation across the nine items. This reinforces the findings from the factor analysis. It is interesting, however, that the absolute value of the average correlation for the two dimensions is substantial higher in the West than in the East. East Germans apparently have a less clear picture of the meaning and context of the individual actions than West Germans. This points to differences that are hidden below the surface of similarities. Furthermore, it should be pointed out that the positive average correlation across the two dimensions (nine items) indicates that both dimensions have an action component in common.[37]

When the results from the 1991 analysis are related to previous findings, it comes somewhat as a surprise that the two-dimensionality emerges so clearly. The most likely explanation for this is that in previous research items had been included that explicitly addressed political violence against persons. If such items are contained in the questionnaire, then the illegal dimension becomes somewhat fuzzy.[38] Similarities and differences in the extent to which East and West Germans consider certain modes of action meant to influence political outcomes are presented in Table 12.7.

In 1991, the willingness of citizens to become involved in unconventional modes of political participation was higher, on average, in the eastern part of Germany than in the western part. The proclivity toward political violence in both parts of Germany is relatively low; the taboo character of violence, however, may have influenced the responses. One should note, though, that East Germans are substantially more inclined (20 percent) than West Germans (12 percent) to participate in demonstrations even if violence might occur.[39] Compared to 1991, East Germans were considerable less likely to engage in demonstrations and citizen initiatives in 1992. This decrease may be explained by the fact that after the "participatory high" which ended in the peaceful overthrow of the SED regime a certain saturation effect has now taken place.

Determinants of Political Participation

Which individual characteristics help to predispose German citizens toward engagement in legal and illegal modes of political participation? Research on political participation over the years has isolated at least three major determinants: socio-demographic characteristics, political orientations, and social context.[40] Regarding the impact of socio-demographic factors, many studies have converged on the so-called standard model: the higher the socioeconomic resource level (usually operationalized as education, occupation, and income), the higher the involvement in political action. This model was found valid for conventional and unconventional participation, including civil disobedience.[41]

Additional socio-structural variables significant for understanding political participation are age and gender. Neither operates in identical fashion, however, with regard to the various dimensions of participation. One important difference is that women, even after having controlled for age and education, are still clearly less inclined to become involved in conventional modes of participation, whereas in the area of unconventional participation the difference between males and females almost completely

Table 12.7
Behavioral Intentions Toward Modes of Unconventional
Political Participation in 1991-92 in East and West Germany
(in percentages)

	East		West	
	1991	1992	1991	1992
A: Legal Modes				
1. Signing a petition	55[a]	51	48	48
	36[b]	36	39	40
2. Taking part in a lawful political	35	25	22	21
demonstration	34	36	34	32
3. Taking part in a citizens' action group	43	39	35	35
	45	43	38	40
4. Taking part in a boycott	10	9	15	16
	28	31	29	34
B: Illegal Modes				
5. Hindering military transports	4	3	4	5
through sit-ins	16	12	14	14
6. Taking part in a demonstration even	4	3	3	3
if there could be violent actions	16	16	9	11
7. Occupying construction sites	6	4	4	4
	18	17	13	17
8. Spraying political slogans on walls	–	1	1	1
	1	2	5	7
9. Damaging property	–	1	1	1
	2	2	4	4

[a]Respondent would surely do so.
[b]Respondent might perhaps do so.

Source: *IPOS Surveys 1991, 1992.*

vanishes even if one controls for age and education. Regarding age, youth-fulness is very important for a supportive attitude toward unconventional political participation. However, if one considers only actual (past) partic-ipation, age loses most of its significance since processes of mobilization and contextual factors influence actual participation.

Taking these findings from previous research as a blueprint against which the East and West German data for 1991 are evaluated, in the following the results from multiple classification analyses will be discussed, using socio-structural factors as independent variables. Furthermore, the position of the respondents on the Left-Right-Scale and the postmaterialist value orientation as measured by the Inglehart index will also be considered. The latter two independent variables were chosen because it has been shown repeatedly that leftist political orientations and postmaterialism are strongly related to unconventional political participation.

Altogether four dependent variables were constructed as additive indices from the nine participation items described in Table 12.7 above. Index I and Index II pertain to the dimension of legal unconventional participation (items 1, 2, 3, 4), the difference between the two being that Index I includes only those respondents who said they would "surely" participate, while Index II includes those who "surely" or "perhaps" participate. Both indices have a range from 0 to 4.

Index III and Index IV include items 5 through 9 which refer to the illegal dimension. This index ranges from 0 to 5. Tables 12.8 and 12.9 below display the differences from the overall mean of the various indices for the individual categories of the independent variables as well as their impact (beta coefficients) on the respective dependent variable and the overall variance explained by the set of independent variables (R resp. R2).

The findings reinforce previous research on determinants affecting legal forms of unconventional participation in western Germany. Age and education show a positive relationship; the effect of gender is small (albeit it is in the expected direction); and leftism as well as postmaterialism have a strong impact on the inclination to become involved. This structure of relationships works for both indices because the mode of construction assures that the positive correlation is strong (r= .61 in the West and .53 in the East). However, age—as one would predict based on previous research findings—shows up stronger in Index II than in Index I.

In the former GDR, the overall explanatory power of the five independent variables combined is clearly lower (beta coefficients .09 resp. .14) than in the West (beta coefficients .21 resp. .21). However, both for Index I and for Index II the relationships in the East point into the same direction as in the West. The largest East-West difference obtains to Index I where age as well as education are less important in the East than in the West. These findings suggest that orientations toward legal unconventional political participation in the East are still evolving, slowly approaching the kind of stable structure typical for the West.

Table 12.8
Structural Determinants of Orientations Toward
Legal Unconventional Political Participation, 1991
(Differences from Overall Means)

Independent variables	Index I		Index II	
	East	West	East	West
Gender:				
(1) Male	.09[a]	.08	.12	.09
(2) Female	-.09	-.07	-.12	-.09
Age:				
(1) 18-24 years	-.04	.21	.27	.33
(2) 25-29 years	-.00	.22	.07	.31
(3) 30-39 years	.07	.19	.14	.17
(4) 40-49 years	-.13	.12	.02	.23
(5) 50-59 years	.16	-.18	-.01	-.05
(6) 60 years and older	-.11	-.23	-.33	-.40
Educational level:				
(1) low	-.06	-.13	-.17	-.12
(2) middle	.01	.11	.07	.02
(3) high	.10	.23	.23	.30
Left-right self-placement				
(1) extreme left	.48	.56	.05	.25
(2) moderate left	.24	.40	.21	.36
(3) medium	-.18	-.20	-.13	-.16
(4) moderate right	-.24	-.13	-.11	-.12
(5) extreme right	-.12	-.33	-.18	-.22
Value orientation:				
(1) materialist	-.24	-.24	-.18	-.26
(2) mixed materialist	-.03	-.10	-.01	-.06
(3) mixed postmaterialist	.11	-.11	.11	.07
(4) postmaterialist	.50	.61	.26	.37
Multiple Classification Analysis: beta coefficients				
Gender	.07[b]	.06	.11	.07
Age	.09[b]	.15	.17	.22
Educational level	.04[b]	.11	.14	.12
Left-right self-placement	.19	.20	.15	.17
Value orientation	.16	.22	.12	.16
Multiple R	.29	.46	.38	.46
Multiple R^2	.09	.21	.14	.21

[a]Deviation from overall mean.

[b]Not significant on the .001 level.

Source: IPOS Survey 1991.

Table 12.9
Structural Determinants of Orientations Toward
Illegal Unconventional Political Participation, 1991
(Differences from Overall Means)

Independent variables	Index III East	Index III West	Index IV East	Index IV West
Gender:				
(1) Male	.00[a]	-.01	.03	.01
(2) Female	-.00	.01	.03	-.01
Age:				
(1) 18-24 years	.15	.29	.41	.64
(2) 25-29 years	.11	-.02	.38	.21
(3) 30-39 years	.03	.04	.08	.17
(4) 40-49 years	-.05	-.05	-.06	-.05
(5) 50-59 years	-.04	-.06	-.15	-.11
(6) 60 years and older	-.04	-.06	-.22	-.32
Educational level:				
(1) low	.02	-.01	-.00	.03
(2) middle	-.00	-.05	-.01	-.14
(3) high	-.06	.10	.05	.13
Left-right self-placement				
(1) extreme left	.25	.89	.34	.25
(2) moderate left	-.00	.02	.06	.22
(3) medium	-.04	-.06	-.09	-.16
(4) moderate right	-.03	-.04	-.09	-.14
(5) extreme right	.29	.04	.57	.17
Value orientation:				
(1) materialist	-.05	-.05	-.11	-.15
(2) mixed materialist	-.04	-.01	-.09	-.02
(3) mixed postmaterialist	.05	-.04	.10	.02
(4) postmaterialist	.18	.10	.46	.27
Multiple Classification Analysis: beta coefficients				
Gender	.01[b]	.01[b]	.03[b]	.00[b]
Age	.12	.19	.20	.25
Educational level	.05[b]	.09	.02[b]	.08
Left-right self-placement	.16	.25	.14	.22
Value orientation	.13	.09	.16	.12
Multiple R	.25	.38	.33	.42
Multiple R^2	.06	.15	.11	.18

[a]Deviation from overall mean.

[b]Not significant on the .001 level.

Source: IPOS Survey 1991.

One might expect important similarities between East and West in the relationship toward illegal modes of participation. A closer look reveals, however, that the correlation in western Germany and eastern Germany between the two dimensions (Index I vs. Index III: r= .36/.32 and Index II and Index IV: r= .43/.39) is only moderate, thereby reinforcing the findings from the factor analyses of the nine individual participation items discussed above. In addition, despite the positive correlations between the two indices (.60 in the West and .59 in the East), substantial differences between East and West as well as between Index III and Index IV exist. This is also visible when one examines the impact of age on Index III and Index IV, respectively, in the East and in the West: the two youngest age cohorts are much more supportive of illegal participation when it is presented as a distant (Index IV) and not a realistic (Index III) option. Second, in the realm of illegal participation, high education in both indices predisposes much less toward action than in the field of legal participation. Third, in terms of the ideological position of the respondent, the data reveal a slight but nevertheless clear indication of curvilinearity in that both the extreme right and the extreme left are most inclined toward illegal modes of action. This finding is especially interesting insofar as it is reminiscent of earlier studies that show that political violence is equally attractive to both ideological extremes.

The comparison between determinants of orientations toward legal and illegal forms of political participation confirms that the political attitudes of East Germans do not show the same distinctiveness and clarity in structure as found in the western part of Germany. The limits of virtual learning without an opportunity for long-time exposure and practice in political involvement may explain this difference.

Conclusion and Outlook

The political situation in the GDR before unification was dominated by citizen dissatisfaction with their economic and political way of life. Naturally, in 1990 East German respondents perceived more deficits in almost all policy areas than West German respondents; this situation lingers on.

If one considers the enormous differences in socio-political structure and context between both parts of Germany for almost half a century, one cannot help but being impressed by the convergence in political orientations for the two populations (provided, of course, one is not dealing with so-called "questionnaire democrats").[42] How deeply these democratic orientations are already ingrained and therefore will persist also in times of crisis remains to be seen.

In early 1990, East Germans were surprisingly more supportive of democratic conflict than West German citizens. However, one year later East Germans had already approached the level of West Germans. It also seems that the magnitude and intensity of political problems in the East have enhanced the feeling that such conflicts require political violence to be solved. This finding commands attention.

The residues of the peaceful revolution in East Germany were clearly visible in 1991 regarding the propensity toward legal forms of unconventional political participation. 1992 witnessed a decline in these orientations. In principle, East and West Germans are driven to unconventional political action by the same factors. Here, as in other areas, the structural patterns in the East are less focused than in the West. This reminds us once more that one should not place too much confidence in findings that highlight similarities in political orientations between East and West Germans.

It is against this background that the prospects for a growing identification with democracy in East Germany must be assessed. In early 1993, the situation in the unified Germany was still marked by substantial economic and social differences between East and West. Undoubtedly, the magnitude of the task to transform the run-down planned economy of the former GDR into a productive market economy has been underestimated by the political elites in both parts of the country. Since the CDU/CSU-FDP government in 1990 had created hopes and expectations that the government later could not live up to, disappointment and frustration seem particularly high. It is an open question whether a more thorough analysis of the situation would have helped to avoid these misjudgments. After all, a large part of the average citizens in East and West Germany had anticipated all along that in the short-run unification would encounter substantial difficulties.

Three years into unification, citizens in the new *Bundesländer* are beginning to feel that the path to safe jobs, a stable economy, and the West German standard of living takes too long. Almost three quarters of East Germans are dissatisfied with what the western part of Germany has done for the East (November 1992). Also, the quality of work by the Trust Agency (the *Treuhand*), whose task is to privatize the former GDR's state property, is sharply criticized by almost everyone. It seems that dissatisfaction and pessimism are merging into a negative climate of opinion which has begun to extend into the area of the "old" Federal Republic. For the first time in mid-June 1992, in the West concern over unification was higher than satisfaction. In this fragile phase in which democratic orientations still have to be firmly established in the former GDR, some people even raise the question whether democracy as a whole is at stake again in the new Germany. In 1992 little more than one third of East Germans were satisfied with the way democracy is presently working in Germany. This problem is aggravated by an increasing feeling among East Germans that they are threatened by increasing levels of crime, an experience they were hardly exposed to in the old socialist days.

East Germans still have difficulties in adjusting to a political system where individuals have a great deal of responsibility for their own life. As a general concept, a market economy, free enterprise, and achievement-dependent salaries seem highly desirable goals. However, the reality makes many East Germans wonder whether they should continue to support such a system. This is particularly unfortunate because East Germans need to build the self-respect that enables them to overcome feelings of powerlessness and the loss of political and personal identity.[43]

Many West Germans have looked at German unification as a distant event with which they identified in principle but which would have little effect on their own way of life. The permanent debate on the necessity to raise taxes and the consequences of the economic recession by now have made every West German aware of the fact that unification not only affects East Germans. In January 1993, almost half of East and West Germans felt that Germany were facing major problems; and 32 percent of those in the West and 43 percent of those in the East even believed that Germany was facing a crisis. In this situation, German democracy confronts its first real test since 1949.

Notes

1. Parts of this chapter are published in Petra Bauer, "Politische Orientierungen im Übergang. Eine Analyse politischer Einstellungen der Bürger in West- und Ostdeutschland 1990/91," *Kölner Zeitschrift für Soziologie und Sozialpsychologie*, 43 (1991): 433-53; and Petra Bauer-Kaase, "Die Entwicklung politischer Orientierungen in Ost-und Westdeutschland seit der deutschen Vereinigung," in Oskar Niedermayer and Richard Stöß, eds., *Wähler und Parteien im Umbruch* (Opladen: Westdeutscher Verlag, 1993).

2. Paul M. Sniderman, *A Question of Loyalty* (Berkeley: University of California Press, 1981), 141.

3. See in particular Francis Fukuyama, *The End of History and the Last Man* (New York: The Free Press, 1992).

4. Daniel Bell, "On the Fate of Communism," *Dissent* (1990): 187-88.

5. Karl-Rudolf Korte, "Deutschlandbilder. Akzentverlagerungen der deutschen Frage seit den 70er Jahren," *Aus Politik und Zeitgeschichte*, B 3 (1988): 45-53, 46.

6. Willi Herbert and Rudolf Wildenmann, "Deutsche Identität. Die subjektive Verfassung der Deutschen vor der Vereinigung," in Rudolf Wildenmann, ed., *Nation und Demokratie. Politisch-strukturelle Gestaltungsprobleme im neuen Deutschland* (Baden-Baden: Nomos, 1991), 71-98, 71; Birgit Szumni, et al., "Datenreport. Die Vereinigung der beiden deutschen Staaten," Zentralarchiv für empirische Sozialforschung, *ZA-Information* 26 (1990): 62-71, 71.

7. Erwin K. Scheuch, *Wie deutsch sind die Deutschen? Eine Nation wandelt ihr Gesicht* (Bergisch Gladbach: Bastei Lübbe, 1991), 260.

8. Wolfgang G. Gibowski and Max Kaase, "Auf dem Weg zum politischen Alltag. Eine Analyse der ersten gesamtdeutschen Bundestagswahl vom 2. Dezember 1990," *Aus Politik und Zeitgeschichte*, B 11-12 (1991): 3-20, 11.

9. Dieter Roth, "Die Wahlen zur Volkskammer in der DDR. Der Versuch einer Erklärung," *Politische Vierteljahresschrift*, 31 (1990): 369-93.

10. The "Basisumfrage 1991" is a special study of the Allbus national survey program which is conducted every two years and jointly administered by ZUMA (Zentrum für Umfragen, Methoden und Analysen e.V., Mannheim) and the ZA (Zentralarchiv für empirische Sozialforschung, Cologne).

11. These data were made available by the Zentralarchiv.

12. Helmut Jung, *Neue Märkte im Osten. Sozialer und politischer Wandel und neue Konsumgewohnheiten in den neuen Bundesländern* (Frankfurt und Dresden: BASISRESEARCH, 1992).

13. Cf. Walter Friedrich, "Mentalitätswandlungen der Jugend in der DDR," *Aus Politik und Zeitgeschichte*, B 16-17 (1990): 25-37; Anne Köhler, "Marschierte der DDR-Bürger mit? Systemidentifikation der DDR-Bevölkerung vor und nach der Wende," in Uta Gerhardt and Ekkehard Mochmann, eds., *Gesellschaftlicher Umbruch 1945-1990. Re-Demokratisierung und Lebensverhältnisse* (Munich: R. Oldenbourg, 1992), 59-79, 62.

14. Rüdiger Thomas, "Zur Geschichte soziologischer Forschung in der DDR," in Heiner Timmermann, ed., *Lebenslagen. Sozialindikatorenforschung in beiden Teilen Deutschlands* (Saarbrücken and Scheidt: Dadder, 1990), 9-35.

15. Petra Bauer, "Politische Orientierungen im Übergang"; and Petra Bauer-Kaase, "Die Entwicklung politischer Orientierungen," in Niedermayer and Stöß, eds., *Wähler und Parteien*.

16. Achim Koch, "Staatliche Eingriffe in die Wirtschaft im Osten hoch im Kurs. Unterschiede und Gemeinsamkeiten in den politischen Einstellungen 'neuer' und 'alter' Bundesbürger." *Informationsdienst Soziale Indikatoren* (ISI) (Mannheim: ZUMA-Publikationen), 6 (1991): 1-5; Bettina Westle, "Strukturen nationaler Identität in Ost- und Westdeutschland," *Kölner Zeitschrift für Soziologie und Sozialpsychologie*, 44 (1992): 461-88, 485.

17. For literature on this topic see, among others, Gabriel A. Almond and Sidney Verba, *The Civic Culture: Political Attitudes and Democracy in Five Nations* (Princeton, N.J.: Princeton University Press, 1963); Max Kaase, "Demokratische Einstellungen in der Bundesrepublik," in Rudolf Wildenmann, ed., *Sozialwissenschaftliches Jahrbuch für Politik*, 2nd vol. (Munich and Vienna: Günter Olzog Verlag, 1971), 119-316; Dieter Fuchs, *Die Unterstützung des politischen Systems der Bundesrepublik Deutschland* (Opladen: Westdeutscher Verlag, 1989); Bettina Westle, *Politische Legitimität. Theorien, Konzepte, empirische Befunde* (Baden-Baden: Nomos, 1989).

18. See David P. Conradt, "The Changing German Political Culture," in Gabriel A. Almond and Sidney Verba, eds., *The Civic Culture Revisited* (Boston: Little Brown, 1980), 212-72; Max Kaase, "Systemakzeptanz in den westlichen Demokratien," *Zeitschrift für Politik* (Special Issue), 2 (1985): 99-125.

19. Fuchs, *Unterstützung*; Westle, *Politische Legitimität*.

20. Kaase, "Demokratische Einstellungen." For similar approaches see James W. Prothro and C.M. Grigg, "Fundamental Principles of Democracy. Bases of Agreement and Disagreement," *Journal of Politics*, 22 (1960): 276-94; Herbert McClosky, "Consensus and Ideology in American Politics," *American Political Science Review*, 58 (1964): 361-82; Herbert McClosky and Alida Brill, *Dimensions of Tolerance. What Americans Believe About Civil Liberties* (New York: Russell Sage Foundation, 1983).

21. Seymour M. Lipset, *Political Man. The Social Basis of Politics* (Garden City: Anchor Book Edition, 1963).

22. Ralf Dahrendorf, *Gesellschaft und Demokratie in Deutschland* (Munich: Piper, 1965).

23. Kaase, "Demokratische Einstellungen," 142.

24. There is, however, some ambiguity in what a "democratic" response for item 9 is. Empirically, this item is only weakly related to the other items. See Kaase, "Demokratische Einstellungen," 151.

25. Rudolf Wildenmann, ed., *Nation und Demokratie. Politischstrukturelle Gestaltungsprobleme im neuen Deutschland* (Baden-Baden: Nomos, 1991).

26. Samuel H. Barnes and Max Kaase, et al., *Political Action. Mass Participation in Five Western Democracies* (Beverly Hills: Sage, 1979).

27. See Helmut Klages, *Wertedynamik. Über die Wandelbarkeit des Selbstverständlichen. Texte und Themen*, Vol. 212 (Zurich: Edition Interfrom, 1988); and Ronald Inglehart, *Culture Shift in Advanced Industrial Society* (Princeton, N.J.: Princeton University Press, 1990).

28. See Petra Bauer, "Freiheit und Demokratie in der Wahrnehmung der Bürger in der Bundesrepublik und der ehemaligen DDR," in Wildenmann, *Nation und Demokratie*, 99-124; Russell J. Dalton, "Communists and Democrats. Attitudes toward Democracy in the two Germanies." Paper presented at the Annual Meeting of the American Political Science Association. Washington, D.C., 1991; and Frederick D. Weil, "The Development of Democratic Attitudes in Eastern and Western Germany in a Comparative Perspective," in Frederick D. Weil, et al., eds., *Democratization in Eastern and Western Europe* (Greenwich: JAI Press, 1993).

29. Weil, ibid.

30. These findings are supported by data collected by the Allensbach Institut für Demoskopie. See Renate Köcher, "Die Einstellungen zur Gewalt ändern sich," *Frankfurter Allgemeine Zeitung*, 264 (1992).

31. Lester W. Milbrath, *Political Participation* (Chicago: Rand McNally, 1965); Norman H. Nie and Sidney Verba, "Political Participation," in Fred I. Greenstein and Nelson W. Polsby, eds., *Handbook of Political Science.*, Vol. 4 (Reading, Mass.: Addison Wesley, 1975), 1-73; and Sidney Verba, Norman H. Nie and Jae-On Kim, *Participation and Political Equality. A Seven-Nation Comparison* (Cambridge, Mass.: Cambridge University Press, 1978).

32. See, e.g., Inglehart, *Culture Shift.*

33. Barnes, Kaase, et al., *Political Action.*

34. A good example is the ongoing debate to amend the German constitution after unification.

35. See Martin Fishbein, "Attitude and Prediction of Behavior," in Martin Fishbein, ed., *Readings in Attitude Theory and Measurement* (New York: John Wiley, 1967), 477-92 and Icek Ajzen and Martin Fishbein, *Understanding Attitudes and Predicting Social Behavior* (Englewood Cliffs, N.J.: Prentice Hall, 1980). The Political Action Study has followed this theoretical logic in designing its measurement instruments. See Barnes, Kaase, et al., *Political Action*, 61-69.

36. For a similar type of analysis see Max Kaase and Friedhelm Neidhardt, *Politische Gewalt und Repression. Ergebnisse von Bevölkerungsumfragen.*, Vol. 4 of Hans-Dieter Schwind, Jürgen Baumann, et al., eds., *Ursachen, Prävention und Kontrolle von Gewalt. Analysen und Vorschläge der Unabhängigen Regierungskommission zur Verhinderung und Be-*

kämpfung von Gewalt (Gewaltkommission) (Berlin: Duncker and Humblot, 1990), 12-14; Bettina Westle, "Politische Partizipation," in Oskar Gabriel with the participation of Frank Brettschneider, ed., *Die EG-Staaten im Vergleich. Strukturen, Prozesse, Politikinhalte* (Opladen: Westdeutscher Verlag, 1992), 135-69.

37. This was emphasized by Barnes, Kaase, et al., *Political Action*, as well as by Allerbeck who had only spoken of one joint dimension of unconventional political participation. Klaus Allerbeck, *Politische Ungleichheit. Ein Acht-Nationen-Vergleich* (Opladen: Westdeutscher Verlag, 1980).

38. Uehlinger as well as Kaase and Neidhardt have interpreted this structure as indicating a "bridging function" of civil disobedience between legal unconventional participation and political violence. See Hans-Martin Uehlinger, *Politische Partizipation in der Bundesrepublik* (Opladen: Westdeutscher Verlag, 1988), 211-17; Kaase and Neidhardt, *Politische Gewalt.*

39. This coincides with findings by Köcher, "Einstellungen zur Gewalt."

40. Lester W. Milbrath and M. Lal Goel, *Political Participation. How and Why Do People Get Involved in Politics* (Chicago: Rand McNally, 1977).

41. See Barnes, Kaase, et al., *Political Action*; M. Kent Jennings, Jan van Deth, et al., *Continuities in Political Action. A Longitudinal Study of Political Orientations in Three Western Democracies* (Berlin and New York: Walter de Gruyter, 1990).

42. See Dalton, "Communists and Democrats," 7.

43. Westle, "Strukturen."

Conclusion

Beyond Unification

Helga A. Welsh
and M. Donald Hancock

The excitement over the fall of the Berlin Wall was short-lived, and sub-sequent celebrations on the day of unification on 3 October are mostly or-chestrated, official acts with little semblance to national holidays in other nation states. In retrospect, unification was and is an act born out of political and economic necessity and, to some extent, solidarity—not one guided by national euphoria. This is fitting, considering the legacies of German history and the anxieties German unification has raised among many European neighbors.

At the time of unification, over forty years had passed since the creation of two separate Germanys. In those years, West German policies toward the GDR changed from non-recognition to increasing levels of interactions. Eventual unification remained the constitutionally prescribed policy of suc-cessive West German governments. Through the 1980s, more than 80 per-cent of the West German population routinely professed the desirability of unification. Yet, most Germans considered the actual chances for unification to be slim at best and certainly not likely to occur in this century. As Jürgen Habermas has observed: "Despite all rhetoric, who would have thought of something like reunification—and was there anybody who still would have wanted it?"[1]

Lacking a strong belief that unification would in fact occur, and having had the hypothetical luxury of asserting that a unified Germany should be modeled closely after West Germany, a favorable posture toward unification on part of the West German population was hardly surprising. Even in the spring and summer of 1990 when specifics regarding unification were ne-gotiated, the lack of any overt political demonstration in favor of unity on the part of West Germans was indeed remarkable but hardly surprising. In countries such as the United States, where political culture and history are characterized by a strong sense of national identity and pride, there seemed little doubt that events following the opening of the Berlin Wall ultimately had to lead to some sort of unification of East and West Germany.

In German history, however, unity was the exception rather than the rule, and regional identities historically have been at least as strong as national identity. In view of the hasty process of unification, it is important to remember that the revolutionary impulse to transform the political and economic system of the GDR was not propelled by nationalism. In a nation divided and darkened by the impact of its historical legacy, efforts at creating a strong national consciousness were politically imprudent. Since the end of the 1960s, the East German leadership had tried to instill a separate German national identity but its efforts met with limited success. Successive West German leaders attempted to diffuse the problem by highlighting processes of European integration and playing down the role of nationalism. More and more it was asserted that West Germany had become a "post-national political community" which had successfully shed its nationalistic past.

The decline of national and nationalist reasoning and the attainment of the desire that all Germans should live in freedom, relinquished any pressing reasons for unification—other than the aspiration that all Germans should live equally well.[2] While economic reasoning might well have deepened an existing, though diffuse, sense of solidarity among West Germans, economic aspects of unification definitely are seen as the driving force in the decision of a majority of East German citizens to vote for the Alliance for Germany and thereby for quick unification. Most East Germans had come to share a growing realization that "indigenous solutions to East German problems were far beyond the reach of GDR resources."[3] From a historical perspective, it is important to remember that Germany's national unification of 1871 was substantially guided by economic forces as well—a "business affair," in the words of a contemporary—and almost completely devoid of emotional sentiment. Ever since then it often has been asserted that in Germany the "identification of nation with the economy left the political system very vulnerable when economic growth failed to deliver the promised degree of integration."[4]

Traditionally, support for democratic institutions in West Germany was closely connected to economic performance, although it is equally clear that the measurement of democratic support is multidimensional.[5] The fusion of politics and economics was particularly pronounced in communist-governed political systems such as the GDR, and the collapse of communism was closely linked to the failure of economic restructuring. The process of democratization is therefore closely connected to the prospect of economic prosperity. For those reasons it is hardly surprising that perhaps no aspect of unification has attracted more attention than the problems associated with the economic restructuring of eastern Germany. The combination of worldwide recession which hit Germany with delay but with great force in 1992, Germany's leadership role in promoting continued economic European integration, and the costs of unification have proven to be a formidable burden with major implications for the domestic and international economy. At the end of 1992 total public debt reached a record high of 1.6 trillion DM as compared to 929 billion in 1989; and 6.6 percent of West Germans and 13.5 percent of East Germans were unemployed, although the actual level of underemployment in the new *Länder* was estimated to be 40.5 percent.[6] Economic growth has declined substantially from 5.1 percent in 1990, 3.7 percent in 1991, and 1.5 percent in 1992. Independent of the question whether the East will become the *mezzogiorno* of Germany or whether it will catch up with the West within a decade or two, the visible difference in economic conditions in the two parts of the country does little to alleviate the alienation between East and West and requires patience on the part of East and West Germans, albeit for different reasons.

As noted in the Introduction to this volume, the literature on regime transitions and democratization emphasizes the element of uncertainty that accompanies the transformation of authoritarian systems to ones that are guided by principles of contestation and participation.[7] Indeed, in Central and Eastern Europe the degree of uncertainty associated with the transformation of highly-structured political systems to democratic pluralism is high, not only because of a lack of previous experience on which to draw. The response to this uncertainty has been different in different countries throughout the region. In this context, the East German situation became unique because of its status as part of a divided nation. Accession to the Federal Republic did prescribe most of the legal parameters and the form the political and economic system would take, but it did not eliminate the introduction of uncertainty into the daily lives of East German citizens. In addition, uncertainty about how unification would affect the lives of East and West Germans and the consistently changing estimates about the magnitude of the financial burden and economic consequences related to unification introduced a high level of apprehension. Predictions about the likely positive long-run implications of unity are therefore received with a heightened sense of skepticism among the general population.[8]

In the intermediate aftermath of unification, Germany continues to suffer from at least two distinct processes which governed the attainment of a national political community: insufficient socioeconomic integration prior to unification, and West German dominance during and after unification.

Insufficient Integration Prior to Unification

The territorial division of Germany after World War II unintentionally had supported the creation of a more homogeneous society in the West, which in turn assisted the achievement and maintenance of democratic institutions and values. For example, the postwar division of Germany included a balance of Catholic and Protestant regions within the Federal Republic, and religion no longer served as a significant social cleavage. The separation from the economic, social, and political problems associated with the vast land holdings in the East (i.e., the territory of the *Junker*) reduced the political division of postwar West Germany, as did the separation from the proletarian centers in Berlin and Saxony. Not the least, land reform, the expropriation of banks and industrial enterprises, a centrally-planned economy, and the discrediting of democratic and legal principles in the eastern part of Germany fostered an ideology of anticommunism among West Germans which provided a lasting bond and helped to instill democratic values. Although contemporary dividing lines in the unified Germany are more the product of industrialization and urbanization processes in divergent political, social, and economic systems than the outcome of traditional divisions, it seems nevertheless true that West Germans nowadays are ill-equipped "to live with the perception of estrangement (*Fremdheit*) among Germans which was still quite common in the first half of this century."[9] Of course, the same statement can be made regarding East German society, which under communism had experienced a substantial politico-economic equalization and homogenization. In 1990 two peoples merged whose political socialization had taken place under substantially different circumstances.

In the German case, unification preceded integration and the process of adjustment originally was conceived as limited only to the former GDR. Viewed from the perspective of federalist and some neo-functionalist theories, longer-term institutional growth and attitudinal changes are the building stones of a new political system based on some sort of supranational decisionmaking system and a shared sense of community. In particular, the process of integration is expected to result in the reciprocal surrender of national responsibilities.[10] In Germany, a unified federal system with one central government, one constitution, and common national symbols and institutions is now in place, but the process of institutional integration—which itself is far from being completed—only provides the shell for the slow but steady process of assimilation and the adjustment of role expectations and attitudes.

To be sure, the process of societal integration—as distinct from institutional integration—did not begin on 3 October 1990: Channels of communications between East and West Germany experienced severe restrictions but never ceased to exist and, indeed, were allowed to expand in the late 1980s. The daily consumption of Western media helped acquaint the East German population with aspects of West German political and popular culture, and a common history and language reinforced the special relationship between the two Germanys. Thus, forty years of political socialization under a communist regime were counterbalanced by exposure and orientation to the West. But decades of separation left deeper traces than had been anticipated by many Germans and outside observers, and commonly-held negative stereotypes often taint the Germans' perception and acceptance of each other. Today, cultural and not material differences are widely perceived as the major stumbling block in the formation of a unified German society with a shared political culture.

Within a few months, the State Treaty on Monetary, Economic, and Social Union and the Unification Treaty were hammered out by delegations of the two Germanys; in its entirety the latter fills 360 pages in the Federal Law Gazette (*Bundesgesetzblatt*). The real and perceived time pressure imposed on political decisionmakers facilitated consensus but encouraged a decisionmaking mode that was characterized by improvisation and centralization and bypassed established channels of consultation and negotiation.[11] In view of the perceived time pressure under which bargaining and negotiation took place, in many cases only general guidelines could be established; in other cases, decisions had to be postponed or later corrected. Decisionmaking overload, a strong belief in swift action which resulted in immediate deadlines and increased time pressures, lack of experience, and insufficient attention to long-term planning have encouraged a piecemeal approach to problem-solving both before and after unification.

West German Dominance During and After Unification

The accession of the German Democratic Republic (GDR) by virtue of article 23 of the Basic Law left no doubt that the unified Germany was supposed to function on the basis of the principles on which the Federal Republic of Germany had been founded. The bargaining over the conditions governing unification reflected this theme as well, since West German negotiators were able to impose much of their agenda on East German politicians. As one scholar observes, the purpose of unification on the part of West Germans "was not so much the *creation* of a new political unit, but the destruction of an old one."[12]

Because of time pressures at work, political elites in East and West were unprepared for the many challenges ahead of them. In any event, the unequal distribution of political experience, institutional expertise, and economic weight favored West Germans then and now. Political legacies of the past—including but not limited to affiliation with the state security (*Stasi*)—and divergent role perceptions and distinct administrative and business cultures have made elite replacement in the eastern part of Germany a particularly difficult task and have led to accusations of West German elite colonization. Many of the top echelons in all areas of life are staffed by West Germans. For example, merely two years after the election of the minister-presidents in the five new *Länder*, three of the four East German office holders had already been replaced by West Germans. Approximately 75 per cent of the employees of the privatization agency (*Treuhand*) are East Germans, but not a single East German is found in top leadership positions.

It may be futile to speculate whether the current economic malaise may have been avoided by more sound economic decisions.[13] But is seems at least reasonable to argue that the shock approach to integrating the East German economy into the West German has aggravated the situation substantially. Decisions were made by West Germans for conditions prevalent in the West German economy. The result has been to make the eastern German economy an "adjunct of another economy."[14] Just as in the political realm, economic integration was based on absorption, assimilation, and synchronization—not on adaptation or adjustment. Whether this strategy was indeed dictated by time pressures and inexperience remains an open question, as does the question of whether developments in both Germanys might have proceeded in different directions had it not been for the fact that 1990 happened to be an election year. In any case, the effects of West German dominance have contributed significantly to the crisis of East German identity and the lack of community-building in the unified Germany. The appeal to solidarity and togetherness seems to be reduced to massive economic assistance and the appeal to economic sacrifices; in many ways political actions have obstructed rather than facilitated the process of societal integration by giving too small a voice to East Germans and by pressing for rapid change that left little to no time for individual adjustment.

Germany and Europe

Unification not only changed the face of Germany but also that of Europe. Germany is now by far the most populous country in Western Europe, although in terms of territory it is still surpassed by France and Spain. Resulting fears surrounding the power of the unified Germany are based at least as much on perception and anticipation as they are on changed reality, though this may change. The unification of Germany did not change its military status as a country without its own nuclear arsenal. Moreover, international agreements ensure the reduction of military manpower during the next several years. At least in the short run, Germany's economic dominance in European business matters—which had already been in place prior to unification—has not been augmented in military or foreign policy spheres.

Power, above all, is not only based on the perception of others but also on the willingness to use it. Germany is in the middle of redefining its role in Europe and in global affairs. A reluctance toward leadership born out of the legacies of two world wars and understandable anxieties on part of its European neighbors meet with increasing expectations to accept leadership roles, particularly so on the part of public officials in the United States. However, increased burden sharing—for example in multilateral peacekeeping operations and in financial assistance—ultimately has to lead to increased decision sharing. The acceptance and reconciliation of these unfolding developments may prove to be difficult—for Germany as well as its international partners.

The process of unification cannot be separated from other European and international developments. German unification proved to a major motivating factor in the acceleration of negotiations that led to the signing of the Maastricht Treaty in December 1991. Now, more than ever, the incorporation of Germany into the European Community (EC) is supposed to diffuse Germany's evolving power position in Europe. However, the concurrence of different strands of global changes also complicates ongoing unification processes. Because of Germany's traditional ties to the East, its special interest in the stability in the region, and its desire to have the Soviet presence removed from the former GDR, the Federal Republic of Germany shoulders most of the financial burden in the provision of aid and assistance to Central and Eastern Europe and to the successor states of the former Soviet Union. Up to February 1993, 100 billion ecu of aid have been promised by the major industrialized countries of the West—of which only roughly one third in fact has been delivered—and Germany agreed to pay 38 billion to the former Soviet Union and 7.5 billion to Central and Eastern Europe.[15] High levels of unemployment, rising inflation rates, and nationalistic excesses which have led to the discrimination of minority groups and outbreaks of violence and war instigated a wave of migration from the former Soviet bloc which has affected Germany more than any country in Western Europe. During 1992 alone, a significant majority of the almost 440,000 people who requested political asylum in Germany came from Central and Eastern Europe, in particular from war-torn former Yugoslavia (122,666) and countries with severe economic and ethnic problems such as Romania (103,787) and Bulgaria (31,540).

In turn, the unprecedented influx of asylum seekers into Germany has created considerable additional domestic tension within Germany. 1992 witnessed the outbreak of over 2,200 crimes against foreigners and electoral successes of right wing parties. In 1993 a trend toward political polarization continued as an increasing number of citizens voted for parties of the extreme right (*Republikaner, Deutsche Volksunion*) and for the Greens. Xenophobia toward foreigners is clearly not limited to the eastern part of Germany, but there are numerous indications that more skinheads and so-called neo-Nazis are active in the eastern part of Germany. Proportionally, membership in right wing extremist parties and movements is higher in the East than in the West. The reasons for this development are manifold and range from past international isolation and lack of contact with foreigners to severe economic and social disruptions which nurture disorientation and frustration. In such a political climate, foreigners easily become scapegoats.[16]

The economic, social, and political implications of unification have created among some Germans a certain nostalgia for the past. Others blame politicians for much of the difficulties that have emerged. The ensuing problems and the seeming lack of strategic planning on part of the major parties have contributed to frustration and disillusionment and have relegated many short- and long-term positive aspects of unification to relative obscurity.

As has been apparent from the beginning of the unification process, the new Germany will be more than the sum of its part. The national identity of its citizens and the future role of Germany in international affairs remain far from settled. The issue of how Germany will come to grips with the pending problems of unification will give important signals about the level and the degree of stability with which democratic norms have become established in both Germanys. To what extent the continued process of unification will be divisive or marked by cooperation, co-optation, and adaptation will be observed carefully not only by Germans but also by an interested and concerned world audience.

Notes

1. *Die Zeit*, 6 April 1990.
2. Gebhard Schweigler, "German Unification: The Social Issues," in Gary L. Geipel, ed., *The Future of Germany* (Indianapolis, Indiana: Hudson Institute, 1990), 2-17, 6.
3. Arthur M. Hanhardt Jr., "Demonstrations, Groups, Parties and the *Volkskammer* Election: Aspects of Political Change in East Germany,"

Paper presented at the 1990 meeting of the American Political Science Association in San Francisco, 40; Dieter Roth, "Die Wahlen zur Volkskammer der DDR. Der Versuch einer Erklärung," *Politische Vierteljahresschrift*, 31 (1990): 369-93.

4. Cf. Harold James, "Germans and their Nation," *German History*, 9 (1991): 136-52, 142.

5. See, for example, Frederick D. Weil, "The Sources and Structure of Legitimation in Western Democracies: A Consolidated Model Tested with Time-Series Data in Six Countries Since World War II," *American Political Science Review*, 54 (1989): 682-706.

6. The numbers are cited in Ilse Spittmann, "Konzeptionslosigkeit," *Deutschland Archiv*, 26 (1993): 1-2.

7. See in particular Samuel Huntington, *The Third Wave. Democratization in the Late Twentieth Century* (Norman and London: University of Oklahoma Press, 1991), 11.

8. For an interesting account of long-run economic benefits associated with unification see Manfred Kops, "Eine vertrags- und föderalismustheoretische Interpretation der Vereinigung Deutschlands," *Staatswissenschaften und Staatspraxis*, 2 (1991): 76-121.

9. Gerhard Lehmbruch, "Die deutsche Vereinigung: Strukturen und Strategien," *Politische Vierteljahresschrift*, 32 (1991): 585-604, 591.

10. Theoretical views on the instutionalization of new integrated political communities are summarized in the Introduction to this volume.

11. Lehmbruch, "Die deutsche Vereinigung," 586-8.

12. Frank Unger, "Discourses of Unity and Some Reflections about Their Aftermath," *German History*, 9 (1991): 172-83. Author's italics.

13. Criticism regarding many aspects of economic unification has been mounting. See, for example, the contributions by Alan Reynolds and W.R. Smyser in Gary L. Geipel, ed., *Germany in a New Era* (Indianapolis, Indiana: Hudson Institute, 1993); Andreas Pickel, "Jump-Starting a Market Economy: A Critique of the Radical Strategy for Economic Reform in Light of the East German Experience," *Studies in Comparative Communism*, 25 (1992): 177-91; Roy Vogt, "Transforming the Former GDR into a Market Economy," *Comparative Economic Studies*, XXXIV (1992): 68-80.

14. Vogt, ibid., 80.

15. "Deutschland zahlt den Hauptteil der Hilfen für Osteuropa," *Deutschland Nachrichten*, 5 March 1993: 5.

16. Karl-Heinz Heinemann and Wilfried Schubarth, eds., *Der antifaschistische Staat entläßt seine Kinder. Jugend und Rechtsextremismus in Ostdeutschland* (Cologne: PapyRossa Verlag, 1992); Marianne Krüger-Potratz, *Anderssein gab es nicht. Ausländer und Minderheiten in der DDR* (Münster and New York: Waxmann Verlag, 1991).

APPENDIXES

Appendix 1

Chronology of German Unification

1989

July	Beginning of refugee flow of East German citizens through Czechoslovakia and Hungary to the West.
7 October	Official celebration of the 40th anniversary of the founding of the German Democratic Republic. Mass protest demonstrations against the SED.
9 October	Demonstration by 100,000 protesters in Leipzig: *"Wir sind das Volk"* ("We are the People").
18 October	Resignation of SED General Secretary Erich Honecker. Succeeded by Egon Krenz.
4 November	One million citizens demonstrate in East Berlin.
7 November	East German government resigns.
9 November	Berlin Wall is opened.
13 November	Hans Modrow (SED) elected new president of the GDR Council of Ministers.
28 November	West German Chancellor Helmut Kohl delivers "Ten-Point Program for Overcoming the Division of Germany and Europe."
1 December	East German Volkskammer deletes the SED's power monopoly from the GDR constitution.
4 December	German question is the central topic at a NATO summit in Brussels.

3-6 December   Egon Krenz resigns from all party and government
                      offices.

7 December   Roundtable talks begin between the SED and
                      opposition parties and groups.

22 December   Brandenburg Gate is opened in Berlin.

1990

10 February   Chancellor Kohl and Foreign Minister Genscher
                      meet with General Secretary Gorbachev in
                      Moscow. They agreed that it is the right of the
                      German people to determine the future of their
                      countries.

13-14 February   Visit by Prime Minister Modrow in Bonn.
                      Chancellor Kohl suggests negotiations on economic
                      and monetary union.

14 February   Agreement by the four wartime Allies and the two
                      German states at a conference in Ottawa to proceed
                      with negotiations on German unification (Two-
                      Plus-Four talks).

18 March   First free elections in history of the GDR. Victors:
                      the "Alliance for Germany" (a coalition of the
                      Christian Democratic Union, Democratic Awaken-
                      ing, and the German Social Union).

12 April   Democratic government formed in the GDR: a
                      "grand coalition" made up of the Alliance for
                      Germany, the Free Democrats (Liberals), and the
                      Social Democrats. Lothar de Maizière is elected
                      prime minister.

18 May   The Federal Republic and the GDR sign a Treaty on
                      Monetary, Economic, and Social Union between the
                      two German states; approved by the West German
                      parliament on 21 June and by the Bundesrat on 22
                      June.

1 July	Treaty on Monetary, Economic, and Social Union goes into effect.
14-16 July	Kohl visits Gorbachev in the Soviet Union; they agree that united Germany shall have the freedom to decide freely on its alliance membership and that German armed forces will be reduced to 370,000 men. The Soviet Union agrees to withdraw its forces from eastern Germany in three-four years.
22 July	The Volkskammer passes a law reestablishing five regional states (*Bundesländer*) in the GDR.
2 August	Election treaty signed between the Federal Republic and the GDR providing for all-German elections to be held on 2 December, 1990.
23 August	The Volkskammer resolves to accede to the Federal Republic on 3 October.
31 August	Unification Treaty is signed in Berlin.
12 September	Conclusion of the Two-Plus-Four talks in Moscow.
19-20 September	East and West German parliaments ratify the Unification Treaty.
1-2 October	Document signed in New York suspending Four-Power rights in Germany.
3 October	Political unification; five new East German states formally created.
4 October	First meeting of an all-German parliament; CDU/CSU-FDP coalition government formed under Chancellor Kohl.
14 October	Elections to state parliaments in the five East German states.
2 December	All-German elections; Christian Democrats and Free Democrats win a majority.

Appendix 2

A Ten-Point Program
for Overcoming the Division of Germany
and Europe

Presented by Chancellor Helmut Kohl
in a speech to the German Bundestag
on 28 November 1989

Since the opening of the intra-German border and the sectoral boundary in Berlin on November 9, relations between the two German states have entered into a new phase which offers new opportunities and poses new challenges. We are all overjoyed about the newly won freedom of movement for those living in divided Germany. We, along with the Germans in the GDR, are glad that the wall and the border fortifications have finally, after decades, been overcome peacefully.

We are also proud that the Germans in the GDR have, with their peaceful intervention for freedom, human rights and self-determination, demonstrated their courage and love of freedom to the world, setting an example which has evoked praise all over the world.

We are deeply impressed by the passionate and unbroken desire for freedom shown by the people of Leipzig and many other cities. They know what they want. They want to determine their own future, in the true sense of the word.

We will, of course, respect every free decision taken by the people in the GDR. Particularly at this time, we in the Federal Republic of Germany stand side by side with our fellow countrymen. At the beginning of last week, Federal Minister Seiters spoke with the chairman of the Council of State, Mr. Krenz, and Prime Minister Modrow about the new leadership's intentions. We wanted to find out how the announced reform program is to be put into effect, and the time-frame for concrete steps which will genuinely benefit the people. . . .

Opportunities are presenting themselves for overcoming the division of Europe and hence of our fatherland. The Germans, who are now coming together in the spirit of freedom, will never pose a threat. Rather will they,

I am convinced, be an asset to a Europe which is growing more and more together.

The credit for the present transformation goes primarily to the people, who are so impressively demonstrating their will for freedom. But it is also the outcome of numerous political developments in the past. We in the Federal Republic have with our policy also contributed substantially to this process.

- First, it was crucial that we pursued that policy on the solid foundation of our integration within the community of free democracies. The alliance's cohesion and steadfastness during the difficult test in 1983 have paid off. By steering a clear course in the Atlantic alliance and the European Community, we have strengthened the backbone of the reform movement in Central, Eastern and South-Eastern Europe by pursuing our clear course within the Atlantic alliance and in the European Community.

- By progressing to new stages of economic and political integration within the European Community we have successfully developed the model of a free association of European nations whose attraction, as anyone can see, extends far beyond the community itself.

- On the other hand, a decisive prerequisite was General Secretary Gorbachev's reform policy in the Soviet Union and the "new thinking" in Soviet foreign policy. Without the recognition of the right of nations and states to determine their own course, the reform movements in other Warsaw Pact countries would not have been successful.

- If Poland and Hungary had not led the way with far-reaching political, economic and social reforms, the dramatic developments in the GDR would not have taken place. The success of the reform movements in those countries is a prerequisite for the success of the reform movement in the GDR. This also means that we must do all we can to ensure that these two countries achieve the goals they have set themselves. . . .

- The CSCE process has also played an important role. We, together with our partners, have always pressed for the elimination of sources of tension, for dialogue and cooperation, and most particularly for respect for human rights.

- Thanks not least to the continuous summit diplomacy of the major powers and the numerous meetings between Eastern and Western heads of state and government, a new trust was able to develop in East-West relations. The historic breakthrough in disarmament and arms control is a visible expression of this trust.

- The federal government's broadly-based contractual policy towards the Soviet Union and all other Warsaw Pact countries has generated strong impulses for the development of East-West relations.

- But our policy to maintain national solidarity is also one of the reasons for the recent changes. If we had listened to those, some of them members of this house, who called upon us to accept the demands made by Mr. Honecker in Gera, we would not have achieved anything like the progress. . . .

Since 1987 millions of fellow countrymen from the GDR have visited us, among them many young people. This policy of small steps has in difficult times kept us aware of our national unity and strengthened the feeling of German fellowship.

The developments of recent years, the well over ten million visitors between 1987 and the summer of this year, refute all the gloomy predictions made in 1983, and constantly since, that this coalition government would usher in a new "ice age" in East-West relations. I mention once more that outrageous insinuation that we are "incapable of fostering peace".

But precisely the opposite has happened. Today we have a greater sense of understanding and community in Germany and Europe than has ever been felt since the end of the Second World War, and we are grateful for it.

Today, as everyone can see, we have reached a new epoch in European and German history. This is an age which points beyond the status quo and the old political structures in Europe. This change is primarily the work of the people, who demand freedom, respect for their human rights and their right to be masters of their own future.

All who bear responsibility in and for Europe have to make allowance for the will of the people and nations. We are called upon to design a new architecture for the European home and for a permanent and just peaceful order on our continent. . . . In this process the legitimate interests of all concerned must be guaranteed. This, of course, includes German interests as well.

We are thus approaching the goal set by the Atlantic alliance in December 1987, and I quote:

No final and stable settlement in Europe is possible without a solution of the German Question which lies at the heart of present tensions in Europe. Any settlement must end the unnatural barriers between Eastern and Western Europe, which are most clearly and cruelly manifested in the division of Germany.

If that is our common foundation then all members of the house will, I hope, be able to agree to the following. We all know that we cannot plan the way to German unity simply in theory or with our appointment calendars. Abstract models may be all right for polemical purposes but they help us no further. Today, however, we are in a position to prepare in advance the stages which lead to this goal. These I would like to elucidate with the following ten-point plan.

1. Immediate measures are called for as a result of events of recent weeks, particularly the flow of resettlers and the huge increase in the number of travellers. The federal government will provide immediate aid where it is needed. We will assist in the humanitarian sector and provide medical aid if it is wanted and considered helpful.

We are also aware that the welcome money given once a year to every visitor from the GDR is no answer to the question of travel funds. The GDR must itself provide travellers with the necessary foreign exchange. We are, however, prepared to contribute to a currency fund for a transitional period, provided that persons entering the GDR no longer have to exchange a minimum amount of currency, that entry into the GDR is made considerably easier, and that the GDR itself contributes substantially to the fund.

Our aim is to facilitate traffic as much as possible in both directions.

2. The federal government will continue its cooperation with the GDR in all areas where it is of direct benefit to the people on both sides, especially in the economic, scientific, technological and cultural fields. It is particularly important to intensify cooperation in the field of environmental protection. Here we will be able to take decisions on new projects shortly, irrespective of other developments.

We also want to extensively increase telephone links with the GDR and help expand the GDR's telephone network. The Federal minister of posts and telecommunications has begun talks on this subject.

Negotiations continue on the extension of the Hanover-Berlin Railway Line. This is not enough, however, and we need to take a thorough look at transport and rail systems in the GDR and the Federal Republic in the light of the new situation. Forty years of separation also mean that traffic routes have in same cases developed quite differently. This applies not only to border crossing-points but to the traditional East-West lines of communication in Central Europe. . . .

3. I have offered comprehensive aid and cooperation, should the GDR bindingly undertake to carry out a fundamental change in the political and economic system and put the necessary measures irreversibly into effect. By "irreversible" we mean that the GDR leadership must reach agreement

with opposition groups on constitutional amendments and a new electoral law.

We support the demand for free, equal and secret elections in the GDR, in which, of course, independent, that is to say, non-socialist, parties would also participate. The SED's monopoly on power must be removed. The introduction of a democratic system means, above all, the abolition of laws on political crimes and the immediate release of all political prisoners.

Economic aid can only be effective if the economic system is radically reformed. This is obvious from the situation in all COMECON states and is not a question of our preaching to them. The centrally planned economy must be dismantled.

We do not want to stabilize conditions that have become indefensible. Economic improvement can only occur if the GDR opens its doors to Western investment, if conditions of free enterprise are created, and if private initiative becomes possible. . . .

Our sincere hope is that the necessary legislation will be introduced quickly, because we would not be very happy if private capital were to be invested in Poland and—with developments progressing so well—even more so in Hungary, which I would also welcome, but not in the middle of Germany. We want as many companies as possible to invest as much as possible.

I wish to emphasize once again that these are not preconditions but simply the foundations for effective assistance. Nor can there be any doubt that the people in the GDR want this. They want economic freedom which will enable them at long last to reap the fruit of their labor and enjoy more prosperity. . . .

4. Prime Minister Modrow spoke in his government policy statement of a "contractual community". We are prepared to adopt this idea. The proximity of the two states in Germany and the special nature of their relationship demand an increasingly close network of agreements in all sectors and at all levels.

This cooperation will also require more common institutions. The existing commissions could be given new tasks and new ones created, especially for industry, transport, environmental protection, science and technology, health and cultural affairs. It goes without saying that Berlin will be fully incorporated in these cooperative efforts. This has always been our policy.

5. We are also prepared to take a further decisive step, namely, to develop confederative structures between the two states in Germany with a

view to creating a federation. But this presupposes the election of a democratic government in the GDR.

We can envisage the following institutions being created after early, free elections:

- an intergovernmental committee for continuous consultation and policy coordination,
- joint technical committees,
- a joint parliamentary body,
- and many others in the light of new developments.

Previous policy towards the GDR had to be limited mainly to small steps by which we sought above all to alleviate the consequences of division and to keep alive and strengthen the people's awareness of unity of the nation. If, in the future, a democratically legitimized, that is, a freely elected government, becomes our partner, that will open up completely new perspectives.

Gradually, new forms of institutional cooperation can be created and further developed. Such coalescence is inherent in the continuity of German history. State organization in Germany has nearly always taken the form of a confederation or federation. We can fall back on this past experience. Nobody knows at the present time what a reunited Germany will look like. I am, however, sure that unity will come, if it is wanted by the German people.

6. The development of intra-German relations remains embedded in the pan-European process, that is to say in the framework of East-West relations. The future architecture of Germany must fit into the future architecture of Europe as a whole. Here the West has shown itself to be [a] pacemaker with its concept of a lasting and equitable peaceful order in Europe.

In our joint declaration of June this year . . . , General Secretary Gorbachev and I spoke of the structural elements of a "common European Home." There are, for example:

- unqualified respect for the integrity and security of each state. Each state has the right freely to choose its own political and social system.
- unqualified respect for the principles and rules of international law, especially [with] respect for the people's right of self-determination.
- the realization of human rights.

- respect for and maintenance of the traditional cultures of the nations of Europe.

With all of these points, as Mr. Gorbachev and I laid down, we aim to follow Europe's long traditions and help overcome the division of Europe.

7. The attraction and aura of the European Community are and remain a constant feature of pan-European development. We want to and must strengthen them further still.

The European Community must now approach the reformist countries of Central, Eastern and Southeastern Europe with openness and flexibility. This was also endorsed by the heads of state and government of the EC member states at their recent meeting in Paris.

This of course includes the GDR. The federal government therefore approves the early conclusion of a trade and cooperation agreement with the GDR. This would give it wider access to the Common Market, also in the perspective of 1992.

We can envisage specific forms of association which would lead the reformist countries of Central and Southeastern Europe to the European Community, thus helping to level the economic and social gradients on our continent. This is one of the crucial issues if tomorrow's Europe is to be a united Europe.

We have always regarded the process leading to the recovery of German unity to be a European concern as well. It must, therefore, also be seen in the context of European integration. To put it simply, the EC must not end at the Elbe but must remain open to the East.

Only in this way can the EC be the foundation for a truly comprehensive European union—after all, we have always regarded the Twelve as only a part, not as the whole, of the continent. Only in this way can it maintain, assert and develop the common European identity. That identity is not only based on the cultural diversity of Europe but also, and especially, on the fundamental values of freedom, democracy, human rights and self-determination.

If the countries of Central and Southeastern Europe meet the requirements, we would also welcome their membership of the Council of Europe, and especially of the Convention for the Protection of Human Rights and Fundamental Freedoms.

8. The CSCE process is a central element of the pan-European architecture and must be vigorously promoted in the following forums:

- the human rights conferences in Copenhagen in 1990, and in Moscow, in 1991;
- the Conference on Economic Cooperation in Bonn, in 1990;
- the Symposium on Cultural Heritage in Cracow, in 1991; and
- last but not least the next follow-up meeting in Helsinki.

There we should also think about new institutional forms of pan-European cooperation. We can well imagine a common institution for the coordination of East-West economic cooperation, as well as the creation of a pan-European environmental council.

9. Overcoming the division of Europe and Germany presupposes far-reaching and rapid steps in the field of disarmament and arms control. Disarmament and arms control must keep pace with political developments and thus be accelerated where necessary.

This is particularly true of the Vienna negotiations on the reduction of conventional forces in Europe, and for the agreement on confidence-building measures and the global ban on chemical weapons, which we hope will materialize in 1990.

It also requires that the nuclear potential of the superpowers be reduced to the strategically necessary minimum. . . .

We are doing our best—also in bilateral discussions with the Warsaw Pact countries, including the GDR—to support this process.

10. With this comprehensive policy we are working for a state of peace in Europe in which the German nation can recover its unity in free self-determination. Reunification—that is regaining national unity—remains the political goal of the federal government. We are grateful that once again we have received support in this matter from our allies in the declaration issued after the NATO summit meeting in Brussels in May.

We are conscious of the fact that many difficult problems will confront us on the road to German unity, problems for which no one has a definitive solution today. Above all, this includes the difficult and crucial question of overlapping security structures in Europe.

The linking of the German Question to pan-European developments and East-West relations, as explained in these ten points, will allow a natural development which takes account of the interests of all concerned and paves the way for peaceful development in freedom, which is our objective.

Only together and in an atmosphere of mutual trust will we be able to peacefully overcome the division of Europe, which is also the division of Germany. This calls for prudence, understanding and sound judgment on all sides so that the current promising developments may continue steadily and peacefully. This process cannot be hampered by reforms, rather by their rejection. It is not freedom that creates instability but its suppression. Every successful step towards reform means more stability and more freedom and security for the whole of Europe.

In a few weeks' time we enter the final decade of this century, a century which has seen so much misery, bloodshed and suffering. There are today many promising signs that the 90s will bring more peace and freedom in Europe and in Germany. Much depends, and everyone senses this, on the German contribution. We should all face this challenge of history.

Appendix 3

Treaty of 18 May 1990 between the Federal Republic of Germany and the German Democratic Republic Establishing a Monetary, Economic and Social Union

THE HIGH CONTRACTING PARTIES,

Owing to the fact that a peaceful and democratic revolution took place in the German Democratic Republic in the autumn of 1989,

Resolved to achieve in freedom as soon as possible the unity of Germany within a European peace order,

Intending to introduce the social market economy in the German Democratic Republic as the basis for further economic and social development, with social compensation and social safeguards and responsibility towards the environment, and thereby constantly to improve the living and working conditions of its population,

Proceeding from the mutual desire to take an initial significant step toward the establishment of a monetary, economic and social union towards national unity in accordance with Article 23 of the Basic Law of the Federal Republic of Germany as a contribution to European unification, taking into account that the external aspects of establishing unity are the subject of negotiations with the Governments of the French Republic, the Union of Soviet Socialist Republics, the United Kingdom of Great Britain and Northern Ireland and the United States of America,

Recognizing that the establishment of national unity is accompanied by the development of federal structures in the German Democratic Republic,

Realizing that the provisions of this Treaty are intended to safeguard the application of European Community law following the establishment of national unity,

Have agreed to conclude a Treaty establishing a Monetary, Economic and Social Union, containing the following provisions.

Chapter I. Basic Principles

Article 1. Subject of the Treaty

(1) The Contracting Parties shall establish a monetary, economic and social union.

(2) Starting on 1 July 1990 the Contracting Parties shall constitute a monetary union comprising a unified currency area and with the Deutsche Mark as the common currency. The Deutsche Bundesbank shall be the central bank in this currency area. The liabilities and claims expressed in the Mark of the German Democratic Republic shall be converted into Deutsche Mark in accordance with this Treaty.

(3) The basis of the economic union shall be the social market economy as the common economic system of the two Contracting Parties. It shall be determined particularly by private ownership, competition, free pricing and, as a basic principle, complete freedom of movement of labour, capital, goods and services; this shall not preclude the legal admission of special forms of ownership providing for the participation of public authorities or other legal entities in trade and commerce as long as private legal entities are not subject to discrimination. It shall take into account the requirements of environmental protection.

(4) The social union together with the monetary and economic union shall form one entity. It shall be characterized in particular by a system of labour law that corresponds to the social market economy and a comprehensive system of social security based on merit and social justice.

Article 2. Principles

(1) The Contracting Parties are committed to a free, democratic, federal and social basic order governed by the rule of law. To ensure the rights laid down in or following from this Treaty, they shall especially guarantee freedom of contract, freedom to exercise a trade, freedom of establishment and occupation, and freedom of movement of Germans in the entire currency area, freedom to form associations to safeguard and enhance working and economic conditions and . . . ownership of land and means of production by private investors.

(2) Contrary provisions of the Constitution of the German Democratic Republic relating to its former socialist social and political system shall no longer be applied. . . .

Article 6. Recourse to the Courts

(1) Should any person's rights guaranteed by or following from this Treaty be violated by public authority he shall have recourse to the courts. In so far as no other jurisdiction has been established, recourse shall be to the ordinary courts.

(2) The German Democratic Republic shall guarantee recourse to the courts, including recourse for provisional court protection. In the absence of special courts for public-law disputes, special arbitration courts shall be set up at ordinary courts. Jurisdiction for such disputes shall be concentrated at specific regional and district courts.

(3) Pending the establishment of a special labour jurisdiction, legal disputes between employers and employees shall be settled by neutral arbitration bodies to be composed of an equal number of employers and employees and a neutral chairman. Their decisions shall be appealable.

(4) The German Democratic Republic shall permit free arbitration in the field of private law.

Article 7. Arbitral Tribunal

(1) Disputes concerning the interpretation or application of this Treaty, including the Protocol and the Annexes, shall be settled by the Governments of the two Contracting Parties through negotiation. . . .

Article 8. Intergovernmental Committee

The Contracting Parties shall appoint an Intergovernmental Committee. The Commission shall discuss—and where necessary—reach agreement on questions relating to the implementation of the Treaty. The tasks of the Committee shall include the settlement of disputes under Article 7 (1) of the Treaty. . . .

Chapter II. Provisions Concerning Monetary Union

Article 10. Prerequisites and Principles

(1) Through the establishment of a monetary union between the Contracting Parties, the Deutsche Mark shall be the means of payment, unit of account and means of deposit in the entire currency area. To this end, the monetary responsibility of the Deutsche Bundesbank as the sole issuing bank for this currency shall be extended to the entire currency

area. The issuance of coin shall be the exclusive right of the Federal Republic of Germany.

(2) Enjoyment of the advantages of monetary union presupposes a stable monetary value for the economy of the German Democratic Republic, while currency stability must be maintained in the Federal Republic of Germany. The Contracting Parties shall therefore choose conversion modalities which do not cause any inflationary tendencies in the entire area of the monetary union and which at the same time increase the competitiveness of enterprises in the German Democratic Republic.

(3) The Deutsche Bundesbank, by deploying its instruments on its own responsibility and, pursuant to Section 12 of the Bundesbank Act, independent of instructions from the Governments of the Contracting Parties, shall regulate the circulation of money and credit supply in the entire currency area with the aim of safeguarding the currency.

(4) Monetary control presupposes that the German Democratic Republic establishes a free-market credit system. This shall include a system of commercial banks operating according to private-sector principles, with competing private, cooperative and public-law banks, as well as a free money and a free capital market and non-regulated interest-rate fixing on financial markets.

(5) To achieve the aims described in paragraphs 1 to 4 above, the Contracting Parties shall . . . agree on the following principles for monetary union:

- With effect from 1 July 1990 the Deutsche Mark shall be introduced as currency in the German Democratic Republic. The banknotes issued by the Deutsche Bundesbank and denominated in Deutsche Mark, and the federal coins issued by the Federal Republic of Germany and denominated in Deutsche Mark or Pfennig, shall be the sole legal tender from 1 July 1990.

- Wages, salaries, grants, pensions, rents and leases as well as other recurring payments shall be converted at a rate of one to one.

- All other claims and liabilities denominated in Mark of the German Democratic Republic shall be converted to Deutsche Mark at the rate of two to one. . . .

(6) Following an inventory of publicly owned assets and their earning power and following their primary use for the structural adaptation of the economy and for the recapitalization of the budget, the German Democratic Republic shall ensure where possible that a vested right to

a share in publicly owned assets can be granted to savers at a later date for the amount reduced following conversion at a rate of two to one.

(7) The Deutsche Bank shall exercise the powers accorded it by this Treaty and by the Deutsche Bundesbank Act in the entire currency area. It shall establish for this purpose a provisional office in Berlin with up to fifteen branches in the German Democratic Republic. . . .

Chapter III. Provisions Concerning Economic Union

Article 11. Economic Policy Foundations

(1) The German Democratic Republic shall ensure that its economic and financial policy measures are in harmony with the social market system. Such measures shall be introduced in such a way that, within the framework of the market economy system, they are at the same time conducive to price stability, a high level of employment and foreign trade equilibrium, and thus steady and adequate economic growth.

(2) The German Democratic Republic shall create the basic conditions for the development of market forces and private initiative in order to promote structural change, the creation of modern jobs, a broad basis of small and medium-sized companies and liberal professions, as well as environmental protection. The corporate legal structure shall be based on the principles of the social market economy described in Article 1 of this Treaty, enterprises being free to decide on products, quantities, production processes, investment, employment, prices and utilization of profits.

(3) The German Democratic Republic, taking into consideration the foreign trade relations that have evolved with the member countries of the Council for Mutual Economic Assistance, shall progressively bring its policy into line with the law and the economic policy goals of the European Communities.

(4) In decisions which affect the economic policy principles referred to in paragraphs 1 and 2 above, the Government of the German Democratic Republic shall reach agreement with the Government of the Federal Republic of Germany within the framework of the Intergovernmental Committee appointed in accordance with Article 8 of this Treaty.

Article 12. Intra-German Trade

(1) The Berlin Agreement of 20 September 1951 concluded between the Contracting Parties shall be amended in view of monetary and eco-

nomic union. The clearing system established by that Agreement shall be ended and the swing shall be finally balanced. Outstanding obligations shall be settled in Deutsche Mark.

(2) The Contracting Parties shall guarantee that goods which do not originate in the Federal Republic of Germany or the German Democratic Republic are transported across the intra-German border in accordance with a customs monitoring procedure.

(3) The Contracting Parties shall endeavour to create as soon as possible the preconditions for complete abolition of controls at the intra-German border.

Article 13. Foreign Trade and Payments

(1) In its foreign trade, the German Democratic Republic shall take into account the principles of free world trade, as expressed in particular in the General Agreement on Tariffs and Trade. The Federal Republic of Germany shall make its experience fully available for the further integration of the economy of the German Democratic Republic into the world economy.

(2) The existing foreign trade relations of the German Democratic Republic, in particular its contractual obligations towards the countries of the Council for Mutual Economic Assistance, shall be respected. They shall be further developed and extended in accordance with free-market principles, taking account of the facts established by monetary and economic union and the interests of all involved. Where necessary, the German Democratic Republic shall adjust existing contractual obligations in the light of those facts, in agreement with its partners.

(3) The Contracting Parties shall cooperate closely in advancing their foreign trade interests, with due regard for the jurisdiction of the European Communities.

Article 14. Structural Adjustment of Enterprises

In order to promote the necessary structural adjustment of enterprises in the German Democratic Republic, the Government of the German Democratic Republic shall, for a transitional period and subject to its budgetary means, take measures to facilitate a swift structural adjustment of enterprises to the new market conditions. The Governments of the Contracting Parties shall agree on the specific nature of these measures. The objective shall be to strengthen the competitiveness of enterprises on the basis of the social market economy and to build up, through the development of private initiative, a diversified, modern economic structure in the

German Democratic Republic, with as many small and medium-sized enterprises as possible, and thereby to create the basis for increased growth and secure jobs.

Article 15. Agriculture and Food Industry

(1) Because of the crucial importance of the European Community rules for the agriculture and food industry, the German Democratic Republic shall introduce a price support and external protection scheme in line with the EC market regime so that agricultural producer prices in the German Democratic Republic become adjusted to those in the Federal Republic of Germany. The German Democratic Republic shall not introduce levies or refunds vis-à-vis the European Community, subject to reciprocity.

(2) For categories of goods in respect of which it is not possible to introduce a full price support system immediately upon the entry into force of this Treaty, transitional arrangements may be applied. Pending the legal integration of the agriculture and food industry of the German Democratic Republic into the EC agricultural market, specific quantitative restriction mechanisms shall be allowed for sensitive agricultural products in trade between the Contracting Parties.

(3) Without prejudice to the measures to be taken under Article 14 of this Treaty, the German Democratic Republic shall, within the limits of its budgetary means and for a transitional period, take suitable measures to promote the structural adaptation in the agriculture and food industry which is necessary to improve the competitiveness of enterprises, to achieve environmentally acceptable and quality-based production, and to avoid surpluses. . . .

Article 16. Protection of the Environment

(1) The protection of human beings, animals and plants, soil, water, air, the climate and landscape as well as cultural and other material property against harmful environmental influences is a major objective of both Contracting Parties. They shall pursue this objective on the basis of prevention, the polluter pays principle, and cooperation. Their aim is the rapid establishment of a German environmental union.

(2) The German Democratic Republic shall introduce regulations to ensure that, on the entry into force of this Treaty, the safety and environmental requirements applicable in the Federal Republic of Germany are the precondition for the granting of authorizations under environmental law for new plant and installations on its territory. For existing plant

and installations the German Democratic Republic shall introduce regulations to bring them up to standard as quickly as possible.

(3) The German Democratic Republic shall, along with the development of the federal structure at Land level and with the establishment of an administrative jurisdiction, adopt the environmental law of the Federal Republic of Germany.

(4) In further shaping a common environmental law, the environmental requirements of the Federal Republic of Germany and the German Democratic Republic shall be harmonized and developed at a high level as quickly as possible.

(5) The German Democratic Republic shall harmonize the provisions governing promotion of environmental protection measures with those of the Federal Republic of Germany.

Chapter IV. Provisions Concerning the Social Union

Article 17. Principles of Labour Law

In the German Democratic Republic freedom of association, autonomy in collective bargaining, legislation relating to industrial action, corporate legal structure, codetermination at board level and protection against dismissal shall apply in line with the law of the Federal Republic of Germany. . . .

Article 18. Principles of Social Insurance

(1) The German Democratic Republic shall introduce a structured system of social insurance, to be governed by the following principles:

1. Pension, sickness, accident and unemployment insurance shall each be administered by self-governing bodies under public law subject to legal supervision by the state.

2. Pension, sickness, accident and unemployment insurance including employment promotion shall be financed primarily by contributions. Contributions to pension, sickness and unemployment insurance shall, as a rule, be paid half by the employee and half by the employer in line with the contribution rates applicable in the Federal Republic of Germany, and accident insurance contributions shall be borne by the employer.

3. Wage replacement benefits shall be based on the level of insured earnings.

(2) Initially, pension, sickness and accident insurance shall be administered by a single institution; income and expenditure shall be accounted for separately, according to the type of insurance. Separate pension, sickness and accident insurance institutions shall be established, if possible by 1 January 1991. The aim shall be to create an organizational structure for social insurance which corresponds to that of the Federal Republic of Germany.

(3) For a transitional period the present comprehensive compulsory social insurance cover in the German Democratic Republic may be retained. Exemptions from compulsory social insurance cover shall be granted to self-employed persons and professionals who can prove that they have adequate alternative insurance. In this connection, the creation of professional pension schemes outside the pension insurance system shall be made possible. . . .

Article 21. Health Insurance

(1) The German Democratic Republic shall introduce all necessary measures to adapt its health insurance law to that of the Federal Republic of Germany. . . .

Article 22. Public Health

(1) Medical care and health protection are of particular concern to the Contracting Parties.

(2) While provisionally continuing the present system, which is necessary to maintain public medical services, the German Democratic Republic shall gradually move towards the range of services offered in the Federal Republic of Germany with private providers, particularly by admitting registered doctors, dentists and pharmacists as well as independent providers of medicaments and remedial aids, and by admitting private providers of independent, non-profit-making hospitals.

(3) The German Democratic Republic shall create the necessary legal framework, for the development of the necessary contractual relations—particularly as regards remuneration—between health insurance institutions and providers of services.

Article 23. Accident Insurance Pensions

(1) The German Democratic Republic shall introduce all necessary measures to adapt its accident insurance law to that of the Federal Republic of Germany. . . .

Article 24. Social Assistance

The German Democratic Republic shall introduce a system of social assistance which shall correspond to the Social Assistance Act of the Federal Republic of Germany.

Article 25. Initial Financing

If, during a transitional period, contributions to the unemployment insurance fund of the German Democratic Republic and both the contributions and the government subsidy to the pension insurance fund of the German Democratic Republic do not fully cover expenditure on benefits, the Federal Republic of Germany shall provide temporary initial financing for the German Democratic Republic within the framework of the budgetary aid granted under Article 28 of this Treaty.

Chapter V. Provisions Concerning the Budget and Finance

Section 1. The Budget

Article 26. Principles underlying the Fiscal Policy of the German Democratic Republic

(1) Public budgets in the German Democratic Republic shall be drawn up by the relevant national, regional or local authorities on their own responsibility, due account being taken of the requirements of general economic equilibrium. The aim shall be to establish a system of budgeting adapted to the market economy. Budgets shall be balanced as regards revenue and expenditure. All revenue and expenditure shall be included in the appropriate budget.
(2) Budgets shall be adapted to the budget structures of the Federal Republic of Germany. The following in particular shall be removed from the budget, starting with the partial budget for 1990 as of the establishment of monetary union:

- the social sector, in so far as it is wholly or mainly financed from charges or contributions in the Federal Republic of Germany,

- state undertakings by conversion into legally and economically independent enterprises.

- transport undertakings by making them legally independent,

- the Deutsche Reichsbahn and the Deutsche Post, which will be operated as special funds.

Government borrowing for housing shall be allocated to individual projects on the basis of their existing physical assets.

(3) National, regional and local authorities in the German Democratic Republic shall make every effort to limit deficits in drawing up and executing budgets. As regards expenditures this shall include:

- abolition of budget subsidies, particularly in the short term for industrial goods, agricultural products and food, autonomous price supports being permissible for the latter in line with the regulations of the European Communities, and progressively in the sectors of transport, energy for private households and housing, making allowance for the general development of income,

- sustained reduction of personnel expenditure in the public service,

- review of all items of expenditure, including the legal provisions on which they are based, to determine whether they are necessary and can be financed,

- structural improvements in the education system and preparatory division according to a federal structure (including the research sector).

As regards revenue, the limitation of deficits shall require, in addition to the measures under Section 2 of this Chapter, the harmonization or introduction of contributions and fees for public services corresponding to the system in the Federal Republic of Germany.

(4) An inventory shall be made of publicly owned assets. Publicly owned assets shall be used primarily for the structural adaptation of the econ-

omy and for the recapitalization of the budget in the German Democratic Republic.

Article 27. Borrowing and Debts

(1) Borrowing authorizations in the budgets of the local, regional and national authorities of the German Democratic Republic shall be limited to 10 billion Deutsche Mark for 1990 and 14 billion Deutsche Mark for 1991 and allocated to the different levels of government in agreement with the Minister of Finance of the Federal Republic of Germany. . . .

(2) The raising of loans and the granting of equalization claims shall be conducted in agreement between the Minister of Finance of the German Democratic Republic and the Minister of Finance of the Federal Republic of Germany. . . .

(3) After accession, debt accrued in the budget of the German Democratic Republic shall be transferred to the assets held in trust in so far as it can be redeemed by proceeds expected to accrue from the realization of the assets held in trust. The remaining debt shall be assumed in equal parts by the Federal Government and the Länder newly constituted on the territory of the German Democratic Republic. Loans raised by the Länder and local authorities shall remain their responsibility.

Article 28. Financial Allocations granted by the Federal Republic of Germany

(1) The Federal Republic of Germany shall grant the German Democratic Republic financial allocations amounting to 22 billion Deutsche Mark for the second half of 1990 and 35 billion Deutsche Mark for 1991 for the specific purpose of balancing its budget. . . .

(2) The Contracting Parties agree that the transit sum payable under Article 18 of the Agreement of 17 December 1971 on the Transit of Civilian Persons and Goods between the Federal Republic of Germany and Berlin (West) shall lapse upon the entry into force of this Treaty. . . . In amendment of the Agreement of 5 December 1989, the Contracting Parties agree that from 1 July 1990 no more payments shall be made into the hard-currency fund (for citizens of the German Democratic Republic travelling to the Federal Republic of Germany). . . .

Article 29. Transitional Regulations in the Public Service

The Government of the German Democratic Republic shall guarantee, with due regard for the first sentence of Article 2 (1), that in collective bargaining agreements or other settlements in the public administration sector the general economic and financial conditions in the German Democratic Republic and the exigencies of budget consolidation are taken into account, with any new service regulations being of a transitional nature only. . . .

Section 2. Finance

Article 30. Customs and Special Excise Taxes

(1) In accordance with the principle set out in Article 11 (3) of this Treaty, the German Democratic Republic shall adopt step by step the customs law of the European Communities, including the Common Customs Tariff, and the special excise taxes stipulated in Annex IV to this Treaty.

(2) The Contracting Parties are agreed that their customs territory shall comprise the area of application of this Treaty. . . .

Article 31. Taxes on Income, Property, Net Worth and Transactions

(1) The German Democratic Republic shall regulate taxes on income, property, net worth and transactions in accordance with Annex IV to this Treaty. . . .

Article 32. Exchange of Information

(1) The Contracting Parties shall exchange such information as is necessary for the execution of their taxation and monopoly legislation. The Ministers of Finance of the Contracting Parties, together with the authorities empowered by them, shall be responsible for the exchange of information. . . .

Chapter VI. Final Provisions

International Treaties

This Treaty shall not affect the international treaties which the Federal Republic of Germany and the German Democratic Republics have concluded with third countries.

Article 36. Review of the Treaty

The provisions of this Treaty shall be reviewed in the light of any fundamental changes in the situation.

Article 37. Berlin Clause

Consistent with the Quadripartite Agreement of 3 September 1971 this Treaty will, in accordance with established procedures, be extended to Berlin (West).

Article 38. Entry into Force

This Treaty, including the Protocol and Annexes I-IX, shall enter into force on the date on which the Governments of the Contracting Parties have informed each other that the necessary constitutional and other national requirements for such entry into force have been fulfilled.

Done at Bonn on 18 May 1990 in duplicate in the German language.

For the   For the
Federal Republic of Germany   German Democratic Republic
Dr. Theo Waigel   Dr. Walter Romberg

Appendix 4

Treaty between the Federal Republic of Germany and the German Democratic Republic on the Establishment of German Unity

Unification Treaty

The Federal Republic of Germany and the German Democratic Republic,

Resolved to achieve in free self-determination the unity of Germany in peace and freedom as an equal partner in the community of nations,

Mindful of the desire of the people in both parts of Germany to live together in peace and freedom in a democratic and social federal state governed by the rule of law,

In grateful respect to those who peacefully helped freedom prevail and who have unswervingly adhered to the task of establishing German unity and are achieving it,

Aware of the continuity of German history and bearing in mind the special responsibility arising from our past for a democratic development in Germany committed to respect for human rights and to peace,

Seeking through German unity to contribute to the unification of Europe and to the building of a peaceful European order in which borders no longer divide and which ensures that all European nations can live together in a spirit of mutual trust,

Aware that the inviolability of frontiers and of the territorial integrity and sovereignty of all states in Europe within their frontiers constitutes a fundamental condition for peace,

Have agreed to conclude a Treaty on the Establishment of German Unity, containing the following provisions:

Chapter 1. Effect of Accession

Article 1. Länder

(1) Upon the accession of the German Democratic Republic to the Federal Republic of Germany in accordance with Article 23 of the Basic Law taking effect on 3 October 1990 the Länder of Brandenburg, Mecklenburg-Western Pomerania, Saxony, Saxony-Anhalt and Thuringia shall become Länder of the Federal Republic of Germany . The establishment of these Länder and their boundaries shall be governed by the Constitutional Act of 22 July 1990 on the Establishment in the German Democratic Republic (Länder Establishment Act) . . . .

(2) The 23 boroughs of Berlin shall form Land Berlin.

Article 2. Capital City, Day of German Unity

(1) The capital of Germany shall be Berlin. The seat of the parliament and government shall be decided after the establishment of German unity.

(2) 3 October shall be a public holiday known as the Day of German unity.

Chapter II. Basic Law

Article 3. Entry into Force of the Basic Law

Upon the accession taking effect, the Basic Law of the Federal Republic of Germany . . . shall enter into force in the Länder of Brandenburg, Mecklenburg-Western Pomerania, Saxony, Saxony-Anhalt and Thuringia and in that part of Land Berlin where it has not been valid to date, subject to the amendments arising from Article 4, unless otherwise provided in this Treaty.

Article 4. Amendments to the Basic Law Resulting from Accession

Resulting from Accession

The Basic Law of the Federal Republic of Germany shall be amended as follows:

1. The preamble shall read as follows:

   "Conscious of their responsibility before God and men,

Animated by the resolve to serve world peace as an equal partner in a united Europe, the German people have adopted, by virtue of their constituent power, this Basic Law.

The Germans in the Länder of Baden-Württemberg, Bavaria, Berlin, Brandenburg, Bremen, Hamburg, Hesse, Lower Saxony, Mecklenburg-Western Pomerania, North-Rhine/Westphalia, Rhineland-Palatinate, Saarland, Saxony, Saxony-Anhalt, Schleswig-Holstein and Thuringia have achieved the unity and freedom of Germany in free self-determination. This Basic Law is thus valid for the entire German people."

2. Article 23 shall be repealed.

3. Article 51 (2) shall read as follows:

"(2) Each Land shall have at least three votes; Länder with more than two million inhabitants shall have four, Länder with more than six million inhabitants five, and Länder with more than seven million inhabitants six votes."

4. The existing text of Article 135a shall become paragraph 1. The following paragraph shall be inserted after paragraph 1:

"(2) Paragraph 1 above shall be applied mutatis mutandis to liabilities of the German Democratic Republic or its legal entities as well as to liabilities of the Federation or other corporate bodies and institutions under public law which are connected with the transfer of properties of the German Democratic Republic to the Federation, Länder and communes (Gemeinden), and to liabilities arising from measures taken by the German Democratic Republic or its legal entities."

5. The following new Article 143 shall be inserted in the Basic Law:

"Article 143

(1) Law in the territory specified in Article 3 of the Unification Treaty may deviate from provisions of this Basic Law for a period not extending beyond 31 December 1992 in so far as and as long as no complete adjustment to the order of the Basic Law can be achieved as a consequence of the different conditions. . . ."

6. Article 146 shall read as follows:

"Article 146

This Basic Law, which is valid for the entire German people following the achievement of the unity and freedom of Germany, shall cease to be in force on the day on which a constitution adopted by a free decision of the German people comes into force."

Article 5. Future Amendments to the Constitution

The Governments of the two Contracting Parties recommend to the legislative bodies of the united Germany that within two years they should deal with the questions regarding amendments or additions to the Basic Law as raised in connection with German unification, in particular

- with regard to the relationship between the Federation and the Länder in accordance with the Joint Resolution of the Minister-Presidents of 5 July 1990.

- with regard to the possibility of restructuring the Berlin/Brandenburg area in derogation of the provisions of Article 29 of the Basic Law by way of an agreement between the Länder concerned,

- with considerations on introducing state objectives into the Basic Law, and

- with the question of applying Article 146 of the Basic Law and of holding a referendum in this context.

Article 6. Exception

For the time being, Article 131 of the Basic Law shall not be applied in the territory specified in Article 3 of this Treaty.

Article 7. Financial System

(1) The financial system of the Federal Republic of Germany shall be extended to the territory specified in Article 3 unless otherwise provided in this Treaty.
(2) Article 106 of the Basic Law shall apply to the apportionment of tax revenue among the Federation as ell as the Länder and communes

(associations of communes) in the territory specified in Article 3 of this Treaty. . . .

(5) Following the establishment of German unity, the annual allocations from the German Unity Fund shall be distributed as follows:

1. 85 per cent as special assistance to the Länder of Brandenburg, Mecklenburg-Western Pomerania, Saxony, Saxony-Anhalt and Thuringia as well as to Land Berlin to cover their general financial requirements and divided up among these Länder in proportion to their number of inhabitants, excluding the inhabitants of Berlin (West), and

2. 15 percent to meet public requirements at a central level in the territory of the aforementioned Länder.

(6) In the event of a fundamental change in conditions, the Federation and the Länder shall jointly examine the possibilities of granting further assistance in order to ensure adequate financial equalization for the Länder in the territory specified in Article 3 of this Treaty.

Chapter III. Harmonization of Law

Article 8. Extension of Federal Law

Upon the accession taking effect, federal law shall enter into force in the territory specified in Article 3 of this Treaty unless its area of application is restricted to certain Länder or parts of Länder of the Federal Republic of Germany and unless otherwise provided in this Treaty. . . .

Article 9. Continued Validity of Law of the German Democratic Republic

(1) Law of the German Democratic Republic valid at the time of signing of this Treaty which is Land law according to the distribution of competence under the Basic Law shall remain in force in so far as it is compatible with the Basic Law, notwithstanding Article 143, with the federal law put into force in the territory specified in Article 3 of this Treaty and with the directly applicable law of the European Communities, and unless otherwise provided in this Treaty. Law of the German Democratic Republic which is federal law according to the distribution of competence under the Basic Law and which refers to matters not regulated uniformly at the

federal level shall continue to be valid as Land law under the conditions set out in the first sentence. . . .

Article 10. Law of the European Communities

(1) Upon the accession taking effect, the Treaties on the European Communities together with their amendments and supplements as well as the international agreements, treaties and resolutions which have come into force in connection with those Treaties shall apply in the territory specified in Article 3 of this Treaty.

(2) Upon the accession taking effect, the legislative acts enacted on the basis of the Treaties on the European Communities shall apply in the territory specified in Article 3 of this Treaty unless the competent institutions of the European Communities enact exemptions. These exemptions are intended to take account of administrative requirements and help avoid economic difficulties.

(3) Legislative acts of the European Communities whose implementation or execution comes under the responsibility of the Länder shall be implemented or executed by the latter through provisions under Land Law.

Chapter IV. International Treaties and Agreements

Article 11. Treaties of the Federal Republic of Germany

The Contracting Parties proceed on the understanding that international treaties and agreements to which the Federal Republic of Germany is a contracting party, including treaties establishing membership of international organizations or institutions, shall retain their validity and that the rights and obligations arising therefrom, with the exception of treaties named in Annex I, shall also relate to the territory specified in Article 3 of this Treaty. Where adjustments become necessary in individual cases, the all-German Government shall consult with the respective contracting parties.

Article 12. Treaties of the German Democratic Republic

(1) The Contracting Parties are agreed that, in connection with the establishment of German unity, international treaties of the German Democratic Republic shall be discussed with the contracting parties concerned with a view to regulating or confirming their continued application, adjustment or expiry, taking into account protection of confidence, the interests of the

states concerned, the treaty obligations of the Federal Republic of Germany as well as the principles of a free, democratic basic order governed by the rule of law, and respecting the competence of the European Communities.

(2) The united Germany shall determine its position with regard to the adoption of international treaties of the German Democratic Republic following consultations with the respective contracting parties and with the European Communities where the latter's competence is affected.

(3) Should the united Germany intend to accede to international organizations or other multilateral treaties of which the German Democratic Republic but not the Federal Republic of Germany is a member, agreement shall be reached with the respective contracting parties and with the European Communities where the latter's competence is affected.

Chapter V. Public Administration and the Administration of Justice

Article 13. Future Status of Institutions

(1) Administrative bodies and other institutions serving the purposes of public administration or the administration of justice in the territory specified in Article 3 of this Treaty shall pass under the authority of the government of the Land in which they are located. . . .

(2) To the extent that before the accession took effect the institutions or branches mentioned in paragraph 1, first sentence, performed tasks that are incumbent upon the Federation according to the distribution of competence under the Basic Law, they shall be subject to the competent supreme federal authorities. The latter shall be responsible for the transfer or winding-up.

(3) Institutions under paragraphs 1 and 2 above shall also include such

1. cultural, educational, scientific and sports institutions
2. radio and television establishments

as come under the responsibility of public administrative bodies. . . .

Article 17. Rehabilitation

The Contracting Parties reaffirm their intention to create without delay a legal foundation permitting the rehabilitation of all persons who have been victims of a politically motivated punitive measure or any court decision contrary to the rule of law or constitutional principles. The rehabilitation of these victims of the iniquitous SED regime shall be accompanied by appropriate arrangements for compensation.

Article 18. Continued Validity of Court Decisions

(1) Decisions handed down by the courts of the German Democratic Republic before the accession took effect shall retain their validity and may be executed in conformity with the law put into force according to Article 8 of this Treaty or remaining in force according to Article 9. This law shall be taken as the yardstick when checking the compatibility of decisions and their execution with the principles of the rule of law. Article 17 of this Treaty shall remain unaffected.
(2) Subject to Annex I, persons sentenced by criminal courts of the German Democratic Republic are granted by this Treaty a right of their own to seek the quashing of final decisions through the courts.

Article 19. Continued Validity of Decisions Taken by Public Administrative Bodies

Administrative acts of the German Democratic Republic performed before the access took effect shall remain valid. They may be revoked if they are incompatible with the principles of the rule of law or with the provisions of this Treaty. In all other respects the rules on the validity of administrative acts shall remain unaffected.

Article 20. Legal Status of Persons in the Public Service

(1) The agreed transitional arrangements set out in Annex I shall apply to the legal status of persons in the public service at the time of accession.
(2) The exercise of public responsibilities (state authority as defined in Article 33 (4) of the Basic Law) shall be entrusted as soon as possible to professional civil servants. Public service law shall be introduced in accordance with the agreed arrangements set out in Annex I. Article 92 of the Basic Law shall remain unaffected.
(3) Military personnel law shall be introduced in accordance with the agreed arrangements set out in Annex I.

Chapter VI. Public Assets and Debts

Article 21. Administrative Assets

(1) The assets of the German Democratic Republic which are used directly for specific administrative purposes (administrative assets) shall become federal assets unless their designated purpose as of 1 October 1989 was primarily to meet administrative responsibilities which, under the Basic Law, are to be exercised by Länder, communes (associations of communes) or other agencies of public administration. Where administrative assets were primarily used for the purposes of the former Ministry of State Security/National Security Office, they shall accrue to the Trust Agency unless they have already been given over to new social or public purposes since the above-mentioned dates.

(2) Where administrative assets are not federal assets under paragraph 1 above, they shall accrue, upon the accession taking effect, to the agency of public administration which, under the Basic Law, is responsible for the relevant administrative purpose.

(3) Assets which have been made available free of charge by another corporate body under public law to the central government or to the Länder and communes (associations of communes) shall be returned free of charge to this corporate body of its legal successor; former Reich assets shall become federal assets.

(4) Where administrative assets become federal assets under paragraphs 1 to 3 above or by virtue of a federal law, they shall be used for public purposes in the territory specified in Article 3 of this Treaty. This shall also apply to the use of proceeds from the sale of assets.

Article 22. Financial Assets

(1) Public assets of legal entities in the territory specified in Article 3 of this Treaty, including landed property and assets in agriculture and forestry, which do not directly serve specific administrative purposes (financial assets), with the exception of social insurance assets, shall, unless they have been handed over to the Trust Agency or will be handed over by law . . . to communes, towns and cities or rural districts, come under federal trusteeship upon the accession taking place. Where financial assets were primarily used for the purpose of the former Ministry of State Security/National Security Office, they shall accrue to the Trust Agency unless they have already been given over to new social or public purposes since 1 October 1989. Financial assets shall be divided by federal law between the Federation and the Länder named in Article 1 of this Treaty in

such a way that the Federation and the Länder named in Article 1 each receive one half of the total value of the assets. The communes (associations of communes) shall receive an appropriate share of the Länder portion. Assets accruing to the Federation under this provision shall be used for public purposes in the territory specified in Article 3 of this Treaty. . . .

Article 23. Debt Arrangements

(1) Upon the accession taking place, the total debts of the central budget of the German Democratic Republic which have accumulated up to this date shall be taken over by a federal Special Fund without legal capacity, which shall meet the obligations arising from debt servicing. The Special Fund shall be empowered to raise loans:

1. to pay off debts of the Special Fund,
2. to cover due interest and loan procurement costs,
3. to purchase debt titles of the Special Fund for the purposes of market cultivation.

(2) The Federal Minster of Finance shall administer the Special Fund. . . .
(5) The Special Fund shall be abolished at the end of 1993. . . .

Article 25. Assets Held in Trust

The Privatization and Reorganization of Publicly Owned Assets Act (Trusteeship Act) of 17 June 1990 . . . shall continue to apply after the accession takes effect with the following proviso:

(1) The Trust Agency shall continue to be charged, in accordance with the provisions of the Trusteeship Act, with restructuring and privatizing the former publicly owned enterprises to bring them into line with the requirements of a competitive economy. It shall become a direct institution of the Federation vested with legal capacity and subject to public law. Technical and legal supervision shall be the responsibility of the Federal Minister of Finance, who shall exercise technical supervision in agreement with the Federal Minister of Economics and the respective federal minister. Stakes held by the Trust Agency shall be indirect stakes of the Federation. Amendments to the Charter shall requirement the agreement of the Federal Government. . . .

Article 26. Special Fund of the Deutsche Reichsbahn

(1) Upon the accession taking effect, the property and all other property rights of the German Democratic Republic and the Reich property in Berlin (West) belonging to the special fund of the Deutsche Reichsbahn within the meaning of Article 26 (2) of the Treaty of 18 May 1990 shall become the property of the Federal Republic of Germany as the special fund of the Deutsche Reichsbahn. . . .

Article 27. Special Fund of the Deutsche Post

(1) The property and all property rights belonging to the special fund of the Deutsche Post shall become the property of the Federal Republic of Germany. They shall be combined with the special fund of the Deutsche Bundespost. Associated liabilities and claims shall be transferred simultaneously with the property rights to the special fund of the Deutsche Bundespost. . . .

Article 28. Economic Assistance

(1) Upon the accession taking effect, the territory specified in Article 3 of this Treaty shall be incorporated into the arrangements of the Federation existing in the territory of the Federal Republic for economic assistance, taking into consideration the competence of the European Communities. The specific requirements of structural adjustment shall be taken into account during a transitional period. This will make a major contribution to the speediest possible development of a balanced economic structure with particular regard for small and medium-sized businesses.
(2) The relevant ministries shall prepare concrete programmes to speed up economic growth and structural adjustment in the territory specified in Article 3 of this Treaty. . . .

Article 29. Foreign Trade Relations

(1) The established foreign trade relations of the German Democratic Republic, in particular the existing contractual obligations vis-à-vis the countries of the Council for Mutual Economic Assistance, shall enjoy protection of confidence. They shall be developed further and expanded, taking into consideration the interests of all parties concerned and having regard for the principles of a market economy as well as the competence of the European Communities. The all-German Government shall ensure that ap-

propriate organizational arrangements are made for these foreign trade relations within the framework of departmental responsibility. . . .

Chapter VII. Labour, Social Welfare, Family, Women, Public Health and Environmental Protection

Article 30. Labour and Social Welfare

(1) It shall be the task of the all-German legislator

1. to recodify in a uniform manner and as soon as possible the law on
   employment contracts and the provisions on working hours under
   public law, including the admissibility of work on Sundays and
   public holidays, and the specific industrial safety regulations for
   women;

2. to bring public law on industrial safety into line with present-day
   requirements in accordance with the law of the European Communities and the concurrent part of the industrial safety law of the
   German Democratic Republic.

(2) Employed persons in the territory specified in Article 3 of this Treaty
shall be entitled, upon reaching the age of 57, to receive early retirement
payments for a period of three years, but not beyond the earliest possible
date on which they become entitled to receive a retirement pension under
the statutory pension scheme. The early retirement payment shall amount
to 65 percent of the last average net earnings. . . .

Article 31. Family and Women

(1) It shall be the task of the all-German legislator to develop further the
legislation on equal rights for men and women.
(2) In view of different legal and institutional starting positions with regard to the employment of mothers and fathers, it shall be the task of the
all-German legislator to shape the legal situation in such a way as to allow
a reconciliation of family and occupational life.
(3) In order to ensure that day care centres for children continue to operate
in the territory specified in Article 3 of this Treaty, the Federation shall
contribute to the costs of these centres for a transitional period up to 30
June 1991.

(4) It shall be the task of the all-German legislator to introduce regulations no later than 31 December 1992 which ensure better protection of unborn life and provide a better solution in conformity with the Constitution of conflict situations faced by pregnant women—notably through legally guaranteed entitlements for women, first and foremost to advice and public support—than is the case in either part of Germany at present. In order to achieve these objectives, a network of advice centres run by various agencies and offering blanket coverage shall be set up without delay with financial assistance from the Federation in the territory specified in Article 3 of this Treaty. The advice centres shall be provided with sufficient staff and funds to allow them to cope with the task of advising pregnant women and offering them necessary assistance, including beyond the time of confinement. In the event that no regulations are introduced within the period stated in the first sentence, the substantive law shall continue to apply in the territory specified in Article 3 of this Treaty.

Article 32. Voluntary Organizations

Voluntary welfare and youth welfare organizations play an indispensable part through their institutions and services in fashioning the socially oriented state described in the Basic Law. The establishment and expansion of voluntary welfare and youth welfare organizations shall be promoted in the territory specified in Article 3 of this Treaty in line with the distribution of competence under the Basic Law.

Article 33. Public Health

(1) It shall be the task of the legislators to create the conditions for effecting a rapid and lasting improvement in in-patient care in the territory specified in Article 3 of this Treaty and for bringing it into line with the situation in the remainder of the federal territory. . . .

Article 34. Protection of the Environment

(1) On the basis of the German environmental union established under Article 16 of the Treaty of 18 May 1990, . . . it shall be the task of the legislators to protect the natural basis of man's existence, with due regard for prevention, the polluter-pays principle, and cooperation, and to promote uniform ecological conditions of a high standard at least equivalent to that reached in the Federal Republic of Germany.

(2) With a view to attaining the objective defined in paragraph 1 above, ecological rehabilitation and development programmes shall be drawn up

for the territory specified in Article 3 of this Treaty, in line with the distribution of competence under the Basic Law. Measures to ward off dangers to public health shall be accorded priority.

Chapter VIII. Culture, Education and Science, Sport

Article 35. Culture

(1) In the years of division, culture and the arts—despite different paths of development taken by the two states in Germany—formed one of the foundations for the continuing unity of the German nation. They have an indispensable contribution to make in their own right as the Germans cement their unity in a single state on the road to European unification. The position and prestige of a united Germany in the world depend not only on its political weight and its economic strength, but also on its role in the cultural domain. The overriding objective of external cultural policy shall be cultural exchange based on partnership and cooperation.

(2) The cultural substance in the territory specified in Article 3 of this Treaty shall not suffer any damage.

(3) Measures shall be taken to provide for the performance of cultural tasks, including their financing, with the protection and promotion of culture and the arts being the responsibility of the new Länder and local authorities in line with the distribution of competence under the Basic Law.

(4) The cultural institutions which have been under central management to date shall come under the responsibility of the Länder or local authorities in whose territory they are located. In exceptional cases, the possibility of the Federation making a contribution to financing shall not be ruled out, particularly in Land Berlin.

(5) The parts of the former Prussian state collections which were separated as a result of post-war events . . . shall be joined together again in Berlin. The Prussian Cultural Heritage Foundation shall assume responsibility for the time being. Future arrangements shall likewise involve an agency that is responsible for the former Prussian state collections in their entirety and is based in Berlin. . . .

Article 36. Broadcasting

(1) The Rundfunk der DDR and the Deutscher Fernsehfunk shall be continued as an autonomous joint institution having legal capacity by the Länder named in Article 1 of this Treaty and by Land Berlin in respect of that part where the Basic Law has not been valid to date for a period not

extending beyond 31 December 1991 in so far as they perform tasks coming under the responsibility of the Länder. The institution shall have the task of providing the population in the territory specified in Article 3 of this Treaty with a radio and television service in accordance with the general principles governing broadcasting establishments coming under public law. . . .

(6) Within the period laid down in paragraph 1 above the institution shall be dissolved in accordance with the federal structure of broadcasting through a joint treaty between the Länder named in Article 1 of this Treaty or converted to agencies under public law of one or more Länder. . . .

Article 37. Education

(1) School, vocational or higher education certificates or degrees obtained or officially recognized in the German Democratic Republic shall continue to be valid in the territory specified in Article 3 of this Treaty. Examinations passed and certificates obtained in the territory specified in Article 3 or in the other Länder of the Federal Republic of Germany, including Berlin (West), shall be considered equal and shall convey the same rights if they are of equal value. Their equivalence shall be established by the respective competent agency on application. Legal provisions of the Federation and the European Communities regarding the equivalence of examinations and certificates, and special provisions set out in this Treaty shall have priority. In all cases this shall not affect the right to use academic professional titles and degrees obtained or officially recognized or conferred.

(2) The usual recognition procedure operated by the Conference of Ministers of Education and Cultural Affairs shall apply to teaching diploma examinations. The said Conference shall make appropriate transitional arrangements.

(3) Examination certificates issued under the trained occupation scheme and the skilled workers' training scheme as well as final examinations and apprentices' final examinations in recognized trained occupations shall be considered equal.

(4) The regulations necessary for the reorganization of the school system in the territory specified in Article 3 of this Treaty shall be adopted by the Länder named in Article 1. . . .

Article 38. Science and Research

(1) In the united Germany science and research shall continue to constitute important foundations of the state and society. The need to renew science and research in the territory specified in Article 3 of this Treaty while pre-serving efficient institutions shall be taken into account by an expert report on publicly maintained institutions prepared by the Science Council and to be completed by 31 December 1991, with individual results to be imple-mented step by step before that date.

(6) The Federal Government shall seek to ensure that the proven methods and programmes of research promotion in the Federal Republic of Ger-many are applied as soon as possible to the entire federal territory and that the scientists and scientific institutions in the territory specified in Article 3 of this Treaty are given access to current research promotion schemes. . .

Article 39. Sport

(1) The sporting structures which are in a process of transformation in the territory specified in Article 3 of this Treaty shall be placed on a self-gov-erning basis. The public authorities shall give moral and material support to sport in line with the distribution of competence under the Basic Law.

(2) To the extent that it has proved successful, top-level sport and its de-velopment shall continue to receive support in the territory specified in Article 3 of this Treaty. Support shall be given within the framework of the rules and principles existing in the Federal Republic of Germany and in line with the public-sector budgets in the territory specified in Article 3 of this Treaty. . . .

Chapter IX. Transitional and Final Provisions

Article 40. Treaties and Agreements

(1) The obligations under the Treaty of 18 May 1990 between the Federal Republic of Germany and the German Democratic Republic on the Estab-lishment of a Monetary, Economic and Social Union shall continue to be valid unless otherwise provided in this Treaty and unless they become ir-relevant in the process of establishing German unity.

(2) Where rights and duties arising from other treaties and agreements between the Federal Republic of Germany or its Länder and the German Democratic Republic have not become irrelevant in the process of estab-

lishing German unity, they shall be assumed, adjusted or settled by the competent national entities.

Article 41. Settlement of Property Issues

(1) The Joint Declaration of 15 June 1990 on the Settlement of Open Property Issues (Annex III) issued by the Government of the Federal Republic of Germany and the Government of the German Democratic Republic shall form an integral part of this Treaty.

(2) In accordance with separate legislative arrangements there shall be no return of property rights to real estate or buildings if the real estate or building concerned is required for urgent investment purposes to be specified in detail, particularly if it is to be used for the establishment of an industrial enterprise and the implementation of this investment decision deserves support from a general economic viewpoint, above all if it creates or safeguards jobs. The investor shall submit a plan showing the major features of his project and shall undertake to carry out the plan on this basis. The legislation shall also contain arrangements for compensation to the former owner. . . .

Article 42. Delegation of Parliamentary Representatives

(1) Before the accession of the German Democratic Republic takes effect, the Volkskammer shall, on the basis of its composition, elect 144 Members of Parliament to be delegated to the 11th German Bundestag together with a sufficient number of reserve members. Relevant proposals shall be made by the parties and groups represented in the Volkskammer.

(2) The persons elected shall become members of the 11th German Bundestag by virtue of a statement of acceptance delivered to the President of the Volkskammer, but not until the accession takes effect. The President of the Volkskammer shall without delay communicate the result of the election, together with the statement of acceptance, to the President of the German Bundestag. . . .

Article 43. Transitional Rule for the Bundesrat Pending the Formation of Länder Governments

From the formation of the Länder named in Article 1 (1) of this Treaty until the election of minister-presidents, the Land plenipotentiaries may take part in the meetings of the Bundesrat in a consultative capacity.

Article 44. Preservation of Rights

Rights arising from this Treaty in favour of the German Democratic Republic or the Länder named in Article 1 of this Treaty may be asserted by each of these Länder after the accession has taken effect.

Article 45. Entry into Force of the Treaty

(1) This Treaty, including the attached Protocol and Annexes I to III, shall enter into force on the day on which the Governments of the Federal Republic of Germany and the German Democratic Republic have informed each other that the internal requirements for such entry into force have been fulfilled.
(2) The Treaty shall remain valid as federal law after the accession has taken effect.

Done at Berlin on 31 August 1990 in duplicate in the German language.

For the   For the
Federal Republic of Germany   German Democratic Republic
Dr. Wolfgang Schäuble   Dr. Günther Krause

Appendix 5

German Elections, 1949-1993

Table 1
Volkskammer Election, 18 March 1990

Party	Percentage	Seats
CDU	40.8	163
SPD	21.9	88
PDS	16.4	66
German Social Union (DSU)	6.3	25
League of Free Democrats (Liberals)	5.3	21
Alliance 90	2.9	12
German Democratic Peasants' Party	2.2	9
Green Party/Independent Women's Association	2.0	8
Democratic Awakening	0.9	4
National Democratic Party	0.4	2
Democratic Women's Association	0.3	1
United Left	0.2	1
Other	0.4	–
Total	100.0	400

Table 2
Bundestag Elections, 1949-1990

Year	KPD/ PDS	Greens	SPD	FDP	CDU/ CSU	Radical Right[a]	Other
1949	5.7		29.2	11.9	31.0	1.8	20.3
1953	2.3		28.8	9.5	45.2	1.1	13.1
1957			31.8	7.7	50.2	1.0	10.3
1961			36.2	12.8	45.3	0.8	5.7
1965			39.3	9.5	47.6	2.0	3.6
1969	0.6		42.7	5.8	46.1	4.3	0.5
1972	0.3		45.8	8.4	44.9	0.6	0.1
1976	0.4		42.6	7.9	48.6	0.3	0.2
1980	0.2	1.5	42.9	10.6	44.5	0.2	0.1
1983		5.6	38.2	7.0	48.8		0.5
1987		8.4	37.0	9.1	44.3		1.4
1990	2.4	5.1	33.5	11.0	43.8	2.1	0.2

Election Results by Territory (December 1990)

	KPD/ PDS	Greens	SPD	FDP	CDU/ CSU	Radical Right[a]	Other
Western Germany	0.3	4.7	35.9	10.6	44.1	2.3	
Eastern Germany	9.9	5.9	23.6	13.4	43.4	1.3	1.0

[a]Includes the National Democratic Party (NPD), the *Republikaner*, and other right wing parties. Since official election results do not always contain detailed percentage results for such parties, support for some splinter radical right parties may be included in the residual "other" column to the right.

Table 3
Landtag Elections, 1985-1993

Year	PDS	Greens	SPD	FDP	CDU	CSU	Radical Right[a]	Other
Baden-Württemberg								
1988		7.9	32.0	5.9	49.0		3.1	2.1
1992		9.5	29.4	5.9	39.6		11.8	3.8
Bavaria								
1986		7.5	27.5	3.8		55.8	3.0	2.4
1990		6.4	26.0	5.2		54.9	4.9	2.6
Berlin								
1985[b]		10.6	32.4	8.5	46.4			2.1
1989[b]		11.8	37.3	3.9	37.8		7.5	1.7
1990	9.2	5.0	30.4	7.1	40.4		3.1	4.8[c]
Brandenburg								
1990	13.4	6.4[c]	38.2	6.6	29.4			5.9
Bremen								
1987		10.2	50.5	10.0	23.4			5.9
1991		11.4	38.8	9.5	30.7		7.2	2.4
Hamburg								
1987		7.0	45.0	6.5	40.5			1.0
1991	.5	7.2	48.0	5.4	35.1		2.0	1.8
1993		13.5	40.4	4.2	25.1		7.6	9.2
Hesse								
1987		9.4	40.2	7.8	42.1			0.5
1991		8.8	40.8	7.4	40.1		1.7	1.1
Lower Saxony								
1986		7.1	42.1	6.0	44.4			.4
1990		5.5	44.2	6.0	42.0		1.5	.8

(continues)

Table 3 (continued)
Landtag Elections, 1985-1993

Year	PDS	Greens	SPD	FDP	CDU	CSU	Radical Right[a]	Other
Mecklenburg-Western Pomerania							
1990	15.7	2.2[d]	27.0	5.5	38.3			11.3
North Rhine-Westphalia							
1985		4.6	52.1	6.0	36.5			0.8
1990		5.0	50.0	5.8	36.7		1.8	0.7
Rhineland-Palatinate							
1987		5.9	38.8	7.3	45.1			2.9
1991		6.4	44.8	6.9	38.7		2.0	1.2
Saarland							
1985	.3	2.5	49.2	10.0	37.3		.7	
1990	.1	2.7	54.4	5.6	33.4		3.5	.3
Saxony							
1990	10.2		19.1	5.3	53.8			11.6
Saxony-Anhalt							
1990	12.0	5.3	26.0	13.5	39.0			4.2
Schleswig-Holstein							
1988	.1	2.9	54.8	4.4	33.3		1.8	2.7
1992		4.9	46.2	5.6	33.8		7.5	2.0
Thuringia							
1990	9.7	6.5	22.8	9.3	45.4			6.3[e]

[a]Includes the *Republikaner*, the *Deutsche Volksunion*, and other right wing parties. Since official election results do not always contain detailed percentage results for such parties, support for some splinter radical right parties may be included in the residual "other" column to the right.

[b]Berlin (West).

[c]Includes 4.4 percent for the Alliance 90/Greens.

[d]Alliance 90/Greens.

[e]Includes 3.3 percent for the German Social Union (DSU).

Select Bibliography

In view of the wealth of publications published in Germany and given the fact that the contributions in this book contain extensive references to German-language literature on the subject of unification, this bibliography refers only to literature that has been published in English.

Adomeit, Hannes. "Gorbachev and German Unification: Revision of Thinking, Realignment of Power." *Problems of Communism* 39 (1991): 1-23.

Alexander, Lewis S. and Gagnon, Joseph E. *The Global Economic Implications of German Unification.* Washington, D.C.: Board of Governors of the Federal Reserve System, 1990.

Anderson, Christopher; Kaltenthaler, Karl; and Luthardt, Wolfgang, eds. *The Domestic Politics of German Unification.* Boulder and London: Lynne Rienner Publishers, 1993.

Ardagh, John. *Germany and the Germans. After Unification.* Revised ed. London: Penguin Books, 1991.

Arnold, Eckart. "German Foreign Policy and Unification." *International Affairs* 67 (1991): 453-71.

Asmus, Ronald D. "A United Germany." *Foreign* Affairs 69 (1990): 63-76.

Bertram, Christoph. "The German Question." *Foreign Affairs* 69 (1990): 45-62.

Bryson, Phillip J. "The Economics of German Reunification: A Review of the Literature," *Journal of Comparative Economics* 16 (1992): 118-49.

Burley, Anne-Marie. "The Once and Future German Question." *Foreign Affairs* 68 (1989/90): 65-83.

Dietz, Raimund. *The Impact of German Unification on the East German Economy.* Vienna: Wiener Institut für Internationale Wirtschaftsvergleiche, 1991.

Doerr, Juergen C. *The Big Powers and the German Question, 1941-1990. A Selected Bibliographic Guide.* New York: Garland Publishers, 1992.

Dunk, F.G. "The Unification of Germany and International Law." *Michigan Journal of International Law* 12 (1991): 510-57.

European Communities Commission. *The European Community and German Unification.* Luxembourg: Office for Official Publications of the European Communities, 1990.

Fawcett, Edmund. "Not as Grimm as it Looks. A Survey of Germany." *The Economist* 323 (1992): 58-67.

Fritsch-Bournazel, Renata. *Europe and German Unification.* New York/Oxford: St. Martin's Press, 1992.

Geipel, Gary L., ed. *The Future of Germany.* Indianapolis, Ind.: Hudson Institute, 1990.

Geipel, Gary L., ed. *Germany in a New Era.* Indianapolis, Ind.: Hudson Institute, 1993.

German Politics and Society. Special Issues: "German Unification: Power, Process, and Problems" (spring 1991); "Economic Aspects of German Unification" (summer 1991); and "Germany and Gender" (winter 1991-92).

Ghaussy, A. Ghanie and Schäfer, Wolf, eds. *The Economics of German Unification.* London and New York: Routledge, 1993.

Glaeßner, Gert-Joachim, and Wallace, Ian, eds. *The German Revolution of 1989. Causes and Consequences.* New York: St. Martin's Press, 1992.

Glaeßner, Gert-Joachim. *The Unification Process in Germany: From Dictatorship to Democracy.* New York: St. Martin's Press, 1992.

Gordon, J.S. "German Reunification and the Bundeswehr." *Military Review* 71 (1991): 20-32.

Goldberg, Gertrude Schaffner. "Women on the Verge: Winners and Losers in German Unification." *Social Policy* 22 (1991): 34-44.

Grosser, Dieter, ed. *German Unification: The Unexpected Challenge.* Oxford and Providence: Berg, 1992.

Hamilton, Daniel. "Dateline East Germany: The Wall Behind the Wall." *Foreign Policy* 76 (1989): 176-97.

Harvard Law Review. "Taking Reich Seriously—German Unification and the Law of State Succession." *Harvard Law Review* 104 (1990): 588-606.

Heisenberg, Wolfgang, ed. *German Unification in European Perspective.* Brussels: Pergamon, 1991.

Heitger, Bernard and Waverman, Leonard, eds. *German Unification and the International Economy.* New York: Routledge, 1993.

Hirschman, Albert O. "Exit, Voice, and the Fate of the German Democratic Republic: An Essay in Conceptual History." *World Politics* 45 (1993): 173-202.

Horn, Hannelore. "The Revolution in the GDR in 1989: Prototype or Special Case?" *Aussenpolitik* 44 (1993): 56-66.

Horn, N. "The Lawful German Revolution: Privatization and Market Economy in a Reunified Germany." *American Journal of Comparative Law* 39 (1991): 725-46.

Huelshoff, Michael G.; Markovits, Andrei S.; and Reich, Simon, eds. *From Bundesrepublik to Deutschland: German Politics After Unification.* Ann Arbor, Mich.: University of Michigan Press, 1993.

James, Harold. *A German Identity, 1770-1990.* London: Weidenfeld and Nicolson, 1989.

Jeffery, Charlie and Savigear, Peter. *German Federalism Today.* New York: St. Martin's Press, 1991.

Jeffery, Charlie and Sturm, Roland, eds. "Federalism, Unification and European Integration." *German Politics* 1 (1992), special edition.

Jeffress, Dorothy A. "Resolving Claims on East German Property Upon German Unification." *Yale Law Journal* 101 (1991): 527-49.

Kaiser, Karl. "Germany's Unification." *Foreign Affairs* 70 (1991): 179-205.

Keithley, D.M. *The Collapse of East German Communism: The Year the Wall Came Down, 1989.* New York: Praeger, 1992.

Kitschelt, Herbert. "The 1990 Federal Election and the National Unification." *West European Politics* 14 (1991): 121-48.

Kopstein, Jeffrey and Richter, Karl-Otto. "Communist Social Structure and Post-Communist Elections: Voting for Unification in Germany." *Studies in Comparative Communism* 25 (1992): 363-80.

Kuechler, Manfred. "The Road to German Unity: Mass Sentiment in East and West Germany." *Public Opinion Quarterly* 56 (1992): 53-76.

Lease, Gary. "Religion, the Churches and the German 'Revolution' of November 1990." *German Politics* 1 (1992): 264-73.

Larrabee, F. Stephen. "Soviet Policy Toward Germany: New Thinking and Old Realities." *Washington Quarterly* 12 (1989): 33-51.

Larrabee, F. Stephen, ed. *The Two German States and European Security.* Basingstoke: Macmillan, 1989.

Lippert, Barbara. *German Unification and EC Integration.* New York: Council on Foreign Relations Press, 1993.

Lipschitz, Leslie and McDonald, Donogh, eds. *German Unification: Economic Issues.* Washington, D.C.: International Monetary Fund, 1990.

Marsh, David. *The Germans: A People at the Crossroads.* New York: St. Martin's Press, 1990.

McAdams, A. James. "Towards a New Germany—Problems of Unification." *Government and Opposition* 25 (1990): 304-16.

McAdams, A. James. *Germany Divided: From the Wall to Reunification.* Princeton, N.J.: Princeton University Press, 1993.

Merkl, Peter. *German Unification in the European Context.* University Park, Penn.: Pennsylvania State University Press, 1993.

Moreton, Edwina, ed. *Germany Between East and West.* New York: Cambridge University Press, 1987.

Neckermann, Peter. *The Unification of Germany, or, The Anatomy of a Peaceful Revolution.* New York: Columbia University Press, 1991.

Noelle-Neumann, Elisabeth. "The German Revolution: The Historic Experiment of the Division and Unification of a Nation as Reflected in Survey Research Findings." *International Journal of Public Opinion Research* 3 (1991): 238-59.

Offe, Claus. "German Reunification as a 'Natural Experiment.'" *German Politics* 1 (1992): 1-12.

Osmond, Jonathan, ed. *German Reunification. A Reference Guide and Commentary.* The High, Harlow: Longman Group UK Ltd., 1992.

Owen, Robert F. "The Challenges of German Unification for EC Policymaking and Performance." *The American Economic Review* 81 (1991): 171-75.

Philipsen, Dirk. *We were the People. Voices from East Germany's Revolutionary Autumn of 1989.* Durham, N.C.: Duke University Press, 1993.

Pickel, Andreas. "Jump-Starting a Market Economy: A Critique of the Radical Strategy for Economic Reform in Light of the East German Experience." *Studies in Comparative Communism* 25 (1992): 177-91.

Plock, Ernest D. *East German–West German Relations and the Fall of the GDR.* Boulder, Colo.: Westview Press, 1992.

Pond, Elizabeth. *After the Wall: American Policy Toward Germany.* Washington, D.C.: The Brookings Institution, 1990.

Pond, Elizabeth. "Germany in the New Europe." *Foreign Affairs* 71 (1992): 114-30.

Randelzhofer, A. "German Unification: Constitutional and International Implications." *Michigan Journal of International Law* 13 (1991): 122-43.

Schmidt, Manfred G. "Political Consequences of German Unification." *West European Politics* 15 (1992): 1-15.

Siebert, Horst. *The Economic Integration of Germany: An Update.* Kiel: Institut für Weltwirtschaft an der Universität Kiel, 1990.

Siebert, Horst. *The New Economic Landscape in Europe.* Cambridge, Mass.: Basil Blackwell, 1991.

Silva, Stephen J. "Left Behind: The Social Democratic Party in Eastern Germany after Unification." *West European Politics* 16 (1993): 24-48.

Singer, Otto. "The Politics and Economics of German Unification: From Currency Union to Economic Dichotomy." *German Politics* 1 (1992): 78-94.

Sinn, Gerlinde and Sinn, Hans-Werner. *Jumpstart. The Economic Unification of Germany.* Cambridge, Mass., and London: MIT Press, 1992.

Smyser, W.R. *The Economy of United Germany: Colossus at the Crossroads.* New York: St. Martin's Press, 1992.

Southern, David. "The Constitutional Framework of the New Germany." *German Politics* 1 (1992): 31-49.

Sperling, James. "The Atlantic Community after German Unification: Cooperation or the Rise of 'Fortress Europe.'" *German Politics* 1 (1992): 200-22.

Stares, Paul B., ed. *The New Germany and the New Europe*. Washington, D.C.: Brookings Institution, 1992.

Stent, Angela. "The One Germany." *Foreign Policy* 81 (1990/91): 53-70.

Stern, Fritz. "Freedom and its Discontents." *Foreign Affairs* 72 (1993): 108-25.

Szabo, Stephen F. *The Diplomacy of German Unification*. New York: St. Martin's Press, 1992.

Thomerson, Michael J. "German Reunification—The Privatization of Socialist Property on East Germany's Path to Democracy." *Georgia Journal of International and Com-parative Law* 21 (1991): 123-43.

Treverton, Gregory F. and Bicksler, Barbara. "Germany and the New Europe." *Society* 29 (1992): 48-56.

Turner, Henry Ashby. *Germany From Partition to Reunification*. New Haven: Yale University Press, 1992 (revised ed. of *The Two Germanies Since 1945*. 1987).

Veen, Hans-Joachim. "German Unity: Public Opinion and Voting Trends." *Washington Quarterly* 13 (1990): 177-89.

Verheyen, Dirk. *The German Question: A Cultural, Historical and Geopolitical Exploration*. Boulder, Colo.: Westview Press, 1991.

Verheyen, Dirk and Søe, Christian, eds. *The Germans and Their Neighbors*. Boulder, Colo.: Westview Press, 1993.

Walker, D.B. "Germany Searches for a New Role in World Affairs." *Current History* 90 (1991): 368-73.

Wallach, H.G. Peter and Francisco, Ronald A. *United Germany: The Past, Politics, Prospects*. New York: Greenwood Press, 1992.

Watson, Alan. *The Germans: Who Are They Now?* London: Thames Methuen, 1992.

Welfens, P.J.J., ed. *Economic Aspects of German Unification: National and International Perspectives*. New York: Springer, 1992.

Wild, Trevor. "From Division to Unification: Regional Dimensions of Economic Change in Germany." *Geography* 77 (1992): 244-60.

Young, M.K. "The Legal Aspects of German Unification." *Foreign Policy Bulletin* 1 (1990): 83-96.

About the Editors and Contributors

Petra Bauer-Kaase is senior researcher in political sociology. She studied architecture, German literature, and political science at the universities of Darmstadt and Mannheim and holds a Ph.D. in political science. She has worked at the Center for European Survey Analyses (ZEUS) and the Forschungsgruppe Wahlen e.V. (FGW), both located in Mannheim. Her current research at the Zentrum für Umfragen, Methoden und Analysen (ZUMA) is in the area of mass communications.

Andreas Falke is a German national who currently works as principal economic specialist in the economics section of the American Embassy in Bonn. He holds a Ph.D. in Political Science from the University of Göttingen and is adjunct lecturer in Political Science at the University of Bonn. He has published widely on American politics, European Community-U.S. relations, and American trade policy. His most recent book is *Washington, D.C., Interdisciplinary Approaches* (together with Lothar Hoennighausen). The views expressed in his chapter are his own and do not reflect those of the American Embassy or any U.S. government agency.

Gert-Joachim Glaeßner is Professor of Political Science at Humboldt University in Berlin. He completed his advanced studies at the Free University of Berlin, where he also served as Assistant and full Professor of Political Science. His most recent publications include *The Unification Process in Germany* (1992) and *The German Revolution* (1992, together with Ian Wallace).

M. Donald Hancock is Professor of Political Science and Director of the Center for European Studies at Vanderbilt University. He is the author of *West Germany: The Politics of Democratic Corporatism* (1989) and co-author and co-editor of *Managing Modern Capitalism: Industrial Renewal and Workplace Democracy in Western Europe and the United States* (1992, together with John Logue and Bernt Schiller). His research focuses on the political economy of Sweden, Germany, and the European Community.

Arthur M. Hanhardt is Professor emeritus of Political Science at the University of Oregon. His publications include *The German Democratic Republic* (1968) and, more recently, a chapter in *From Bundesrepublik to Deutschland: German Politics after Unification* (1993, co-edited by Michael G. Huelshoff, Andrei S. Markovits, and Simon Reich).

Michael G. Huelshoff is Assistant Professor of Political Science at the University of New Orleans. His research has appeared in *German Politics* and Society, the German Studies Review, Comparative Political Studies, the International Journal, and the Political Research Quarterly. His most recent publication is a co-authored and co-edited volume, From Bundes-republik to Deutschland: German Politics after Unification (1993, to-gether with Andrei S. Markovits, and Simon Reich).

Henry Krisch is Professor of Political Science at the University of Con-necticut. Since 1989, he has been President of the Eastern German Studies Group (formerly the GDR Studies Association). His publications include German Politics under Soviet Occupation (1974), the German Democratic Republic: The Search for Identity (1985), and Politics and Culture in the GDR (1990). His current work deals with the relationship of political cul-ture to the changing role of the ruling party in the former GDR.

Johannes L. Kuppe received his Ph.D. in Political Science from the Uni-versity of Munich. Prior to its dissolution, he directed the division "Politics and Contemporary History" at the All-German Institute (Gesamtdeutsches Institut) in Bonn which was affiliated with the former Ministry for Inner-German Relations. He is now one of the chief editors of the weekly newspaper, Das Parlament, in Bonn. His publications deal with issues in German politics, with particular emphasis on German-Ger-man relations and German foreign policy.

Peter H. Merkl is Professor emeritus of Political Science at the University of California, Santa Barbara. His most recent books include German Uni-fication in the European Context (1993); Encounters with the Contempo-rary Radical Right (1993, co-edited with Leonard Weinberg); The Politics of Economic Changes in Postwar Japan and West Germany (1993, co-edited with Haruhiro Fukui, Hubertus Müller-Groeling, and Akio Watan-abe); and Developments in German Politics (1992, co-edited with Gordon Smith, William F. Paterson, and Stephen Fadgett). His current research interests include radical right movements in Continental Europe and a comparison of political generations in Germany and Japan.

Michaela W. Richter teaches comparative politics at the City University of New York, College of Staten Island, and at the Center of European Stud-ies, New York University. Her work on German politics focuses on the complex relationship between political parties and democracy in both the Weimar and the Federal Republics. As a Volkswagen Fellow (1992-93) at the American Institute for Contemporary German Studies and the German Historical Institute in Washington, D.C., she conducted research on the formation of West Germany's distinctive "democratic party state" for a forthcoming book comparing the roles played by the major parties in the difficult transitions to democracy in Germany after 1945 and after 1989.

James Sperling is an Associate Professor of Political Science at the Uni-versity of Akron. He is co-editor of The Federal Republic of Germany and NATO: 40 Years After (1992, together with Emil J. Kirchner) and is currently co-authoring a book on the institutions of the emerging European security order.

Helga A. Welsh holds a Ph.D. in Political Science from the University of Munich and for several years was a research fellow at the Institute for Contemporary History in Munich. She has held visiting appointments at the University of South Carolina and the University of Arizona, and is currently Visiting Assistant Professor at Wake Forest University. She specializes in European politics and has published in the areas of German history and politics and in comparative East European Studies.

Gunnar Winkler studied Economics of Industrial Relations at the Karl Marx University in Leipzig and the Martin Luther University in Halle-Wittenberg. He received his Ph.D. in 1967 and his Habilitation in 1974. After having held a professorship at the Gewerkschaftshochschule Bernau, he became Director of the Institute for Sociology and Social Policy of the Academy of Sciences in Berlin (East). He has published numerous articles and several books on issues of social policy in East Germany.

About the Book

The East European revolutions of 1989 led to momentous changes throughout the region. Nowhere were they felt more dramatically than in Germany, where unification unexpectedly became reality, unfolding with breathtaking speed, unhindered by major obstacles. However, joy over the fall of the Berlin Wall and the opening of the borders was soon dampened by the daunting political, economic, and social challenges ahead.

One of the first major efforts in English to analyze the process of unification and to assess some of the problems facing a united Germany, this book offers a synthesis of opinions. In it distinguished experts from Germany and the United States examine the deep-seated issues of political identity, painful economic adjustments, and Germany's redefined international role.

Index

Abortion laws, 86, 235
Adenauer, Konrad, 36-38, 46, 165, 246
Alliance 90, 104, 122, 124, 129, 147, 149, 151, 154, 156, 256
Alliance for Germany, 121-2, 141, 124, 146-7, 150, 286, 314
Allianz für Deutschland. See Alliance for Germany
Allied rights. *See* Four Power rights
Alternative Youth List, 122
Asylum issue, 187, 245, 250-51, 255-6, 288, 290, 319-20
Authoritarianism, demise of, 7, 10, 18-19, 24. *See also* communism, collapse of
Authority, erosion of, 23-24, 27-30, 55, 117. *See also* legitimacy

Bahr, Egon, 39
Baker, James, 264
Basic Law
and European unification, 269
prohibition against anti-democratic behavior, 256-7
provisions for German unification, 35, 85-86, 124, 140, 152, 174-5, 177, 317
reform of, 152
Basic Treaty, 28, 42-44, 166-7, 286
Becker, Helmut, 107
Berghofer, Wolfgang, 115
Berlin
Berlin Accord, 42
Berlin aid, 181
Berlin question, 37, 39-41, 165-6
Berlin Wall
construction of, 28, 38-39, 97, 286
opening of, 63, 81-82, 85, 93-94, 100, 104, 117, 172, 313-4
Biedenkopf, Kurt, 150, 190, 210
Biermann, Wolf, 56
Bloc parties. *See also* Christian Democratic Union; Democratic Peasants' Party; Liberal Democratic Party of Germany;

National Democratic Party of Germany; party system
history of, 94-97
renewal of, 79, 101, 110-3, 117, 123, 140, 144-5
Böhme, Ibrahim, 107-108
Bohley, Bärbel, 79, 103-4
Brandt, Willy, 39-43, 100, 108, 145, 246
Breuel, Birgit, 207-8, 214
Brezhnev doctrine, rejection of, 74, 77
Brezhnev, Leonid, 38, 43
Brittan, Sir Leon, 182
Bündnis 90. See Alliance 90
Bulgaria
asylum-seekers from, 319
Bulgarian Communist Party, 24
demonstrations in, 18
lack of reform in, 18, 77
West German policy toward, 39
Bund freier Demokraten. See League of Free Democrats
Bundesbank. *See* German Federal Bank
Bundeswehr. *See* German Federal Army
Bush, George, 83, 272

The Carnations, 122, 124
CDU. *See* Christian Democratic Union
Ceausescu, Nicolae, 24
Chirac, Jacques, 270
Christian Democratic Union (CDU, all-German), 142, 158, 250-1
Christian Democratic Union of Germany (CDU-East), 79, 95-96, 104, 112-3, 117, 120-1, 142, 150-1, 208. *See also* Alliance for Germany; bloc parties; de Maizière, Lothar
Christian Democratic Union (CDU-West), 107, 123, 125, 141-2, 147. *See also* Adenauer, Konrad; Kohl, Helmut

Christian Social Union (CSU), 121,
123, 141, 150
*Christlich-Demokratische Union
Deutschlands. See* Christian
Democratic Union of Germany
Christlich Soziale Union. See
Christian Social Union
Churches, role of in the GDR, 28,
100. *See also* Protestant Churches
Citizen movements. *See* civic
movement
Civic movement, 45, 56-7, 62, 93,
101-10, 125, 148. *See also*
opposition
Collectivization, 202
Comecon. *See* Council for Mutual
Economic Assistance
Communism, collapse of
in Central and Eastern Europe, 5,
17-30, 35, 97-98
in the GDR, 35-36, 42, 55-56,
74-82, 149, 226, 314
Communist Party of Germany
(KPD), 95
Community, political, 1-4, 7-8, 11,
65, 315, 318
Commonwealth of Independent
States (CIS), 212
Comparisons between East and
West Germany
income differentials, 214, 233, 249
political culture, 288-307, 317
political and economic
conditions, 27, 44, 55-56, 81-82,
98-100, 125-6, 223-4, 226, 228,
234, 306, 315, 317
Confederation, 7-8, 37, 153, 169.
See also Ten-Point Program
Conference on Security and
Cooperation in Europe
Helsinki Final Act, 28, 42, 84,
98, 105
and security policy in Europe,
263, 265-9, 274
Constitution (Federal Republic of
Germany). *See* Basic Law
Constitution (GDR)
and expropriation, 202
revision of, 61, 64-65, 140, 152-3
Corruption. *See* leadership
Council for Mutual Economic
Assistance (Comecon)
collapse of, 155

and German Democratic
Republic, 76, 167, 180-1
relations with European
Community, 165-6
CSCE. *See* Conference on Security
and Cooperation in Europe
CSU. *See* Christian Social Union
Currency union. *See* economy; State
Treaty
Czechoslovakia
developments in 1968, 38, 40, 77
lack of reform in, 18
opposition in, 18, 102
privatization in, 211-2
West German policy toward, 39

DBD. *See* German Peasants' Party
Delegitimation. *See* legitimacy,
erosion of
Delimitation, policy of, 42
Delors, Jacques, 172-3, 175-6, 183
de Maizière, Lothar, 112, 123, 151,
154-5, 204, 206, 209
Democracy. *See also* pluralism;
transitions to democracy
attitudes toward, 291-6, 305-6
socialist democracy, 20-21
pluralist, 57
Democracy Now, 102, 104-5, 110,
122, 147-8, 204. *See also*
Alliance 90
Democratic Awakening, 102, 106-
7, 109-10, 121, 123, 141, 151.
See also Alliance for Germany
Democratic centralism, 96, 152
Democratic Peasants' Party (DBD),
96, 113, 122, 124, 130, 141-2,
147, 204. *See also* bloc parties
Democratic Women's Association
of Germany (DFD), 106, 124
Demokratie Jetzt. See Democracy
Now
*Demokratische Bauernpartei
Deutschlands. See* German
Peasants' Party
Demokratischer Aufbruch. See
Democratic Awakening
Demonstrations, 76, 79, 80-81, 83-
84, 87, 93, 99, 101, 103, 139, 285
Détente. *See* East-West relations
Deutsche Forumpartei. See German
Forum Party
Deutsche Soziale Union. See
German Social Union

Deutscher Gewerkschaftsbund. See German Confederation of Trade Unions
Deutschlandpolitik. See inter-German relations; *Ost- und Deutschlandpolitik*
DFD. *See* Democratic Women's Association
DGB. *See* German Confederation of Trade Unions
Diestel, Peter-Michael, 147
Dissent. *See* civic movement; opposition
DSU. *See* German Social Union

East-West relations. *See also* North Atlantic Treaty Association; security policy
 and Cold War, 36, 96
 change in, 19, 26-28, 38, 40-42, 44-45, 47, 98, 165-6, 261
Ebeling, Hans-Wilhelm, 146
Economic and monetary union. *See* State Treaty
Economy. *See also* privatization; State Treaty; Trust Agency, unemployment
 economic conditions (GDR), 23, 55, 98, 140, 179, 213, 229
 economic growth, 208, 245, 249
 loss of export markets (in Eastern Europe), 155, 189, 213, 229, 248
 performance and policies after unification, 157-8, 213-6, 245, 249-50, 258, 314-5
Election, all-German (December 1990), 10, 85, 142, 151, 158, 210, 286
Election (March 1990)
 electoral law, 120-1
 outcome, 83-84, 93, 100, 125, 127, 141, 143, 149-51, 127, 151, 158, 175, 247, 286
 scheduling of, 10, 83, 104, 118-20,
Elections
 of 1946, 95
 communal (1989), 24, 27, 75
 communal (1990), 86
 state (1990), 151, 156
 state (1992), 187, 250-1
 to Volkskammer (prior to 1990), 96

Electoral alliances, 104, 106, 120-2, 141, 143-9, 147, 149
Electoral behavior, 11, 149-51
Electoral pacts. *See* electoral alliances
Elites, political. *See also* leadership and reform, 18, 24-27
 role of in democratization and integration, 4, 8, 10-11, 245-6, 257-8, 291, 317-8
 material privileges for, 25-6, 214, 224
Emigration (from East Germany), 27-28, 44, 77-78, 84-85, 99, 102, 117, 128, 149, 153, 213, 247, 285. *See also* travel regulations
Engholm, Björn, 250-1, 257
Environmental problems, 56, 63, 168, 180
Eppelmann, Rainer, 106-7
Erhard, Ludwig, 39, 246
European Community. *See also* Delors, Jacques; France; Great Britain; Maastricht Treaty; Western European Union
 agricultural policy, 170, 179-80
 attitudes toward German unification by individual members of, 163-4, 168-72, 176-7
 decisionmaking within, 171-7
 democratic deficit, 9
 and Eastern Europe, 8, 181, 186-9
 and European integration, 4, 46, 110, 185-9, 245, 253, 262, 314-5, 274
 and European Parliament, 174, 186, 188
 Germany's role within, 170, 186-7, 269, 319
 integration of former GDR into, 163-89
 and integration theory, 4-5
 and relations with GDR, 8, 166
 and security policy, 263-70
 and social policy 225, 227-8
Exodus. *See* emigration

Falcke, Heino, 106
FDGB. *See* Free German Federation of Trade Unions
FDJ. *See* Free German Youth
FDP. *See* Free Democratic Party
Federal Constitutional Court
 and abortion, 235

and Basic Treaty, 43
and prohibition against anti-
democratic behavior, 257
and restitution, 201
Federal states, 156-7, 170. See also
elections, state
Federalism, 2-3, 6, 8, 246, 316.
Forck, Gottfried, 106
Four Power rights, 8, 38, 42-43, 74,
82-83, 86, 95. See also Two-
Plus-Four talks
France. See also European
Community; Four Power rights
attitude toward unification, 83,
87, 164, 168-9, 172
and European security, 269-73
Free Democratic Party (East), 122-
3, 141, 143, 151. See also League
of Free Democrats
Free Democratic Party (West), 111,
122, 123, 125. See also
Genscher, Hans-Dietrich
Freier Deutscher Gewerk-
schaftsbund. See Free German
Federation of Trade Unions
Free German Federation of Trade
Unions (FDGB), 200, 224
Free German Youth (FDJ), 122,
200
Freie Deutsche Jugend. See Free
German Youth
Functionalism, 2-3, 6, 8. See also
integration, theories of; neo-
functionalism

Geissler, Heiner, 210
Genscher, Hans-Dietrich, 45, 86,
100, 122, 126, 173, 185-6, 264,
247, 257, 264, 266-7
Gerlach, Manfred, 111, 120
German Confederation of Trade
Unions (DGB), 253
German Federal Army, 86
German Federal Bank, 85, 155,
176-7, 185
German Forum Party, 104, 122,
141, 143, 153. See also League
of Free Democrats
German Social Union (DSU), 106,
121, 123, 141, 145-7, 150-1, 156.
See also Alliance for Germany
Glasnost. See Gorbachev, Mikhail;
Soviet Union
Götting, Gerald, 112

Gohlke, Reiner, 209
Gorbachev, Mikhail, 18, 21, 26-7,
35, 43, 56, 60 74, 77, 80, 83, 86-
87, 94, 98-99, 126, 143, 166,
247, 266. See also Soviet Union
Government of National
Responsibility (January-March
1990), 102, 119
Grand coalition
in the Federal Republic of
Germany (1966-1969), 39-40
in the German Democratic
Republic, 140, 145, 151-2, 158
possibility of future, 294
Grassroots democracy. See civic
movement; political participation
Great Britain. See also European
Community; Four Power rights
attitude toward unification, 83,
87, 164, 168-9
and European security, 271-3
Green Liga, 105
Green Party, 102, 105, 109, 122,
141, 148-9
The Greens, 123, 129, 148-9, 151.
See also Greens/Alliance 90
Greens/Alliance 90 256, 258
Grotewohl, Otto, 37
Grüne Liga. See Green Liga
Die Grünen. See The Greens
Grüne Partei. See Green Party
Gutzeit, Martin, 107
Gysi, Gregor, 114, 150

Hallstein doctrine, 37-38
Hallstein, Walter, 165
Harmel doctrine, 265
Hartmann, Günter, 113
Haussmann, Helmut, 210
Havel, Václav, 211
Havemann, Katja, 103
Heinemann, Gustav, 41
Helsinki Final Act. See Conference
on Security and Cooperation in
Europe
Henrichs, Rolf, 78-79
Herger, Wolfgang, 81
Heym, Stefan, 56
Homann, Heinrich, 113
Honecker, Erich, 23-28, 42, 44-45,
55-57, 77, 79-80, 99, 144
Horn, Gyula, 77
Hülsemann, Wolfram, 106

Hungary
  Hungarian Socialist Workers'
    Party, 24
  opening of border, 18, 77
  privatization, 210-1
  reform policies, 18, 26-28, 59,
    73, 77-78, 95, 109, 125, 285
  West German policy toward, 39
Husák, Gustáv, 24

Identity, national, 6-7, 30, 320
Ideology, erosion of, 58, 64, 66
Independent Women's Association
  (UFV), 102, 105-6, 122
Information. *See* media; travel
  regulations
Initiative for Peace and Human
  Rights, 102, 104-5, 110, 122,
  147, 150. *See also* Alliance 90
Initiative für Frieden und
  Menschenrechte. *See* Initiative
  for Peace and Human Rights
Integration. *See also* European
  Community
  theories of, 1-5, 8-9. *See also*
  federalism; functionalism; neo-
  functionalism; pluralism
  West German into Western
  community, 36-37
Intelligentsia, literary, 56
Inter-German relations, 35-47, 78,
  110. *See also* intra-German trade;
  Ost- und Deutschlandpolitik;
  policy of rapprochement
International recognition of GDR,
  28, 37, 42, 44
Intra-German trade, 163, 165-8
Iron curtain, dismantling of, 18, 77

Kádár, János, 24
Kaiser, Jakob, 36
Keßler, Heinz, 81
Khrushchev, Nikita, 37
Kiesinger, Kurt Georg, 39-40
Kinkel, Klaus, 257
Kirchner, Martin, 112
Kohl, Helmut, 7, 43, 45, 79, 84-87,
  100, 115, 121, 126, 141, 155,
  169, 173, 175, 185-6, 215, 247,
  250, 253, 256, 263, 266, 270-1,
  273, 286
KPD. *See* Communist Party of
  Germany
Krause, Günter, 154

Krenz, Egon, 75-76, 80-81, 100,
  103, 111, 114, 144
Kunze, Reiner, 56

Labor unrest, 252-3. *See also* Metal
  Workers' Union; Public
  Employees Union
Lafontaine, Oskar, 85, 146, 247
Lambsdorff, Otto Graf, 122, 257
LDP. *See* Liberal Democratic Party
  of Germany
LDPD. *See* Liberal Democratic
  Party of Germany
Leadership. *See also* elites, political
  corruption of, 114, 127, 144, 257
  in the GDR, 10, 21-23, 26, 28, 120
  succession, 24, 28
  renewal of in unified Germany,
    257
League of Free Democrats, 121-2,
  124, 141, 143, 149, 151
legitimacy
  and democratization, 10
  erosion of, 18, 30, 55, 61, 66, 74,
    98
  question of, 22-23, 46-47
  refusal to acknowledge East
    Germany, 37-40
Liberal Democratic Party (LDP).
  See Liberal Democratic Party of
  Germany
Liberal Democratic Party of
  Germany (LDPD), 79, 95-6, 104,
  111-3, 117, 120-2, 141-3. *See*
  also bloc parties; League of Free
  Democrats
Liberals. *See* League of Free
  Democrats
Loest, Erich, 56
Luxemburg, Rosa, 99

Maastricht Treaty, 185-6, 188, 245,
  253-4, 272-3, 319
Maleuda, Günther, 113
Marshall Plan, 36
Meckel, Markus, 107, 145
Media (Western), influence in
  GDR, 7, 26-27, 56, 99, 103, 288,
  296, 317
Menzel, Bruno, 143
Metal Workers' Union (*IG Metall*),
  251-3, 257
Migration. *See* emigration
Mittag, Günter, 80

Mitterrand, François, 83, 169, 172,
    270-1
Modrow, Hans, 81-82, 116, 118,
    120, 153, 209
Möllemann, Jürgen, 251
Monetary union. *See* State Treaty

NACC. *See* North Atlantic
    Cooperation Council
National Democratic Party of
    Germany (NDPD), 96, 113, 120,
    122, 124, 141, 143. *See also* bloc
    parties
*National-Demokratische Partei
    Deutschlands. See* National
    Democratic Party of Germany
Nationalism, 30, 314
Nationalization of property, 200-2
NATO. *See* North Atlantic Treaty
    Organization
NDPD. *See* National Democratic
    Party of Germany
Die Nelken. See The Carnations
Neo-functionalism, 2-4, 6, 8, 316.
    See also functionalism;
    integration, theories of
Neues Forum. See New Forum
New Forum, 62-63, 79, 83, 102-5,
    108, 110-1, 119, 122, 147-8. *See
    also* Alliance 90
Noack, Arndt, 107
North Atlantic Cooperation Council
    (NACC), 264-6
North Atlantic Treaty Organization
    (NATO)
    and German membership in, 36,
       261, 263
    German policies toward, 263-75
    and German unification, 83, 86,
       169
    in integration theory, 6
    redefinition of mission, 261, 264-5

Opposition. *See also* civic move-
    ment; Protestant Churches
    attitudes toward opposition, 293-4
    in Central and Eastern Europe, 18
    in the GDR, 9-10, 28, 74-76, 78,
       82, 93-94, 99, 110, 116, 285-6
Ortleb, Rainer 111, 143
Ost- und Deutschlandpolitik, 38, 41,
    79, 286. *See also* inter-German
    relations

Pahnke, Rudi, 106
Parliament, all-German, 286
Participation. *See* political
    participation
Party of Democratic Socialism
    (PDS), 29, 64, 82-84, 117, 122-5,
    127, 141, 143-4, 149-51, 154,
    203, 256. *See also* Gysi, Gregor;
    Modrow, Hans; Socialist Unity
    Party
Party system (GDR)
    development of, 93-161
    transformation after WWII, 95-97
    transformation in 1989/90, 100-61
    westernization of, 101, 107, 111-
       2, 115-27, 140, 158-9
PDS. *See* Party of Democratic
    Socialism
Pensioners
    effects of unification on, 237-9
    standard of living of, 238
Perestroika. See Gorbachev,
    Mikhail; Soviet Union
Pluralism, 2-3, 6, 8, 17, 19. *See
    also* integration, theories of
Pöhl, Karl-Otto, 85, 213
Poland
    and German unification, 84, 155-6
    Polish United Workers's Party, 18
    privatization, 210-1
    reform policies in, 18, 24, 26-28,
       73-78, 102, 109, 125, 285
    Solidarity movement in, 18, 56, 59
    West German policy toward, 38
Policy of rapprochement, 44
Political culture
    culture shift, 28, 57, 66
    comparison East vs. West
       German, 286-307
    and political socialization, 26-29
    postmaterialist values, 28, 149,
       302-4
Political participation. *See also*
    civic movement; opposition
    attitudes toward, 296-300
    demands for, 8-9, 19-22, 60, 62-
       63, 65-66, 108, 152
    determinants of, 300-5
    limits of, 20-22
    and local government, 60
    modes of, 298-305
    voter turnout, 251
Political unification. *See*
    Unification Treaty

Privatization. *See also* Trust
Agency
in Eastern Europe, 210-1
in former GDR, 118, 189, 201,
203-16, 229-30, 232, 247, 255
Property rights. *See* collectivization;
nationalization; privatization
Protestant Churches. *See also*
churches
21, 63-64, 101-3, 106, 285
Public Employees Union, 252

Real existing socialism, 55, 63,
100, 128, 223
Realsozialismus. See real existing
socialism
Reform. *See also* Hungary; Poland;
Soviet Union; third way
economic and political, 19-20,
55-66, 76
and human rights, 58
lack of, 18, 22-23, 30, 62, 78, 99
and modernization, 19-20, 30
and social science research, 56-61
Reich, Jens, 63
Restitution. *See* privatization
Reunification. *See* unification
Revolution, theory of, 74-75, 87
Richter, Edelbert, 106
Ridley, Nicholas, 169
Rohwedder, Detlev Karsten, 205-7,
209-10, 214
Romania
asylum-seekers from, 250-1, 319
lack of reform in, 18, 77
popular upsurge in, 18
Romanian Workers' Party, 24
West German policy toward, 39
Romberg, Walter, 153
Roundtable discussions, 10, 18, 64-
65, 82, 94, 98, 101-5, 112, 116-
20, 152, 204, 227, 285
Rühe, Volker, 121

Satellite parties. *See* bloc parties
SBZ. *See* Soviet Zone of
Occupation
Schabowski, Günter, 81
Scharping, Rudolf, 257
Schmidt, Helmut, 43-44
Schnur, Wolfgang, 107
Schorlemmer, Friedrich, 106
Schürer, Gerhard, 23
Schumacher, Kurt, 36

SDP. *See* Social Democratic Party
Security policy, 261-76
SED. *See* Socialist Unity Party
Simonis, Heide, 257
SMAD. *See* Soviet Military
Administration
Social policy. *See also* social
structure
history of (GDR), 223-4
social security, 236-40
and women, 228, 234-6
and unification, 224-40
SPD. *See* Social Democratic Party
of Germany
Social Democratic Party in the
GDR (SDP), 62, 79, 102, 106-10,
119, 145. *See also* Social
Democratic Party of Germany
(SPD-East)
Social Democratic Party of
Germany (SPD, all-German),
210, 250, 255
Social Democratic Party of
Germany (SPD-East), 95-96,
108, 119-20, 122, 124-5, 128,
145, 151, 155 147, 150, 206
Social Democratic Party of
Germany (SPD-West), 38, 40,
45, 107-10, 146, 158. *See also*
Brandt, Willy
Socialist Unity Party (SED), 10,
20-21, 25, 29, 39, 45, 63 113-5,
143, 200, 203. *See also* elites,
political; Honecker, Erich;
leadership; Party of Democratic
Socialism
Social contract, erosion of, 22-25
Social structure, changes in, 229-33
Solidarity
between East and West Germans,
313, 318
in GDR 126
Solidarity Pact, 255
Soviet Military Administration
(SMAD), 95-96
Soviet Union. *See also* East-West
relations; Gorbachev, Mikhail;
security policy; United States
attitude toward unification, 82-85,
140
policy toward Eastern Europe,
19, 27, 43. *See also* Brezhnev
doctrine

policy toward GDR, 76-77, 80-
81, 95, 126
policy toward Germany, 37, 83,
86-87, 95-96. *See also* Berlin
policy toward the West, 40-41
reform thinking in, 56-58, 60, 74-
76, 78, 80, 87, 98, 101, 144
Soviet Zone of Occupation
communization, 246
expropriations, 200-1, 204
land reform, 201, 204
party developments in, 95-96, 145
*Sozialistische Einheitspartei
Deutschlands*. *See* Socialist Unity
Party
Staatssicherheit. *See* state security
service
Stalin, 36-37
Standard of living. *See also*
comparisons between East and
West Germany; economy
demand for equal, 155
in the Federal Republic of
Germany, 246
in the GDR, 25, 28, 233
development since unification,
157, 233-4
Stasi. *See* state security service
State security service
agents of, 144, 203, 209, 318
and GDR opposition, 56, 63, 80
102-3, 106-7, 110,
property of, 206
reform and dissolution of, 82,
118-20, 156
role of, 76, 127, 144, 224, 318
State Treaty, 8, 27, 85, 124, 153-6,
163, 173, 178, 204, 209, 212-3,
226, 238, 249, 317
Steinkühler, Franz, 251
Stolpe, Manfred, 150, 157
Stoltenberg, Gerhard, 265
Stoph, Willy, 40, 42
Streibl, Max, 251
Süssmuth, Rita, 107
Suhr, Heinz, 214

Teltschik, Helmut, 79
Templin, Wolfgang, 151
Ten-Point Program, 7-8, 83, 100,
105, 107, 115, 169, 172, 286
Thatcher, Margaret, 169, 176
Thierse, Wolfgang, 146

Third way 30, 57, 64, 81-82, 87,
93, 105, 125-26, 285
Tiananmen Square demonstrations,
24, 27, 76
Transitions to democracy, 1-2, 9-11,
17-19, 22, 128, 159, 285, 291-6,
314-5. *See also* democracy; party
system; reform
Travel regulations, 26, 28, 44, 56,
77-78, 81. *See also* emigration
Treaty on the Establishment of
German Unity. *See* Unification
Treaty
Treaty Establishing a Monetary,
Economic, and Social Union. *See*
State Treaty
Treaty on European Union. *See*
Maastricht Treaty
Treuhandanstalt. *See* Trust Agency
for the People's Property
Truman doctrine, 36, 96
Trust, erosion of, 18, 26-27, 83, 117
Trust Agency for the People's
Property (*Treuhandanstalt*), 118,
182, 199, 204-16, 248-9, 252,
306, 318. *See also* privatization
Two-Plus-Four talks, 84, 86-87,
156, 201. *See also* Four Power
rights

UFV. *See* Independent Women's
Association
Ulbricht doctrine, 39
Ulbricht, Walter, 25, 28, 40-42, 56, 61
Ullmann, Wolfgang, 104, 204
Unabhängiger Frauenverband. *See*
Independent Women's
Association
Unemployment
in Eastern Europe, 319
and economic reform, 19
elimination of, 25, 232
within European Community, 254
within Germany, 207, 215, 227-
31, 245, 249, 315
among women, 232-5, 249
Unification (Germany). *See also*
communism, collapse of;
election; European Community;
security policy; State Treaty;
Unification Treaty
attitudes toward, 29, 124-25,
313-4
causes of, 35-6, 82, 85

consequences of, 289, 315-9
demands for, 7, 62, 81-82, 100
historical legacies and, 1, 11, 78
313-4
and international role of
Germany, 318-9
models of, 5-8
perceived advantages and
disadvantages of, 288-9
redefinition of Germany's role, 319
Soviet security interests, 86-87
steps toward, 74-87, 151-59
Unification, constitutional options.
See Basic Law
Unification Treaty (second State
Treaty), 8, 65, 86, 153, 156-8,
203, 207, 214, 226-7
United States. *See also* Four Power
rights
and European security, 261-6
and German unification, 83, 86-
87
relations with Soviet Union, 38,
43, 83, 86
United Left, 102, 106, 110, 124

Vereinigte Linke. See United Left
Volkskammer activities, (1990)
153-4, 156
Volkskammer election. *See* election
(March 1990)

Walesa, Lech, 211
Walter, Vernon, 78
Walther, Hansjoachim, 146
Warsaw Pact. *See* Warsaw Treaty
Organization
Warsaw Treaty Organization
(WTO), 6, 38-39, 76, 86, 100,
261, 264, 266
West Berlin. *See* Berlin
West German policy toward GDR.
See Basic Treaty; intra-German
trade, *Ost- und Deutschland-
politik*
Western European Union. *See* also
security policy
and European security, 263-4,
266-7, 270-3
German attitude toward, 269-73
WEU. *See* Western European Union
Winzer, Otto, 47
Wolf, Christa, 56, 65

Women. *See also* Independent
Women's Association
abortion, 86, 235
and child care facilities, 234
effects of unification on, 236-7
and literature, 56
and pension adjustments, 228,
238-9 rights of 63, 228, 234-6
and unemployment, 232-5, 249

Youth, 28-29, 55, 74

Zhdanov, Andrei, 36
Zhivkov, Todor, 24
Zwickel, Klaus, 257